1ST GO

Edward Glover, M.D.

*Selected Papers on
Psycho-Analysis, Volume* I

ON THE EARLY
DEVELOPMENT OF MIND

SELECTED PAPERS ON PSYCHO-ANALYSIS VOLUME I

ON
THE EARLY
DEVELOPMENT
OF MIND

EDWARD GLOVER

INTERNATIONAL UNIVERSITIES PRESS, INC.

New York, N. Y.

ACKNOWLEDGEMENT

Acknowledgement is made to the Editors of the Journals in which various articles have appeared; as follows, *The International Journal of Psycho-Analysis*, *The British Journal of Medical Psychology*, *The Proceedings of the Royal Society of Medicine*, *The Journal of Mental Science*, *The British Journal of Educational Psychology*, *The British Journal of Psychology*, *The British Medical Bulletin*, *Horizon* and *The British Journal of Delinquency*. Full reference is given in the title footnotes.

NOTE

Abbreviations used in this volume are in accordance with the *World List of Scientific Periodicals* (Oxford, 1950). Numerals in bold type refer to volumes; ordinary numerals to pages. Further abbreviations are *C.P.=* Freud, *Collected Papers* (5 vols.), Hogarth Press, London, 1924-50.

CONTENTS

viii   CONTENTS

PREFACE

The custom of issuing volumes of 'Selected Papers' during the life-time of the author has no doubt many motivations in common with the practice of writing autobiographies, and, as in the case of an autobiography, can be justified only on the assumption that the author's remains are worth preserving. At first a sanguine belief shared by author and publisher, this sometimes naïve assumption must sooner or later be submitted to the public for judgment.

Under these circumstances the least the author can do is to save the reader unnecessary trouble by cutting out the redundancies inevitable when papers dealing with various aspects of the same subject are originally published at haphazard. Surveys of the literature, often but by no means always indispensable to the argument of a given essay, are in any case mostly out of date by the time the collection of papers is made: they too can be omitted. The same applies to much material of an expository kind. An exception may sometimes be made when the paper is of historical interest and has maintained its position in lists of standard reference. It is for this reason that I have included in this collection the gist of two early papers on the oral phase of libido-development. When I started to make clinical observations in course of everyday psycho-analytical practice, little was known or written about this subject apart from the work of my tutor, the late Karl Abraham. At the time it surprised me that such simple observations had not been made many years before: but since the oral phase has recently become a storm centre of controversy regarding early mental development, I may be excused for reprinting what may now appear a somewhat time-worn exordium.

The problem of arranging collected papers is not easy to solve. Inevitably a great variety of factors determines the choice of subject; for example, the writer's own predilection for a particular theoretical or practical aspect of the work, the type of clinical material that comes his way, the impact of current discoveries or controversies, or the need to supply extraneous demands for expository articles. In spite therefore of the practical advantage of ordering sections under subject-headings, I have chosen to present the various papers in chronological order, and trust that the effect will not be too disjointed. After all, although the subject matter may vary widely, the individual approach of the writer is likely to prevail over other influences and provide a conceptual thread on which the various issues can be strung. In fact the great majority of the papers reprinted here are concerned with one aspect or another of the *early development of mind*, e.g., early libidinal stages, early structural and functional activities, the inter-relations of psychic mechanisms, etiological and developmental classifications of and researches on mental disorders. A few more general papers have been included which though not bearing directly on mental development have exploited mainly developmental criteria. For the same reason I have included two articles on the psychology of the psycho-therapeutist and on the indications for psychoanalysis which might otherwise have been more appropriate to a book on technique.[1] Some other breaks in the conceptual thread are due to the fact that a number of articles on theoretical and clinical aspects of mental development have already been published in monograph form.[2]

A more important source of confusion lies in the modifications in theory that have occurred throughout a span of thirty years. During this period the range of psycho-analytical thinking has widely extended and in fact is increasingly disturbed by crises of controversy. For some years before the death of Freud psychoanalytic theory had already begun to follow a rudderless course; and since his death some of the more erratic of these tendencies have acquired the sanction of sheer repetition. Most of these speculative efforts have consisted of hypothetical reconstructions of early phases of mental development concerning which we can have no direct psycho-analytical information; and since there is a world of difference between, on the one hand, the correlation of theory with established clinical findings and, on the other, the moulding of theory in accordance with individual speculations, it was inevitable that many of the later papers published here should be concerned with the basic principles and methods of research

[1] *The Technique of Psycho-Analysis*, Baillière, Tindall & Cox, London, 1955.

[2] *An Examination of the Klein System of Child Psychology* (in 'The Psycho-Analytic Study of the Child', Vol. I, Imago Publishing Co., 1945); *Psycho-Analysis and Child Psychiatry*, Imago Publishing Co., 1953.

by which alone theoretical speculations of this sort can be satisfactorily controlled.[1]

To this it may be added that my own views have undergone
various modifications in the course of time. I was, for example,
mortified to find, when arranging the papers in chronological
order, how long I had given unthinking assent to that specious but
almost totally misleading concept of a 'part-object', a term the use
of which has debauched so much recent psycho-analytical thinking.
And I have sought to correct this, and other, misapprehensions in
footnotes. Moreover it is impossible to observe the course of
mental disorders without looking at the same time for the 'kernel-
complexes' which they have in common and for the characteristic
variations which are responsible for clinical differences and for
different degrees of accessibility to treatment. The danger of this
dual incentive is of course that one may confuse variable with
standard factors, and so distort the presentation of a presumably
orderly progress of mental development. Such contradictions as
the reader may discern are, I think, due largely to this faltering in
perspective. In the long run the acid test of theory is its consonance
with clinical observations. But since in psycho-analysis the observer is constantly concerned to get behind the clinical facts, there is
not the same possibility of checking his essays in reconstruction;
the best he can do is to see that these neither outrage psycho-
biological probability nor flout the basic concepts on which the
whole science of psycho-analysis is founded.

EDWARD GLOVER.

[1] See also *Basic Mental Concepts*, Imago Publishing Co., London,
1947.

I

THE SIGNIFICANCE OF THE MOUTH IN PSYCHO-ANALYSIS*

[1924]

As has been suggested in the Preface, this article is something of a museum piece. Written at a time when concepts of an 'oral phase' were merely rough generalizations, it was, after Abraham's, one of the first attempts to give body to the term. Needless to say the material was easy to gather: indeed it was surprising that the oral phase had not been exhaustively described long before, equally surprising that it was not quickly amplified afterwards. The truth is that psycho-analytical terms tend to develop into clichés: once the rough generalizations have been accepted they are handed down from one generation to another without either very close inspection or adequate amplification. To this day terms such as 'oral primacy', 'oral fixation', 'oral sadism' are bandied about as if they described amply the first eighteen months of mental activity, and as if they were the result of direct analytical observation: whereas in fact they are merely loose inferences drawn partly from observational data and partly from the direct analysis of cases from the age of four years upwards. Even so they give only a vague idea of the multiplicity of needs and mental impressions current during the suckling period. The only progress that can be reported during the past thirty years is that analysts are at last prepared to make actual observations of infant behaviour and to draw from these observations such conclusions as to primary mental processes as their pre-conceptions permit. The conclusions are however still subject to gross error.

From the psycho-analytic point of view, mouth activities can be classified into three main groups. The first of these, and by far the most completely understood of the three, is comprehended in the

* Read before the Medical Section of the British Psychological Society, April 30, 1924 and published in *The British Journal of Medical Psychology*, Vol. IV, pt. 2, 1924 [here slightly abbreviated].

familiar phrase – the oral stage of *libido* development. The second includes the laying down of certain mechanisms which determine and help to delimit the corporeal ego, afterwards providing a basis for character formation. We might say that these activities constitute the oral stage of *ego-development*, were it not for the fact that throughout a large part of the period involved it is scarcely accurate to talk of a distinct ego-formation. The difference between the second and first group can be expressed more clearly if one thinks of the play and interplay of self-preservative and libidinal impulses.

Of the nature of the third group we can only say here, that it coincides with the significant period of mouth activity after birth, but cannot be immediately distinguished by direct observation. It includes the *isolation or fusion through preservative or libidinal channels of the impulses to destruction* which, as Freud has shown, represent one side of the primary instinct antithesis of life.

Roughly speaking, then, libidinal activity, self-preservative activity (including orientation) and mechanisms for fusing or diverting primary instincts form the functional groundwork of the mouth or oral stage.

The necessity of division into stages was born of empirical investigation of libido development. It will be remembered that Freud's division of libido organization was based partly on his isolation of the component sexual impulses and partly on the dynamics of choice of a love-object. So that the first division was between an autoerotic stage where these component impulses found gratification of an 'anarchic' type, as Ferenczi[1] has aptly said, on the body itself without reference to a definite object, and a stage of genital primacy, when the component impulses are subordinated ultimately to the purposes of reproduction. Freud's study of paraphrenia then led to the recognition of a narcissistic stage where a definite object is chosen, but one coinciding with the self. The analysis of obsessional neurosis resulted in a delimitation of a third stage, when component impulses are directed towards an outer object, but not under genital primacy. The primacy involved is rather one of anal-erotic and sadistic impulses. Still later, in a reprint of the *Three Contributions to Sexual Theory*,

---

[1] Ferenczi: *Versuch einer Genitaltheorie*, I.P.V., 1924 [Thalassa: *A Theory of Genitality*, Psa-Q, Inc., N.Y., 1938].

he sketched out the earliest stage of libido organization, giving it the name of oral or cannibalistic stage.[1]

In considering the deeply sedimented and remotely accessible stages of oral development, it is highly necessary to follow the pharmaceutical device of introducing into any mixture certain correctives or adjuvants. In the present instance the most important of these is the idea of *relative primacy* of any one zone. We have to keep in mind that the erotogenic zones, mouth, anus, skin, musculature, etc., represent points of concentration of libidinal energy but that the whole organism can also be regarded as a reservoir of libido generally distributed. In the case of the mouth the association of self-preservative needs, not clearly distinguished as such, serves to accentuate the gratification of combined hunger and libidinal tensions. At the same time, however, other gratifications of organ pleasure, especially of the muscular system, are in full swing: even in genital primacy, where a centralization of libido into a common 'accumulation and discharge' system has taken place,[2] this accumulation is only relative, and even the most indifferent parts of the body are to some extent libidinally autonomous, and are capable in times of stress of taking over centralizing functions, as can be seen in conversion hysteria when genital primacy is denied and a backward displacement to the organic libido systems occurs.

The early primacy of the mouth is then purely relative, and this fact in turn gives rise to the question of *periodicity*: Is there in the case of pregenital primacies a general or individual period necessary for the sufficient working out of gratification? Apart from

---

[1] This development can be traced in the following of Freud's publications: *Drei Abhandlungen zur Sexualtheorie*, 1st to 5th editions (1905–1922), Deuticke, Wien [*Three Essays on the Theory of Sexuality*, Imago Publishing Co., London, 1949]; 'Eine Kindheitserinnerung des Leonardo da Vinci' (1910) [*Leonardo da Vinci, A Psychosexual Study of an Infantile Reminiscence*, Routledge & Kegan Paul, London, 1922]; 'Psychoanalytische Bemerkungen über einen Fall von Paranoia', *Sammlung kleiner Schriften*, 3te Folge ['Psycho-Analytic Notes upon an Autobiographical Account of a Case of Paranoia (Dementia Paranoides)', in *C.P.* Vol. III]; 'Zur Einführung des Narzissmus'; 'Die Disposition zur Zwangsneurose', *Sammlung kleiner Schriften*, 4te Folge, 1918 ['On Narcissism: An Introduction'. Hogarth Press, *C.P.*, IV] ['The Predisposition to Obsessional Neurosis', *C.P.*, II]. See also 'The Infantile Genital Organisation of the Libido', *Int. J. Psycho-Anal.*, April, 1924 [*C.P.*, Vol. II].

[2] See Ferenczi's views on genital function, op. cit.

biological speculations as to periodicity (Fliess) and views on the influence of race history on individual development, there seems to be little question that, especially with suckling gratifications, there is an *optimum* period with individual variation, the shortening or prolongation of which constitutes either a traumatic experience, or a situation of fixation. I should be inclined to say that shortening of the period is almost invariably traumatic, whilst the effect of lengthening depends on the stage of ego development reached in the civilization concerned, since we find that in certain more primitive areas (e.g. of Serbia, Macedonia) suckling is sometimes carried on right into childhood (5–9), is associated with smoking in its later stages but given up when wine drinking is permitted.

For the present we must content ourselves with one special consideration; if we assume that an insufficient or over-great gratification of an earlier primacy *can* take place and can give rise to an individual oral *disposition*, or *character*, how may this affect later primacies, such as the pregenital anal or phallic primacies? Normally it would seem that the primary gratification of one stage becomes subsidiary in the next, until under full genital primacy these are all represented in the preparatory fore-pleasure of coitus. May there not then come about in abnormal cases a struggle on the part of the earlier primacy to retain its dominating influence, thereby inhibiting the free working out of the next primacy by continuous archaic modification, e.g. may the oral impulses not seek displaced and condensed 'working out' at the anal level, giving rise to cumulative inhibition all along the pregenital series? Here again, it would seem that, although in the normal case gratifification of a later stage seems to compensate for renunciation of an older pleasure, some such cumulative disturbance does take place in those constitutionally or individually fixated. How then does this disturbance take effect? Here we are faced with alternative possibilities. The first and most familiar implies the use of certain mechanisms of displacement and condensation, whereby libido energy is withdrawn from one point to invest another, in the case of regression, to reinvest another. This is the *quantitative* point of view and would account for the recurrence of oral characteristics in other erotic, e.g. urinary, situations as an overflow occurring at some point in common which permits or stimulates unconscious identification. Ferenczi[1] has recently put forward another

[1] Ferenczi, op. cit.

view, that the 'handing on' is not only quantitative but *qualitative* and sees in the genital act itself a merging of certain pregenital characteristics, for which he has coined the term 'amphimixis'. The rhythm of coitus, for example, is regarded as an oral blending, eating during defaecation an oral-anal blending, etc.

Whichever point of view one takes, the facts of experience and analytic investigation can only be understood on the basis of *some* kind of displacement, and that, not only forwards but backwards, i.e. regressive. Displacement and regression form the keystone to all oral investigations.

It would seem reasonable to suppose therefore that to understand and explore oral development we have only to work back with the help of ordinary exploratory methods. Unfortunately the matter is not quite so simple. In the first place the system of word presentation essential to direct psychical remembering is not developed until the primacy of the mouth is over. Hence, with the exception of visual, olfactory and plastic representation, *we can know nothing of the primary mouth situations, except by repetition through later situations akin in some way to the first.* The early mouth positions are not only deeply sedimented and compressed, they are layered over by later deposits. More important still, in these later stages the ego is becoming more formed and is about to receive the final character imprint of the Oedipus situation. Consider for a moment what this means; the barring of all uninhibited erotic impulses towards the parent, the repression of the anal-sadistic organization together with all contemporaneous infantile sexual theories, that is to say, the very stages from which we might hope to gain information as to the significance of the mouth, form a battle-ground of guilt-conflict, following which all primitive systems can gain expression only in disguise. Any view of the oral stage is not only blurred as seen through opaque glasses, it is more or less boarded off by this intervening repression, and our main source of information remains a study of abnormal states, as it were an oblique reflection from a distorting mirror.

Now the influence of relative primacy and of repression are more matters of internal economy, and leave out of account a dynamic function of mouth activity which is perhaps more easy to appreciate since it concerns the 'stage setting' in which the drama of suckling is enacted. Just how far the abrupt termination of intrauterine life by the act of birth has been underestimated in conscious thinking can be gathered by a study of the opposite point of view contained in a recent treatise by Rank.[1] Apart, however, from the validity of such speculations or their possible application, we have to note three main considerations. First that by the act of birth the antithesis of pleasure-pain has been established; second that a trauma requiring psychical fixation or binding has taken place. The oral stage commences with certain prescribed functions to perform, to sweeten the pill of existence and to afford repetition situations, such as the ever repeated gratification and privation of suckling and hunger whereby the catastrophic primal experience of birth is worked through. Both of these serve a third purpose, viz. to link the subject more and more to the outer world. The first is the libidinal, the second the repetitive and the third the reality function of oral development.

We may now proceed to review certain details of the actual process of *suckling*, the full significance of which is made apparent when they are encountered during post-oral stages of development. The pictorial setting must obviously depend on the method of feeding and especially whether bottle feeding has been adopted from the outset. Even with breast feeding there is wide scope for variety of experience owing to varying physical and mental characteristics of the mother. In all cases, however, the smell of the mother's body, especially of the armpit, of exhalations from bed and body clothes, warmth of skin and the rhythmic movements of maternal respiration provide the atmosphere of the mouth stage. In breast feeding there is a gradual appreciation of a dome-shaped pillow with an especially sought-after projection, an exquisite pleasure centre vaguely orientated but having continuity *in experience* with prenatal existence. Later on comes the mystifying appreciation of two domes each like a face with an eye in the middle, together with the intervening gulf, chasm or cleft. With increasing visual appreciation there gradually resolve out of chaos certain more definite impressions, a circumambient whiteness, a cosmic vantage point of brown, the areola, and a red or pink-tipped organ from which warm sweet whitish fluid can be extracted. On suitable treatment by the mouth this organ is erected and responds to rhythmic jaw-pressure with increased

[1] Rank, *Das Trauma der Geburt*, I.P.V., 1924 [*The Trauma of Birth*, Routledge & Kegan Paul, London, 1924].

supplies. It is rough, and is studded round with pimple-like excrescences, calling for the erasing ministrations of baby finger-nails. At times when the nipple is cracked there is mingled with milk a taste of blood. It is easy to imagine how significant must be the wide variations in physical shape of the breast in different mothers, the size, degree of projection and erectility of nipples, the firmness or flaccidity of the mammae, and the ease with which breasts can be exhausted. This varies with different mothers and in the case of the first-born with the same mother. The technique of suckling, too, varies from the incorrect introduction of the nipple alone to the correct offer of the pendant breast.

We must remember that although the suckling reflex is in all probability present prenatally, the child has often to be taught to take the nipple, indeed sometimes has the nipple forced upon it. Quite apart from the fact that children injured at birth and those with nasal obstruction suck with difficulty, a broad distinction can be drawn as to the manner of sucking, from a purely passive torpid reaction to active and distinctly aggressive jaw activity.[1] During suckling some peculiar movements of the body occur, a slow stretching and bending of the upper and lower limbs, a crooking of legs and drawing up of toes which are seen again in life during recumbent masturbation, during the recumbent lover's kiss and in the privation stages of restlessness with drug takers. During and towards the end of the process urine is frequently voided, and regurgitation may take place from oversatisfaction or faulty technique. The change over from breast to bottle produces reactions of varying intensity from easy acquiescence to violent protest, and in accordance with the teat used can favour a more passive type of suckling. The bottle lends itself to grasping activities but is deficient in other erotic respects. During the first year whilst jaw-pressure is constantly used, sucking and swallowing predominate, biting is more especially associated with dentition, and mastication does not usually date till premolar eruption (end of second year). It is important to note that whilst miniature weanings are constantly taking place, the final weaning occurs at a time when the biting apparatus is definitely developed. Ferenczi[2]

[1] [Note (1955): The first extended analytic study of suckling was not published until 1941: see Middlemore: *The Nursing Couple*, Cassell, London.]

[2] Ferenczi, op. cit.

holds that eruption of teeth is largely responsible for weaning and with certain exceptions this seems to be the case. At any rate, quite apart from the reaction to pain caused by fissured and inflamed breasts, it is certain that many of the initial slaps administered to the baby are associated with aggressive biting at the nipple. In other words, weaning ends in an atmosphere of punishment or at least loss following aggression. Erotic play with the nipple during actual suckling is a significant feature and equally so sadistic irregularity on the part of the mother, or the definite association of suckling as a means of stilling pain. Indeed, the complicated reactions of the mother particularly in the direction of erotic gratification or aversion during suckling are of the utmost consequence for future instinct modification: these, together with the side-tracking of erotic play by the infant to dummy and thumb would require a lecture in themselves. One particular drama deserves more than passing attention, it occurs with increasing frequency when night feeds are discontinued and suckling is preceded by partial undressing. At the critical moment a crack or gap appears in the unbroken curve of the mother's body from which protrudes a large white organ with a brown centre and a pink tip, tiny hands clutch upwards from the immeasurable distance of the lap and the child climbs magically. After a pleasure eternity the baby is once more at a distance, the protruding organ disappears and the chasm closes up, leaving the curve of the body again unbroken.

So much for the individual experience of suckling: only for family Benjamins, however, does the matter rest here. For the others, at a time usually coinciding with the anal-sadistic phase, there is in store the mortification of discovering that from another unbroken maternal curve another organ with a red poll appears – the rival baby, during the suckling of which by the fickle mother oral memories are reactivated, although on this occasion with a clearer perception of objects and a more complicated emotional valuation on the part of the jilted child.

Inadequate as these pictures are, they may help us to form certain generalizations. The first has been put very suggestively by Ferenczi,[1] viz. that the child at this stage behaves as a direct ectoparasite, the mother's body constituting the first nutritive

[1] Ferenczi, op. cit.

material. The second is the close relation of suckling followed by sleep to prenatal absolute narcissism, and the third that the nipple provides a point of focus for aggressive and libidinal impulses, a focal point which is ultimately beaten out into a path towards the outer world. This last generalization really follows from the first two and brings us to the relations between *instinct-development and object-formation*, the purpose served by the object in instinct economy and the part of instinct deflection in object formation.

To begin with, we must remember that instinct tensions are continuous and are only altered by some form of discharge, hence they can be contrasted with stimuli from the outer world from which flight can provide suitable relief. It is this contrast which gradually conduces to separation of the outer world from the self, but the only reality involved is the reality of pleasure and pain. The most urgent of these inner tensions, hunger, is precisely that which brings about the most intimate connection with the nipple object which is, however, not distinguished as an object but as part of the pleasure self. Now whilst these hunger tensions recur constantly, developing an increasing erotic tone, gratification does not follow the same course; it becomes more arbitrary or at least is associated with certain motor expressions such as crying. Even this becomes in time less effective, and the displaceable part of the tension, the erotic part, is side-tracked and gratified autoerotically on the fingers or toes, thereby founding an additional criterion for the outline of the subject, the self – in the sense that one pleasure centre partly refuses to obey the omnipotent will, whilst other centres do obey unconditionally. Here is an enormous step forward: a part of the pleasure self is recognized as detachable, is associated with pain and thwarting. Moreover, it supports the fiction that all sources of inner tension (unlust, pain) can be attributed to outside sources. We can see in this gradual separation of a pleasure ego from a painful outer world the play of mechanisms of projection and introjection whereby inner and outer, originally one, are distinguished, although at first inaccurately. We might say that self-preservative instincts, at first fused with erotic components, have become isolated into hunger gratification and erotic gratification, whilst owing to lack of differentiation of a real ego, libido has been attached, as it were, by mistake to the object, which becomes progressively more distinct and more multiform. A path has been found for love. At the same time the original destructive instincts of the organism have, in the form of mastery instincts, become tinged erotically, i.e. a fusion has taken place which is ultimately represented by the sadistic component of sexual gratification. A path has been found for hate. This again might be said to have been deflected by mistake on the part of the self. Nevertheless, these misapprehensions serve a useful function in that they widen the interest of the self in the outer world. The child seems to find in the outer world a pleasure-pain system, which can be identified with the pleasure and pain of instinct gratification and tension.

It is easy to see how such considerations are of more than theoretical importance. We have only to remember that the fusion and separation out of ego and sex instincts is a gradual continuous process throughout this stage, to realize how a *libidinal* regression to oral stages at a later period is capable of lighting up the *ego* point of view appropriate to the earlier period, more particularly the old pleasure-pain point of view of what is outer and what is inner.[1]

We must now consider the relation of the mouth to the fully formed *ego-characteristics*. This can be expressed simply in the series incorporation, introjection, identification. It will be seen that the primary autoerotic objectless stage contributes that feeling of unalterable conviction which is the basis of all future identifications. It is the unconscious character of such identifications that the objects identified *are* the same: in the first instance the subject and all objects *are* the same for the child. We have seen that following this unity of self and outer world the isolation and investment of objects commences with the breast, so that, as Freud puts it, in the primitive oral phase, object investments and identifications can scarcely be distinguished from one another.[2] Moreover, the manner of dealing with the object is unique in that the object is actually taken into the mouth, a process of incorporation which has its psychical analogue in the introjection of objects

[1] For a clear understanding of instinct modification and the polarities of instinct, reference should be made to Freud's fundamental essay, 'Triebe und Triebschicksale', *Sammlung kleiner Schriften*, 4te Folge ['Instincts and their Vicissitudes', *C.P.*, Vol. IV]; also to his *Beyond the Pleasure Principle*, Hogarth Press, 1922, and *The Ego and the Id*, Hogarth Press, 1927. In addition, see Ferenczi, 'Introjection and Transference' and 'Stages in the Development of the Sense of Reality', in *Contributions to Psycho-Analysis*, Hogarth Press, 1916.

[2] Freud: *Beyond the Pleasure Principle* (ibid.); see also *Group Psychology and the Analysis of the Ego*, Hogarth Press, 1922.

into the ego. That this is something more than a mere resemblance has been shown by Freud in his study of cannibalistic activities and totemistic ceremonials.[1] Here we find a phylogenetic link which helps to fill the gaps in observation of child development: the swallowed food is believed by the primitive to bring about an alteration in the character of the subject, actual introjection has been followed by psychical identification. These primary identifications are of a different nature from the identi- fication of the child with parent which occurs later when these parent objects and certain of their qualities are more definitely recognized, but they contribute enormously to the strength of these later *complete* object identifications. In a similar way the oral stage may be regarded as moulding all subsequent object relations by fusing love and aggression towards one and the same object. At the mouth stage an inner tension, hunger, is dealt with aggressively by muscular movement towards and incorporation of what ultimately proves to be an outer object. But the fact of gratification makes this object a love object: as Freud puts it, at the oral stage of libido organization amorous possession is still one and the same as annihilation of the object.[2] In this sense, whilst the nipple provides a path both for love and hate, we can also say that hate precedes and finds a path for love. Keeping in mind, then, the close connection between this archaic ambivalence, introjection and identification at the oral stage, we are better able to appreciate what may happen when, in the course of *later* identification of *complete* objects, a sexual striving leads to the formation of love choice towards the complete object of the opposite sex, in other words, we can trace the influence of oral development in the Oedipus situation. In the first place, the erotic striving towards the parent of the opposite sex leads to a hostile attitude towards the parent of the same sex – so that, as Freud puts it, the ambivalence implicit in the original identification becomes manifest.[3] The second oral contribution occurs when later this erotic striving is abandoned. A tendency then exists to regress

[1] Freud: *Totem and Taboo*, Routledge & Kegan Paul, 1919. [See also Ferenczi: 'A Little Chanticleer', in *Contributions to Psycho-Analysis*, ibid.; Markuszewicz: 'Beitrag zum autistischen Denken bei Kindern', *Int. Z. Psychoanal.*, **6**, 1920.]
[2] Freud: *Beyond the Pleasure Principle*, ibid.
[3] Freud: *The Ego and the Id*, ibid.

to the oral method already mentioned of introjection and identification, the boy adopting feminine characteristics, the girl masculine. In this description we have obviously singled out special
aspects of the Oedipus situation to illustrate oral mechanisms, but
we might add that in Freud's view all other abandoned object
investments are dealt with in this way: it is, as he says, a kind of
regression to the oral phase, and to it is due in large part the
formation of character.[1]

It must be clear, of course, that *other erogenous zones* influence
this ambivalent attitude towards objects in addition to playing a
part in character formation, and it is essential for us to consider
how far these can effect mouth mechanisms. Take, for example,
the relation to anal activity. In its primary form mouth gratification consists in swallowing and retention, anal gratification in
expulsion. Later on we find a significant change: retention has
become one of the anal pleasure features and, although less notable,
rejection either in vomiting or breast refusal one of the modes of
expression of the mouth. Both are associated with a more definite
appreciation of the object and both can express ambivalence
towards the object. In the mouth, however, the association of
aggression with the eruption of teeth serves to mask this fusion of
anal characteristics, so much so that Abraham[2] divides the oral
stage into an earlier purely autoerotic suckling stage, when there is
no object and no ambivalence, and a later narcissistic cannibalistic
stage, when ambivalence is expressed for the first time in total
incorporation and destruction. As Abraham points out, such
divisions are arbitrary in nature and although ambivalence obviously implies the existence of an object, differences in jaw activity
from birth would suggest that in the first stage strong dispositions
exist which help to determine the degree of later ambivalence.
Here again Abraham[3] makes the interesting suggestion that the
retention activity of the anal sphincter muscles is largely contributed to by the repression of oral ambivalence, or more correctly,
of the sucking components.

We have seen that thwarting of the mouth zone from without

[1] Freud: op. cit.
[2] Abraham: *Versuch einer Entwicklungsgeschichte der Libido*, I.P.V., 1924.
[*A Short Study of the Development of the Libido viewed in the Light of
Mental Disorders*, in Selected Papers, Hogarth Press, 1927].
[3] Abraham, op. cit.

leads to increased interest in other zones at first more independent or autoerotic in nature. It is easy to understand that the act of urination, especially for the male child with his nipple-like penis, provides many compensations for oral loss; here is an organ which produces precious fluid to command. Not only is this product equated with mother's milk, but, in common with other bodily secretions and excretions, it plays an important part in the infantile sexual theories, especially in the theories relating to baby-manufacture. Hence the urinary stage not only provides both direct and regressional autoerotic compensation, but, by the process of identification, continuity between suckling and the ejaculation of semen is established. The oral compensation in ejaculation is more obviously regressive in the case of the male, more in keeping with introjective identification with the mother: insemination provides the woman with direct compensation by the equations: penis=nipple; semen=milk. As far as my observation goes, in cases of *ejaculatio praecox* where emission is not only premature but lacks the usual spasmodic quality, there is in addition to strong urinary interests, a marked oral disposition; it is in this respect a reaction of oral 'impatience'. Other displacements of oral activity are to be found in the fore-pleasure stages of coitus: the kiss, the playful bite, the embrace, the enfolding represents a repetition with varying ambivalence of the swallowing or incorporation stage. In the technique of coitus, the immission of penis, perineal contractions which produce vaginal sucking, the ejaculation of semen and its retention or partial ejection, we have again mouth-nipple parallels which permit direct compensation of oral loss in the case of the woman and regressional identification compensation in the case of the man. Moreover, in the act of suckling, whilst the man can only obtain vicarious satisfaction in viewing the act, the woman has a double source of satisfaction, identifying with the mother and again, this time regressively, identifying with the father by the same penis-nipple equation.

We have now to consider the relation of oral activities to *component impulses*. It is perhaps simpler to regard these as forming a kind of ring, on the analogy of the ring formulae of organic chemistry, where the ultimate compound is determined by the nature of concentrations at one or more points in the ring. It has already been noted in describing the oral pictorial setting that touch, taste, sight and smell are more closely associated with

the mouth than with any other erotogenic zone. Now, with the
exception of auditory channels, these comprise the full set of
instruments of projection and object formation. Thus the earliest
act of viewing associated with instinct tension and gratification is
the gradually increasing apprehending of the contours and colours
of the breast area, whilst later on the elaborate ritual of uncovering
the breast is sufficient to stamp the action of uncovering with
pleasure memories. Here the association with touching is very
close, and one has only to recall their equally intimate relation in
sexual fore-pleasure and in the perversions, e.g. the pleasure in
viewing, handling and punishing those other twin cupolas, the
buttocks, or again the satisfaction of the boy (and envy of the girl)
aroused by the somewhat obstetrical ceremony of being assisted to
urinate by his mother; or again the early forms of sexual assault at
puberty by 'feeling'. Here we are encroaching on the territory of
the sadistic-masochistic couple.

In early infancy the expression of aggression and mastery
through special parts of the musculature, the jaw and hands is
combined with stimulation of other highly erogenized tissues, the
mucous membrane and skin, and is associated in particular with
certain smell memories including sweat and blood. Moreover,
whilst suckling provides erotic gratification for the mother,
evidence in itself of the child's mastery over the object, scratching
and biting especially at fissured nipples or inflamed breasts, give
rise to maternal reactions which, although confirmatory evidence
of mastery, are in striking contrast to pleasurable acquiescence.
The immediate result is some degree of restraint which may end
either in withdrawal of the nipple or actual retaliation on the child
or both. At all events there is an association of loss (tension –
'unlust' – pain) which is heightened where biting has had no
relation to the supply of milk but has been rather an aggressive
play. Teething and painful mouth affections help to fuse erotic
gratification with the infliction and enduring of pain, a fusion
which is being at the time reinforced by experiences at the anal
aperture. As has been said, Abraham[1] holds the view that biting
constitutes the original form of the sadistic impulse.

If we now correlate these two developmental activities, viz. the
displacement of interest between one erogenous zone and another,
and the association and mutual modification of different com-

[1] Abraham, op. cit.

ponent impulses, we are in a position to understand, *not* the causal mechanisms of *perversions*, but what helps to determine the end product. It is useful to remember here that at the oral stages feeling is directed not so much towards the whole object as towards part objects – also that in regressive identification the part can be taken to represent the whole. In fellatio, for example, in addition to the later regressive displacement of interest from vagina to mouth, we have a mother-child situation where, in accordance with previous dispositions, biting, sucking or both these activities can be gratified on a magnified nipple. In cunnilingus, in addition to the proximity of the breast-like buttocks and the secretions and odours of the parts, there is a special sucking interest to which we will shortly have occasion to refer. The method of flight from incest phantasies represented in the perversions brings us naturally to consider the castration complex. And here we find yet another more direct link between oral development and the Oedipus complex. In birth we have the prototype of situations where a state of pleasure is followed by loss and tension; later this is repeated constantly in suckling and defaecation at a time when objects are in reality only part objects. Especially in the later stages this loss has a suspicious resemblance to punishment. Now the castration complex by definition represents the nexus of phantasies with associated affect relating to loss or injury of the phallus as a punishment for incestuous wishes. Hence weaning is one of the important factors in forming the pre-castration disposition. The essential difference is that in the castration situation a complete object is involved whilst the injury to the subject is either apprehended or phantasied: in pre-castration situations the loss is a real loss connected with a part object inside or outside the self (faeces-nipple). In orally fixated cases the loss of the penis-like nipple can colour the true castration complex to the extent of obscuring the essential guilt situation behind the latter.[1]

[1] Although the technique of psycho-analytic treatment does not come within the scope of this paper, it may not be out of place to emphasize how understanding of the early stages of ego and libido development are necessary for effective handling of 'resistances'. The anxiety of castration is to be understood as one of the manifestations of incest-guilt; to regard it merely as an expression of penis-envy is to underrate its use in defence or assuagement of guilt. A further stage of defence exists where castration reactions are expressed entirely in terms of oral loss or grievance. On the

Study of the oral pictorial setting sheds much light on the formation of *castration theories*. It explains in large part the firmly
rooted belief in the 'woman with the penis', with its modifications,
'the woman with the hidden penis, the disappearing penis and the
reappearing penis'. It adds an additional motivation to the sucking
activities in cunnilingus (i.e. to recover by suction the hidden
phallus) whilst a passive reversal of a sadistic oral impulse,
together with a projection on to the female genital of destructive
mouth impulses can be traced in the fear that the female genital
will, during coitus, tear away and suck in the male genitalia.[1]
Again the duplicate breasts give unconscious reality to the compensatory reassurance of polyphallic symbolism.[2] Continuing the
study of flight reactions, we are inevitably faced with the problem
of homosexuality. We are already familiar with one of the main
mechanisms involved whereby renunciation of the incestuous
object is dealt with by introjection on the oral pattern, the boy
adopting female, the girl masculine characteristics. Another factor
contributed from oral sources is the degree of activity or passivity
standardized in suckling technique. In the case of passive technique we have direct continuity with the attitude of the male
passive homosexual. Again, active homosexuals of both sexes are
able to represent in their object relations an identification with
both suckling mother and suckled child. In both these situations
the atmosphere of jealousy and rivalry has an additional historical
setting where suckling of the rival brother or sister has been
observed. Finally, in reference to the narcissistic valuation of the
penis in homosexuality, we have only to remind ourselves of the
original carry-over from suckling, via urination to the penis.
When this carry-over has been fixed in the narcissistic stage of
object love (i.e. self+penis) the influence of the mouth has at any.

other hand, an actual regressive expression of 'oral' guilt is a factor of the
utmost importance in cases bordering on a manic-depressive state: hence
it is essential to have some idea as to whether an oral fixation applies
solely to libidinal organization or has affected the process of ego-development (see further: – Horney: 'On the Genesis of the Castration Complex
in Women', *Int. J. Psycho-Anal.*, Jan. 1924; Abraham, op. cit.; and
James Glover: 'Notes on an Unusual Form of Perversion', *Int. Psycho-
Analytical Congress*, April, 1924). [*Int. J. Psycho-Anal.* **8**, 1, 1927].

[1] See also Boehm: *Zeitschrift für ärztliche Psychoanalyse*, **8**, 3, 318.

[2] See also Flügel: 'Polyphallic Symbolism and the Castration Complex',
Int. J. Psycho-Anal., April, 1924.

rate left a strong imprint on the situation, where it is represented in some degree of fear of, contempt for and anger against the absence of the penis in the woman.

The same sequence of events, viz. carry-over from oral to urogenital interests plays a large part in the technique of *mastur-bation*, which has to be considered not only biologically but as a flight reaction from Oedipus gratifications. A situation of oral revenge is often observed in masturbatory technique, whereby the penis is punished by the act itself: the elusive nipple is at last at the mercy of the one-time baby: it is driven to produce milk and its ultimate collapse after orgasm is regarded at the same time as a just punishment. A reversal of this situation is seen in cases such as one described by Abraham where cessation of masturbation was followed by depression and extensive sweet-eating.

Finally no reference to the psycho-dynamics of the mouth would be complete without mention of various infantile theories. One need hardly mention the most vital connection, viz. the theory of impregnation and delivery by the mouth. Again the nexus of phantasies of watching parental coitus has had the soil well prepared where suckling of the new baby is carried out before the chagrined rival.

I propose now to refer as briefly as possible to the more systematic description of *mental disorders* in which the mouth plays a part. It will be well to remind ourselves again that an oral fixation may refer to purely libidinal activity or to the stage of separation of ego from outer world which exists during the height of mouth gratification. In both instances the development of psychic mechanisms is rudimentary, and motor discharge is the easiest way of dealing with tension. We may also assume that psychic recalling of experience has some of the reality quality which is experienced in hallucination. In the case of *conversion hysteria*, we can see that the ego development has proceeded satisfactorily, hence that object investment, too, has been effective. Indeed, it has been carried forward to the genital stage and even in the most marked regression the subject-object relation is not really broken. The outstanding feature of these cases is the disorder of libido development. It is obviously difficult to disentangle from the advanced libido mechanisms involved in *hysteria*, the factors which are due more essentially to mouth disturbance, but the

influence of a purely libidinal oral fixation can be easily understood. Moreover, we have only to reverse the libido path from
mouth to genital to see how in regressive reinvestment, genital
expression can be easily attained at the mouth end of the body,
the more so that this displacement upwards serves to avoid
implicating directly the anal-sadistic pregenital stage. It will be
seen, too, that the part played by the mouth in infantile sexual
theories of birth gives wide scope to the series of conversion
symptoms which affect the upper part of the alimentary tract.

In the *obsessional neurosis*, the primacy of the anal-sadistic
organization and the play of ambivalence determine the familiar
formations, and it is not hard to see how oral difficulties which are
exquisitely ambivalent will serve to sharpen this ambivalence in a
cumulative sense. But it is specially interesting to note that whilst
the disturbance in obsessional neurosis is mainly libidinal, the
subject-object relation is also affected. The attitude to the object
has never been really that of *love of a whole object*, but is rather one
of part-love (as Abraham terms it[1]); that is to say, it is reminiscent
of the early stages of object development when parts of the self,
faeces, or parts of the object, nipple, contributed to the pleasure-
pain organization.[2] Here we have a critical point in the develop-

[1] Abraham, op. cit.

[2] [Note (1955): In this and other earlier papers of the present series,
the concepts 'part-object', 'complete object' and 'part-love' were taken
over from Abraham, without, as I later realized, adequate consideration
of the metapsychological confusion to which they give rise. They illustrate also the fallacies that spring from the injection into infantile
thinking and theory of the (adult) observer's (pre)conscious valuations.
A 'part-object' is an object's view of an object. The true object of an
instinct is that on which the original aim of the instinct is gratified. It is
in itself 'complete'. The term 'part-object' can be legitimately used as a
descriptive term only when the subject already recognizes the 'complete'
object. Thus, we can say that when the child, or neurotic adult loves an
object 'with exclusion of the genital', he is in a state of 'part-love' of a
'part-object'; but this state of modification of aim is better described by
the term 'aim-inhibited impulse'. Similarly the term 'part-repression' is
accurate enough when applied to the selective action of repression but
cannot be regarded as an 'early' form of repression. In any case the term
'complete object' as used by the adult is a (pre)conscious synthesis of
visual impressions, which ignores the multiplicity of instinctual aims
that may bind 'subject' and 'object' at any given moment. Recent 'object-
in-the-ego' psychologies illustrate the confusion that arises from unthinking adoption of these terms.]

ment of the individual – another step back and we are amongst the psychoses. Indeed, it is to Freud's[1] penetrating study of *melancholia* and the elaborate investigations of Abraham[2] that we owe most of our understanding of mouth mechanisms. The two primary factors to be recognized are a constitutional increase in mouth erotism and a special fixation of libido at the oral stage of development. Here again we have a disturbance of early ego-relations to the object, but one infinitely more grave. By far the greater part of object investment has remained at the stage of part-love, whilst the remainder has been attached to the whole object on a narcissistic basis (i.e. the self as object). Hence it is not surprising to find that when in addition an infantile narcissistic love injury has been reactivated by some later love injury, the slender narcissistic threads tend to snap and the object is lost. But not entirely lost; the same mouth mechanism which found the object in the first instance by way of cannibalistic love, helps to retain it now, but at the ransom price of identification. The object is incorporated into the ego and once inside the ego is subjected to hostility and criticism in keeping with the full blast of primary oral ambivalence. It is in this sense that we must translate the self-reproaches, viz. the castigation of the object in the self, as well as the self-reproach for the intolerable cannibalistic wish, which latter is expressed in a more dramatic form in the refusal of nourishment.

Passing on to the mechanisms of *paranoia*, we can only note a recent formulation by Abraham that whilst the libido development has never got beyond the anal-sadistic stage, the relation of ego to object has not passed the stage of part-love, and that in the paranoic regression a part-introjection of the object, penis, faeces and probably breast, takes place as compared with the complete intro-jection of melancholia. At any rate we can readily imagine that as object relations have never been stable in these cases, the formation of the ego-ideal must necessarily be even more unstable, and indeed we can see in the delusional formations, how the ego-ideal has

[1] Freud: 'Trauer und Melancholie', *Sammlung kleiner Schriften*, 4te Folge ['Mourning and Melancholia', *C.P.*, Vol. IV].

[2] Abraham: 'Die psychologischen Beziehungen zwischen Sexualität und Alkoholismus'; 'Ansätze zur psychoanalytischen Erforschung und Behandlung des manisch-depressiven Irreseins u.s.w'; 'Untersuchungen über die früheste prägenitale Entwicklungsstufe der Libido'; *Klinische Beiträge zur Psychoanalyse*, I.P.V., 1921. These earlier researches are amplified in his *Versuch einer Entwicklungsgeschichte der Libido*, op. cit.

deteriorated and crumbled until criticism is once more heard as the voice from without.

This deterioration of the ego-ideal leads naturally to the consideration of an interesting group of conditions, where there is no psychotic appeal to the mechanism of projection but where, nevertheless, normal introjection of the criticizing instances has not been completely effected. The voice from without, however, is a real voice and the punishment no less real, in the one instance social obloquy and in the other the ministrations of the penal code. The most fascinating examples are *alcoholism* and *drug taking*, and in no conditions can we find greater wealth of illustration of mouth influences in development. Needless to say, here as elsewhere the root of the matter lies in the overcoming of traumatic experience at the Oedipus stage, but the venue of the conflict has been widely displaced, and a factitious integrity of the genital system has been preserved by flight to socially infantile regressions whilst unconscious guilt is appeased by social criticism, ostracism or punishment. Indeed, if we go back to the ancient codes, we can see punishment reflecting an unconscious appreciation of the infantile structure behind these habits. A Chinese Edict of 1100 B.C. institutes the death penalty (symbolic castration) for drunkenness, and in the Laws of Manu it is said, 'any twice born who has intentionally drunk the spirit of rice (*sura*) through perverse delusion of mind, may drink more spirit in flame and atone for his offence by burning his body: or he may drink boiling hot, until he die, the urine of a cow or pure water or milk or clarified butter or juice expressed from cow dung'[1].

It is curious to note that whilst in both conditions a flight from homosexual impulses plays a large part in determining the nature of the habit, in the case of drug-taking by mouth, there is, as far as my observation goes, a deeper repression of the active impulses and a corresponding increase in the heinousness of the habit. In both instances there is an exceedingly strong oral libido-fixation, and as a consequence a strong precastration setting. It is interesting to observe how frequently in the series of adolescent taboos, the mouth plays directly or indirectly a constant part: masturbation, of course, stands by itself in this respect, but the series of adolescent prohibitions roughly runs in the order, swearing, smoking, drinking,

[1] *Institutes of Hindoo Law: Ordinances of Manu* (Wm. Jones). Allen & Co.

gambling and direct sexual intimacies, the earliest of which are kissing and hugging (pseudo-incorporation). Smoking itself forms an interesting transition study, not only on account of its special technique but because in the judgment of modern society adult indulgence stands midway between alcoholism and some other mouth gratifications, such as tea-drinking and sweet-eating which are either regarded as normal or when excessive as indications of at the most a neurotic character. Here, again, there are distinctions within the habit. Like all other gratifications, it provides condensed expression for libido-formations arising at other erogenous areas and dating from more advanced stages of development, but special habit forms may be contributed largely from one special zone or stage. Thus whilst cigarette, cigar and pipe-smoking obviously mingle gratifications of an anal type with displaced genital representation, tobacco-chewing is much more subject to an anal-sadistic taboo.[1]

Considerations of this sort add to the difficulty of distinguishing between neurotic or perverted formations associated with the mouth and the neurotic mouth characteristic, which itself shades off gradually into mouth character traits. Theoretically the distinction can be drawn by a consideration of the instinct mechanisms involved[2] together with an appraisement of the degree of ego-ideal formation. Thus in alcoholism we find evidence of miscarriage of repression, together with a strenuous attempt to prevent the 'return of the repressed', whilst the ego-ideal formations, as has been suggested, are unstable and tend to seek reinforcement from without. At the same time, by overstepping what are socially regarded as the necessities of the case, they clearly place themselves in the category of abnormal states. We may say roughly that what distinguishes the neurotic character from these more severe conditions is the fact that whilst the *libidinal* gratification of impulses is direct and real, it is seldom recognized as such by the individual, whilst the punishment situation is less directly associated with social blame and more with individual consequences. The dynamic situation, however, is essentially the same: repression, reaction-formation and sublimation have not been entirely effective, whilst the ego-ideal exhibits some degree of instability.

[1] See also Brill: 'Tobacco and the Individual', *Int. J. Psycho-Anal.*, **3**, 1923; and Hiller, ibid.

[2] Freud: 'Die Disposition zur Zwangsneurose', op. cit.

In the case of *oral neurotic character*, as with all other neurotic character formations, there are two main streams, one in which the gratification is in the 'thing' itself, activities associated with the self or object, and one where gratification is obtained through 'word'-presentations. A very brief study of speech formations will serve to show that in the colloquial and formal use of words, wide gratification is permitted the oral subject. Indeed, they are capable of loose subdivision in accordance with developmental instinct activities. The oral sadist not only adopts incisive speech to eat up his victim but revels in the use of words which describe the biting process; his sarcasm is biting, he flavours his sharp-tongued speech with corrosive wit, a process which usually ends in feeding-up his opponent. Less aggressive types chew the cud of reflection, whilst others, still more passive, prefer to drink in the distillations of wisdom. In Isaiah the word of God is likened to wine and milk.[1] We assimilate and digest information or, according to taste, eschew and spue it out of our mouth; too voracious reading ends, as we are accustomed to hear, in mental indigestion. One of the innumerable colloquial equivalents for coitus describes it as 'a cut off the joint'.

It is impossible to do more than mention the multiformity of gratifications in action; they penetrate into every nook and cranny of our daily life. One generalization, however, can be made; all gratifications are capable of distinction in accordance with the satisfaction of *active* or *passive aims*: they stamp respectively the biter or the sucker. Study the mouthpieces of pipes, the stub ends of pencils, observe the reactions of your friends to hard and soft foods, the degree of incorporation of the soup-spoon, or the noisy sucking in of soup, and in a few minutes you will be able to hazard a guess as to instinct modification after birth which may require the deepest analysis to bring home to the individual. Even in the melancholic atmosphere of the vegetarian restaurant, you will find the conscientious biter at his nut cutlet, the sucker at his Instant Postum.

To the next stage in classification of oral characteristics we have already alluded in the more exaggerated form of alcoholism: there is, however, a minor degree of indulgence in eating and drinking, the feature of which is that whilst not notably neurotic, it does not conform to the mere necessities of self-preservative appetites. Here, as has been suggested, we will find the café frequenter, the

[1] Isaiah, lv. i.

diner-out, the theatre addict who, like the baby, combines viewing with sweet eating. There is just a trace of compulsion in their make-up, and around the public houses of a Sunday evening, one can invariably find a small crowd in a minor state of optimistic impatience, whose nursery cries for a drink once rent the fretful watches of the night. Amongst the third group, where mouth habits bear no relation to self-preservative appetite, we can include paper chewers and blanket suckers, gum masticators, and a horde of other miniature mouth perverts.

We have the key here to one other generalization about mouth traits, viz. that the necessities of self-preservation and the tolera-tion extended to ceremonial eating provide a screen behind which purely erotic activities can take cover and defy the censoring attentions of the ego-ideal. An immediate consequence of this is that there is not so much necessity for displacement on to a psychical plane, such as exists with the anal and urethral impulses which, being more definitely under suspicion and infinitely less tolerated, must attain gratification in the disguise of psychical character traits. But oral psychical traits do exist and have been neglected merely because they so closely resemble the so-called urinary character. Indeed we can add quite definitely that the same intermingling of erotogenic influences from mouth, urethra and anus takes place in character trait formation which we have already noted in neurotic mechanisms. Impatience, envy and ambition constitute the oral triad: a sense of immediate urgency, a necessity to 'get the thing over', an accompanying motor restless-ness, an envy of the achievement of others, a desire to climb, a hankering after the plums, and yet behind it all a feeling that the silver spoon is or ought to have been in the mouth. This fact, indeed, does help to distinguish oral from urethral ambition. As Abraham has pointed out,[1] the ambition of the oral erotic always tends to security and regularity; in the case of the permanent official we see one who quietly, calmly and diligently sucks at the regularly proffered nipple of the public purse. There is, moreover, an echo of the old oral omnipotence to be traced in the ambition of the oral erotic. If the worst comes to the worst, it is, he con-

---

[1] Abraham: 'Beiträge der Oralerotik zur Charakterbildung', *Inter-national Psychoanalytic Congress*, April, 1924 ['The Influence of Oral Erotism on Character Formation', in *Selected Papers*, Hogarth Press, 1927].

ceives, his inalienable claim on society to be supported. He is in that sense an optimist; something is bound to turn up and doubtless he clings in the secret recesses of his mind to the magic formula, 'Table! Cover thyself'. But there is another side to his character; let reality come too perilously near, if he but guess that society is prepared to let him go wanting, that the nipple he confidently anticipated is only a dummy, immediately the sponge is thrown up; he turns his back on the unfaithful bosom and drifts into that irresponsibility which borders on primal narcissism. Or, again, he may turn in a rage on society and seek to get his rights by force, as once on a time he furiously clawed at his mother's bodice. Even in the absence of dire necessity this aggressive reaction can be noted, and oral impulses are seen to emerge in the less urgent gesture of kleptomania.

One more mode of oral representation demands our attention, the autoplastic, or, to limit it to one variety, the physiognomic.[1] Abraham has remarked on the surly expression of anal erotics, the raising of the upper lip and contraction of the nasal wings as if in the act of smelling. Oral physiognomy need hardly go beyond the lips and jaw musculature. At this point the stern-jawed hero of romance comes into his own and testifies to a lifelong steadiness of oral purpose in striking contrast to the darling of the music-hall with his slack jaw and loose bibulous lips. These, indeed, speak louder than words, and in their firm or loose line, pursed or tremulous set, pout or pucker, moistness or dryness, bear silent witness to the instinct tendencies of life as they existed in the first few months after birth.

[1] Abraham: 'Ergänzungen zur Lehre vom Analcharakter', *Int. Z. Psychoanal.*, I, 1923 ['Contributions to the Theory of the Anal Character' (1921), in *Selected Papers*, ibid.].

NOTE

With the exception of one reference to Freud's *Totem and Tabu*, no mention has been made of the researches of applied psycho-analysis on the present subject. These will be found to provide a series of interesting ethnological and other parallels to many of the mechanisms described. The researches of Roheim are particularly interesting, e.g.: 'Nach dem Tode des Urvaters', *Imago*, 9, 1, 1923; as are those of Jones: 'The Symbolic Significance of Salt'; 'The Madonna's Conception', *Essays in Applied Psycho-Analysis*, Baillière, London, 1923. Other references to the subject are to be found in Rank: *Beiträge zur Mythenforschung*, I.P.V., No. 4, 1922; Riklin: *Wunscherfüllung und Symbolik im Märchen*, 1908, etc.

II

NOTES ON ORAL CHARACTER FORMATION*
[1924]

Concerning psycho-analytical characterology, two legitimate comments may be made, first, that in its time it completely revolutionized normal psychology, and, second, that it is now in need of radical revision. Like many original psycho-analytical discoveries, what appeared at first to be a set of irreducible formulations proved in the long run to be rough approximations capable of both expansion and sub-division. The same may be said of the concept of a series of 'primacies' of libidinal components on which all psycho-analytical characterologies have so far been based. A purely libidinal characterology was in any case marked out for revision as soon as the effect on early ego-structure of 'primacies of mental mechanisms' could be established. Similarly the distinction of 'positive' and 'negative' character reactions and of 'positive' and 'reactive' formations has to be amplified in the light of our knowledge of 'combined' mechanisms and of early ego manifestations. Not only so, it is high time that the influence of instinctual components other than those exerting a 'primacy' were adequately described. To which it may be added that the earlier characterological essays were without exception influenced too much by (pre)conscious valuations of 'end-products'. They were too sophisticated and reflected a tendency, only too common in psycho-analytical circles, to project backwards on the infant the more elaborate and fused products of later childhood and sometimes of adult life. Incidentally study of the primary character formations is a valuable field for research which promises to tell us much more of the developmental phases of early mental life than do most 'reconstructions' based on the analysis of children and adults. At the very least they provide us with a suitable check on the fallacies of uncontrolled 'reconstruction', which in recent times have so grievously hindered the progress of psycho-analytic theory and practice, and, in their more absurd forms, have brought them into disrepute.

* Read before the British Psycho-Analytical Society, Oct. 15, 1924, and published in *The International Journal of Psycho-Analysis*, Vol. VI, pt. 2, 1925 [here abbreviated].

Whilst the groundwork of psycho-analytic characterology was based on the results of empirical observations, uninfluenced by any theoretical considerations, it is only natural that recent advances should be closely associated with deeper understanding of stages in ego and libido development. The expansion of characterology in the direction of the oral character, for example, was not made until a previously sketched oral phase of libido development had been submitted to elaborate clinical investigation. Thus, Jones, writing in 1911, suggested a relationship between excessive mouth erotism and definite character traits, similar to the relationship described by Freud between anal erotism and character formation. He pointed out that mouth erotism was almost invariably associated with over-strong mother identification and anal erotism; the association of oral and anal erotism was due to their common relation to the alimentary tract and to the intimate connection between smell and taste. The results of fixation varied according to sex, leading in men to exaggeration of female components (through mother-identification and the equation: mouth=vagina); in women on the other hand no tendency to inversion was present owing to similarity in function of these orifices. No systematic description of the oral character was made, however, until 1924, when Abraham[1] read a paper on this subject at the International Psycho-Analytic Congress. His description of the oral character-imprint confirmed and expanded greatly some tentative observations made by the present writer during the analysis of some cases of alcoholism and drug addiction, and in the present communication the conclusions arrived at by Abraham have been drawn upon freely.

At this point it may be well to emphasize some of the *peculiarities of the oral stage of libido development*. In their most general terms these might be described as, first, the chaotic state of subject-object relations, and second, the incomplete nature of instinctual differentiation and deflection prevailing during that stage. In particular we have to note the gradual differentiation of inner and outer on a pleasure-pain basis and the mutual support afforded each other by self-preservative and libidinal impulses at this zone. Moreover, the relations to the object are all important, in the first

---

[1] Abraham: 'Beiträge der Oralerotik zur Charakterbildung', *Psychoanalytische Studien zur Charakterbildung*, I.P.V., 1925 ['The Influence of Oral Erotism on Character-Formation', in *Selected Papers*, Hogarth Press, 1927].

place because the primary deflection of destructive impulses towards what ultimately proves to be an 'object' (nipple, later mother) is merged with a libidinal relation towards that object, hence that we have the most archaic and strongest ambivalence in the individual's history. The second factor is of at least equal importance, viz. that just as the differentiation of self and not-self is not effective, so the complete nature of the object of ambivalent strivings is not appreciated.[1] So much so that Abraham has differentiated between an earlier oral stage, the 'sucking' oral stage, which he regards from the love point of view as objectless and therefore pre-ambivalent and a later cannibalistic stage, associated with dentition, where total incorporation represents the relation to the object and true ambivalence begins. We might say, however, that ambivalence is implicit in the earlier stage and that pre-ambivalence is due also in part to the relative absence of differentiation of ego and object. We have to remember, too, the almost negligible degree of instinctual control which exists during the greater part of the oral primacy, how little delay exists between the accumulation of tension and its discharge through the motor systems, the concurrent gratifications of muscle and skin erotism and the fact that most of the instruments of object-differentiation and of projection, touch, taste, sight and smell are very closely associated with oral activities.

Some other matters merit consideration before coming to a definite formulation of oral characteristics. The first is specially familiar to us from Ferenczi's[2] work on *stages in the development of the reality sense*, viz., the state of relative omnipotence which endures throughout the oral phase. Character traits of omnipotence are usually associated with their anal manifestations but, as we shall have occasion to see, there is a close connection between oral and anal characteristics, the former constituting the groundwork to be modified later by anal influences. Moreover, the urgency associated with hunger tension, although not in itself convertible into anxiety, may not be without influence on the allied oral libidinal impulses and may serve to strengthen that state of compulsion which is under certain conditions the reaction to anxiety arising from thwarted libido. A morphine addict, whose method

---

[1] [Note (1955): See footnote on 'part-object', Chap. I, p. 18.]

[2] Ferenczi: 'Stages in the Development of the Sense of Reality', *Contributions to Psycho-Analysis*, Badger, Boston, 1916.

consisted in having the drug introduced into a white-coloured indigestion mixture which he carried in his pocket, drinking invariably directly from the bottle mouth, described his reaction to the idea of abstinence in the following terms: 'When I think of stopping drugs, the idea appears to me not only as something unthinkable and impossible but as being clearly contrary to common sense. It is as if some one were to suggest that I should not eat when I feel hungry.' Like many drug addicts he never did feel hungry, and regarded food generally with the grudging distaste usually associated with the taking of medicine.

The second point is of considerable importance when we come to discuss the 'blending' of characteristics produced by the pregenital stages and the more complicated problem of characteristics which distinguish each of these stages from the others. It is, in fact, the question of *oral disposition* and how far such dispositions may affect subsequent pregenital stages. It will be agreed that the so-called 'oral primacy' of libidinal gratification is only relative and, further, that there is an individual optimum period, shortening or prolongation of which may give rise to an 'oral fixation'. In the writer's opinion shortening of this period is more likely to prove traumatic: the effects of prolongation seem to depend not so much on lengthening of the suckling period – except in extreme cases – as on the amount of libido-play between subject and object which is associated with this lengthening. When one considers the significance of 'spoiling' in this respect, it will be seen that 'oral spoiling' is intimately associated with erotic play between mother and child; suckling is often continued by the child and permitted by the mother long after hunger has been stilled, and the mother often makes deliberate use of the act to alleviate other kinds of thwarting, to say nothing of the unconscious expression of maternal sadism in irregular feeding and the conscious limitation of the infant's 'biting sadism' by withdrawal of the breast.

A third factor is the *variation in types of suckling*. Not only are there various extrinsic causes why suckling can be associated with pain or difficulty, in other words with deficient pleasure, but there is a distinct cleavage in the type of suckling between a passive and an active type. There seems good ground for the assumption that dispositions of this kind are inherited and are subsequently reinforced during individual development.

Keeping these factors in mind, it would be no difficult matter to surmise what the general character reactions of the oral stage would be, and, by a process of caricature, to hazard a guess as to the reactions of those with whom the oral stage has in some respect or other been abnormal. One would expect to find, either in positive or negative form, the characteristics of omnipotence, ambivalence in object relations, sensitiveness in regard to 'getting' and to the maternal function of environment, quick emotional discharge, alternation of mood and rapid motor reactions, together with character traits associated with viewing, touching, smelling, etc.

Taking the first-mentioned characteristic, that of *omnipotence*, we find that the usual unconscious manifestations[1] of this are well marked in the analysis of oral subjects but that there is in addition a distinct type of character presentation, namely, an excess of optimism which is not lessened by reality experience. This, Abraham points out, is the reaction of the orally gratified type. Such individuals feel that they will always get what they want and are confident in the omnipresence of the generous mother or nipple. Hence they are in reality lazy and inactive. In contrast to this we find the *pessimism* of the orally dissatisfied type, the forerunner, as Abraham suggests, of the anal pessimist. Sometimes this is accompanied by a prevailing mood of *depression* and an attitude of *withdrawal*, but more often the aggressive component has not been dealt with entirely in this way, and the attitude can be best described by saying that they invariably expect to get what they want and consider that it is somebody's fault if they don't. In the writer's experience, there is almost always present this unalterable conviction of their right to be supported by society. In his fascinating study of a seventeenth-century neurosis of dæmonic possession, Freud[2] described this special characteristic as being the attitude of the 'eternal suckling'. In the analysis of drug-addicts one comes across various blendings of the two attitudes described above, i.e. satisfied and dissatisfied reactions. The most common

[1] Jones: 'Hate and Anal Erotism in the Obsessional Neurosis'; 'Anal-erotic Character Traits', in *Papers on Psycho-Analysis*, Baillière, London, 1923, 'Einige Fälle von Zwangsneurose', *Jahrbuch für Psychoanalyse*, 5, 1913, p. 73; see also 'The God Complex', in *Essays in Applied Psycho-Analysis*, 1923, Hogarth Press.

[2] Freud: 'A Neurosis of Demoniacal Possession in the Seventeenth Century', *C.P.*, IV., 1925.

attitude in such cases is, not as in the gratified type a feeling of
certainty, but rather an *uncertainty* which swings from conviction
that luck is coming their way to a feeling of pessimistic depression.
They are always certain of their right to be supported by society,
and much of their seeming shiftlessness is due to this conviction.
They exhibit, moreover, *quick motor reactions* to any situation of
disappointment. In the morphine case already mentioned there
was a standardized reaction to disappointment of any kind, one of
drumming with hands and feet and impulses to dash persons or
objects to the ground or to punish them by scratching, a type of
motor reaction which is not only characteristic of the oral stage
but seems to be an almost universal accompaniment of drug
taking. In this particular instance, the habit of dashing objects
was usually vented on half-smoked cigarettes, whilst he frequently
experienced the sudden impulse to dash his drug bottle to the
ground, an impulse which was partially gratified in the frequently
repeated slip action of pulling the bottle violently from his pocket
so that the cork came loose and part of the contents was spilled on
his clothes or on the floor.

Before going further it will be well to concede that those interested in urinary, anal and passive homosexual characteristics have
every right to claim these and similar attributes, such as the
method of absorbing and imparting information, as also characteristic of these phases of development. They are doubtless correct, but it is nevertheless significant that in oral types such reactions are found to be especially accentuated, and that they can, so
to speak, 'feed' the later reactions. This problem of character
displacement will be considered in detail later. Returning in the
meantime to oral reactions of disappointment, we find that these
obtain varying forms of expression in everyday life, and especially
in relation to business affairs. For example, the expression of
ambitions differs from that of the gratified type. Instead of the
sanguine expectation of the latter, we meet with an intense desire
to climb, as it is often expressed, together with a conviction of
unattainability, a feeling of difficulty in achievement and of the
insuperable, which is frequently represented in a grudging incapacity to get on. Moreover, one often observes a sort of *rhythm* in
their reaction to business. Either a business is chosen which
involves periodic states of affluence with intervening fallow
periods or an occupation bringing steady remuneration is con-

ducted with varying degrees of energy resulting in the same fluctuation. In a case coming under my notice this reaction seemed to have played a constant part in the choice of occupation. At one time or another means of livelihood reminiscent of various infantile sexual interests had been chosen in rapid succession, acting, dancing, catering, etc. The element of fluctuation was represented in the first instance by alternation in employment and unemployment, but when he finally settled down to a steady occupation, this took the form of a series of ventures in which his unconscious conditions were fully satisfied, i.e. there were definite periods of affluence with inevitable lean periods. 'I cannot plod in business', he said, 'like a cow chewing the cud in a field': he must have periods of aggressive activity ending in superabundant success. If this was achieved he would relapse into inactivity looking forward in a dreamy way to 'the *next* time'. Abraham has remarked on this rhythmic character of oral reactions, illustrating it with examples from more passive types.

We have already noted a tendency to motor reactions of *impatience* among drug addicts, and it is no exaggeration to say that character traits of impatience are almost invariably exhibited by disappointed oral types. As one would naturally expect, it often gains expression through an increased sensitiveness on the matter of time and particularly about keeping appointments. We are of course familiar with the view of time taken by omnipotent anal types,[1] and in oral subjects, too, the influence of omnipotence is very great. It is, however, accompanied by states of impatience which can scarcely be prevented from gaining some motor expression. Oral subjects are usually keen on keeping appointments and often adopt precautionary measures towards this end, e.g. always setting their watches fast, but their main concern is that the *other* party should not be a second late. Should any delay take place, they are overcome by a fury of impatience usually accompanied by phantasies of violence. Even when they have ample time in hand they usually hurry to keep an appointment, tend to walk faster and faster until sometimes they find themselves breaking into a run as the objective is approached. Psycho-analysts have unique opportunities for studying sensitiveness on the matter of appointments. One need only instance unconscious manifestations of rage exhibited by patients over any delay, or any alteration in

[1] Jones, op. cit.

the accustomed hour, or again a jealous guarding of 'privileged' hours, e.g. the first morning or last evening appointment.

Whilst dealing with various types of oral rhythm, one might mention a particular reaction to intellectual activity which, although mainly anal in origin, has an obvious oral component. It belongs to that group of bedtime activities which seem to be a condition for falling asleep. Sleep can in such instances be successfully wooed after a certain amount of reading. This amount varies considerably, but in certain cases a fixed dose is ingested regularly before sleep, a 'nightcap', the directly oral equivalent of which is familiar to most.

Reverting to the feeling of just claim on support and the strength of hostile reactions to neglect, it is not surprising to find abundant evidence amongst disappointed types of *grudge, feelings of injustice, a sensitiveness to competition, acute envy and a dislike to share*. Some time ago Eisler[1] called attention to the oral significance of *envy*, and Abraham has shown how this is ultimately represented by lack of capacity for social adaptation. A typical example came to the writer's attention during analysis, where a male patient whose envy had been aroused by observing the suckling of rival children, and who till an advanced age had been permitted the use of a dummy, found himself with a strong interest in teaching, but only under certain conditions. He could only impart information to individual pupils, who had to be narcissistic replicas of himself. Another case enjoyed teaching so long as it did not involve handing on any specialized knowledge which had been imparted to him individually. This he felt bound to keep to himself. Characteristically he hated dining with his wife in a public restaurant.

Indeed we cannot go far with any consideration of oral characteristics without some broad view of reactions to giving, keeping and getting; and this, in turn, is impossible without some reference to the *interrelations of oral to urethral and anal activities*. Abraham has expressed the relationship in the simplest way by associating the oral, anal and genital stages respectively with the verbs 'to get', 'to keep' and 'to give up'. Further, he indicates the point at which a carry-over from oral to anal reactions occurs, viz. the

[1] Eisler: 'Pleasure in Sleep and Disturbed Capacity for Sleep', *Int. J. Psycho-Anal.*, **3**, 1922.

reinforcement of sphincter retention from sucking. Forsyth[1] made a similar suggestion concerning a carry-over of biting in the familiar anal play with fæces. Abraham regards the retention of avarice as having an oral component, or, more precisely, that anal avarice is based on abnormal oral erotism. In other words, the 'getting' of suckling persists owing to deficient pleasure premium, and is expressed in the form of anal 'keeping', which is thus inevitably exaggerated. This accentuation is reflected in social adaptation by an incapacity to earn a livelihood, energy being used up in keeping what the subjects already possess.

Here again we find characteristics the nature of which depends on whether impulses are merely deflected or opposed by reaction barriers. In one instance a patient was not satisfied by getting up early in the morning, he had to be the first of the household to rise and loved to think that he could potter about in his fruit garden before anyone else was awake; he required to be first served at meals, which he ate hurriedly; he was distinctly averse to the sharing of any kind of crockery, reluctant to communicate any fresh piece of information, and could not take part in any conversation in which the remarks were not addressed to himself in the first instance. In other cases one meets with a liberality towards suitable objects which usually has a slight tendency to excess or may even be accompanied by the desire to force acceptance on the object, a refusal being reacted to with deep depression. This represents not only a vicarious satisfaction of oral wishes, but gives vent to a strong sadistic tendency. It is well observed in certain sanguine-tempered individuals who are generous in 'standing' intoxicating drinks; they brook no denial, but behind the cloak of generosity there sometimes lurks a sadistic wish to degrade the object which is expressed in pleasure at any sign of intoxication on his or her part. In others, again, one finds a blending of stinginess in actual hospitality with a liberality in speech; generous presents of personal reminiscence are given, and there is always on tap a copious supply of information, ex cathedra opinion and gratuitous advice.

Indeed, as with all other stages of development, we see reflected in *speech characteristics* and in the play with words the influence of the oral stage. Not only do we find the usual omnipotent valuation

[1] Forsyth: 'The Rudiments of Character', *Psychoanalytic Review*, **8**, 1921.

of speech, but a variation in output from extreme verbosity to extreme taciturnity: words are poured out in a constant flow or, on the other hand, there is a tendency to dwell on special phrases which are treated like choice morsels and rolled round the tongue. Ambivalent selection and use of words is also a striking characteristic and there is an obvious preference for the use of terms descriptive of mouth activities, particularly of biting activities, the effect being commonly described as 'incisive speech'. On occasion this choice of oral phraseology is only expressed by slips of the tongue, a common example of which is the substitution of 'mouth' for 'mind'. One particular patient had constant difficulty with the word 'drugs', which he would render impartially either as 'jugs' or 'dugs'. As we have seen, this variation from liberality to economy is also expressed in regard to intellectual activities. A curious example of the reaction to reproducing information was that of a student with strong oral interests who, during examinations, had great difficulty in putting to paper facts with which he was quite familiar. When the difficulty was acute he would suddenly have an orgasm, and, although this reaction was greatly overdetermined, it was strongly linked to situations of disappointment, to soiling phantasies and to the memory of suckling of rival children. In this connection it is interesting to note that early libidinal situations can be reflected at the same time in the technique of sexual gratification and in stereotyped character reactions. In the case of oral reactions the parallel expression is often obtained through mechanisms of 'disappointing'. The desire to disappoint others is reflected in numerous social reactions, of which perhaps the commonest is to invite some 'rival' to dine and on the appointed day forget all about it, perhaps even clinching the affair unconsciously by dining at some third person's establishment. On the other hand, in ejaculatio præcox we find a combination of soiling and depriving phantasies leading back on analysis to a fundamental attitude of oral revenge. A patient suffering from this condition and identifying his sexual partners with his mother had the impulse to say to them 'You wouldn't give me the nipple when *I* wanted it: now you shan't have *my* milk'.

The intimate relationship between character reactions and the *technique of sexual gratification* is also illustrated by an attitude in which the oral qualities of omnipotence, impatience, envy and apprehension are all expressed. It is very common to find amongst patients with a strong oral disposition a desire for rapid mastery of any object or objective, with which is combined the wish to get the process over as quickly as possible. This is usually associated with anger over any delay in mastery, but in some instances there is also a degree of apprehension, a feeling that if they are not 'quick about it' something or other will be lost. This may even amount to a state of panic, and in a few cases the writer has investigated, the idea was connected with the feeding of a rival child. Now it is interesting to note that in cases of alcoholism and drug addiction, the same attitude is taken up in the love relation to objects. In autoerotic technique a desire is felt to master the penis, together with an impatience to get through with the affair as quickly as possible. One patient described the process as a situation in which he had the once refractory nipple at his mercy: he could make it produce milk to order, and the subsequent flaccidity of the organ was regarded as a just punishment. Such individuals adopt the same method in coitus. The love object must be quickly mastered, coitus must be hurried to an abrupt conclusion, and in one instance ejaculation was accompanied with the impatient command 'Take it' which the patient associated with scenes of his younger sister being fed. Delay in the process is regarded with apprehension, often cloaked under the rationalization that protracted coitus is alleged to be harmful. This association of mastery, impatience and panic in relation to all object activities is the more interesting that it illustrates how individual oral characteristics may become stereotyped in complex formation and, although subsequent stages must contribute largely to the final form of the attitude, the fundamental reactions are clearly of an oral type.

Reviewing this rough presentation of oral characteristics, two *criticisms* suggest themselves. First, that there is too wide variation amongst the traits described, that one cannot expect anything more than vague and unformed character tendencies to represent the deeply sedimented oral stages. This variation in characteristics is not so wide as it appears. There are three main reasons for the seeming complexity, first, the varying degree of modification which the impulses have undergone, e.g. they may have been merely deflected or represented by reaction formations; secondly, the broad distinction of active and passive oral impulses, and thirdly, the distinction of two phases in the oral stage, sucking and biting phases respectively. Abraham has endeavoured to simplify the presentation by distinguishing between character traits of the sucking and of the biting phases. Amongst the former he includes intense covetousness and push, impatience, liberality, cheerfulness and sociability, together with an accessibility to new ideas; associated with the biting phase he finds covetousness, with an added tendency to destroy, envy and jealousy, hostility and acerbity. These are subsequently modified in the carry-over from oral to anal interests, with the result that we ultimately find a characteristic lack of vigour in 'getting' with obstinate retention, procrastination and avarice. The type is surly, reserved and conservative, inaccessible to new ideas.

This brings us to the second criticism: namely, that the alleged oral characteristics are really borrowed from the reactions to later stages of development. In particular we must consider the relation of oral to urinary character traits, for it will be seen that by appropriating envy, impatience, ambition, liberality, etc., as oral characteristics, we have in one sense depleted the urinary character. Now it must be admitted that there can be no question of isolating characteristics from oral, urethral or anal stages in order to produce what Abraham calls a pure culture from any one phase: knowledge of the mechanisms of identification and displacement is in itself sufficient to deter us from any such procedure. Moreover, it is reasonable to expect that the oral stages can at best provide only a primary modification to be elaborated later. Nevertheless we must bear in mind here two other considerations. The first concerns the nature of 'handing on' or 'carry-over'. Here we have two main possibilities, that an oral fixation, like any other, fosters the tendency to regression during later stages and that unsatisfied oral tendencies may endeavour to attain realization during later stages at any point where identification permits. In either case, of course, the ultimate result would be the same, that, for example, an accentuated anal characteristic would from the first contain certain definite oral elements. The second factor concerns the amount of direct gratification of pregenital libido formations which occurs in adult life. From this point of view there is a vast difference between the oral and the anal-urethral stages. Sheltered behind impulses of self-preservation there is considerable direct gratification of oral libido in innumerable habits, customs and idiosyncrasies of eating and drinking. On the other hand, derivatives of anal and urethral libido are much more subject to repression, hence there is a stronger drive towards gratification through character traits. It is true there is also direct gratification, but it is much more limited and, if continued beyond a certain point, must take the form of abnormality in function, as witness the irregularities incident to the urinary and bowel passages. This would seem to suggest that however much the oral stage contributes to later characteristics, it is nevertheless these later traits, especially anal traits, which deserve our main attention. On the other hand it would seem reasonable to suggest that a stage which can be responsible for such dramatic changes as manic-depression can also produce specific character formations. As a matter of fact, those who study patients with strong oral interests cannot fail to be struck with the labile nature of their moods. They are sanguine and optimistic and moody and depressed by turn: if anything, an easy relapse into pessimistic depression is more often noticeable.

Returning now to the influence of *regression* or of 'handing on' in character development, we may note that Ferenczi[1] has recently familiarized us with the conception of a qualitative handing on which he terms 'amphimixis'.[2] According to this view, the nature of genital activities is determined in part at any rate by characteristic qualities which are contributed from the pregenital stages. It is perhaps too soon to express any opinion on the validity of this conception, but the question might certainly be asked whether our knowledge of regression and displacement is not capable of explaining most of the phenomena he describes. For instance, if we regard 'handing on' as an attempt to complete an unsatisfied oral cycle at the next level, making use of the symbols valid at that

[1] Ferenczi: *Versuch einer Genitaltheorie*, I.P.V., 1924 [Thalassa, 'A Theory of Genitality', Psa-A Quarterly, 1938].

[2] As Tansley has pointed out (*Brit. J. med. Psychol.*, 4, 1924), the term 'amphimixis' is rather unfortunately chosen, inasmuch as it has already a precise biological connotation, viz. the complete mingling of the gamete nuclei in conjugation. Moreover, whilst Ferenczi describes similar mergings of other erotisms, he regards an amphimixis of urethral and anal erotisms as the main determinant of the act of coitus. Even if we were to exclude any specific character from genital erotism, we could scarcely be content with an explanation of coitus based solely on the mingling of anal and urethral characteristics. As we have seen, the relation of oral erotism to 'giving', 'keeping' and 'getting' is all-important.

level, it might not be necessary to assume a qualitative displacement of cathexis. Moreover, if we consider how often in the transference neuroses symptoms are short-circuited to the mouth end of the body, and how on the other hand intolerable forms of oral aggression get expression in anal terms, e.g. in coprophilic phantasies, it will be seen that we cannot wholly estimate the significance of characteristics either by their accentuation or by the chronological order of their development.

At all events, one must be chary that in so doing one does not overlook the economic function of *mutual modification*. This problem can perhaps be more easily stated by illustration from two different types which have come under the writer's observation. One has a liberal disposition, is hospitable, spends freely without any tangible return, is impatient and rather irritable; the other is stingy, grudging in hospitality, spends reluctantly and rarely without some tangible form of property in return, is equally irritable but displays the patience of obstinacy. The former has excellent bowel function, but has numerous functional urinary difficulties; the latter has no urinary difficulties, but suffers from chronic constipation. In both cases oral characteristics are accentuated and mouth satisfactions much sought after; both are strongly mother-fixated. We cannot, of course, pursue this comparison too closely, but, as the oral stage seems to have been almost equally important in both individuals, the question arises how far the influence of later libido primacies was decisive in modifying their ultimate social adaptability. In the one case there must have been strong urinary interests, and it is conceivable that this accounted for the exaggeration of the oral trait of liberality; in the other, less emphasis seems to have been laid on urinary gratifications, and the anal stage evidently resulted in emphasizing the retention aspect of oral activity. It is apparent that, owing to the superficial morphological resemblance of nipple and penis and to the unconscious identity of fluids secreted or excreted, urination is excellently adapted to compensate for insufficiency in oral pleasure, and it may well be that the urinary stage performs the useful function of mitigating oral injuries, thus ensuring subsequently a certain efficiency of genital function. The same would apply to character formations, and, for example, it would depend largely on other evidence of fixation whether one regarded liberality as an indirect oral or a direct urinary characteristic.

The more one attempts to correlate various character traits, the more apparent it becomes that we have to deal with *imprints from all stages of ego and libido development*; from these imprints we can gather reliable information as to the influence on the particular individual of the various pregenital stages, the relative importance of different leading zones, of the component impulses, and finally the nature of object relations. In the case of the oral zone, which is intimately associated with early gratification of viewing in direct relation to the taking of nourishment, with exhibitionism, with active attempts at mastery of what is gradually proving to be an external object and with numerous pain and disappointment mechanisms, there is bound to be some trace left of the influence of component impulses and of erotogenic zones other than those already mentioned. As a matter of fact, in cases with a strong oral disposition one frequently finds social manifestations connected with viewing and exhibitionism either directly or in reaction formation. Curiosity over trifling domestic details is often combined with more abstract interests: in one instance, a strong preoccupation with psychological mechanisms and treatment was found to be based mainly on oral situations, a view which was corroborated by an interesting slip of the tongue whereby the word 'psychology' was rendered as 'suckology'. In this and other cases the necessity for a short cut to knowledge, referred to by Jones,[1] was a condition of interest. Along with this abstract interest one often finds a scepticism with regard to any finding which cannot be given concrete representation. The individual will not believe anything he does not see; there must be something he 'can get hold of'.

Regarding, then, character formations as superimposed impressions of various stages in ego and libido development, it might be inquired *whether some use can be made of the results of character analyses in prognosis and treatment*. At this point we have to be clear as to the use of the terms 'character trait' and 'neurotic character trait'. Freud[2] has given us a theoretical basis for differentiation where he points out that what distinguishes character development from the mechanisms of neurosis is the absence of any miscarriage of repression or of the 'return of the repressed'.

[1] Op. cit.
[2] Freud: 'The Predisposition to Obsessional Neurosis' (1913), *C.P.*, II.

'Repression', he says, 'either does not come into play in character formation, or it easily attains its goal, the substitution of the repressed by means of reaction formation and sublimation'. Elsewhere he points out that ideal formation is the condition for repression on the part of the ego: hence, before describing a character trait as 'neurotic', we would expect to find, not only evidence of some breakdown of repression, but of an inadequate ego-ideal system. Now whilst in many instances these conditions are easily demonstrable, in others it is by no means easy to draw the distinction accurately, and the earlier the stage of ego development, the more difficult it is to distinguish between a normal and an abnormal character trait. Thus the 'castration' character, reflecting advanced relations between ego and object, lends itself more easily to gratification in reality of a repressed system. The libidinal relation to complete objects is more recent, more clearly defined, and the inadequacies of the 'ideal' system, which in themselves constitute a historical 'document', can be gathered from a study of the individual's stereotyped attitudes to life. That is to say, the castration character is not merely a reflection or exaggeration of genital characteristics. In the case of oral traits, the 'neurotic mouth character', if we can use the term, must be mainly an exaggeration of normal mouth characteristics. For this reason the castration character, although difficult enough to influence, is much more amenable to analysis, and gives less real cover to narcissistic gratifications than oral or anal characteristics. The study of oral activities is in fact specially helpful in arriving at a prognosis or in directing treatment in difficult cases since, owing to their intimate association with self-preservative appetites, they are much less concealed and more capable of subdivision than those of other stages. Observation of the eating and drinking activities sanctioned by usage soon shows that libidinal components are much more extensively gratified than is at first apparent, e.g. the choice of food, its consistency and preparation, table manners, gratification of appetite, etc. When the libidinal element is over-stressed we find numerous small encapsulations in the form of 'habits', and finally are able to distinguish an ascending series, commencing with minor indulgencies (characteristically described as 'fondnesses') and culminating in pronounced tobacco, alcohol and other drug habits. There is, however, a distinction to be observed in the mechanism of different habits. In more extreme addictions the punishment system is rarely based on injurious effects alone and the necessity for assuaging guilt by the disapproval of external objects is most marked. In the case of more larval indulgences, the addiction is to what is generally recognized as a 'food', and the injury or individual consequences, e.g. a bilious attack, seem to meet the necessity for punishment. Yet both in minor and major habits the inadequacy of 'ideal' control is soon apparent.

But regression factors alone do not provide a complete explanation of the conditions mentioned: we have to consider cases where the advance to complete ideal-formation has never been made. The distinction is important both for prognosis and for treatment. To take an example: one frequently observes situations in analysis, where a homosexual flight from the Oedipus complex, involving the analysis of anal character traits and the recovery of anal experience and phantasy, is covered by a rearguard of oral phantasies and preoccupations. Patients familiar with analytic literature are quick to offer a seemingly disinterested explanation of this phenomenon; they will assure the analyst in a spirit of mingled resignation and bitterness that they are incurable since they 'have an oral fixation'. The question arises whether there is any means of distinguishing this flight by regression from the true archaic oral disposition. In general, of course, there is always the fact that the true archaic is by no means forthcoming with his oral phantasies; on the contrary, these are very stubbornly defended, and even fractional analysis is associated with strong affect. Nevertheless, it is often by no means easy to be certain whether one is dealing with a defence or with the results of a true fixation. One has the impression, however, that by a close study of character traits, useful information on this point can be obtained. For example, in the presence of character traits of the positive, gratified type, it is unlikely that even exaggerated preoccupation with oral phantasies indicates a grave fixation. It is perhaps too soon to come to any fixed conclusions on this matter, but the writer would like to make two suggestions of a very tentative kind, viz. that the archaic oral disposition does not result merely in an exaggeration of oral characteristics, but in an overstress of all the associated characteristics, omnipotence, narcissism, viewing, etc., and that an exaggeration of the motor accompaniments of oral activity is of special significance. This might almost be called a kind of 'muscle-speech': it includes not merely the usual displacements of sucking to fingers, outside objects, etc., but certain motor activities during the periods of depression which are so often a feature of oral subjects. These are shown not only in the technique of eating and drinking, which becomes exceedingly archaic, but in primitive forms of play with the buccal cavity, e.g. paroxysms of teeth grinding, attempts to thrust the hand in the mouth, etc. These occur mainly during periods of unconscious privation, and it is conceivable that when the fixation is at a later stage the results of privation and regression show a similar 'homing' tendency, and hence may afford some criterion for differentiation.

If we could gain more precise information as to means of character differentiation, it might be possible also to guide analysis in different cases without having recourse to 'congestive' methods (Ferenczi's active therapy).[1] Even when oral characteristics are accentuated by way of flight from Oedipus conflict, one has the impression that states of privation can be brought about *indirectly*, an analysis of which can affect genital libido positions favourably.

In a case of morphinism where drug-taking increased in inverse ratio to masturbation, a stagnation period arose which seemed to be due to leakage through promiscuous genital activities. Repeated analysis of the latter position brought about no change in tactics on the part of the patient, but it became clear that his sustenance relationships to his parents, his food idiosyncrasies and his characteristics of social adaptation (e.g. his distinctly oral habits of conducting business) provided a more fundamental gratification. Analytic attention was then directed to these activities, in the first instance to his attitude of dependence on his parents, which bore little relation to his financial position. The position was explained from the privation point of view, but no direct prohibition was given. After a period of resistance the patient set up an independent establishment, a step which coincided with the appearance of transitory symptoms based on fellatio phantasies. The next indirect interference was to draw attention to the libidinal gratification covered by his idiosyncrasies to food, and again the idea of voluntary privation was accepted by the patient, followed by an increase in homosexual and pregnancy phantasies. Throughout both of these phases an alteration took place in his attitude to the love-objects who had been chosen on a narcissistic basis, and on whom he had, up till then, practised a genital technique on a strikingly oral pattern. He was less quarrelsome and did not so frequently arrange unconscious situations

[1] Ferenczi u. Rank: *Entwicklungsziele der Psychoanalyse*, I.P.V., 1924.

of disappointment; on the other hand, certain sadistic components began to tinge his genital activities and analysis was able to resume its ordinary course.

Bearing then in mind the fact that *some* relatively unmodified Id gratification is a pleasure premium for reality adaptation, it becomes conceivable that *character formations, as well as providing resistance-cover in neurotic flight, may function as a first line of defence when breakdown of repression is threatened.* This might be regarded merely as another way of saying that repression is only one of the mechanisms dealing with instinct excitations and that failure to sublimate is one of the contributing factors in falling ill. But this reminds us that the position of sublimation and reaction formation has never been very precisely defined in psycho-analytic literature: character formation, for example, is sometimes referred to under the heading of sublimation, sometimes as an independent instinctual modification. Two conclusions can, however, be drawn, that the aim of both processes is to enable the ego to control the Id and, secondly, that if distinctions can be drawn, these must turn to some extent on the manner in which instincts have been controlled or modified prior to the building up of the ego-ideal system. From this point of view a study of character formations is of the greatest value. If one regards them as end-products, they can be simply classified either as sublimations or as reaction formations. If, however, we correlate character formations with developmental stages, a distinction might be drawn as to their economic function. The closer the association of the original activities to the overcoming of the Oedipus phase, hence the more elaborate the ego-structure, the less likely are characteristics to provide cover for only slightly modified Id-excitations, although this is counterbalanced by an easier capacity for regression. The earlier the stage represented by the character traits the more cover there is for Id satisfactions. As we have seen, many oral traits are sheltered behind self-preservative necessities, hence they are well adapted to gratify narcissistic libido and possibly to ease the strain of instinctual control thrown on the ego-ideal system.

[NOTE (1955)]

In a recent book [1], Eysenck, one of our most enthusiastic and skilled laboratory psychologists, describes in some detail what he regards as 'the first attempt to apply factor-analysis to psycho-analytic hypotheses'. This was made by Goldman-Eisler [2], and the particular hypothesis chosen was 'concerned with oral character traits as outlined more particularly by Karl Abraham and E. Glover'. 'Two main syndromes', Eysenck continues, 'are posited by these writers to emerge from the experiences of gratification or frustration attached to the oral stage of development. One of these is the orally gratified type (late weaning) . . . and the other the orally un-gratified type (early weaning).' [Here is interpolated a description of the types drawn from the above article and the papers of Abraham.] Eysenck continues as follows: 'We have thus two hypotheses, (1) certain traits correlate together in a well defined way so as to give rise to a factor of "orality", and (2), the position of a person on the continuum defined by this factor is determined by his experiences of early and late weaning.'

Goldman-Eisler examined an experimental population of 115 middle class adults on the basis of intercorrelated scales, mostly of a question-naire type, and a factor analysis was carried out, the result of which seemed to confirm the first hypothesis. An analysis of 'variances' was then carried out on 'early weaners' and 'late weaners', also on 'early weaners' and 'very late weaners'. In both cases the results were in the expected direction. These and other factorial investigations seemed to permit the conclusion that 'both hypotheses had been verified: we have found the hypothetical type to exist roughly as posited, and we have found this type to be related to weaning in the predicted direction at a high level of confidence'.

Eysenck then advances the following criticisms: first, that 'the structure of the traits found is very similar to that which has given rise to the hypo-thesis of an introvert-extravert dichotomy'. And since 'for Jung and his followers extraversion and introversion are largely determined by consti-tution, while for Freud and his followers the "oral" type is determined entirely in terms of early childhood experience, the results of the factorial study do not confirm Freud any more than they confirm Jung: as far as the crucial difference between them is concerned the results are neutral.'

Regarding the correlation with weaning, Eysenck then remarks that a correlation of .3, even though it be fully significant, 'cannot under any circumstances be given a causal interpretation'; that if, for example, introverted mothers tend for genetic reasons to have introverted children, and if, for lack of 'exo-cathexis' (which apparently is synonymous with 'extraversion') introverted mothers tend to wean their children earlier, a correlation between early weaning and the child's introversion would arise which might 'all too easily mislead the investigator to believe in some principle of direct causation'. Eysenck then maintains that in the absence of a crucial experiment between the rival hypotheses '. . . all that the Goldman-Eisler study has done is to confirm in a very impressive manner Abraham and Glover's original observation of a correlation. The interpretation of that correlation is not affected in any way by her experiment, and it would be indicative of an "environmentalist" pre-judice to interpret it as favouring the Freudian view, just as it would be evidence of a "heredetarian" prejudice to interpret it as favouring the Jungian view'.

It is tempting to join issue over Eysenck's comments: to say, for example, that his criticisms do not give evidence of close acquaintance with the text of the original papers, or, for the matter of that, of very close acquaintance with Jung's omnibus concepts of extraversion and introversion, to say nothing of the complications introduced by Jung's subdivision of 'attitude types' in terms of 'functional types', 'superior' and 'inferior functions', 'polar opposites', 'compensations' and 'regressions', It is perhaps sufficient to point out, (1) that the concepts of oral libido, oral sadism and of the primacy of an oral phase (which seem to be subsumed under Eysenck's term 'orality') were not derived from the study of oral character: on the contrary the concept of oral character was an offshoot from the already established concepts of an oral phase of development and is supported mainly by observations of ego-reactions; (2) that oral frustration is not attributed by the Freudian solely to the factor of weaning; (3) that so far from the oral type being attributed by Freudians entirely to environmental factors, the importance of constitutional factors and of a number of unconscious endopsychic factors has been constantly emphasized by them; (4) that the Jungian concepts of constitutional extraversion and introversion have been broken down by the Freudian in terms of specific individual libidinal and reactive factors. In this connection it may be remembered that Jung, although distinguishing a 'nutritional' phase during which the child may have a few 'problems', maintains that the child is not aware of them and indeed does not consciously distinguish its ego from that of its parents until puberty. [3]

Sound as these counter-criticisms are they do not invalidate the methods employed by Goldman-Eisler and explicitly approved by Eysenck, and which indeed might be applied with advantage to any psycho-analytical concept capable of standard definition and statistical expression and control. They do suggest however that when academic psychologists apply factorial techniques in the investigation of psycho-analytical conclusions, it would not be a bad idea for them to enlist the co-operation of psycho-analysts themselves, who might conceivably assist in isolating the most reliable units of comparison, in framing the most pertinent questionnaires and in interpreting the statistically confirmed correlations. This is all the more essential since, as has been indicated in the preamble to this Chapter, psycho-analytical characterology is itself in need of radical revision and wide amplification. In the meantime the analyst is himself in the best position to indicate to the statistician the most reliable of his provisional observations.

Be that as it may it is gratifying and not a little significant to find that correlations arrived at by two analysts round about 1922, on the strength of a few uncontrolled observations of a few cases, have been confirmed by the extensive and intensive statistical investigations of two experimental psychologists writing round about 1950. Perhaps this time-lag will be reduced in future by team-investigators, a getting-together which (although this is perhaps too sanguine an assumption) might even lead to a closer agreement on the vexed and vexing question of interpretation. The relations of psycho-analysis to experimental and statistical psychology are considered in more detail in Chap. XXVI (Research Methods in

Psycho-Analysis), and Chap. XXVIII (The Frontiers of Psycho-Analysis) also in a paper entitled 'Team Methods of Research in Delinquency' (*Brit. J. Delinq.* 4; 3 *Jan.* 1954).

[1] H. J. Eysenck: *The Scientific Study of Personality*, Routledge & Kegan Paul, London, 1952.

[2] F. Goldman-Eisler: 'Breast-feeding and character formation', *J. Personality*, 1948, 17, 83.
    'Breast-feeding and character formation: the etiology of the oral character in psycho-analytic theory', *J. Personality*, 1950, 19, 189.
    'The Problem of "Orality" and of its origin in early childhood', *J. Ment. Sci.*, 1951, 97, 765.

[3] Edward Glover: *Freud or Jung*, Allen & Unwin, London, 1950, pp. 67, 89–106, 126–8.

III

THE NEUROTIC CHARACTER*

[1925]

If it is legitimate to distinguish specific developmental factors in the formation of 'normal' character, it is a logical step to enquire what 'abnormal' character formations can be traced to fixations occurring at the same points of development and whether these play a part in mental economy similar to that of the corresponding symptom-formations. And since psycho-analysts had always paid special attention to the psycho-neuroses, it was equally natural to enquire whether there existed character-formations having the same developmental origins as the classical hysterias and obsessions. Hence the term 'neurotic' character. On the other hand examination of the so-called psychopathic character reveals disorders of personality, varying from neurotic to near-psychotic, which are frequently associated with sexual disorders and emotional instability, and which are apparently traceable to frustration crises occurring from birth to the end of the infantile period of development. Clearly then the 'neurotic character' case cannot be described as a psychopath, nor the psychopath as a case of 'neurotic character'. Indeed it would be absurd to expect to classify character disorders under a few simple headings, for the same variety of factors go to their formation as in the case of normal character. The isolation of 'neurotic character' was however a step in the right direction.

Reviewing this paper after a lapse of thirty years two main flaws in the presentation are apparent, one clinical and the other etiological. In the first place I cannot quite understand why I paid so little attention to that most exquisite form of 'neurotic character', namely, the 'obsessional personality', in which, although the patient manifests little or no sign of obsessional 'symptom-formation', his everyday reactions to love, work and social contact are patently governed by obsessional mechanisms. In the second, the

* Read before the Medical Section of the British Psychological Society, Nov. 25, 1925, and published in *The British Journal of Medical Psychology*, Vol. V, pt. 4, 1925 [here slightly abbreviated].

attempts to include a great variety of character idiosyncracies under the heading of 'neurotic character' and to trace these to disorders existing at a great number of stages of development, were much too ambitious. The purveying of 'omnibus' etiologies is indeed one of the besetting sins of psycho-analysts and is due, no doubt, either to absence of wide clinical experience or to a plain neglect of clinical criteria. I think now it would be much better to confine the term (a) to personality disorders in which neurotic mechanisms are obviously exploited and (b) to those which are dynamic 'equivalents' of neurosis, i.e. have similar fixation points and perform like defensive functions. A purely masochistic character, for example, deserves to have a clinical label of its own. Incidentally, although the system should be subordinated to broad clinical classifications, the method of using literary captions is often the only satisfactory means of designating highly specialized types of character defect.

From time to time the psycho-analyst is called upon to treat certain individuals of both sexes whose illness cannot be classified under the usual categories. In some instances it is ostensibly a matter of matrimonial difficulties, in others an incapacity for social adaptation bringing with it a crop of emotionally tinged situations, in others again a tendency to 'breakdown' in phases of life requiring decisive action. Preliminary investigation does not bring much positive information: symptom-formations of a dramatic sort may be absent, although leading questions in many cases may uncover some larval disorders; for example, a tendency to hypochondriacal preoccupation, mild forms of compulsive doubt, slight phobia constructions, lesser conversion or pathoneurotic symptoms or in some instances abnormal jealousy reactions together with indications that the patient's projective systems are being overworked, attitudes of exaggerated suspicion, a tendency to regard himself as the victim of conspiring circumstances. Some form or other of psycho-sexual inhibition is usually present although it may not have been regarded as such by the patient. Two facts however can usually be elicited without much difficulty, first that the individual is faced with a series of crises which recur constantly and seem to have a stereotyped form even although the environmental setting may vary: secondly, that the most acute of these crises are associated with changes in the libidinal *milieu*, separations from or losses amongst the family circle, problems of marriage or of marital life, changes in occupation or decisions regarding a fixed career, sudden variations in social conditions or sudden assumptions of responsibility.

Should the case proceed to analysis it is not long before some of the preliminary surmises are easily confirmed. The analytic situation with its potentialities for libidinal satisfaction is accepted with suspicious alacrity, and analysis often proceeds with that smoothness and intellectualistic avidity which indicates unconscious libido gratification and portends the most stubborn of affective resistances. Nevertheless from the mass of preconscious material which is produced, it becomes more and more obvious that the situations of difficulty, doubt or emotional conflict have some patent resemblance. They may indeed be so identical as to merit the description 'repetitive'; but even where both stage setting and actors are widely different, the theme is worked out along identical lines, indicating an underlying mechanism common to all of the situations. Moreover, it can sometimes be seen that the situations themselves, although seemingly arising by chance, are in fact unconsciously engineered to meet periodic stresses of instinctual tension.

The next point to be noted is the frequency with which everyday social contingencies are woven into an emotional climax. Two stock situations are observed; in one of these, owing to a seemingly perverse and malignant environment, the patient is 'injured' in some way; in the other, seemingly from no fault of his own and with the best of conscious intentions he brings unhappiness to significant persons in his environment. In many respects the situation is similar to that existing when, within the family circle, the neurotic is the victim of misunderstanding and at the same time inflicts considerable damage on his own capacities and on those of his family. In the latter instance however the area affected is a comparatively circumscribed one, whereas with the type we have mentioned the family circle has been widened to include the whole range of his acquaintance, indeed society as a whole represented through laws, customs, business conventions and so forth.

By way of illustration, let us consider the following case:

A male patient whose reasons for coming to treatment were ostensibly concerned with some hypochondriacal symptoms and some obsessive thoughts, soon indicated that what aroused most of his concern was a feeling of ineffectiveness in life and a considerable preoccupation with money affairs. In addition it was clear that, although married, his psycho-sexual life was very much inhibited. It gradually transpired that as well as occupying his attention, financial affairs constituted almost his sole activity. They seemed to be of two sorts, a concern with speculations which were intended to fulfil dreams of quickly amassed wealth but which in practice failed in their purpose or even ended in sometimes substantial loss. In these matters he played a lone hand although the consequences sometimes involved others. But there was another group in which he acted as a kind of fairy godmother to other people, mostly men, and embarked on a series of ventures which again resulted most often in loss to himself although not to his protégé. A third situation was that of rescuing certain types in financial distress. The striking feature of the case was the persistent way in which, ignoring all previous experience, he would bring about precisely similar situations, entering anew on speculations, being drawn into new ventures and successfully sponged on by an always needy entourage. Even when his operations were successful he usually made it the occasion to transfer substantial sums to other members of the family, i.e. he was no longer in pocket. It was as if the amassing tendency was inevitably opposed by a tendency to rid himself of masses, which ultimately gained the upper hand and resulted in quite appreciable losses. With almost uncanny precision he would dally with speculative dreams until the moment for effective action was past and would then fling himself into the market to be left with a 'parcel' of stock, which he could only realize at a loss.

Another case showed a somewhat similar reaction:

He could allow himself to be effective to an appreciable extent but after these periods of success would bring himself to the verge of actual ruin. Again and again he would exhibit great skill in building up a business; this would be followed by periods of foreboding and ultimately by disaster which in the retrospect was seen to have been avoidable. He would then start all over again with a fresh venture. In both cases described the actual steps taken were however at the time based on seemingly unassailable rationalizations. This repetitive play with means of subsistence can be enacted with every possible variation. It is seen, too, although in less dramatic form, with persons who turn from one occupation to another, always abandoning one activity when a certain degree of efficiency or futility has been demonstrated. An artist becomes an actor, takes up singing, dabbles in lecturing, turns to teaching and ends in so-called nervous breakdown.

We might include here, too, individuals such as those described by

Stekel[1] and Abraham[2], who spend their lives in dramatic representation of some quality or other which is suggested by their own surname, or who unconsciously model their behaviour on the pattern of some famous personage whose name or surname they happen to share.

Other common types are those who, although not necessarily unsuccessful in business affairs, expend much energy and ingenuity in getting into stereotyped emotional situations. Their lives seem to be a running series of clashes with authority, successfully engineered rebellions and superfluous martyrdoms. Others again involve themselves in a series of social situations where they deem themselves to be slighted, passed over or wronged; they bring themselves periodically to states of emotional misery and inflict not a little suffering on the involuntary actors in their dramas. Their reactions resemble very closely the reactions of a large group of seemingly normal persons whose love-life is made up of a series of repetitive affairs with different love-objects, the ultimate end of which is disappointment on one or both sides and a compulsive drive towards the next entanglement. In this connection Freud shrewdly remarked how unhappy marriages, loss of money or bodily infirmity may resolve an otherwise refractory neurosis.[3] On the other hand, although usually associated with some mild form of neurotic symptom, their general reactions do not conform to the accustomed modes of neurotic symptom formation. In fact from both descriptive and psycho-genetic points of view, it has been found convenient to distinguish the conditions with the special designation of 'neurotic character'. As we shall see, there are other character abnormalities of a more glaring and compulsive nature which would seem to indicate the necessity for subdivision of the neurotic character, or for a separate category, or again for inclusion in a psychotic character grouping. The types illustrated have three features in common: first that the character reaction is pathological, secondly that it is diffused throughout everyday life, and thirdly that it is supported by a framework of cast-iron

---

[1] Stekel, W.: 'Die Verpflichtung des Namens', *Zeitschrift für Psychotherapie und medizinische Psychologie*, 3, Ht. 2, 1911.

[2] Abraham: 'Über die determinierende Kraft des Namens', *Klinische Beiträge zur Psychoanalyse*, 1921. [*Selected Papers*, Hogarth Press, 1927].

[3] Freud: 'The Economic Problem of Masochism', *C.P.* Vol. II.

rationalizations, which on many occasions satisfy the onlooker as well as the patient.

Now it might well be argued by those familiar with the handling of neurotic patients that this so-called neurotic character is no more than a sort of neurotic 'aura'. This would seem to be borne out by the frequency with which repetitive situations occur in the love-life of the neurotic and by the fact that in particular neuroses there is a notable accentuation of certain character traits, e.g. in obsessional neurosis an accentuation of anal character traits which are repetitive in type. Against this we have to put the facts that many pathological character changes do exist without symptom formations and particularly that treatment of character changes can give rise to a temporary exacerbation of larval neurotic symptoms.

It is scarcely necessary to recall here the pioneer work in psycho-analytic characterology carried out by Freud,[1] Jones[2] and Abraham.[3] Freud's original classification of orderliness, obstinacy and avarice as anal character traits was abundantly confirmed and amplified in numerous respects by all three writers. Almost simultaneously urethral character changes – ambition, envy and impatience – were described, some of which were later traced back to a primary character-stamp affixed during the oral stage of libido development.[4] During the same period much individual work had been done on more general character peculiarities. Freud,[5] for example, in his description of the obsessive disposition, called attention to the remarkable character changes occurring at the climacteric, how the sweet maiden, loving woman and tender mother may deteriorate into the 'old termagant', becoming quarrelsome, peevish, argumentative, petty and miserly. The observation was not in itself original but Freud's explanation was both original and illuminating, namely, that it represented a post-genital regression to the former pre-genital anal-sadistic phase,

[1] Freud: 'Character and Anal Erotism', C.P. Vol. II.

[2] Jones: 'Anal-erotic Character Traits', in Papers on Psycho-Analysis, Baillière, London, 1923.

[3] Abraham: 'Contributions to the Theory of Anal Character', Int. J. Psycho-Anal., 4, 4, 1923 [In Selected Papers, Hogarth Press, 1927].

[4] Abraham: 'The Influence of Oral Erotism on Character Formation'. ibid. 6, 3, 1925. Edward Glover: 'Notes on Oral Character Formation', ibid, 4, 2, 1925 [see Chap. II this volume].

[5] Freud: 'The Predisposition to Obsessional Neurosis', C.P. Vol. II.

and that what distinguished the character change from an obsessional change was the absence of conflict, or of any struggle against the regression by means of reaction formations or compromise symptom constructions. At a somewhat later date Freud[1] described analytically 'resistant' types claiming to be 'exceptions', exempt from all restrictions of the pleasure principle. These were shown to be individuals who had suffered libidinal thwarting during the infantile period. Women of this group who felt that they had been unfairly injured in childhood had moreover an unabsorbed castration situation. Still more striking was his analysis of patients who appear to wreck themselves on attaining success in life. It seems that in such cases unconscious wishes are tolerated so long as there is no appearance of fulfilment in reality. When, however, reality seems likely to gratify the forbidden phantasy, conflict breaks out and the consequent inner deprivation becomes pathogenic. Another important character study is that on 'The God-Complex' by Ernest Jones,[2] which in effect deals with certain transition types between normal and neurotic characteristics.

The next development in psycho-analytic characterology is illustrated by Abraham's[3] work on the female castration complex. It belongs to the same group as descriptions of anal, urethral and oral characteristics, but, dealing as it does with situations centring round the Oedipus phase, we are shown more complicated specific reactions to external situations and objects. Alexander[4] also described the part played by the castration complex in moulding a patient's love, business and general social attitudes, and discussed the relation of character formation to symptom formation, in the light of the ego psychology available at the time. Shortly afterwards in *The Ego and the Id* Freud provided a stable framework in which earlier fragments of characterology could be pieced together, jigsaw fashion. Briefly he distinguished three systems in the psyche. First comes the Id, a reservoir system or hinterland of instinct tendencies. A part of this Id-system is highly modified, is ranged

[1] Freud: 'Some Character Types met with in Psycho-analytic work', *C.P.* Vol. IV.

[2] Jones: 'The God-Complex', in *Essays in Applied Psycho-Analysis*, Hogarth Press, 1923.

[3] Abraham: 'Manifestations of the Female Castration Complex', *Int. J. Psycho-Anal.*, **3**, 1, 1922.

[4] Alexander: 'The Castration Complex in the Formation of Character', *Int. J. Psycho-Anal.*, **4**, 1 and 2, 1923.

round perceptual consciousness as round a nucleus and is essentially corporeal. This highly modified part constitutes the ego, includes the preconscious system and guards the approaches to motility. The ego, however, comes to be sharply separated from the repressed, which therefore is included within the Id. Now *here we have a fact of fundamental importance for character study*. On the one hand the ego is separated from the repressed: on the other the ego, being a modified part of the Id, is not sharply separated from it and is in fact infiltrated by the Id, especially in its more primitive formations. So that there is possible a roundabout way of communication between the repressed and the ego, namely at the region where the Id infiltrates the ego. There is, however, a third system to be bargained with, the ego-ideal or super-ego, which is set up as the result of individual struggle with the Oedipus situation. Its exact structure and tendency depends on the nature of primary identifications with the parents and the fate of erotic strivings towards the parents, but it illustrates the special mechanism whereby abandoned Id-strivings towards an object are dealt with by introjection and identification. It is known of course that all object relations leave some imprint on the ego, but this particular series is unique in that it, so to speak, incorporates the parents in the individual and continues to function as an instigator of repression.[1]

For example, when the Oedipus phase in a boy or girl is overcome, it is sometimes possible to observe an accentuation of masculine characteristics on the part of the girl and of feminine in the boy. This illustrates not only one of the ways of dealing with the Oedipus complex but represents the typical mechanism of *character formation by introjection*, after an erotic striving has been abandoned. Coming back to the formation of the super-ego, we have to note that its activities are of a twofold nature represented in the imperatives 'Thou shalt' and 'Thou shalt not'. The latter imperative gives us a hint as to what is happening when an individual is shattered by success. Now whilst the formation of the super-ego represents a climax in character processes, the ground has been by no means unprepared previously. Throughout each

[1] Freud: 'On Narcissism, an Introduction', *C.P.* Vol. IV; *'Beyond the Pleasure Principle'; Group Psychology and the Analysis of the Ego*, Hogarth Press, London, 1922. *Das Ich und das Es*, I.P.V., 1923 [*The Ego and the Id*, Hogarth Press, 1927].

of the phases of infantile libido development, similar imperatives have been urged from without and have been accepted from within although on a strictly business footing, the terms being, so to speak, the hard cash of libidinal gratification. In this way manifestations of component sexual impulses have been partly controlled so that, when the final stage is reached, there is already in existence a loosely organized system of primitive morality which in normal individuals is then welded together. Ferenczi[1] has in fact described the development of various sphincter controls as a kind of sphincter morality, a physiological forerunner of the super-ego. It is easy to see, however, that in the early stages of scattered ego formation, direct Id components must be more strongly represented, ego control must be less effective, reaction formations more crude and real sublimation rudimentary. A bird's-eye view of character formations at the end of the infantile period might well be compared with a geological formation, each stratification bearing a typical imprint, increasing in complexity from the most primitive post-natal impressions, through the auto-erotic, narcissistic stages to the point at which the struggle over love and hate of the parents, is reached and passed.

The nature and outline of surface formations will depend partly on the underlying order and partly on the age and vicissitudes of the individual. We know that from childhood onwards the ego is less pliable to character alteration or is somewhat selective. It is, of course, common experience that the process of introjection and ego alteration still holds to some extent for emotionally significant personages in later life, as we can see in the gradual character absorptions which take place between married couples, but of course, unconscious selective processes have already been at work here. Again we are familiar with the regressive character changes already mentioned when libido involution lights up pregenital character traits.

In the case of neurotic character we would expect to find either exaggeration or distortion of the imprint at one or all of the primitive levels, having in either case the same ultimate result, a warping of characteristics acquired during the Oedipus phase. To return to the case first described:

We have seen that this patient showed exaggerated reactions to

[1] Ferenczi: 'On the Psycho-Analysis of Sexual Habits', *Int. J. Psycho-Anal.*, **6**, 4, 1925.

money affairs, and brought about states of financial self-punishment. His methods of getting rid of money were particularly reminiscent of the neurotic reaction described by Abraham,[1] where states of anxiety are met with by disbursing sums of money. The opposing tèndencies to acquire and to get rid of accumulations seemed to dominate his activities and it was not surprising to find that these tendencies were illustrated by reactions dating from different pregenital stages of development. As might have been surmised from his interest in specu- lation, there was a definite accentuation of oral reactions. On the one hand he would show signs of anxiety when eating or drinking with strangers or in a crowd, and on the other would so order his social life that he gave hospitality to people who either had no means or no inclination to return it. At the same time his speculative interests were always attracted by concerns dealing with natural products and food- stuffs, whilst his phantasy life was busy with luxuriant tropical pictures of lands where food exists in abundance and is obtained without effort. The usual character traits of the anal stage were quite patent in his case, but there was in addition an elaborate series of anal reactions which penetrated into every detail of his daily life. As a matter of interest, his excretory tempo varied from constipation to diarrhoea, and he observed a mild series of excretory rituals of a contamination sort, which were definitely exaggerated but not sufficiently pathological to be called obsessional ceremonials. He had innumerable peculiarities in regard to money, apart from the major reactions described. They seemed in- variably to centre round ideas of affluence and philanthropy or of poverty and rescue. He would typically go about with no change in his pocket and would depend on some female member of the household to rescue him from numerous minor financial embarrassments. At the same time accumulations of money disturbed him. This was paralleled in other activities by apprehensions about every conceivable variety of stoppage. Traffic blocks excited him strangely and he had constant intestinal preoccupations of a like sort. Obviously this was associated with pregnancy phantasies but here again he could find vent for his ideas in financial activities, dwelling particularly on anticipations of luxuriant growth of speculations. On the other hand, loss of money would immediately stimulate phantasies of falling into consumption. His incapacity feelings were clearly associated with castration anxiety and unconscious passive homosexuality and again his reactions were exhibited in everyday life, his ethical and political views and prejudices, his relations to family, friends and acquaintances, his games and

---

[1] Abraham: 'Das Geldausgeben im Angstzustand', *Klinische Beiträge zur Psychoanalyse*, 1921 ['The Spending of Money in Anxiety States', in *Selected Papers*, Hogarth Press, 1927].

hobbies. Finally his love-life had been determined on the same basis and his marriage represented a climax in his attempts to reproduce and yet avoid the Oedipus situation.

In short the whole of his life was honeycombed with character peculiarities representative of a thwarted pregenital and genital development.

So far we have produced no working definitions of either normal or neurotic character. To understand the function of normal character and the pathological nature of neurotic character we must turn our attention to the position of the neurotic and psychotic symptom. Perhaps the simplest approach to this subject is to consider what happens when a situation of instinct tension arises in any individual. This tension necessitates some modification, calculated to bring about relief. Instinct tension being a tension from within, modification can conceivably take place within the individual (e.g. in meeting sexual need by autoerotic discharge). This is the *autoplastic* method, to use the phrase coined and adopted by Ferenczi and Freud.[1] But as the ego develops instinct tension has come to be bound up with outer objects. Hence effective discharge involves modification of environment. This is the *alloplastic* as opposed to the autoplastic method. Now modification of external environment implies a sound reality sense, and effective displacement; but even if these are not sound or effective, it is still possible to deal with tension through environment by giving up reality, and projecting on to environment an emergency reality. This is the psychotic method. The neurotic has, however, in effect an unimpaired 'sense of reality testing', as can be seen by contrasting the subjective attitudes of patients to a phobia and to a delusion respectively. The neurotic knows that he cannot justify his fears, the delusional case gives the full force of reality conviction to his reactions to environment. What then has the neurotic done? He has abandoned the normal alloplastic modification of instinctual tension in favour of an autoplastic modification. He has regressed to older methods of gratification but, as these are of a forbidden nature and contravene the imperative injunctions of the super-ego, he has to produce them in a disguised symptom form, that is to say, at the cost of illness. He gives up real gratification but retains a practically unimpaired sense of reality

[1] Freud: 'Neurosis and Psychosis' and 'The Loss of Reality in Neurosis and Psychosis', *C.P.* Vol. II.

testing. The result is that his symptom solution is completely out of touch with the ego, it is irrational and dissociated. The psychotic, on the other hand, has ignored reality and at considerable cost substituted a reality of his own. Again, the neurotic by adopting the autoplastic method has obviously localized his solution to his own personality, and in the actual mode of symptom formation may localize it still further to a particular part or activity of his body. The psychotic may succeed in some degree of localization, as in paranoia, but it invariably involves the environment in some projective respect.

These two considerations enable us to take some measure of the neurotic character. It will be seen that whereas the neurotic can only tolerate an autoplastic solution of instinct tension and the psychotic solution involves giving up reality, *the neurotic character takes advantage of the social situation disguising his solution, broadly speaking, under accepted social conventions.* In so doing he is aided and abetted by the environment, in that society up to a point tolerates character abnormalities and the patient's rationalizations tend to be accepted at face value. In other words, the neurotic character justifies himself as the delusional case does, but his justifications, unlike those of the psychotic, are to some extent accepted by society. Clearly there is an absence of any localization in the neurotic character and there is a deficient sense of reality proving. Hence there have arisen two views as to its gravity, the first put forward by Alexander,[1] who says that the neurotic character makes life his neurosis, that his life is interwoven with neurosis, and the second by Ferenczi who regards character abnormalities as private psychoses tolerated by the ego.[2]

Without taking sides in this discussion we may go on to consider other aspects of the neurotic character. As we have seen, the neurotic character not only makes positive demands on environment but sees to it that the demands are periodically refused, or still further that the environment should inflict injuries upon him. This is of course reminiscent of neurotic self-punishment, the difference being that in the symptom we can trace a symbolic punishment, whereas with the neurotic character, although the injury has also a symbolic significance, it is a real injury which seems to be almost deliberately inflicted by circumstances or other

[1] Alexander, op. cit.
[2] Ferenczi, op. cit.

objects, persons, parents, Gods, Fates, etc. This implies either that the super-ego in neurotic character has never been firmly established or that the neurotic character represents a regression to a more archaic level of super-ego formation and is dependent on environment for the drive which in other cases comes from within. Here we have an obvious link with the perversions. The pervert carries out Id-tendencies quite directly, not through disguised symptom formations, yet, as Sachs[1] has reminded us, he invokes a punishment situation which is real and is carried out definitely by environment. In fact the pervert's solution is emphatically rejected by society. Another resemblance between perversion and the neurotic character has been pointed out by Freud when considering by what means the ego can reconcile the claim of the Id and of the super-ego respectively. He remarks that the ego can avoid a rupture of its relations by deforming itself and goes on to say, 'Thus the illogicalities, eccentricities and follies of mankind would fall into a category similar to their sexual perversions for by accepting them they spare themselves repressions.'[2]

Here we are reminded of another link between neurotic character and the psychoses. We have said that the delusional idea is rejected more in sorrow than in anger by society, but there are cases where wide tolerance of psychotic characteristics is displayed. Freud[3] has pointed out concerning jealousy that although, strictly speaking, this is not a normal reaction from the point of view of reality adaptation, nevertheless the condition can be regarded as a normal competitive reaction to the loss of an object. His next grouping is a projective one, when the individual's own faithlessness is obscured by an exaggeration of unconscious signs of infidelity on the part of the object, e.g. where the unconsciously faithless husband interprets his wife's social relations in terms of infidelity. The third grouping is that of delusional jealousy where, to conceal an unconscious love for objects of the same sex, the man is convinced of his wife's love for other men. This last represents a paranoic state. Now to take an extreme instance, whilst expressions of ordinary suspicion may be based on good rationalizations, many paranoics regard themselves as supremely normal, and, what is

[1] Sachs: 'Zur Genese der Perversionen', *Int. Z. Psychoanal.*, **9**, 2, 1923.

[2] Freud: 'Neurosis and Psychosis', *C.P.* Vol. II.

[3] Freud: 'Certain Neurotic Mechanisms in Jealousy, Paranoia and Homosexuality', ibid.

more, are regarded by others as supremely normal. Many people, however, although not paranoic, are paranoidal in type and we find that in the neurotic character exaggerated forms of suspicion exist, which, although essentially psychotic in type, are often accepted at their face value by others.

Apparently then it is going to be a difficult matter to define the neurotic character, without formulating at the same time an additional grouping of *psychotic characters*. This difficulty becomes more pressing when we meet with character types which have been studied and grouped together by Reich under the designation of 'triebhaft' (governed by instinct) character.[1] Reich includes these definitely under the heading of neurotic characters, but distinguishes them from instinct-inhibited characters on several grounds. The most important of these are (1) that they have a closer relation to the *repetition compulsion*, (2) that they give more direct expression in *action* to *unmodified* instincts in contrast to distorted expression, (3) that there is no single fixation point, but on the other hand a specific developmental disturbance of the ego. His cases exhibited manifest ambivalence without reaction formation, faulty repression, sadistic actions unaccompanied by guilt and were usually associated with manifest perversions. In addition neurotic symptoms were quite a prominent feature, and although psychotic formations were not always present, the patients frequently presented schizoid characteristics.

The question immediately arises whether the types Reich describes can be included under the neurotic character, or whether they are not mixed types capable of further subdivision in accordance with their resemblance to severe neuroses, perversions, psychoses, etc.[2] On the other hand, in Alexander's description of the neurotic character the irrational and apparently senseless behaviour of patients is emphasized, which would to some extent separate them from the types presented in this paper, with whom a feature of the situation is the existence of almost cast-iron rationalizations. Difficulties of this sort may be met to some extent

[1] Reich: *Der triebhafte Charakter*', I.P.V, 1925.

[2] [Note (1955): It is pretty clear that Reich was concerned with cases which the criminal psychiatrist now designates as 'psychopathic': but apparently he was anxious to describe them under an analytical label. This no doubt can be done, so long as clinical criteria are employed which prevent the confusion of 'instinct-ridden' with 'neurotic' characters.]

in one or all of three ways. They may be regarded as the result of variation in intensity of character discharges, lighting up, so to speak, increasingly archaic levels of adaptation. Or broad differences in types of neurotic character may be correlated with the nature of the super-ego formation, e.g. the more positive and unmodified the instinct drive the more compulsive and less rationalized the character reaction and vice versa. Or again, the difficulty might be lessened by isolation of a special group of 'psychotic characters'. For example, one of my cases went through a constantly recurring series of situations which ended in the abandonment of one occupation or hobby in favour of a new but symbolically related activity. Analysis showed that underlying each situation there was a network of ideas which were not distinguishable from delusions of reference. The patient had in early life experienced substantial positive gratification of component impulses, especially of an exhibitionistic sort, and had evidently solved the problem of Oedipus deprivation and guilt by a concealed system of spying ideas. It seems probable that with a more adequate reality sense, this case would have developed either a severe neurosis or a manifest perversion.

But whatever justification there may be for a psychotic character grouping, it is evident that we have not advanced far enough to deal effectively with the classification of types whose reactions border closely on psychotic mechanisms, to say nothing of the social groups vaguely called defective and criminal.[1] Nevertheless, we cannot escape from the necessities of a neurotic character grouping in which the whole personality is permeated with reactions which, if localized and concentrated, would irresistibly remind us of a neurotic symptom. The fact that these permeations can in some cases be distinguished only with great difficulty from normal character formations is far from being a drawback to the classification. It is only another illustration of the commonplace that we can learn much of normal function from a study of exaggerated or positively abnormal function.

It has already been noted regarding normal character traits that they represent the imprint of various stages in ego and libido

---

[1] [Note (1955): It is interesting to note that the clinical classification of pathological delinquents is still very much in arrears, and that the concept of psychopathy is still extremely confused and confusing.]

development, and that character reactions constitute an active exercise directly and indirectly of Id-gratifications and ego reaction formations. A typical example would be that of the reaction formations of social pity and humanitarianism, which express the barrier against cruelty and yet by insisting on penalties for cruelty, give a certain scope for retention of the original impulse. We can recall here the fact that the ego does not circumscribe the Id but is rather a localized, so to speak, external construction which guards the approaches to motility but is to some extent – a much greater extent than we like to imagine – infiltrated by the Id. From the point of view of rationalization, we might say that it forms a kind of veneer which draws attention to the finished surface, irrespective of the quality, grain or warp of the substructure. The simile is, however, too rigid to suggest the function of normal character. This might, very inadequately, be compared with a coarse surface filter made of some elastic sponge-like substance, which holds back the major incompatibilities of the Id-reservoir, but retains in its own interstices varying amounts of the same material which can then evaporate imperceptibly into reality. With too large a mesh or too much pressure from below we are faced with the neurotic character. To pursue the comparison further; if we regard normal character processes as having a kind of respiratory function in the psyche, acting, so to speak, as a pulmonary system, neurotic character could be compared to the laboured respirations of active and passive hyperaemia.

At any rate we have here the idea of a *protective system* with sufficient elasticity and 'give' to meet stresses both from within and without, operating normally as a sort of capillary anastomosis between the Id and reality. When for any reason there is an obstruction to the libido stream of the individual, this system can function as a collateral circulation, but at the possible cost of hypertrophy, i.e. of neurotic character. Should this collateral circulation fail, the psyche gets into a state of libido congestion calling for further repression, and in the absence of effective repression the road to symptom formation is open. As Freud[1] pointed out, what distinguishes character formations from neurosis is the absence or miscarriage of repression. It is conceivable then that *in normal character processes we have a boundary formation which prevents the establishment of a vicious circle in libido economy.*

[1] Freud: 'The Predisposition to Obsessional Neurosis', *C.P.* Vol. II.

This is in keeping with Freud's view that failure to sublimate is one of the contributing factors in falling ill.

At any rate, if we are not in a position to define neurotic character with precision, our knowledge of it is sufficient to permit of increasingly exact formulations concerning normal character processes. We might provisionally define these as a *set of organized behaviour reactions founded on and tending to preserve a stable equilibrium between Id-tendencies and submission to Reality: they are characterized by more or less satisfactory adaptation along lines of displacement.* What strikes every observer of character processes, is not only their almost compulsive nature but the way in which they repeat over and over again the same situation. In the language of metapsychology we would say that the individual's actions are governed to a large extent by the 'compulsion to repeat' which is a characteristic of instinct and is seen in a milder form in habit. But this is only to give academic form and understanding to that more terse generalization – 'Character is Destiny'.

Consideration of the prognosis and treatment of neurotic character affords a welcome opportunity of emphasizing that neurotic character studies are essentially tentative and have no claims to finality. Nevertheless, we are already in a position to formulate certain points of agreement and to indicate sharp cleavages of opinion on these matters. For example, it is generally agreed that character-analyses are more difficult and prolonged than the analysis of the transference neuroses, and Ferenczi[1] has added the rider that analysis of so-called 'normal' persons is for the same reason really much more difficult than has been imagined. There are many good reasons why this should be so. To take the last-mentioned factor, the influence of the repetition compulsion: where this compulsion is very strong there is a greater tendency to repeat in action than to remember. Obviously then the prognosis would depend on whether the repetition compulsion can be got into the transference. For example, a blind repetition in external situations provides an easy escape from recognition of repressed alloerotic tendencies in transference. Besides we have the additional difficulty that this blindly repetitive solution can be camouflaged as a real and thoroughly rationalized reaction to an actual problem.

The problem of neurotic character formation is essentially an

[1] Ferenczi, op. cit.

ego problem and to be certain about the nature of prognosis or treatment, we must have definite information concerning the strength of super-ego formations and the efficiency of the ego in reality proving. In fact we have to reconsider the relation of neurotic character to normal character, to neurosis and to psychosis. Now here we find a very definite cleavage in opinion. Whereas all observers seem to be agreed that there is no sharp distinction between an exaggerated character trait and neurotic character, Alexander[1] holds that the latter is midway between health and neurosis, and that each neurotic character contains the germ of a neurosis. As opposed to this, Reich[2] believes that the neurotic character is more serious than neurosis, and that neurosis represents a peak standing out from a mountain group of neurotic character formation. This prognosis is therefore more grave. Now, whilst Ferenczi,[3] as has been said, regards character abnormalities as private psychoses tolerated by the ego, it is clear that he does so only for descriptive and not for prognostic purposes, because he advocates for character analysis a form of 'active' treatment which is contra-indicated in the psychoses.

This variance amongst authorities would seem to suggest that no definite prognosis can be given in any case until a preliminary investigation of an analytical nature has been carried out. This is to some extent true and it is obviously good practice to delay opinion until one has taken measure of the patient's sense of reality proving and noted the exaggeration or otherwise of mechanisms of projection. But there is still a rough and ready method of arriving at prognosis. It is the relation of character peculiarities to symptoms and the nature of the symptoms if any. To take extreme cases, a severe neurotic character would appear to have more serious prognosis where there was neither insight nor any subjective signs of neurosis. Where, however, signs of neurotic illness were present the prospects of influencing character peculiarities would appear more favourable. Again the presence of neurotic symptoms associated with libido defect of late origin, e.g. phobias, anxieties, conversions, etc., would in many instances be regarded as a favourable factor.

It was indeed this relation between symptom formation and

[1] Alexander, op. cit.
[2] Reich, op. cit.
[3] Ferenczi, op. cit.

character alterations which drew increasing attention to the possibility of treating character peculiarities by psycho-analysis. Four definite observations have been made in this direction; first, that deliberate analysis of character peculiarities arouses not only vigorous transference resistances but is associated with transitory symptom formation; second, that the analysis of neuroses is sometimes accompanied by temporary regressions of character to more primitive levels; third, that reduction of neurotic symptoms is frequently associated with improvement in character abnormalities; and fourth, that improvement in cases of manic-depressive insanity has been observed by Abraham[1] to coincide with the appearance of obsessional characteristics, implying advance from a primitive oral fixation to the anal-sadistic level. This would seem to suggest that as in the milder psychoses (Abraham) and in the curable perversions (Sachs) a middle stage may be necessary for the alteration of neurotic character, viz. the transformation of alloerotic impulses into neurotic symptoms and the uncovering of primitive forms of guilt and anxiety.

It is a commonplace of analytic practice to say that character analysis is often refractory and always difficult, and it is not surprising that various suggestions have been made concerning the employment of *auxiliary devices*. Two of these seem to be in direct opposition to one another yet have this in common that they represent purposive attempts to modify the structure of the ego ideal or super-ego. The first is the so-called 'active' method of Ferenczi, which is intended to produce increased libido tension by the imposition of various libido frustrations. They are directed mainly against certain set habits and concealed gratifications and are imposed under transference authority in order to force repressed material to the surface. The second, suggested by Reich for his 'instinctive' character cases, consists of a preliminary educational phase for the purpose of stabilizing the unbalanced super-ego, to be followed by the usual analysis[2]. A third method is

[1] Abraham: 'Versuch einer Entwicklungsgeschichte der Libido', I.P.V., 1924 ['A Short Study of the Development of the Libido Viewed in the Light of Mental Disorders', in *Selected Papers*, Hogarth Press, 1927].

[2] [Note (1955): Although Reich's techniques are no longer regarded as psycho-analytical, it is interesting to note that he anticipated a method subsequently pursued by some child-analysts and nowadays followed extensively in the psycho-therapy of pathological delinquents].

suggested by the work of Wälder[1] on psychotics and of Aichhorn[2] on reformatory cases, the judicious encouragement of sublimatory activities during analysis. All of these methods are in the experimental stage and do not as yet justify definite conclusions. Nevertheless, we can say definitely concerning the treatment of neurotic character that the ultimate success of any treatment depends on classical psycho-analytic methods which do not shrink from subjecting the seemingly banal routine of everyday life to detailed scrutiny.

[1] Wälder: 'The Psychoses: their Mechanisms and Accessibility to Influence', *Int. J. Psycho-Anal.*, **6**, 3, 1925.
[2] Aichhorn: 'Über die Erziehung in Besserungsanstalten', *Imago*, **9**, 2, 1923 [see *Wayward Youth*, Imago Publishing Co., 1951].

IV

FREUD'S THEORY OF INHIBITION, SYMPTOM-FORMATION AND ANXIETY*

[1926]

It was some years before Freud's work Hemmung, Symptom und Angst *was available to English readers. The following article constituted the critical part of a general digest of the book.* Hemmung *has never been a very popular work amongst analysts, partly because it was largely devoted to a tidying-up of loose ends in psycho-analytical theory, and partly because of the involved nature of the presentation. Its greatest value lies in Freud's re-statement of the theory of anxiety. That it was also a refutation of Rank's 'Birth Trauma' theory is of little interest nowadays, though it may well serve as a caveat to ambitious purveyors of one-factor etiologies.*

CRITICAL SUMMARY

Those addicted to 'ding-dong' methods of scientific controversy ought to make a point of reading this book whether their interest in psycho-analysis is purely academic or openly hostile. Thanks to psycho-analytical investigation we now know by what displacement of forces the simple joys of partisan discussion come to have such an overwhelming appeal, and why they are so inept and arid of result. Their ineptitude in the province of psychology is particularly obvious and it is of more than passing interest to find that in the present work they have given place to a purely scientific method, that of original contribution to the subject in dispute. Freud has shown us a brilliant example of the renunciation of 'tu quoque' gratifications in favour of more fruitful sublimation of energies.

* Being the second and critical part of a Descriptive Notice of Freud's *Hemmung, Symptom und Angst*. 'Internationaler Psychoanalytischer Verlag'. Leipzig, Wien, Zürich. 1926: first published in *The British Journal of Educational Psychology*, Vol. VI, pt. 2, 1926 ['Inhibitions, Symptoms and Anxiety, Hogarth Press, 1936].

Although perhaps a matter of domestic interest, it has to be noted that this book owes its existence to a difference of opinion on a point of psycho-analytical importance, viz. the relation of the trauma and anxiety of birth to neurosogenesis. Those who have read Rank's book *Das Trauma der Geburt* (1924) will be aware that he holds somewhat original views on this subject. They cannot be recapitulated here, but it may be said that his fundamental contention, that the anxiety of birth is the model of all later anxieties, was never in dispute. It was originally Freud's own view and had been accepted by all psycho-analysts. When however he related the subsequent development of neuroses to individual variations in abreaction to a birth trauma, general exception was taken to this point of view[1]. Much discussion followed, but lively as it was, no immediate part was taken by Freud himself, although such participation would not have been unnatural since Rank's views, if accepted, would have necessitated a radical revision of psycho-analytic teaching and therapy. Instead of defending his own theories by means of polemic against any undermining, a course which he could have followed with easy success, Freud has given us an illuminating and comprehensive study of the whole problem of anxiety. It is one of the most complete refutations of scientific error which one could imagine. Reconstruction has taken the place of rejoinder and on cursory reading it is difficult to realize that the book had its origin in controversy. Rank's hypothesis has been reduced to its proper proportions and psycho-analysis has benefited by what is in effect a solution of the problem of anxiety.

It has to be admitted that this problem had never been satisfactorily solved. Freud's original view of neurotic anxiety (that it arose directly from the libidinal charge (cathexis) of a repressed excitation) had never found complete assent. Jones, for example, had some difficulty in accepting the explanation as satisfactory in that it did not seem to be in keeping with a biological view of fear instinct. It is a most striking feature of the present treatise that at no point is the psychological view in conflict with a biological one: on the contrary it conforms completely to what we have been

[1] [Note (1955): This is not quite accurate. Rank's prestige amongst psycho-analysts was such that his views were hastily accepted, and only after some time quietly abandoned. The first public repudiation of them took place in the British Psycho-Analytical Society after a critical review by James Glover and myself].

led to expect from processes of adaptation. Thus we have now a satisfactory correlation of real anxiety to neurotic anxiety, of outer to inner danger, which at the same time accounts for the appearance of neurotic anxiety in the human species. Considering the matter first of all from the point of view of adaptation, it is clearly in the interests of self-preservation to get as far away from traumatic situations as possible; it is a better adaptation to be able to steer clear of possibilities of a traumatic situation: it is still further protection if we prick up our ears at the hint of a possibility of a traumatic situation. Now our standards of a traumatic situation have already been fixed by the peculiar experience of birth, where we are helpless in the face of an overwhelming breakthrough of excitations. And our reactions have been standardized by the same experience, so that when we see anything which recalls the one we revive the other, that is to say, we develop a state of anxiety. But the more anxiety we develop, the more likely we are to experience once more an actual traumatic state, so that some further adaptation is necessary. Taking as an illustration the proverb, 'Once bit, twice shy', let us assume that we have been bitten by a dog and found ourselves quite unable to escape from the attack. When next we see a dog, a vivid memory of the mauling is revived. If this is so vivid as to paralyse action, we are likely – provided we have not made a mistake about the dog – to be mauled once more. If, however, we can fly (or attack), then the revived memory, i.e. the anxiety, has been of service; it has been turned to advantage as an adaptation. It is still, however, rather on a par with burning down the house to get roast pig, which in this case is freedom from trauma. It involves too many risks. If, however, we are alert to observe any evidence of the near existence of any dog, as for example a notice board warning us to 'Beware of the Dog', we are guaranteed a memory sufficiently vivid to make us take action but unlikely to inhibit our flight or protective plans. The warning notice is the hint of the possibility of a trauma. The reduced memory of the original affect is the reaction to the hint, the affective signal for action.

If now we imagine a child being protected from a second and all subsequent chances of attack by the intervention of an adult, it is easy to see that the hint of possibility of trauma is represented by the absence of the protecting object. Advantageous as these adaptations are they present possible drawbacks. If we continue to go on the assumption that all dogs are wild, we are liable to react to tame or stuffed dogs in a needlessly inhibited way. This enables us to understand one of the important differences between real and neurotic danger. To illustrate the case of adaptation to real danger, we have only to consider the reaction of a hawker, who has come to realize that the notice 'Beware of the dog' is often merely an equivalent for 'No hawkers'. He then reacts by ignoring the notice. But in neurotic danger owing to the action of repression and other mechanisms of defence no opportunity exists of taking a fresh measure of the situation. So we must constantly repeat the reaction of flight or suffer anxiety. But as Freud points out, in the case of neurotic anxiety we cannot escape and even if we plan counter-attacks we only succeed in muzzling ourselves. The position of the patient who attempts to take flight from instinctual danger by means of the neurotic symptom, is similar to that of a person who ties up a dog in a kennel and proceeds to drag the kennel about on the end of a chain.

Freud has given a very clear idea of the gradual modification of conditions for danger in different stages of ego-development. This is valuable in two directions; first of all we can observe the point at which adaptation to inner dangers becomes unsuitable. For example, there is still some adaptation value in the early phobia reactions of the infant, as in crying in the absence of the mother, but it is greatly reduced from that stage onward. Secondly, we can see how important a part is played by infantile sexuality in neuroso-genesis. Just when the danger situation has been narrowed down to the genital organization, as in the phallic stage, the action of repression puts a check on effective adaptation. Modification of the conditions for danger does not cease, the super-ego is formed at the same time and we approach a situation where conditions for danger are completely internalized, hence where flight on an external pattern is still less effective. There is still of course a slight adaptation value in anxiety concerning loss of love from the super-ego, e.g. where social anxiety insists on meticulous correspondence to local convention. But the capacity for regression is quick to neutralize and outweigh this adaptation remainder.

The function of the symptom in preventing anxiety, or as Freud now prefers to put it, in removing the ego from a situation of danger, is now comprehensible, and the view that neuroses are not illnesses in the strict sense but rather maladaptations is confirmed.

Recognition of actual lessening of instinctual danger being precluded by defence, e.g. repression, the process of flight is maintained on the archaic, autoplastic level, indeed cannot be otherwise, because although ejected from the ego, the excitations remain in the Id, of which the ego is only the organized portion. The fact that a symptom is a sort of boundary formation where Id and ego meet, though not on terms of equality, made it necessary to draw a distinction, otherwise unimportant, between a symptom and an inhibition. The inhibition, Freud says, comes from the ego, limits or modifies function and serves to avoid conflict. The symptom is a compromise of actual conflict, existing outside the ego, and capable, in accordance with the intensity of Id-excitations, of aggrandizement at the expense of the ego. So far the distinction is quite clear, and in dissecting a typical phobia Freud separates out the pure inhibition element and dismisses it from further consideration. It is perfectly true that in relation to the continuance of danger situations the inhibition is on a different plane from the symptom. It does not provide any positive gratification of repressed instinct excitation like the symptom, hence is not repudiated by the ego. On the other hand, it does not bind anxiety in the same way as the symptom. At this point the distinction between inhibition and symptom becomes less effective. Freud agrees that in so far as the inhibition prevents anxiety, every inhibition can be called a symptom, so that for general clinical purposes, the distinction has lost significance and we are thrown back on dynamic considerations. Freud has not elaborated the point any more than is necessary for purposes of his argument, but it would have been interesting to follow the matter further, in view of the fact that he has given a more detailed description and correlation of various methods of defence.

We now have to distinguish under the main heading of defence several mechanisms, e.g. repression, regression, reaction formation, 'undoing', isolating, etc. Further we are given the hint that these have probably some particular relation to stages of development and types of neurotic reaction. Repression, for example, is regarded as a genital form of defence, and associated closely with hysteria. Reaction formation is also present in hysteria but is directed against perceptions from without which stimulate; the reaction formation of obsessional neurosis is directed against inner stimuli. Freud also holds that in each neurosis there is probably a characteristic condition for danger, e.g. loss of love from the object being the condition for anxiety in hysteria as castration in phobias and super-ego anxiety in obsessional neuroses. The tendency to distinguish other mechanisms of defence from repression has already been heralded in Laforgue's description of the process of 'scotomization', which Freud considers as identical with his hysterical form of reaction formation, or outer anti-cathexis. The association of regression and inner reaction formation in obsessional neurosis is quite in keeping with the auxiliary function of regression alongside repression. Both are forms of flight, but regression combines with flight, the advantages or disadvantages of gratification at an earlier level of development.

It is obvious that Freud has contented himself here with indicating certain possibilities and fruitful lines of research. No attempt has been made to present a worked out plan or to gloss over possible difficulties in correlation. It is very probable that the first fruits of his suggestions will be the segregation of numerous mechanisms of defence which have not before been regarded from this point of view. In two instances the way seems already clear. For example, difficulties regarding symptoms and inhibitions might conceivably be cleared up by investigating the place of inhibition as a mechanism of defence, not as a result of defence. Comparing repression, for example, with inhibition, it might be said that repression interferes at an early stage of defence by withdrawing cathexis from the preconscious presentation, whereas inhibition interferes, in motor instances at any rate, at the outside margin of ego-control, the approach to motility. Correlating this with the reaction to danger we might say that whilst inhibition avoids conflict, it does so rather after the fashion of the animal which avoids danger by immobility, by shamming death, etc. An obvious difficulty here would be the position of so-called thought inhibition. But as there are some resemblances between thought inhibition and amnesia and scotomization respectively, this difficulty might not prove insuperable. A clinical example may serve to illustrate the above view of the relation of inhibition to defence. In certain cases of anxiety hysteria, we can observe during analysis that solution of psycho-sexual difficulties brings about a transitory disturbance of sexual function or a variation in existing disturbances. A patient, for example, who owing to conflict over adult sexuality has never entered into adult object relations, may, on gaining courage to face the situation, find that he is for the time being entirely or partly impotent. Repressions have been loosened, inhibitions have increased, and defence is offered at the margin of motility.

A second mechanism, the defensive possibilities of which might be explored, is that of introjection. We are familiar with this mechanism in its oral form and, at the Oedipus stage, during the process of super-ego formation. In the latter instance, it is clear that compensation for loss of an outer object is gained by an inner substitution. It seems probable that this compensation persists and that in the case of grief over loss of objects, the loss being not only reminiscent of conditions of danger of trauma, but an actual injury, introjection has an immediately defensive purpose.

Returning to the main problem of anxiety we can see that Freud's abandonment of his earlier views on the nature of anxiety is not so much a repudiation as a reorganization. Anxiety is the reaction to danger, and can have either a controlled or an uncontrolled expression. If the ego is given any say in the matter we have a controlled reaction, together with measures to prevent its spread. If the danger develops in the Id the control system cannot be put in operation and the ego tends to be overcome with repetitive anxiety, as in the state of undischarged excitation of the actual neurosis. In the latter case, the change over from undischarged libido to anxiety is direct because an immediate situation of helplessness has arisen. When on the other hand the ego perceives the danger and is able to give a signal, this signal does not come from libido but is a repetition, a slight re-experience of the ego's original reaction to trauma. The ego may still employ the energy of libido in the anxiety discharge, but this is a state of affairs, viz. the ego operating with energy originally libidinal in nature, with which we are quite familiar, e.g. in the processes of sublimation. A new set of problems arises here. What happens to excitations in the Id-system? The answer to this one question will keep psychoanalysts busy for some considerable time to come.

[1938]

The following review[1] was published twelve years later, following the publication of the book in English translation. It is of some

---

[1] *Inhibitions, Symptoms and Anxiety* (Hogarth Press, London, 1936). The review was first published in the *Int. J. Psycho-Anal.*, **19**, pt. 1, Jan. 1938.

interest to observe the effect of intervening controversies regarding stages in the development of ego- and super-ego on theories of anxiety. For this reason I have abandoned at this point the arrangement of these papers in chronological order.

The review is also of some historical interest in that it adumbrated the idea of 'fusion' of primary affects to form secondary affects, later expanded in 'The Psycho-analysis of Affects' (see Chap. XIX).

The appearance, after a lapse of twelve years, of the first English translation of *Hemmung, Symptom u. Angst* affords a tempting opportunity to re-assess the significance of this remarkable book. For there is no question that the book is a remarkable one. It contains some of the most important of Freud's later contributions to psycho-analytical theory; it provides an outstanding illustration of his capacity to revise his own theory whenever he feels that the facts warrant revision; and it is without doubt the most disjointed presentation ever published by one who has so often proved himself a master of orderly exposition.

One of the circumstances contributing to this disorder is not so extenuating now as it seemed at the time. Two years before, one of Freud's favourite pupils had signalized his coming defection from psycho-analysis by publishing a book on the Trauma of Birth, the argument of which – if widely accepted – would have arrested the growth of that science. Interestingly enough, Rank's theory was, in fact, hastily swallowed by a number of analysts whose enthusiasm and sense of prestige had outrun their scientific discretion. [On the publication of *Hemmung* they surreptitiously disgorged the forbidden fruit.] Freud, more cautiously and temperately took the whole problem to avizandum, and produced a book which served the double purpose of refuting Rank's views and advancing a new theory of anxiety. We now know that the first of these aims was scarcely worth the trouble. In earlier times the defection of any important adherent was a serious matter, but by 1926 psycho-analysis had reached the stage when it could weather any defection. Indeed, it is interesting to reflect that had the Jung and Adler schisms occurred about the same time, the Zürich school would not have come to figure quite so prominently in the public eye as it does, and the Adlerian system would, in all probability, have been stillborn.

But even if Rank had never produced the birth-trauma theory it would have been necessary for Freud to write a book on anxiety. His earlier theories of anxiety had never been entirely satisfactory, and they could be maintained only so long as simpler views of mental structure prevailed, e.g. the concept of an 'unconscious system' shut off from the ego by a 'repression' barrier. Having given himself more elbow room by his tripartite division of the psyche (ego – super-ego and Id), Freud was faced with the task of readjusting and amplifying his earlier and over simple meta-psychology. It is this process of readjustment that Freud presents to us in a characteristic way. He thinks aloud. The orderliness of this thinking depends very much on the nature of the problem and the degree to which he has already predigested the material. In most cases it is a method he has used with conspicuous success. In the case of *Hemmung* the issues were peculiarly involved, touching not only on the central problem of anxiety, but on ego structure, symptom formation, the nature of affects, and so forth. Almost inevitably the thinking-aloud method added to rather than reduced this complication. Faced with a number of weak places in the line of his theory, he had to keep moving back and forward, reinforcing at some points, reconstructing at others, and at others again staking a claim for future research. In short, the material Freud crammed into one short book would have justified a series of separate volumes. And it is a thousand pities he did not write them. For except in two particulars, viz. the early structure of the ego and the early content of the unconscious, the progress of analysis since 1926 has been extremely slow. Most of the hints and suggestions thrown out in this book have fallen on stony ground, no doubt waiting for someone of Freud's own calibre to develop them. So far that portent has not appeared in the psycho-analytical sky.

Despite the complex nature of the material, the book stands or falls by its theory of anxiety. And there can be no doubt that, in most essential respects, his revised theory has stood the test of time. The relations of anxiety to instinct, to ego-structure, to mental defence mechanisms and ultimately to symptom formation are soundly described. No better theory has been put forward in the intervening ten years, nor is it likely that one will appear in the next twenty. The dangers of excessive excitation, the existence of defence barriers, the traumatic situation arising when these

barriers are broken down, the danger situation existing when
trauma is threatened, the exploitation of doses of anxiety as a
danger-signal system, and the displacement of signalling from the
danger situation to the condition threatening danger, all this is
still extremely plausible. On the other hand, the assessment of
external and endopsychic factors in real and neurotic anxiety
respectively, the correlation of different types of anxiety with
different phases of development, and in particular the relation of
phobia formation to super-ego development do not carry the
same conviction as formerly. As I have indicated, these criticisms
do not invalidate the theory but they do make one wonder why
one part of the theory should have proved less firmly founded than
the rest.

One reason for this patchiness is not difficult to detect. Reading
the book afresh in translated form one cannot but be impressed
with the old-fashioned nature of the clinical material from which
Freud's thread of argument is drawn. It has always been his habit
to extract the last ounce from his clinical material, and it is part of
his genius to make an unusually large percentage of accurate
generalizations from a single case or even from one aspect of a
case. In its time the analysis of Little Hans was a remarkable
achievement and the story of the analysis constitutes one of the
most valued records in psycho-analytical archives. Our concepts
of phobia-formation, of the positive Oedipus complex, of ambivalence, castration anxiety, and repression, to mention but a few,
were greatly reinforced and amplified as the result of this analysis.
But it was scarcely exhaustive enough to provide the basis for far-
reaching conclusions as to the nature of anxiety. In any case the
pregenital stages still remained unexplored territory. What we
knew of them was derived mostly from obsessional cases and some
studies of melancholia. And that knowledge was somewhat confusing. Obsessional cases experienced unconscious conflict over
pregenital interests, yet these neuroses were supposed to date after
the appearance of infantile hysteria. Apparent contradictions of
this sort might well have been avoided by a provisional confession
of ignorance. Unfortunately, this course was not followed, and,
for some time before *Hemmung* was published, views on pregenital
stages, on the etiology of hysteria and obsessional neurosis, and
on symptom structure had come to be accepted without question.
There is ample evidence in *Hemmung* that these old views were

taken over without any modification. Discussing the primary phobias of infants Freud adopts an old-fashioned classification and jumps from these early stages to the symptomatic phobias of a five-year-old. Now the simplest behaviouristic observation of infants shows that by the time they can talk they exhibit a considerable number of phobias. During the second, third and fourth years these phobias go through elaborate development. Sometimes they disappear spontaneously. Sometimes they merge in fresh formations. Sometimes they become fixed and potentially symptomatic. Admittedly, observations of children were then very rudimentary [despite an increase in the number of analytic observations of small children, child study is still one of the most neglected branches of psycho-analysis]; they were not improved by the analyst's habit of selective examination, looking only for facts that would confirm conclusions already reached in the adult field. In short it may be said that Freud's analysis of anxiety situations was handicapped by lack of sufficient clinical observation of children and by bias in favour of those analytical conclusions derived from study of adults.

The second source of error is even more interesting. It was actually the neglect to employ systematically enough a form of approach which he himself had just won for psycho-analysis. The importance of repression and of the relation between the repressed and the unconscious had led to a formulation of mental structure which, as I have suggested earlier, was proving inclastic. Freud in this very book had swept the old system almost completely away. He described repression as one of a series of defence functions, gave a definite place to reaction-formation, regression, undoing, and sought to associate these mechanisms with characteristic clinical pictures. [*A propos* of the mechanism of undoing, devotees to restitution-psychology, of whom there are not a few in this country, should note that Freud himself is the Father of Restitution-psychology. He places it along with other expiatory and ritualistic phenomena in the department of obsessional religiosity.] It is the more remarkable that in his analysis of anxiety formations Freud should have neglected the part played by projection and introjection. All the more remarkable since he was the first to describe and explain these very mechanisms. And although nowadays the elaborate phantasy content of projection and introjection systems has been more fully recorded we have not added to Freud's original description of their origin and function. It is now clear that for theoretical purposes phobia formations cannot be analysed solely in terms of reaction to castration anxiety. The balance of real and unreal anxiety must from the very first months of life be influenced by processes of introjection and projection. This does not mean that the clinical reading of a five-year-old phobia in terms of castration anxiety is inaccurate. Given reasonably efficient diagnosis and the exclusion of early psychotic tendencies it is in all probability extremely accurate. But one should not confuse the clinical assessment of a symptom with the analysis of its structure and development.

The third difficulty is of the same order as the second. Obviously if the super-ego dated from the passing of the Oedipus complex, it would be easy to describe a rapid transition from external to purely endopsychic sources of anxiety. But the time was already ripe to modify this view. So-called pre-Oedipus stages had always been treated by psycho-analysts with a lack of imagination almost as great as that exhibited by academic psychologists in their handling of adults. After all, if the passing of the genital Oedipus phase produced a strong introjection pattern there was no reason to suppose that the passing of earlier phases of libido did not produce characteristic introjection patterns in which the object, as conceived at each phase, would be set up in the ego. But this would mean that endopsychic fear of the super-ego would exist from early phases of development and would contribute a degree of unreality to more realistic estimations of external objects. Behaviouristic evidence was much in favour of this view, for despite a tendency to regard obsessional patterns as of comparatively late development, there are almost as many varieties of obsessional action in the second year of life as there are varieties of anxiety in the first.

I have gone into these blemishes in some detail because a book such as this should be assessed by the effect it produces on research. During the twelve years following its publication the progress of analysis has not only been slow but uneven. Sharp divergences of opinion have appeared, which reflect accurately the mixture of old and new views present in this book. This can easily be tested by reading the journals of the period. Contributions from the more orthodox branches on the Continent have reached a high peak of monotony. In this country an early break away from tradition gave rise to a few fruitful years of research, but now threatens to defeat its own aims. Recent work shows some of the same rigidity of outlook which prevented advance along the more orthodox lines. Introjection and projection mechanisms are now treated with some of that fetichistic reverence formerly reserved for repression. Repression has quite unjustifiably lost caste and with this for a time, anyhow, has gone some depreciation of libidinal factors in neurosogenesis. Fortunately, there is a pendulum swing in all such movements, and whereas in Continental circles the most recent movement is in the direction of rediscovering the early super-ego, in this country in recent years the tendency has been to rediscover the early libido. It is indeed remarkable how much energy is spent in all psycho-analytical groups in rediscovery as distinct from restatement.

Some of these differences are, no doubt, due to inadequate study of the literature by both sides, but in any case they could have been reduced had more attention been paid to what is, after all, the main concern of this book, viz. *the analysis of affect*. It is an interesting fact that as far as the therapeutic results of analysis are recorded or can be studied directly, there is little to distinguish the results obtained by analysts holding different theoretical views. It is true that analysts now attempt more difficult cases than formerly, but this is due less to increased efficiency of analytical ideas than to decrease of timidity in handling pre-psychotic types. The moral is, of course, that therapeutic results are due less to length of analysis or level of interpretation than to the speed and success with which the patient's affective states (actual or potential) are ventilated and reduced. Granted that the importance of affect has been stressed from the very earliest 'carthartic' days, it is nevertheless a fact that analysis of affect has not kept pace with analysis of ego-structure, of unconscious content, or of defence-mechanisms. By comparison it has been woefully neglected. For this reason alone, *Hemmung* will always be one of the most important books of analytical reference. It contains not only a penetrating analysis of anxiety, but enters into the relation of anxiety to pain and grief. Freud's approach to this problem is one which might well have been applied to the problems of depression, jealousy, envy, to say nothing of more positive affects of the elation group. To a varying extent all scientists are suggestible creatures. Analysts are no exception to this rule. They incline to be seduced by the fashions of the moment. Long ago the catchwords were 'anxiety' and 'libido' – later they changed to 'guilt' and 'sadism', and nowadays the choice lies between 'guilt' and 'bad objects', or 'restitution' and 'good objects'. But anxiety and guilt are not simply affective states: they are the father and mother of a large progeny of affects. That is to say: although anxiety and guilt can be experienced in a diluted form as current affects their greatest contribution to mental activity lies in instigating secondary affects which in their turn become attached to ideational systems. Guilt, as Freud said, is no doubt a special modification of anxiety, but its origins are so remote that it deserves the label of a primary affect. Even so, anxiety and guilt are not the only primary affects. To analyse depression solely in terms of guilt or of guilt-release is to ignore the multiplicity of affective sources existing from birth, to say nothing of the affect-fusions that occur later. We cannot expect to understand the use made of different mechanisms at different stages of development unless we know just what are the combinations or contrasts of affect with which the child's mind has to deal. Reviewing this book in some detail twelve years ago I pointed out that the mechanism of introjection had to be regarded not only as a response to the anxiety-aspect of psychic loss of object occurring in infancy, but as a mechanism employed constantly to mitigate the reality of pain and grief. I went on to indicate, however, that behind all problems of the relation of mechanism to affect lay one major issue: what happens to excitations in the Id-system? Is it the case, as Freud has suggested, that the primary cathexis of unconscious constellations can become spontaneously reduced? At that time I wrote – 'the answer to this one question will keep psycho-analysts busy for some considerable time to come'. The expectation was over sanguine. Nothing has been added to the tentative formulations set down by Freud. Yet until this problem is solved a number of controversial issues must remain unsettled – questions of etiology, of analytical as distinct from clinical diagnosis, of prognosis – to say nothing of the theory of therapeutic results. I hesitate now to prophesy about the researches of the next ten years, but I have no hesitation in saying that this issue of Id-excitation has first claim on our attention.

V

THE ETIOLOGY OF ALCOHOLISM*
[1928]

The progress of clinical psycho-analysis has been greatly influenced by the incidence of mental disorders. Statistically speaking it was natural enough that the psycho-neuroses should receive priority of attention and it was extremely fortunate that their structure should permit a pretty full description of the stages and mechanisms of symptom-formation. Only another step was needed, viz. to correlate the psycho-neuroses with specific stages of mental development. Once that was achieved the incidence factor became irrelevant: it was much more important to examine conditions which, however infrequent in incidence, lay between the great disorder groups. These 'transitional' states, as I have called them, tell us more of the gradual process of mental development than the major groups of mental disorder which merely represent milestones on the route of mental evolution.

The vicissitudes of consulting practice drew my attention at an early stage to the conditions of alcoholism and drug addiction, and at first I was concerned to systematize the etiological factors of alcoholism in terms of the then existing knowledge of symptom-formation. This paper may be compared with the paper on drug addiction (Chap. XII). It is systematic and plays for etiological safety, whereas the paper on drug addiction attempts to establish appropriate mental content for the transitional group and to relate it to some forms of sexual perversion. At the same time it is a significant fact that although alcoholism constitutes on the whole a transitional group, it is nevertheless itself capable of sub-division in terms of varying depth of defence, e.g. hysterical, obsessional, depressive and paranoid types.

When psycho-pathologists discuss with psychiatrists 'the etiology

* Contributed to a Joint Meeting of the Psychiatric Section of the Royal Society of Medicine and the Medical Section of the British Psychological Society, and published in the *Proceedings of the Royal Society of Medicine*, Vol. XXI, Section of Psychiatry, pp. 45–50, 1928.

of alcoholism', both parties must realize clearly the differences in their methods of approach. The psycho-pathologist approaches his problem with a roving commission. His interest in 'diseases' is largely secondary, dictated by considerations of convenience in discussion; he prefers to describe as *maladaptations* the various groups of neurotic and associated disorder which come to his notice. He abandons the term 'patient' and starts work with a conception of the ego as a psychic organ developed to sample stimuli from the external world and to register inner psychic stimuli (instincts). The alterations effected by the ego in response to these stimuli are described as adaptations, and may take the form of alterations in the individual or in environment. When the individual alteration is detrimental to the interests of the ego it is termed a 'maladaptation'.

In approaching alcoholism, the psycho-pathologist asks: to what development of instinct life is this a response? Secondly, how does it affect the individual's relation to environment? Thirdly, what individual and environmental factors contribute to the choice of alcoholism as a (mal) adaptation? His problem is primarily one of individual psychology. He is concerned less with statistics of age-incidence than with the reason why any individual should become alcoholic at a particular age. If the alcoholism is uncomplicated he desires to find out why the instinctual difficulties were capable of such direct solution: if the alcoholism is part of a wider symptom-complex he wishes to know how the alcoholic response dovetails into other precautions. He then considers certain social factors, to see how far they obscure the individual problem, and the distillate of his combined observations may be regarded as a valid contribution to the psycho-pathology of the condition.

GENERAL PSYCHO-PATHOLOGICAL ASPECTS

No sooner do we consider the case material than a second difference in approach becomes apparent. The clinician wants to distinguish entities and to show his skill in differential diagnosis. The psycho-pathologist is concerned to discover, for example, what *psychic mechanisms* are common to chronic alcoholism, dipsomania and Korsakow's psychosis, and *then* to discover the mechanisms causing clinical differences.

For if we consider clinical manifestations from the point of view of an individual caught between his instinctual urges and the pressure of reality, it becomes apparent that all the primary features of alcoholism represent fundamentally the individual's attempt to extricate himself from an impasse. As far as environment is concerned they are attempts at *flight from reality*, whilst as far as instincts are concerned, this flight coincides with an obvious *increase in phantasy formation*. Clinical differences can then be related to the *completeness* of the withdrawal and to its *periodicity*. The habitual drunkard adopts continuous flight, in contrast to the periodic bouts of the dipsomaniac: neither can compare with the flights in alcoholic hallucinosis or delirium tremens. There is one subjective factor which hinders adequate appreciation of the extent of phantasy activity. The investigator is apt to describe much of the drunkard's phantasy life by calling him an 'inveterate liar' and at the same time to obscure the significance of phantasy in psychotic states by calling it 'confabulation'. Lying, romancing, boasting, obscene wit, illusion, confabulation, hallucination and delusion, all are results of overcharged phantasy.

But hallucinations and delusions also indicate an attempt to *substitute a new reality for the old*, or at least to *project* into reality the more painful elements of phantasy life. So we must inquire to what extent the alcoholic's overcharge of phantasy life leads to *actual gratification* in *real* life. What is generally called weakness of will, lack of decency, and moral deterioration in the chronic alcoholic can then be described in psycho-pathological terminology as the gratification of previously inhibited impulse. In any case terms such as 'weakness of will' combine diagnosis with moral judgment in much the same way that the phrase 'obstinate constipation' combines an accurate psycho-physiological diagnosis with an expression of the diagnostician's annoyance.

But it is not enough to say that withdrawal from reality increases or activates phantasy; it activates phantasy corresponding to definite *layers of psychic development*. This element of *regression* can be studied behaviouristically over years in chronic alcoholism, or over a few hours in acute intoxication. The regression of intoxication is plainly heading towards an infantile end, and the ultimate picture is scarcely distinguishable from that of a suckling, who, after an ample feed, might be described as 'blind to the world'.

The next step in investigation is to catalogue the *instincts or component instincts* gratified in alcoholic regression. Impulses of *aggression* with their accompanying attitudes of hate are freely expressed (irritation, quarrelsomeness, assault). Again, there is accentuation of *sexual impulse* and especially of *component sexual impulses*. Exhibitionism (lack of decency, exposure, obscene wit), scopophilia (sexual curiosity), sadism (acts of sexual violence), fetichistic activities, manifest expressions of homosexuality, can all obtain representation in alcoholism. On the other hand, in simple intoxication it is easy to find not only direct but *displaced* (and) or *rationalized* expressions of the same impulses (vanity, boasting, anecdotage, exchange of confidence, argumentation, sociability and general 'heartiness' towards members of the same sex). Moreover, in alcoholic hallucinosis or paranoia, we see the same impulses in the form of accusations of sexual perversion or delusions of infidelity.

To the *mechanism of projection* involved in the latter instances we will return: meanwhile we may note that it is characteristic of all alcoholic states. The chronic alcoholic shelves responsibility, attributes his drink habits to social or marital difficulties, is suspicious, distrustful and generally 'on guard', especially against non-drinkers; the sufferer from delirium tremens may even attack his anxiety hallucinations in the environment.

SOCIAL ASPECTS

Coming to the social aspects of the problem, not all psychopathologists are agreed on the etiology of alcoholism. Some authorities consider that in many instances the unconscious factors can be ignored; they regard social drinking customs, habit, idiosyncrasy, or economic conditions as prime etiological factors; but the Freudian school holds that external frustration owes its apparent pathogenicity to internal (instinctual) frustrations. Social drinking habits have the same etiological relation to alcoholism as a pandemic of mild itch would have to acute eczema: moreover, if we examine them closely we can scarcely resist the conclusion that they are socially sanctioned measures of instinctual gratification or defence: witness the joviality of a 'stag party' with its scarcely concealed bonds of homosexual interest.[1]

[1] Abraham: 'The Psychological Relations between Sexuality and Alcoholism', in *Selected Papers*, Hogarth Press, 1927; Boehm: 'Beiträge zur Psychologie der Homosexualität', *Int. Z. Psychoanal.*, 6, Ht. 4, 1920; 8, Ht. 3, 1922.

The true pioneers of behaviouristic etiology are the alcoholics themselves, who are always ready to give rationalistic explanations of their habits. If diagnosticians are to avoid the charge of unconscious collusion, they should be prepared to pay attention to the unconscious significance of *rationalizations*, to say nothing of the language of *symbolism* (compare the homosexual significance of 'snake' hallucinations in delirium tremens).

SYSTEMATIC PSYCHO-PATHOLOGY

The results of psycho-analytical investigation must be considered from three points of view: (*a*) the modification of instinct, (*b*) the ego's relation to instinct, and (*c*) the relation of instincts and ego to environment.

(*a*) *The Modification of Instinct*

A feature of the analysis of alcoholism, drug addiction and manic-depressive insanity is intense preoccupation with *oral* images and phantasies[1]; these are concerned with mouth-breast gratification, or with scenes of frustration accompanied with rage affect. They may be finally expanded into fellatio, cunnilingual, coprophagic or cannibalistic phantasies. The unconscious preoccupations and character traits of the alcoholic indicate either that he has brought about an unobstructed *oral regression* or that his libido has never completely abandoned the oral stage, i.e. that he is *orally fixated*. This fixation is rarely complete even in manic-depressive cases, but we are safe in saying that the alcoholic is *partially fixated*. But since all individuals have oral erotic interests and undergo oral frustration, why are these of special importance in alcoholism? The first reason is that, apart from the gratification of self-preservative urges, oral activities represent the earliest form of libidinal gratification and are associated with the earliest form of aggression and destruction. This particular combination, described as *oral sadism*, is specially accentuated in the alcoholic. The second reason is that excessive frustration in this primitive phase

[1] Abraham: *Selected Papers*, pp. 248, *et seq.*; 393, *et seq.*; 418, *et seq.*; op. cit.; Freud: 'Drei Ahhandlungen zur Sexualtheorie' (5te Auf.) [*Three Essays on the Theory of Sexuality*, Imago Publishing Co., 1949]; 'Mourning and Melancholia', *C.P.* Vol. IV; Glover, E.: 'The Significance of the Mouth in Psycho-Analysis', *Brit. J. med. Psychol.*, **4**, 1924 [Chap. I, this volume].

makes the relations to objects (primarily nipple-mother) exceed-ingly difficult, and *all future relations to objects tend to be coloured by this oral ambivalence.*

The alcoholic then has made a bad start, and whether this is exaggerated by *constitutional* factors or not, he is hampered thence-forward by a tendency to psychic *regression* which produces inertia in development. But matters go from bad to worse. The next stage of libidinal development, the *anal* stage, has more severe frustra-tions in store. In the alcoholic, *anal erotism* is heightened, again owing to partial fixation, whilst *anal sadism* is correspondingly increased. The result is that when the potential alcoholic reaches the third or infantile genital stage he is faced with a double difficulty: his genital impulses towards objects preserve an archaic sadistic quality, and his reaction to thwarting and disappointment is appropriately severe. His genital libido is impoverished and when the incestuous climax to infantile sexuality is shipwrecked on castration anxiety, the *tendency to regression is fully established.* The ground is thus prepared for miscarriages of sexual instinct in adult life. Most characteristics of alcoholism depend on the *distri-bution* of this regressional interest. Anal sadistic fixation and regression supply the driving power to *homosexual* impulses,[1] which play so large a part in the analysis of alcoholism. Together with other fixations on component sexual instincts, these help us to understand in part the close relation between alcoholism and *perversion.*[2] Finally, the accentuation of genital (castration) anxiety in the alcoholic sheds light on the acute anxieties of alcoholic deliria and psychoses. *One of the dire necessities which drive the individual to alcohol is the need to overcome these excessive charges of*

[1] Abraham, op. cit.; Clark: 'A Psychologic Study of Some Alcoholics', *Psychoanalytic Review*, **6**, 1919; Ferenczi: 'Homosexuality in the Patho-genesis of Paranoia', Contributions to Psycho-Analysis, Hogarth Press, 1916; 'Alkohol und Neurosen', *Jb. psychoanalytische Forsch.*, **3**, 1911; Freud, op. cit., 'A Case of Paranoia', *C.P.* Vol. III; Juliusburger: 'Beitrag zur Psychologie der sogennanten Dipsomanie', *Zentralblatt für Psycho-analyse*, **2**, 1912; Riggall: 'Homosexuality and Alcoholism', *Psycho-analytic Review*, **10**, 1923; Wholey: 'Revelations of the Unconscious in a Toxic (Alcoholic) Psychosis', *American Journal of Insanity*, **74**, 3, 437.

[2] Sachs: 'Zur Genese der Perversionen', *Int. Z. Psychoanal.*, **9**, 1925; Glover, J.: 'Notes on an Unusual Form of Perversion', *Int. J. Psycho-Anal.*, **8**, 1, 1927.

castration anxiety. In the early stages of chronic alcoholism it is partly overcome; the drunkard's boastfulness affords compensation for inner insufficiency or impotence (symbolic castration): when however the ego is temporarily or permanently damaged the anxiety breaks through in massive charges.

(b) The Development of the Ego

When the real ego begins to develop and become consolidated, a large part of libidinal interest is directed on the self as object (narcissism). Each thwarting produces narcissistic injury, increases ambivalence to objects and makes it more difficult to establish object relations. The most advanced pleasure-producing zone (genital) becomes the centre of narcissistic interest. But this is the zone thwarted in primitive object relations. So between narcissistic fixation, anxiety and regression, the ego of the alcoholic is over-charged with narcissistic libido. Relations with objects are of course established, but the ego hardly dares love anyone who cannot be identified with the self. In some cases identification depends upon the object possessing the same genital, incidentally another clue to the homosexual fixations of the alcoholic. When a true object is chosen it is more often than not for unconscious purposes of revenge, as witness the misery of the alcoholic's marital life.

A second factor in the variety of alcoholic manifestations is, therefore, *the stage at which the ego began to lag in development*. Evidence of narcissistic regression is found in the increased use of the defence mechanism of *projection*. The ego overworks that primitive method of flight from painful excitations which it cannot master, projecting them into a 'painful' outer world. This is characteristic of all alcoholic states, although the manifestations vary from vague suspicion to hallucinatory certitude. Some subjects go so far as to pursue these excitations in the outer world and attempt to destroy them (assault, homicide).

(c) The Ego and Environment

Many of the guilts and anxieties of alcoholics indicate interference with the function of conscience. The constant use of projection makes it appear as if their consciences were turned inside out. The alcoholic paranoic detects malignant influences outside himself and rushes to destroy (punish) them; the chronic drunkard feels that everyone else is to blame, especially the virtuous members of his group. Again, the euphoria of alcoholism suggests that relief has been obtained from an intolerable burden, whilst the disregard of social usages indicates temporary suspension of conscience.

Analytic investigation of both normal and alcoholic types shows that what we recognize as conscious conscience is only the peak of a more *primitive conscience*, which operates unconsciously. This archaic conscience (super ego)[1] is a protective organ developed during the gradual wrecking of infantile sexuality: it instigates inside the ego the inhibiting activities at first associated with the parents. Built up when the child's reality sense is weakly developed and when its instincts are exceedingly primitive, this super-ego has primitive characteristics; it demands the repression of incestuous impulse and failing successful repression exacts primitive punishments. Now as the alcoholic tends to remain fixated or to regress to primitive impulses, we must expect to find *either that he has a more severe primitive conscience than normal or that he is unable to cope with the drive of primitive impulse and lands himself in situations of self-punishment.* Both difficulties can be observed in alcoholics. The former is seen in the depressed secret drinker and in more psychotic types whose bout may end in suicide. Up to a point alcohol counters the depression by inducing relative euphoria. This cycle reminds us of the manic-depressive states, and the labile moods of alcoholics are well known. The second mechanism, where inhibition fails and punishments are instituted, is still more obvious. The chronic alcoholic gratifies tendencies which previously may have been foreign to consciousness, and the punitive response elicited from environment varies from moral reprobation to capital punishment. *With the collusion of society the alcoholic has established and for a time reinforced the function of primitive conscience.* The abuse of alcohol leads inevitably to self-punishment (organic illness, economic failure); it promotes projected self-punishment (aggression towards environment) and this ultimately provokes punishment of the self by environment. In this sense *alcoholism is a disastrous attempt to cure abnormalities of primitive conscience.* Should the alcoholic attempt to break through primitive inhibitions he risks the integrity of his ego (compare the sequence, latent homosexuality, alcoholism, abstin-

[1] Freud, op. cit.; *The Ego and the Id*, Hogarth Press, 1927; Rickman: 'Alcoholism and Psycho-Analysis', *British Journal of Inebriety*, **23**, 1925.

ence, paranoia)[1]; if he maintains an uneasy balance by means of alcohol he is compelled to keep to a course which also ends in physical and mental disintegration.

WHY ALCOHOL?

To answer this question we must recall (1) the compulsive element in alcoholism; (2) its close connection with sexual instincts and their components, in particular its compensatory relation to impotence; (3) the fact that sexual instincts are to a large extent capable of displacement; (4) that alcohol is unconsciously identified with bodily secretions and excretions (milk, urine, saliva, semen and blood), and plays a part in unconscious imagery as a medium of sexual assault and as a procreative fluid. It is not too much to say then that *alcohol is chosen as a surrogate of sexuality or, at the least, as a method of short-circuiting sexuality, a method which at the same time releases the pressure of repression and reverses processes of sublimation.*[2]

INTER-RELATIONS OF ALCOHOLIC STATES

To sum up: three main etiological factors have to be considered in alcoholism. (*a*) the partial fixation of libido at oral or anal sadistic levels of development; the alcoholic maintains ambivalent object relations at the price of alcoholism.[3] (*b*) the constant tendency to regress to a narcissistic ego organization which automatically sets primitive mechanisms (projection) in action. (*c*) the disorders of primitive conscience which lead to a fruitless exploitation of the same mechanism of projection. We have already noted the resemblance between alcoholic lability and manic-depressive insanity; some forms of alcoholism might be called artificial manic-depressive states. The manic-depressive, however, has a more severe oral fixation of libido, his super-ego is more disordered and his sadism is completely inverted. On the other hand, with a stronger anal-sadistic element, a more primitive narcissistic regression and a disintegrated super-ego, the picture becomes one of paranoia; alcoholic paranoia, however, has originally maintained slightly stronger object relations than non-alcoholic. In the next

[1] Ferenczi, op. cit.
[2] Abraham, op. cit.; Freud, op. cit.
[3] Glover, J., op. cit.

place the dipsomaniac exhibits some of the characteristics of an obsessional neurotic, although alcoholic ceremonial is more apparent in the social drinker. Again, although alcohol brings out many 'perverse' sexual tendencies it may itself function as a surrogate of component sexuality. As we know, the essential mechanism of perversion depends on the canonization of one or more component sexual impulses in order that the remainder of infantile sexuality can remain repressed. Alcoholism is in this sense a 'pseudo-perversion'.[1] Finally its close relation to psycho-sexual impotence brings us back to the fundamental significance of castration anxiety. We must not forget that the essential problem in depressive states, in obsessional neurosis, fetichism, homosexuality and impotence, is one of infantile guilt and anxiety. Alcohol owes most of its attraction to the fact that it is primarily well adapted to overcome castration anxiety, although in the long run it defeats its own end by bringing about impotence and death (symbolic castration).

[1] Glover, J., op. cit. See also Kielholz: 'Analyseversuch bei Delirium Tremens', *Int. Z. Psychoanal.*, **12**, Ht. 3, 1926; Rado: 'Die psychischen Wirkungen der Rauschgifte', ibid. ['The Psychic Effects of Intoxicants, *Int. J. Psycho-anal.*, **7**, 1926]; 'Das Problem der Melancholia', ibid., **13**, Ht. 4, 1927 ['The Problem of Melancholia', ibid., **9**, 1928].

VI

THE PSYCHOLOGY OF THE PSYCHO-
THERAPEUTIST*
[1929]

It is to the credit of the psycho-analyst that, following the injunctions of Freud, he pays more attention to the 'fallibility of the instrument' than any other variety of psychologist, more sometimes than the physical scientist. The history of his endeavours in this direction are contained in the literature of 'counter-transference' towards which indeed there has recently been manifested a degree of almost fetichistic over-estimation. Yet the phenomena of counter-transference do not exhaust the motivations of the psychotherapeutist. The following paper represents an attempt to bring order into the wider ranges of the subject. It constitutes a useful preamble to the study of the concept of normality (Chap. XIV); for even if we assume that psychotherapeutists as a whole are normal persons – a somewhat sanguine assumption – it is evident that the range of normality is both elastic and variable and that it includes a respectable number of peculiarities of function.

Although the subject is one that concerns closely the processes of psycho-therapy, I have chosen to include it in the present series in illustration of the practical uses of a developmental approach. There are few problems in clinical psychology which cannot be clarified by the application of developmental criteria.

A cursory glance at the syllabus of any representative body of psychologists is sufficient to remind us how rarely psychotherapeutists inflict on themselves the discipline of self-examination. Papers on the subject-matter of clinical investigation are as plentiful as blackberries, but only once in a while is the instrument of investigation, the psychotherapeutist himself, subjected to purposive scrutiny. This is scarcely to be wondered at. In the

* An address from the Chair at a meeting of the Medical Section of the British Psychological Society on Dec. 19, 1928, first published in *The British Journal of Medical Psychology*, Vol. IX, pt. 1, 1929 [here slightly abbreviated].

first place much of the psychotherapeutist's energy is spent in the almost hectic isolation of his consulting-room, listening to and participating in the conflicts of others: when he does emerge to discuss current problems, his energy is further depleted by critical, not to say controversial, examination of psychological data. Naturally, after all this expenditure of effort, there can be little drive left over for subjective searching of heart. Indeed, in many instances it is an open question whether some of the psychothera-peutist's sustained capacity for professional objectivity is not purchased at the ransom price of refractoriness to self-inspection; or, to put the matter in another way, whether relative freedom from the irritation of self-questioning does not play a part in the psychotherapeutist's choice of a profession.

Now whatever views one may hold on the desirability of making subjective examination a first consideration in the training of every psychologist, there can be little doubt that it is impossible to understand psychological treatment without some grasp of the function of the therapeutic instrument. The first step in this in-vestigation can be taken on the common ground of behaviouristic approach. And there is some advantage to be gained for the moment by broadening the basis of enquiry to include the be-haviour of the general physician during his therapeutic efforts; for, regarded from the psychologist's point of view, the conduct of the general physician borders on the pathological. Starting then with the concept of a 'normal' psychotherapeutic activity, involving an approach to illness from a psychological angle and the employ-ment of psychological means of treatment, we may fairly say that any pointed and consistent endeavour to *exclude* psychological factors constitutes a 'pathological' manifestation. Now with certain exceptions the field of general medicine represents an almost un-broken line of defence against psychological means of approach, and the persistence with which obvious psychological factors in treatment are plastered with the labels of organic therapy shows a lack of reality feeling which at first sight seems little short of psychotic. But the general physician is not strictly speaking psychotic in this respect: his lack of reality feeling approximates more closely to that exhibited by cases of conversion hysteria. For example, when a childless woman states her psychological require-ments in terms of amenorrhoea, the general physician enters into her conspiracy by attributing the condition to, shall we say,

bloodlessness. But he is not content with endorsing this symptomatic disguise; he plays up to the situation by administering by
mouth or by injection some drug in the potency of which he has
profound conviction. Fortified by the rationalizations of scientific
diagnosis, he initiates or carries through symbolic ceremonials of
impregnation, showing that whilst he accepts his patient's conversion mechanism at her own valuation, he can return a Roland
for her Oliver. Stripped of their rationalizations, his therapeutic
convictions are seen to be of a magical order. Irreproachable as
his organic diagnostic methods may be in their own sphere, they
have been exploited on this occasion to endorse the therapy of
white magic, although the recovery of his patient, should that
ensue, is regarded as a tribute to scientific method. This latter
assumption is not simply a venial expression of pride: it is an
essential part of the system by which he screens from himself his
thaumaturgic proclivities. He is of course not limited to this one
form of defence: the aspersions cast by general physicians on the
scientific validity of psychological methods illustrates the operation
of another defence mechanism, viz. projection of the unconscious
self-criticism engendered by their own psychological myopia.

But let us assume that the case does not prove to be a tractable
one: suppose for example that after an unsatisfactory marriage a
woman develops gastro-intestinal disorder, or genito-urinary
trouble or cardiac arrhythmia. If the results of scientific organic
therapy, that is to say, in terms of our present analysis, if the
disguised magical methods prove unsuccessful, the chances are
that the patient will be treated in one of two ways. The more
summary of these is based on the method of treating foreign
bodies in the eye: the offending patient is 'removed' in some way
or another, sent to another practitioner or consultant, or perhaps to
a physician-substitute such as a spa, or transplanted to surroundings of symbolic significance, the seaside, mountains, the south or
west. In short the physician's reaction of impatience ends in a
negativistic gesture.

The second mode of response is not so extreme: nevertheless, it
represents a considerable deviation from the original attitude of
scientific detachment. The patient is not actually excommunicated,
but the therapeutic means employed are sufficiently tedious or
far-fetched as to suggest an unconscious punitive intention. It is
no exaggeration to say that if the teeth have not already been

extracted, they will be drawn now. More convincing, however, is the appearance of an obvious emotional reaction: the patient is liable to be wheedled or cajoled, or a tone of persistent exhortation is adopted which may not stop short of downright bullying. The most crass example is to be observed when the physician is called upon to treat conditions which he of his own accord diagnoses as functional or neurotic: one need hardly recall how barely the refractory hysteric escapes the ultimate argument of a pail of water, or how the obsessional neurotic, having out-pointed his physician in debate, is finally given peremptory instructions to remember his family ties and pull himself together.

Summarizing these quite commonplace observations of the behaviour of organic therapeutists, we see that, apart from realistic reactions, by which in their case is implied a true objective attitude to the diagnosis and treatment of uncomplicated organic disease, there are four main types of reaction to be considered, viz. magical, persuasive, exhortative and negativistic reactions. One cannot but recall here the systems of the primitive medicine man described by Prof. Malinowski in a recent lecture to this Society. The main difference is that whereas the medicine man frankly stakes his reputation on magical and suggestive procedure, the modern clinician, whilst pluming himself on an entirely realistic approach to disease, takes advantage of the elaborate façade of modern empirical medicine to gratify his unconscious predilection and natural gift for magical procedure.

Turning now to the reactions of the psychotherapeutist, it might appear that the latter's openly professed interest in psychological data and methods of treatment would automatically entitle him to immunity from scrutiny, on the ground that this interest constitutes a guarantee of realistic approach in the psychological sense. This is far from being the case. In the first place I imagine that every psychotherapeutist at one time or another is aware of a tendency to backsliding, by which I do not mean so much flirtation with endocrinology as an impulse to give 'the benefit of the doubt' to organic factors in illness. This impulse to be 'fair' differs only in a quantitative respect from the general clinician's gross favouritism and has, I imagine, identical motivation, viz. unconscious bias in favour of the disguises and mechanisms of conversion hysteria. It represents a vicarious flight into illness, corresponding with the direct flight favoured by his patients.

Even leaving out of account these tendencies to periodic regression, the devices actually employed by psychotherapeutists are capable of a loose classification not unlike that already indicated for organic therapeutists. That persuasive and exhortative forms of technique exist will scarcely be denied: one need only recall the familiar descriptive labels 'suggestion', 'persuasion', 're-education', etc., attached to methods of treatment which absorb a large proportion of psychotherapeutic energy. And these methods are at times difficult to distinguish from more peremptory systems, which have been aptly described by the term 'gingering'. Gingering in its turn is often a preliminary to still more negativistic reactions, for there seems to be no doubt that when pushed into a corner the psychotherapeutist is liable to have recourse to that ultimate defence against intruders on his peace of mind which is to counter-attack and show them the door.

But whilst it is easy to multiply instances of exhortative or negativistic attitudes, it is a more delicate matter to apportion the magical and realistic components of psychotherapeutic tendency. Before attempting to do so it would be well to remind ourselves that we are not concerned with the validity or empirical advantages of any one method, but with the subjective attitude represented by any particular form of therapeutic behaviour. The exponent of persuasive systems might argue with some force that he used entirely realistic and objective methods in diagnosis and then, convinced of the empirical advantages of persuasive therapy, exploited that form of treatment for purely realistic reasons. The correctness of that view does not concern us here. All we need take into account for the moment is the *behaviour* of the therapeutist: the fact remains that he does sooner or later adopt a persuasive or exhortative attitude to his patient, hence that a large proportion of his daily time and energy is spent in the gratification of this particular tendency.

In the same way, when we come to investigate the type of behaviour favoured by analytical therapeutists, we are not concerned with any virtues or defects their methods may possess. We are faced with the fact that the analyst goes out of his way to avoid any semblance of persuasion or exhortation in his relations with a patient: one might say that his attitude of diagnostic objectivity is maintained throughout his therapeutic labour, that his ideal for his patient is the development and maintenance of a like objectivity. In this sense we may say that his energies are for the most part expended in both direct and vicarious pursuit of psychological objectivity. Of course it might be argued that the analyst is simply attracted by the empirical advantages of an objective attitude and is prepared to sacrifice his own natural tendency to exhort. This is a criticism which deserves careful attention.

Coming now to methods which imply an omnipotent or magical attitude to patients, it must be admitted that it is difficult to give such convincing illustrations as are possible when observing the conduct of general medical practitioners. After all the psychotherapeutist is more familiar with the history of magic than the clinician and he is less likely to adopt a crudely magical technique. Nevertheless I should be inclined to suggest that particularly in some of the expedients for producing a hypnotic state we can recognize rationalized remainders of magical ritual, remainders which are nevertheless still felt to be of an 'uncanny' order. Admittedly the same might be said concerning the technique of an ordinary consultation. It is generally agreed that both the stage setting of the consulting-room and the personal characteristics of the consultant are invaluable assets in inducing the proper atmosphere for suggestive work, but I think it might be said that in the exploitation of glance, gesture and spoken word the technique is essentially omnipotent and therefore magical in character.

To recapitulate: a clinical survey of subjective therapeutic tendencies indicates that there is, *mutatis mutandis*, a close resemblance between the attitudes of the general physician and those of the psychotherapeutist. In both cases the maximum amount of objectivity is exhibited on consultation and possibly at the commencement of treatment, but sooner or later this is liable to be brushed unceremoniously aside by an open 'wish-formation'. The tendency both direct and indirect is to convert an objective situation of illness into a subjective emotional crisis (a phenomenon described in analytical circles as 'counter-transference') and to react to this crisis in some characteristic way. The most highly rationalized attitude might be expressed affectively in these terms: 'Do please get well for my sake'; a more authoritative attitude says, 'Come now, I insist'. These are on the whole parental in type. Failing success, these may be followed by regression to an omnipotent magical attitude, an attitude which corresponds closely to that adopted by the obsessional neurotic when faced by a disturbing excitation. In some cases the therapeutist's reaction of impatience to thwarting is so strong that he takes up an omnipotent attitude from the outset. Finally the stimulus of an unfulfilled wish may become pathogenic and lead to the severance of therapeutic relations. In both instances regression to primitive attitudes is skilfully cloaked by an access of apparent objectivity, but should this defence prove inadequate, the therapeutist is prepared to ease pressure by a system of projection. One can well understand why many organic physicians are frankly contemptuous of what they consider the obscurantist attitude of the psychotherapeutist, or why the psychotherapeutist regards the clinician on occasion as a superstitious apothecary. We have only to reverse such projections to see that there is an irritant grain of truth at the core of these and other pearls of emotional catharsis. The clinician must defend his own tendency to gratify magical leanings in pharmacological disguise: the psychotherapeutist has more difficulty in adopting open magical means, but compensates for this by a tendency to lapse into a physiological outlook during psychological crises, especially to give assent to the disguises of conversion hysteria. So he maintains uneasy peace of mind by castigating the inadequacies of his more physiologically-minded colleagues.

At this point it becomes necessary to abandon the mainly behaviouristic approach to our problem. If we are sufficiently positive to say that illness provokes a group of specific reactions on the part of the psychotherapeutist we are under some obligation to account for this phenomenon. It is not enough to suggest that these reactions are merely a reflection of the therapeutist's character or temperamental type. Undoubtedly this must be to some extent accurate, but since any one therapeutist may exhibit at different times all the reactions described, it seems reasonable to suggest that these reflect the existence of distinct and more or less stable systems of mental organization. Admittedly the problem of mental organization is a controversial one, but I imagine that a temporary safe-conduct may be granted those who enter a controversial field with the best of empirical intentions. The theory of mental organization I propose to consider is the conception of tripartite mental structure which has been advanced by Freud. It may be advantageous to recall the main features of this system.

Starting with the function of the ego, the view is held that the

ego of any individual represents a boundary organization which
deals with the continuous claims of instinct and samples the
impinging stimuli of the external world: its function is to satisfy
the claims of instinct, in so far as its control of external circumstance will permit. But it is immediately apparent that on many
occasions when the claims of instinct are insistent and when the
external world responds with an 'As you please', the ego interferes
on its own account and ceases to promote the release of tension.
And we are compelled to attribute this interference to a special
ego system, which on account of its administrative function has
been called the super-ego. To a formulation of this sort there
would doubtless be little opposition, were it not for the fact that,
in tracing the origin of these institutions, Freudian theory sets on
one side their relation to conscious experience and introspection.
The super-ego for instance is regarded as being in the greatest
part unconscious and is related to the first critical struggles of a
weak and dependent ego with the primitive infantile phases of
sexual instinct. But this weak and dependent ego is the sadder and
wiser descendant of a primitive pleasure ego whose relation to the
urgencies of instinct is that of a devoted flunkey. To start from
the other end of the series we have a hypothetical reservoir of
instinct, the Id, loosely contained in a primitive pleasure ego;
from this is gradually developed at first a weak and helpless real
ego which in the unequal battle between instincts and external
frustrations preserves a certain degree of integrity by the cession of
territory. Henceforth, this territory is the preserve of an archaic
morality, the unconscious super-ego. The promotion of peace
between these striving elements is a task to which the expanding
real ego devotes its available energies. Always on the side of peace
and compromise the ego makes free play of its peculiar defensive
mechanisms of repression, reaction formation and continues to
daub the finished product with a liberal varnish of rationalization,
leaving here and there breathing holes which at one time give vent
to eruptions from a more volcanic primitive core, at another release
those super-ego rumblings which we are accustomed to recognize
as pangs of conscience.

Provided we accept these farther-reaching formulations, the
approach to our problem is greatly simplified: our first task is to
strip off the varnish and cement of rationalization. Having done so
the problem can be stated in questionnaire form: firstly, what Id

drive provides the energy for psychotherapeutic activity? secondly, how far is this directly gratified according to the primitive patterns of the pleasure ego? thirdly, how far are the archaic moral counter-drives of the super-ego represented? and lastly, what are the contributions of the real ego?

It is an easy matter to identify the hallmarks of the primitive ego. As has been indicated, its original function is to provide for almost immediate relief of tension; failing immediate relief it has recourse to magical omnipotent means of inducing release, and there is only a short interval between the failure of magic and the appearance of violent reactive tendencies. It is reasonable to assume therefore that the more summary methods of psychotherapy can trace direct descent from this primitive pleasure system. Many years ago, in a study of various narcissistic and omnipotence characteristics, Jones shrewdly commented upon the significance of a certain kind of interest in psychology. Certainly the desire for an immediate cure by command, the reaction of impatience to thwarting, the browbeating of psychoneurotics, their banishment from the presence, in fact the whole system of psychological gingering together with its aftermath seems to correspond with our conception of primitive ego functioning.

But it must not be assumed that the primitive ego is only to be found expressed in one therapeutic system. *I imagine there is no system of psychotherapy the practice of which does not involve either direct expression of primitive character traits or the use of special precautions to eliminate their expression.* For example, whilst much has been written as to the nature of suggestive phenomena, comparatively little has been said on the phenomena exhibited by the suggestionist. Viewed solely from the angle of the primitive ego he can be regarded as an individual with a fundamental belief in the magical power of the spoken word, who seeks to banish the ills of his patient but is actually under a more urgent need to get rid of the uncomfortable tension produced in himself by his patient's illness. This is of course a refracted view which must in fairness be corrected by other considerations. To take another case: the analyst who quite consciously aims at complete objectivity in treatment has clearly abandoned that objectivity should he feel any tendency to plume himself on his own particular choice of a profession. The slightest suspicion of a feeling of analytic virtue, the merest assumption of esoteric privilege, or, to take a simple

example of analytic negativism, even a tendency to drowsiness
during the dog-days of an analysis should be a warning to him
that the paths of regression to primitive narcissism are still
invitingly open.

Equally simple to recognize are the components contributed to
psychotherapeutic behaviour by the super-ego. In its most primitive form this is an organization for the issue of fiats and anathemas:
even that part of the super-ego which we recognize in consciousness
as conscience is constantly using reality as a peg on which to hang
a system of ethical and moral injunctions and can be heard busily
commanding, exhorting, persuading, wheedling or reproaching
the ego. So that whilst the gingering type of psychotherapy can
be related to the functioning of a primitive ego, it is evident that
some of its exhortative and reproaching tendencies must be laid
at the door of the super-ego. Nevertheless, the forms of therapy
which represent as it were the purest culture of unmodified super-
ego tendencies are those contained in the suggestion group.
Although these methods have a considerable stiffening contributed
by the primitive ego, they are less hampered by the negativistic
readiness of the latter, hence a more complete identification with
the patient is possible. If time permitted it would be interesting
to consider how far we might supplement certain psycho-
analytical theories which have been advanced to account for the
phenomena of suggestion. For example, it seems likely that the
subjective virtue of any suggestionist depends on the unconscious
wholeheartedness with which he *offers* the patient his own super-
ego and the degree to which he is able to keep out of the picture
the more arbitrary and imperative primitive ego components.
Admittedly this involves the assumption that the unconscious of a
patient can penetrate the disguises of the physician's ego, and without involving the processes of conscious judgment sum up his
capacity for identification or transference.

And here we must come to grips with the problem of the real
ego's contribution to psychotherapeutic tendency. In the first
place it is undeniable that the real ego does contribute something
to all therapeutic systems. It enables the therapeutist to take stock
of the patient's situation with some degree of objectivity and it
tends to give him rationalistic support for his own system of treatment. The problem whether the ego by its own unassisted efforts
can ever take a purely objective view is one which involves too

many controversial arguments to be discussed here. But I would remind you that one of the functions of the real ego is to make an effective compromise between internal conflicting systems. The least controversial comment one can make is that the objective integrity of the real ego depends on the degree to which it is free from the embarrassment of unrecognized primitive drives and super-ego counter-urges. Two extreme cases may be stated: either the Id and super-ego systems dominate, and, if need be, disrupt the ego, in order to gain direct expression in the behaviour of the individual, or they are subordinated to the realistic purposes of the ego, and are expressed through the real ego.

It is conceivable for example that a dispute might arise between those who believe in methods of total or partial 're-education', 'logical persuasion' or 'ego synthesis' and those who believe (as psycho-analysts do) that given sufficient freedom from unconscious drives and counter-drives the ego will proceed with its own affairs of adaptation with increasing efficiency. Both schools might claim that their psychological therapies were entitled to be described as real ego therapies, free from any gross admixture of super-ego or Id elements.

Before commenting on these claims it is necessary to revert to a problem already stated earlier in this discussion, viz. is the psycho-analyst so very objective after all or does he merely offer up his own tendencies to exhort on the altar of opportunism? I think it cannot be denied that there is a constant danger of his reacting in this way. For this reason it is a prerequisite for his therapeutic success that his own super-ego and Id systems should have been as fully explored as possible. Moreover, it is incumbent on him throughout his therapeutic labours to practise what I have called elsewhere the 'analyst's toilet' in order to maintain the measure of real objectivity he has attained. Whilst therefore it might be superficially true to say that both methods of re-education or logical persuasion and methods of psycho-analysis appear to derive their characteristics from the real ego, the differences would still be fundamental. The analyst does not deny the part played by the real ego in persuasion, but he does believe that the particular real ego activity exploited is that of rationalization, and that the more psychologically scientific the rationalized façade the more successfully is the emotional rapport (or transference relationship) concealed. In the same way whilst the analyst regards education as in many respects an adaptive ego process, he considers re-education methods or methods of ego synthesis to be the result of unmodified super-ego drives, in which the standards are set by the physician's own super-ego.

Indeed, I believe that a good part of the psycho-analyst's reputation of being stiff-necked and contumacious, a die-hard in the ditches of analytical purism, is due less to esoteric aloofness than to the necessity he sees of drawing a fundamental distinction which will strike to the roots of transference phenomena. As is well known, he goes so far as to distinguish the methods of psycho-analysis from methods which incorporate or adapt analytic procedure, and he does so in the belief that so long as the essential super-ego drives and Id content are not adequately uncovered, the relation of physician to patient remains of necessity a transference relationship.[1] Hence we have what appears the sweeping psycho-analytical generalization that psychotherapy is in the long run either psycho-analytic or suggestive therapy. With this statement I find myself in general agreement, although, as I have tried to set out, I believe there is some advantage to be obtained by sub-dividing suggestive procedure in accordance with the extent to which the primitive ego or the primitive super-ego contributes to the subjective drive, and to the choice of suggestive method.

To sum up: I believe that a study of the different components of mental structure enables us to classify the main tendencies of psychotherapy, and possibly, though this does not concern us at the moment, the main tendencies of psychology. It might be said that the heterogeneous group of psychotherapeutists could be roughly subdivided according to tendency into ego psychologists, super-ego psychologists, and Id psychologists (or, as the anthropologist might call them, 'Medicine Men'). This sweeping generalization must be qualified by the statement that every psychotherapeutist exhibits qualities derived from all three systems and according to his method is bound either to exploit these qualities or to take steps to eliminate them.

I feel tempted to add here some reflections on the nature of psychological controversy in general and in particular on the urge

[1] [Note (1955): This implies of course that failure to uncover these factors adequately places the 'analysis' in the category of 'rapport-therapy' (see Glover: *The Technique of Psycho-Analysis*, Baillière, London, 1955.]

to found an irreproachable 'scientific' psychology. Of course, the characteristics of the primitive ego and of the super-ego are reflected in all controversies, psychological or otherwise; they are represented by hostility, antagonism, dislike of new ideas, the exploitation of scientific discussion in the interests of internal conflict and so forth. But the most interesting reaction to study in relation to psychological controversy is that of the real ego. One would expect that the contribution of the real ego would be that of scientific outlook and objectivity. Nevertheless, I think it is extremely unsafe to assume that the idea of 'scientific psychology' which perpetually hovers over psychological discussion is simply the result of a realistic demand for objectivity. We are warned against such a rash assumption by several important considerations. To begin with, our suspicions should be aroused by the mere fact that our critics, the organic therapeutists (who, it is suggested, are often saved from conversion hysteria by their interest in organic disease), constantly reproach psychologists for their lack of scientific method. But in fact these reproaches very frequently arouse guilt on the psychologist's part. Much of the feverish energy and psychological scrupulosity which has been and is still devoted to statistical method and measurement can be regarded as the psychologist's obsessional technique of pleading guilty to the charge.

Now the view of the real ego that I have endeavoured to present is that of a psychic organ constantly engaged in processes of adaptation but as constantly interfered with by importunate inner claimants (Id impulses) and imperious inner taskmasters (super-ego urges). It is as if a microscopist busy with histological research were constantly having his elbow jogged by a humanitarian, or an antivivisectionist or a 'lab' boy anxious to go off duty, and was forced for the sake of peace to include their protestations and demands under disguise in his next histological report. The real ego is driven to cover up the traces of the less objective components of the mind and one of the most effective disguises of its embarrassment is a clamorous insistence on scientific method. In other words the core of the real ego is a primitive Id system, speaking a primitive language and adopting a primitive magical technique: hence the drive to be 'scientific' must be in part a counter-drive calculated to banish magic or refuse it countenance.

But it would be manifestly one-sided to leave the problem of

psychotherapeutic tendencies without some reference to what is
in many respects the crux of the matter, viz. the nature of the
subjective instinctual forces involved and the characteristic
mechanisms employed in controlling them. In reviewing these
forces it is customary to refer to various 'component instincts'.
All schools of opinion would agree that impulses of curiosity and
viewing tendencies play a large part in determining psychological
interests and they are certainly gratified in some stage or other of
all psychotherapeutic processes. Others again who believe in oral
stages of libidinal development hold that psychotherapeutic
labour involves considerable gratification of oral tendencies. But
in the brief space remaining at my disposal, I think we might with
advantage limit ourselves to the consideration of one group, viz.
the impulses of aggression, mastery and destruction which when
existing in combination with libidinal impulses have been described as the sadistic impulses.

In the first place, whatever urges have driven the psychotherapeutist to psychotherapy, the objective situation with which he is
faced is one of illness or maladaptation presented by his patient. In
so far as this represents injury to or damage of his patient's personality, it is bound to stimulate some characteristic reaction on the
part of the therapeutist. In one simple case it can be seen that the
result is an access of open aggression. The more violent forms of
psychotherapeutic exhortation, especially when accompanied by
direct or implied reproach and criticism, represent the most
primitive form of reaction. It is true that some degree of contact
with the patient is maintained, but it is a violent, and, one might
say, sadistic form of contact. The patient's illness is a source of
inner irritation to the therapeutist and since the latter cannot
escape by flight, i.e. by refusing to have anything to do with the
case, he aims at an immediate and violent cure, viz. the cure by
attack. By so doing he provides a psychotherapeutic parallel to
systems of clinical therapy which the lay public with considerable
insight has described as 'kill or cure'. The dangers inherent in this
situation are obvious: should the therapeutist have difficulty with
his own sadistic urges, the existence of illness and suffering in the
external world provides him with a focal point on which to project
his own difficulties. The temptation then exists to avoid curing the
patient in order to preserve the external excuse for projection. This
reaction is most clearly illustrated in clinical medicine by those

physicians whose main interest is in diagnosis and whose treatment is somewhat on the perfunctory side, the rationalization being that 'patients really heal themselves'.

Next in order of interest is the situation where the therapeutist does not permit any outward exhibition of sadism but as the result of reaction formations against sadistic drives is hampered by the necessity of alleviating external situations of suffering. I say hampered advisedly, because compulsive reactions of this sort tend to be satisfied by any change which can be read as a sign of improvement whether the change is actually to the patient's interests or not. Much of the drive to 'alter' patients' character traits or 'improve' them is of this nature. On the other hand, when sadistic drives have been modified by the mechanism of 'turning on the self' and when the therapeutist forges a bond of masochistic identification with his patient, the therapeutic outcome is almost as precarious and uncertain as when he has a positive sadistic urge to satisfy. In fact the whole problem of the patient's 'negative therapeutic reaction', in both suggestive and analytic procedure, requires to be constantly checked by reference to the subjective mechanisms of the therapeutist. That certain types of patient are inaccessible in this respect is undeniable, but I hesitate to say how many cases are ultimately filed *in statu quo* because of the therapeutist's own sadistic difficulties.

A cognate problem arises when one comes to consider the part played in the pursuit of psychotherapy by neurotic or psychotic formations existing in the therapeutist himself. It is a common analytic finding that, at a certain stage of treatment, patients express the desire to become analysts themselves, and whilst we are not concerned with the technical aspects of this defence, the fact remains that the attitude is essentially a defensive attitude. And it is significant that many applicants for training are clearly inhibited by subjective neurotic or psychotic reaction. On the whole they resolve themselves into three groups, an anxiety group, an obsessional group and a paranoidal group, but in all cases the test remains – how far do they exploit mechanisms of introjection or projection respectively? I believe it is no exaggeration to say that the most dangerous group from the point of view of therapeutic success is the obsessional group. Whatever the method employed, whether one exploits the affective dispositions of the patient or seeks to uncover and analyse these affective dispositions, the key to therapeutic success lies in the affective factor. And this is the factor which the obsessional type, by pitting one drive against another, succeeds in neutralizing. In spite of all the marching and counter-marching, the aim of the obsessional type is always to preserve the *status quo* and the obsessionally-minded therapeutist, gifted though he be in archaic psychic dialects, is liable to exact toll for this gift in the form of refractory results.

To conclude: I believe that whilst all psychotherapeutists exploit or are liable to exploit subjective psychic reactions characteristic of all three great mental systems, the Id, the super-ego and the real ego, they may be roughly grouped in accordance with a preponderating tendency in favour of any one system. I believe that the suggestion group exhibits the most spontaneous and involuntary exploitation of unmodified super-ego tendencies with a continuous drag towards the methods of the primitive Id system. And I believe that the differences between psycho-analysis and other analytic methods depend on the degree to which the rationalizing tendencies of the real ego are allowed to cover unmodified super-ego interests. So much from the point of view of mental organization. As far as instinctual drives are concerned, I believe that the most important group is the sadistic group and that the type of modification these drives undergo plays a large part in the choice of any one form of psychotherapy. Finally, I believe that, major neuroses apart, every therapeutist tends to exploit (or must take steps to avoid exploiting) character traits patterned on anxiety, hysterical, obsessional or paranoidal mechanisms.

It might reasonably be asked, do these views help us to advise any prospective psychotherapeutist as to the type of therapeutic procedure he should pursue? Speaking purely as a psycho-analyst, I am sufficiently sceptical of rule of thumb formulations to say that they do not help us very much *in a positive direction*: on the other hand it is conceivable that with some regard to the classification given above *we might be able to indicate certain courses to be avoided*. For example, if one detected open manifestations of an urge to 'improve' people, one might possibly save a good deal of subsequent heartburning by diverting this devotee of projection from analytical pursuits to the practice of suggestion or re-education. At any rate he could be warned that analytical activity would involve as a prerequisite the careful investigation and, if necessary, resolution of this 'synthetic' urge. I am not in a position to say whether those who teach suggestive psychotherapy find it necessary to eliminate refractory students with an inconvenient taste for investigating transference phenomena: but I imagine it would be worth while at any rate to come to some rough estimate of the aggressive make-up of candidates and to guide the more draconic types in the direction of those forms of hypnotic or suggestive procedure most suited to their talents. In this connection one last observation falls to be made. It has often been suggested by distinguished representatives of all schools of psychotherapy that a suitable mixture of analytic, suggestive and hypnotic techniques might be compounded in order to deal expeditiously with the existing overwhelming mass of psychic disorder. It appears an eminently reasonable proposition. The difficulty in all these schemes is however not entirely the objective reaction of the patient; even more important is the subjective *impasse* of the therapeutist. If the views I have presented here have any validity, it follows that there is a fundamental subjective incompatibility between the tendencies gratified in transference manipulation and those gratified in transference resolution. Any mixing of methods must be in the nature of an unstable emulsification liable to separate out in moments of stress.

VII

THE 'SCREENING' FUNCTION OF TRAUMATIC MEMORIES*

[1929]

Commenting recently on the technical aspect of screen-memories, I had occasion to point out that actual memories of traumatic events happening in childhood should be carefully scrutinized, on the ground that they are well adapted to the defensive purpose of covering repressed material. The ordinary screen-memory can scarcely avoid arousing analytical suspicion because the nature of the memory image does not account for its persistence over a number of years or for its frequent repetition during the earlier stages of analysis. When, however, the memory image is in itself of a sufficiently traumatic nature there is some possibility that its credentials may be too easily accepted at their face value. The following example illustrates with some precision this screening function of infantile traumatic memories.

The case was one of severe and protracted impotence. The early stages of analysis were characterized by profound amnesia covering the events of early childhood and extending well into the latency period. As is to be expected, the great majority of memories which had persisted from these periods were typical screen-memories; they referred to seemingly insignificant events and unimportant places, but it was possible in most instances to uncover a more elaborate and emotional substratum. Some emotionally tinged events were recalled by the patient, scenes of domestic conflict and correction, e.g. quarrels with a sister, punishment by his mother, but they were few and far between. Some details of illnesses in boyhood were remembered, but there was no special affect during their recital. One of these seemed to be a little more significant from the analytic point of view in that it had occurred in earlier childhood. It was a memory of having his hand burned on the kitchen stove.

* First published in *The International Journal of Psycho-Analysis*, 1929, Vol. X, pp. 90–93.

At the time, however, the patient paid no special attention to this 'burn' memory, and the analysis continued its ordinary course. It was marked by phases of intense resistance. He gave a somewhat grudging intellectual assent to any explanation of the infantile nature and exciting cause of these resistances and his progress was extremely slow. Gradually some infantile phobias were uncovered and this led inevitably to the interpretation of his castration-anxiety. Several months passed before it transpired that he had been circumcized in childhood. Some comment was made on the importance of this historical fact, together with the significance of its omission from his historical material. This elicited the reply that, so far as he knew, the circumcision had been performed in early infancy, in all probability within a few months of birth. It had not occurred to him to mention the fact because it did not appear to be of any consequence; it was a natural hygienic operation, etc. His system of rationalization was watertight.

Within a few days the situation had altered considerably. Stimulated, no doubt, by this discussion, the patient of his own accord had instituted some inquiries and learned indirectly from his mother that the circumcision had actually taken place when he was between the ages of three and a half and four years. The immediate result was to induce an altered attitude to the subject of infantile amnesia. The patient was startled into dragging his infantile years for further recoveries, but, as is not surprising, with little result. In particular he was unable to recall anything at all about the circumcision, in spite of the fact that he could remember quite clearly some events which took place prior to the alleged date of the operation.

Again the analysis resumed its course, the resistances against castration images being, if anything, a little more pronounced. The second discovery was made a month or so later, when the patient had an opportunity of going into the matter with his mother in person. The facts elicited were as follows. During his infancy his mother was from time to time advised on matters of child hygiene by a medical practitioner who was a close relative of her own. He seems to have had a mania for performing the operation of circumcision, and very few children who came within his ken escaped this fate. His own children were circumcised. In spite of the fact that our patient's prepuce and glans were normal in every respect, this surgeon never failed to impress on the patient's mother the inestimable advantages to be obtained from circumcision. There were evidently good psychological reasons for this vicarious sacrifice on his part, but, except in so far as these contributed to a somewhat intimidating personality and thereby increased the child's apprehensions concerning this father substitute, they need not concern us. He seems to have been a man of sombre disposition, with a heavy, overbearing manner, and the patient as a child was not slow to accept the uneasy valuation of his possibilities current amongst his holiday playmates, the doctor's own children. On the occasion of a particular holiday visit the mother's scruples were finally overcome, and she consented to have the circumcision performed on her child. The final step in gaining her consent took the form of visiting the nursery. The patient was awakened out of his sleep by having the bedclothes abruptly pulled away; he woke up to find the sinister figure of the doctor leaning over the bed. His penis was unceremoniously seized by the surgeon's left hand, with the right the motion of cutting was imitated and the mother, who stood on the opposite side of the bed, was asked to note how simple a matter it was to cut off the foreskin, or words to that effect. She was rather concerned at the whole performance, and observed that her son showed signs of panic, but she did not interfere with the demonstration. On the following morning the circumcision was performed. The technique must have been rather crude, because the process of healing was delayed. The wound had to be dressed daily, and each dressing aroused agonized anticipations and was followed by wailing protestation. One protestation in particular took the form of a reproach directed at his mother. The day after the operation he is said to have cried out to his mother, 'Why did you let him cut it off?' After a week's dressings the wound began to heal by granulation, and there is no exact record of its subsequent course. There was, however, no doubt in the mother's mind that the experience was an agonizing one for the child, and for a long time afterwards she regretted giving her consent to the operation.

Shorn of a certain amount of elaboration, the main facts were as given above, but, in spite of the most circumstantial detail, the patient was still unable to remember one iota of the whole affair. He added the following important comment: 'It surprises me very much that I cannot remember at all about my circumcision, because I can remember very well something that happened at the very same visit: *it was during that visit that I burned my hand on the stove. I now remember the whole thing perfectly, and that I had to have my hand dressed for some days.*' He was certain that there could be no mistake. They had only once visited that particular house, a fact which the mother confirmed.

The possibility had still to be considered that the whole burn story was a substitution, and on this point it was hard to obtain absolutely convincing evidence. The patient could not remember whether the burn took place before or after the circumcision, although, judging from the duration of stay and the period of circumcision dressing, it seems likely that it occurred before the operation. The mother's testimony was not very satisfactory, because in the first instance she could not remember the burn and was mainly concerned with the circumcision. On the other hand, the patient was able to recall many incidents relating to the same visit, including games and conversations with the sons of the house: his recollection of the circumstances of the burned hand, the occasion of the accident, its cause, the stove, the dressings, and of many other confirmatory details was unshakable. The amnesia for the circumcision, however, remained absolute.

VIII

GRADES OF EGO-DIFFERENTIATION*

[1930]

Reading this paper twenty-five years later I find that in spite of a certain naïveté in the metapsychological presentation, it has some points of historical interest. It was written only five years after Freud at the Berlin Congress had given birth to the concepts of the Id and super-ego; in the interim psycho-analysts had celebrated their enthusiastic acceptance of the new ideas by anthropomorphizing them. On all sides one heard talk of 'severe super-egos', 'imperious Ids', 'helpless egos', 'panzers' and other members of a new pantheon of theoretical concepts. All this had as much to do with metapsychology proper, as the car designer's engaging habit of calling his latest model 'she' has to do with the principles of internal combustion, differential transmission or other products of mechanical engineering.

About the same time the first signs of a cleavage between what is now known as the Klein school of child-psychology and the 'classical' (Viennese) school of child-analysis had become increasingly evident. This paper in fact set out to examine whether or not these differences were irreconcilable, and what were their respective metapsychological tendencies. At that time Kleinian views on early Oedipus formation and on the importance of early sadism in mental development had begun to percolate through the British Society though not elsewhere. Despite this acceptance however, it was clear that a controversial issue of some magnitude was at stake, namely the nature and origin of the Real-ego. And it is interesting to note that already in this paper the main flaws in the Klein system were indicated, flaws which led in later years to the development by the Klein group of a pseudo-mystical type of religious psycho-biology, which I have outlined and discussed in a monograph entitled 'An Examination of the Klein System of Child-Psychology'. Not only so, it was also apparent even at this early date that sooner or later

* Read before the Eleventh Psycho-Analytical Congress at Oxford, July 27, 1929, and first published in *The International Journal of Psycho-Analysis*, Vol. XI, pt. 1, Jan. 1930 [here abbreviated].

the Id would be credited with organized ego-characteristics and that a confusion would arise as to the overlap of primary and secondary processes. There is now ample evidence that both of these anticipations have been realized. [See Chapter XX.]

Finally the paper has some interest in that it adumbrates at one point the nuclear theory of ego development which I formulated shortly afterwards. At the time this seemed to me one of the ways of getting round the difficulties following on the postulation of a primitive pleasure ego; although it was only later that the possibility of utilizing a nuclear theory in the classification of mental disorders occurred to me.

Not long after Freud first published his systematization of psychic structure in terms of the ego, the super-ego and the Id, a tendency manifested itself amongst psycho-analytic writers, to convert what had been of necessity a fluid presentation into a more rigid and refractory medium. Moreover, in their exposition of this concept of tripartite psychic structure some writers had recourse to terms which, although suggestive enough in themselves, evaded the more disciplined usages of academic statement. One might quote, for example, phrases such as that coined by Alexander of a 'secret alliance' between Id and super-ego, or again, the statement that a psychic formation can be 'Id-syntonic'. Useful as such phrases may be for purposes of description, they are unsatisfactory in many other respects: they tend to gloss over the difficulties of a precise statement of mechanism and may ultimately give rise to theoretical misconceptions. Thus we are left to form our own opinion whether we can or must postulate some degree of Id organization in order to express the idea of regression to some common point in development or to some common functional reaction.

As usual Freud was himself the first to see this danger: in his original essay he warned us that from the topographical point of view, although the Id and ego systems could be illustrated by a conventional diagram, a system such as that of the super-ego did not lend itself to diagrammatic representation; and again he entered a mild caveat against taking abstractions too seriously when (in *Hemmung, Symptom und Angst*) he warned us against regarding the mental systems as armed camps. It may be profitable therefore to review the existing structural conceptions to see to

what extent their manifest advantages are offset by certain difficulties in formulation.

The first step in such a review is to consider *what advantages are
actually obtained by the formulation of an Id concept*. To begin with,
the concept of the Id made an end once and for all to the confusion
arising from the use of the same term (i.e. unconscious) to
designate a special mental system and a characteristic applicable
to two out of three mental systems. It enabled us not only to
distinguish between the old *ucs* and the unconscious components
of the ego but between the 'repressed' and the remainder of the
ucs system. Further, it clarified the position of what up to then
had been called the ego-instincts, a somewhat urgent matter since,
as Mitchell[1] pointed out, the use of the term ego-instinct had
become somewhat precarious after the separation of the ego-libido,
and more so after the self-preservative instincts were assigned to
the Eros group. Indeed, whatever view one might hold as to the
clinical usefulness of postulating Life and Death instincts, it was
impossible to make theoretical use of these postulates, without
formulating the concept of an instinct reservoir such as the Id.
Naturally once the Id concept had been established, the ego was
necessarily reduced to the status of a regulating institution, formed
originally on a reactive pattern, with a capacity for exploiting
perceptual function and an adequate sensitiveness to affective
danger signals. Incidentally, it may be noted that the modern
concept of the ego is in the deterministic sense as impersonal as
that of the Id itself. Finally, the concept of an Id matrix provided
an asylum for the preservation of phylogenetic experience and
temporarily at any rate rescued the theory of primal impressions
from some unclarities with which it was beset.

As far as the ego was concerned it was an organization derived
from this psychic matrix but without any clear line of demarcation
from the Id. At a later date the fact that the Id itself was no
organization had to be restated in *Hemmung, Symptom und Angst*.
The necessity for this reminder itself suggests that the Id system
was being credited with some features more characteristic of an
ego system; in other words, that an anthropomorphizing tendency
was eating into a scientific concept.

Now the pre-Id view of the relation of the ego to instinct and
stimuli prevented this anthropomorphizing tendency, in so far as

[1] *Problems in Psycho-Pathology*, London, Kegan Paul, 1927.

it related the development of the ego to a primary separation of inner and outer world based on experiences of instinct tension and of the mastering of stimuli. This primary functioning is gradually complicated by the expansion of the pleasure-pain principle. This in turn leads to exploitation of the special reactive function of projection and hence to the formation of the primary pleasure ego as distinct from a painful outer world. With the clearer differentiation of objects and the consequent frustration and foundering of impulses directed towards those objects, ego differentiation receives much stronger impetus. It is at this point that we are justified in speaking of a super-ego system and in describing its function. By the development of the super-ego system, the ego is placed in the advantageous position of being able to delegate some of its primary activities: the super-ego becomes the instigator though not the executant of inner inhibition. At this point also we are entitled to speak of the Real ego. Having delegated the exhausting task of scrutinizing certain instinct derivatives, the Real ego can exploit its capacity for watchfulness as an organ of adaptation to external stimuli.

The formulation of the Id concept does not involve any alteration in these fundamental views of ego development, but the postulate that the ego had no sharp lines of demarcation from the Id has resulted in some blurring of the *concept of the primary pleasure ego*. As has been suggested, in spite of the fact that the Id is to be regarded as an unorganized psychic mass, the tendency exists to attribute to it characteristics which imply some degree of organization, and hence are more appropriately reserved for a primary pleasure ego. Moreover, it has the delayed result of obscuring what are the ontogenetic and functional relationships between the ego and the super-ego. Thus, for example, even if we ignore the infiltration of ego by the Id and content ourselves with the rough formulation of distinct Id, ego and super-ego systems, we are bound to assume that since the ego is a structure imprinted on the Id by external necessity, and since the super-ego is a differentiated part of the ego, there is a sort of historical precedence of the ego over the super-ego.

Now in view of the close connection (inferred from clinical data), between the Id and super-ego system, this is a precedence which can by no means be taken for granted.

A good deal of confusion is due to the fact that perceptual

consciousness and the instruments of projection are at the service of the most primitive ego formations. In the sense of organized reactive function we are entitled to say that a 'real'-ego system exists from shortly after birth. In spite of hallucinatory and other pleasure aberrations which obscure its reality function, this system is maintained unbroken down to the final formation of the actual Real-ego. That battles are fought for the possession of these instruments is seen in the phenomena of split-personality and is implied in, for example, paranoidal personalities.

But apart from these sources of confusion I think it can be shown that *our interpretation and formulation of infantile stages of development has been affected by our theoretical conceptions.* Isaacs has reminded us in her paper on 'Privation and Guilt'[1] that according to the accustomed view there is a definite temporal relationship between the passing of the Oedipus complex, the formation of the super-ego and the onset of latency. According to this view we have an approximate date of *completion* of super-ego formation, viz. the onset of latency (leaving out of account of course the processes of consolidation which take place during latency and after). The *onset* of super-ego formation is not so precisely indicated, but is nevertheless bound by the view that true castration anxiety cannot occur until the phallic phase of infantile organization has set in. Even if we allow for precocity in attaining the phallic phase, this view gives rise to certain diffi-culties. The analysis of obsessional neurotics has shown that it is possible for the ego to achieve a high degree of differentiation (in the super-ego sense) under the primacy of the anal-sadistic phase, and the presence of distinct obsessional traits in a large number of so-called 'normal' individuals suggests that this early differentiation is a common occurrence. In the second place there has long been clinical evidence to support the view that in certain cases (until recently regarded as exceptional) organized Oedipus impulses could manifest themselves in the first year, that is to say, at a time when the Real ego is obviously undeveloped. If then the existing views are strictly adhered to, we must assume that super-ego differentiation of unconscious components of the ego takes place only at the stage of final renunciation of the Oedipus wishes – a time when by ordinary standards the Real ego is already developed. But if the Real ego is the end result of renunciation of

[1] *Int. J. Psycho-Anal.*, 1929, **10**, p. 335.

the pleasure principle it is difficult to see how it can take proper shape until incest wishes are renounced, i.e. until the new reality principle has been finally established. If this contradiction is something more than a mere nosological confusion we are thrown back on certain assumptions. We may say, for example, that the super-ego develops simultaneously with the ego, a differentiation in function becoming more obvious with each stage of development. Or if we prefer it, we can say that both super-ego and ego are struck out of a primitive pleasure ego, itself derived from the Id, or we may say that the super-ego is first differentiated from the primitive pleasure ego, the Real ego being as it were an important by-product of conflict between the super-ego and the primitive pleasure ego. What seems to cause confusion and difficulty is the postulation of an unorganized Id, and an organized ego from which the super-ego is ultimately differentiated.

The final resolution of these problems must obviously depend on the results of future psycho-analytical research, but there are three particular lines of investigation which appear especially promising in this connection. These are, first, direct analysis of young children; second, analysis of borderline psychotic personalities and, third, the working hypotheses of psycho-analytical anthropology.

As far as the analysis of young children is concerned, the only available evidence at the moment is that derived from the findings of Klein and her school. The main contentions of the Klein school are: (*a*) That super-ego formation commences in the second half of the first year of life – and that at first the super-ego is hardly differentiated from the Id. (*b*) That the growth of this system is stimulated by an early efflorescence of primary sadistic charges which, when linked to purely libidinal charges, set up a vicious circle of frustration and tension. (*c*) That this reactive system, patterned on unreal primitive object-imagines, can itself promote tension, and that as the result of these tensions an impetus is given to Real ego and real object formation.

From the structural point of view the logical outcome of her views might be put rather crudely in this way: *So far from the super-ego being a later differentiation of an organized ego, the ego in its relation to real objects is hammered out of the Id by the super-ego.*

With regard to the *validity of these views*, it seems to me that there is one argument in favour of their acceptance, provided of course we admit the accuracy of Klein's primary observations, and the correctness of most of her primary interpretations. It is that, apart from the special time relationship between super-ego and Real ego implied by her, and apart from the fact that she derives the super-ego almost directly from the Id, the early processes of super-ego formation she describes differ in no fundamental respect from the processes described and accepted by all analysts for what Klein would call later stages. For example, it might appear that the processes of object introjection she describes would be vitiated by the partial and rudimentary nature of these objects, and that the decisive element of abandonment of object cathexes cannot be presumed. Now whilst it may be true that, in Abraham's sense, real object formation does not commence until the second of the anal-sadistic phases, this does not invalidate the conception of introjection of 'part-objects'. The term part-object is after all an object's view of an object. The completeness of an object depends on the whole-heartedness of instinctual aims. The only true sense in which early pregenital objects are part-objects is in so far as libidinal strivings are polymorphous. If we agree that the primacy of the earliest stages of libido development is an oral primacy, then the object of that libido is correspondingly as complete as the object of genital libido. Similarly if we agree that one primacy gives way to later primacies, whether by frustration or as the result of processes inherent in development, or both, we are bound to concede that the abandonment of this libidinal aim is as complete and as liable to give rise to introjection as a later abandonment of genital aims to a 'complete' Oedipus object. The difficulty is due to a confounding of perceptual syntheses with the objects of libidinal aims.

In short, I believe that when all due corrections have been made [1] the most important of Klein's findings will remain unchallenged, viz. the pre-phallic Oedipus phase, and the pre-genital phase of super-ego formation. Even granting this, we are no better off as far as the primitive phases are concerned. Indeed, the tendency of her work is one of super-ego aggrandizement at the expense of the concept of the primitive ego. The primitive ego is suggested simply as a weak ego as little differentiated from the Id as the super-ego.

---

[1] e.g.: free use of the term 'sadism' is liable to obscure our understanding of early modifications of the destructive impulses, together with their influence on development.

Now the mere suggestion that the early super-ego is very little differentiated from the Id necessitates careful examination. *Is it permissible to say that a super-ego is an immediate derivative of the Id?* The reply might be made that if it is justifiable to regard the ego system as a whole as being a differentiated part of the Id, it is at any rate conceivable that the super-ego system represents some of the more direct modifications. To do so, however, is to put a certain amount of strain on the topographical aspect of Freud's psychic systematizations. An Id concept is after all the expression of ideas concerning instinct and concerning phylogenetic ego inheritance; apart from its special relationship to the 'repressed' its main justification in theoretical description is the extent to which it simplifies and clarifies the concept of an organized ego system, and Freud has been content so far to represent the idea of an Id-ego boundary in the most elastic terms. The expression of the aims of Id instincts and the record of Id tensions automatically constitute the groundwork and reckoning apparatus of the primitive ego. To put the matter crudely: if we did not already possess the concept of a primitive ego it would be as necessary to invent one as it is to postulate a primal ego in anthropological study.

If now we define the function of the ego as that of regulating psychic tension, involving primarily the employment of reactive instincts for this purpose, and proceed to re-examine the course of events leading up to the formation of the primitive super-ego, it will be observed that the *primitive ego* not only plays a large part in this process but that it must itself have attained a relatively high degree of organization before it could play this part. What is described briefly as the cumulative charge of sadistic impulses leading to super-ego formation can be translated in terms of the primitive ego as a turning point in a *protracted history of reactive ego functions*. These have arrived at a stage where they tend to defeat their own aim of reducing tension, and in face of defeat the *primitive ego develops in self-defence* a specialized protective and inhibiting institution, viz. the super-ego. The ultimate factor responsible for the threatened defeat is the failure of the primitive mechanism of projection. But projection is by no means the only protective measure of the primitive ego. To mention only two other systems, the discharge through the sensory end of the psychic apparatus is constantly exploited and continues to be exploited throughout the dream life of the individual. Again the distribution of the reactive tensions through systems other than the oral system performs a protective function.

Apart from these considerations, if we view the actual processes of object formation and introjection, it appears that these would be liable to founder but for peculiarities of primitive ego organization, e.g. *primary identification*. Like the concept of the Id, *primary identification is a necessary descriptive formula*. It forms the basis of all later systems of identification and introjection by virtue of the fact that for the primitive mind all states having the same pleasure tone tend to bring about identification of the objects connected with these states. But we must not treat this primary identification in a one-sided way – for although by wrongly including the object, primary identification leads the way to introjection, it is also true that by faulty differentiation of the ego the primitive ego arrives at object formation. *Indeed, it might be held that the concept of a primitive ego itself requires further elaboration. It is conceivable that at the stage we usually describe as that of primary identification, there are as many primary egos as there are combinations of erotogenic zones with reactive discharge systems: in other words, it is conceivable that the so-called primitive ego is originally a polymorphous construction.*

Finally, with regard to the *rôle of the super-ego in promoting object formation* the views held by Klein seem to imply that the early formation of the super-ego with the resultant loosening of anxiety promotes closer adaptation to reality, hence stimulates real object formation. That under favourable circumstances an early super-ego ultimately promotes objectivity cannot I think be denied, but the processes of adaptation remain essentially ego processes, and in this sense are simply reinforced varieties of mechanism already put in operation by the primitive ego. Possessed as it is by the instruments of cognition, the primitive ego is driven by inner tension to make sharper perceptions of objects. It is, moreover, the primitive ego which by virtue of its tendency to aversion gradually develops the system of denial which, as Freud points out, is the first step in the acceptance of objects associated with pain. It is the primitive ego's first libidinal drive towards incorporation, which is the first step in adaptation to the outside world, and, as Ferenczi has suggested, it is the fusing or the defusing of libidinal and destructive drives which promotes objectivity as distinct from the mere recognition of objects.

Lastly, it is the primitive ego's capacity for identification on a pleasure or pain basis which promotes displacement and maintains a sufficient spread of discharge. In short, *it is difficult to avoid the presumption that the primitive ego has attained a highly complicated stage of organization before the development of more complicated aims towards objects necessitates a sub-division of labour, which is achieved by the formation of the super-ego and the splitting of libidinal drives.*

Considerations of space prevent more than a cursory review of the two other sources of evidence I have mentioned. A *study of psychotic personalities* shows, however, that in every case *two* factors have to be estimated: first, the amount of disorder of super-ego formation and, second, the extent of regression to a primitive ego organization. In a paper given at the Innsbruck Congress on suicidal mechanisms I endeavoured to show that the suicidal act, although primarily the result of destructive forces directed through the super-ego, *could not* come about without a regression of the ego to primitive animistic levels and the adoption of primitive autoplastic methods of dealing with tension based on the processes of primary identification.

With regard to the third group of data, the evidence of *psycho-analytical anthropology* is so familiar as hardly to require recapitulation. Nevertheless, it is curious to note how little attention has been paid to a discrepancy between anthropological views and the customary teachings of a temporal relation between ego and super-ego. If we had no evidence to consider other than the evidence of anthropological data, one would have presumed from the sequence animism and magic, religion and objective science, that the super-ego was a decisive factor in Real ego formation and real object formation. But we would also have to realize from the finished product of the primitive personality how far the primitive ego had advanced in organization and in the exploitation of primitive mechanisms before the development of guilt finally instituted a drive towards culture.

To conclude: it would seem that a number of difficult theoretical problems can be resolved provided we do not set out on investigation with too rigid preconceptions as to psychic structure. There would appear to be a certain over-estimation of the ego in the customary teaching and an under-estimation of the primitive ego in Klein's teaching. It is true to say that forces directed by the super-ego drive the ego to the grindstone of objectivity, but it can still be held that the super-ego is a differentiated part of the primitive ego, through which it maintains its close connection with the Id. The alternative to this view is to postulate a readiness for differentiation in the Id, whereby early super-ego formations gather impetus directly from racial impressions in the Id.

IX

'AN INTRODUCTION TO THE STUDY OF PSYCHO-ANALYTICAL THEORY'*

[1930]

Next to unconscious resistances the study of psycho-analytical theory is one of the main stumbling blocks in the training of candidates, and since the great majority of candidates ultimately become full members of analytical societies it follows that theoretical understanding is not conspicuous even amongst practising analysts. The following six extracts from an Introductory Lecture on the subject may therefore still be regarded as pertinent. They deal with (1) Subjective sources of difficulty in assimilating theory, (2) aids to theoretical understanding, (3) the 'complexity' of analytical theory, (4) the rediscovery of analytical principles during psycho-analytical practice, (5) the requisites of psycho-analytical theory, (6) the use and abuse of 'conceptual thinking'.

(1) Subjective Difficulties

Subjective difficulties in regard to theory can be divided into two main groups, viz. an anxiety group and an obsessional group. The reactions in question need not necessarily indicate the presence of an anxiety hysteria or an obsessional neurosis; in many cases they are simply characterological reactions. The main features of the anxiety group are that analytical theory functions as a substitutive anxiety idea, and a degree of fear of theory is exhibited together with over-estimation of it. The student approaches theory with the conviction that it is extremely difficult and complicated; he believes that he will never understand it; that he has not a fair chance; theory has gone too far ahead. As a corollary, he imagines that others do understand it or will understand it more thoroughly than he ever will. From this he develops the idea of hierarchies

---

* Extracted from the first of a series of lectures on theory given at the Institute of Psycho-Analysis, London, May–July, 1930, and first published in *The International Journal of Psycho-Analysis*, Vol. XI, pt. 4, p. 471, 1930.

within the science and may in time experience jealousies over the publications of contemporaries. In the obsessional group we again encounter displacement and over-estimation, but in place of anxiety reactions there is much preoccupation with theoretical questions. The preoccupation may be of the philosophic type or of the sort which is best expressed in the German word *grübeln*. Persons in this group are prone to regard theory as excessively important; it is, in their view, essential for practical reasons to be closely conversant with it; as a rule they feel that they have themselves a flair for theory and tend to believe that others, more obtuse or more unregenerate, cannot or will not understand it.

In both groups the mechanism involved is one of displacement, and in both groups the source of the trouble is that some more archaic personal hostility is screened by hostility to an abstract system. It is characteristic of the anxiety group that those concerned have some difficulty in *remembering* theory; in the obsessional group a tendency exists to *doubt* theory and to meet it with destructive criticism.

Some time ago I reported the case of a medical practitioner who was greatly exercised on reading in a current journal of the possibility of extirpating a particular ego system which we call the super-ego. His criticism was doubtless sound, but the animus exhibited, together with other associative material, clearly indicated that this theoretical possibility had stimulated his castration anxiety. Another example: fear of the unconscious (which we know to be universal) may take the form of an anxious desire to be able to prove its existence, covering, of course, the hope that it does not exist. A variant of this is where fear of the inside of the mother's body activates all fear of the unknown, including ultimately fear of unknown theory. There are, of course, many other types of subjective reaction, such as a 'virginal' reaction of students to theory, or a tendency to regard it like the Ark of the Covenant as a sacred untouchable structure. In the former case theory is reacted to as an agent of seduction that might loosen temptations and stimulate habits; in the latter the importance of 'father-attributes' is obvious. Now these reactions are not by any means unique: if you happen to analyse students of the so-called exact sciences you will come across the same reactions. But they are more easily elicited in the case of students of psycho-analysis. May I cite here a good example of a reaction which is patent in most students? It is a reaction of modified hostility: the reasoning is that, since a certain percentage of scientific findings are likely in the long run to prove erroneous, the student in question will devote himself to purging the science of inaccuracies and irrelevancies.

(2) Aids to Theoretical Understanding

At this point one may ask whether there are any extra-analytical activities which might contribute to the understanding of analytical theory. Let us be clear first of all that these interests are not to be identified with the basis of psycho-analytical matriculation, i.e. an adequate training in scientific methods together with a sufficient familiarity with biology and medicine. Nor are we concerned with branch sciences, as for example, anthropology, courses in which are part of your analytic training. Apart from these two groups, the choice of an auxiliary interest or hobby is very much a matter of personal inclination. I would suggest, however, that an interest in the development of meaning in words is of considerable value, and in two directions. Familiarity with shades of meaning promotes a feeling for the proper significance of theoretical terminology. Secondly, a study of the use of familiar words soon discloses the existence of a vast field of naïve or folk psychology embodied in the mother tongue. Freud has often drawn from these springs of knowledge to support and refresh his own terminology. A good example is the close parallel between the psycho-analytical and the popular use of the word 'love'. Of course, it is again a matter of taste whether one acquires this knowledge by the formal study of etymology or simply in the course of general reading.

(3) The Complexity of Theory

The idea that analytical theory is too complicated also justifies reassurance. The structure of analytical theory is certainly not more complicated than the structure of physiological theories concerning the function of the liver. At the present moment we might almost say that it is less complicated. In the same way the idea that theory has already gone too far ahead, or that the beginner will never be able to 'catch up' is not justified in reality. Indeed, this is an attitude which calls for special comment. It is remarkable how relatively little has been added to the structure of analytical knowledge from the time of Freud's earlier revolutionary formulations. This is no reflection on recent research activities; it is rather a tribute to the gigantic strides made in the early days of the science. In the next place there has always been a smouldering edge to the researches of analysis: or to put it another way, psycho-analytical theory has always been a living structure exhibiting processes of growth, adjustment and disuse atrophy.

Actually the reaction in question has its roots in processes of over-estimation. If we consider what constitute at present the pillars of psycho-analysis we are bound to say that these fundamental conceptions have undergone little alteration. They are in fact (1) the existence of a structural and dynamic 'unconscious' (now the Id), (2) repression (now an example of 'defence'), (3) the concept of libido and infantile sexuality and (4) mental conflict. The great bulk of recent research is in a sense a specialization of problems. Apart from work on instinct problems and on ego-differentiation (the dynamic function of the super-ego) the great bulk of research has been in the nature of buttress work.

(4) The Re-discovery of Principles

In the case of psycho-analytic teachings there are two means of absorbing ideas, first of all by the usual conceptual channels and secondly by a process of actual discovery during the experiences of analytic work. Many writers have noted this relationship between psycho-analytical theory and practice, and Ernest Jones, in particular, has drawn my attention to the significance of this constant re-discovery of psycho-analytical principles. But it has at times disconcerting consequences. The more voluminous the literature of psycho-analysis, the greater the tendency to concentrate on the most recent publications and to remain content with digests of earlier literature. The result is that as each new-comer approaches clinical work he is apt to have frequent outbursts of exultation over apparently fundamental discoveries. A little more reading may, however, lead to the rather dashing realization that the discovery is one of Freud's accepted observations. If, however, the earlier literature is neglected it is just possible that unwitting plagiarism may be committed. As a general rule then it is a mistake to underestimate Freud: there is very little in psycho-analysis that does not owe its recognition to Freud's activities, and I recommend constant browsing in his earlier works before proceeding to publish discoveries. It is an interesting and sobering exercise to allow one's fancy free play with concepts of mental structure and function in terms of the latest theories and then to read once more the chapter in 'The Interpretation of Dreams' which contains the earliest formulations on those subjects.

One can only add that, altogether apart from the necessity of personal analysis, knowledge of theory is no guarantee of practical capacity. This is more true of psycho-analysis than of any other science, although of course it is a commonplace observation in other applied sciences. One finds in psycho-analytic 'controlled' work the same tendencies operative which drove a clever contemporary of mine in an obstetric class to diagnose locked twins on his first examination of a normal pregnancy.

(5) The Requisites of Theory

Before going any further we may well pause to ask: under ideal circumstances what do we really require of psycho-analytical theory? I think we may safely impose three conditions: (a) that it should be a convenient and compact systematization of existing data, (b) that it should present as sparingly as possible those conclusions which appear to have stood the test of time, (c) that the theoretical structure should not be too cramped or rigid. It should be sufficiently elastic to permit of modification without collapse, and it should stimulate speculative and research activities. You will note that special attention is paid in this scheme to the part played by speculation. It is only natural that the science which first described the mental activities of unconscious and preconscious mental systems should pay tribute to that end-product which is usually suspect in other sciences. Provided you have ascertained that you have no unconscious axe to grind, speculate as much as you please. Of certain ideas, Freud remarks that they can only be worked out by 'combining facts with pure imagination many times in succession', although, as he says elsewhere, 'the basis of the science on which everything rests . . . is observation alone'.

(6) Conceptual Thinking

But there is one other difficulty in approaching analytical theory which cannot be dealt with by reassurance. It is inherent in the nature of the mental apparatus and is therefore a permanent obstacle. It is the difficulty of thinking psychologically. When we come to study the nature of 'memory traces', of 'thing' traces and 'word' traces, we shall be in a position to express this difficulty in psycho-analytical terms. In the meantime it can be best expressed by saying that there is a tendency to regress from conceptual modes of mental function to those perceptual modes which retain a more vigorous charge of interest. To avoid involving ourselves in a philosophic discussion of the relation of concepts to perceptual fluxes let us take some simple examples of confusion liable to arise in psycho-analytical thinking.

When we think of our relations to an 'external object', in the sense of a person to whom we have deflected interest from ourselves, we are usually prepared to say that this object is really something 'in our mind', an 'image' if we like, or, if we wish to be more precise, the charging and lighting up (cathexis) of a 'memory trace'. So far our psychological behaviour is beyond reproach. But let us assume that in any given crisis an 'object' disappoints us, does not come up to our expectations, and that we allow ourselves to dwell on the 'might have been', we are prepared to say that this imagined behaviour is a product of our phantasy, that we are thinking of an 'ideal' or 'phantasy object'. This is where our mind tends to slip: we think of the 'phantasy object' as a mental presentation, but tend to treat the 'real object' as something outside our mind. If we do so we are abandoning psychological thinking at the behest of a mental mechanism which 'projects' painful representations.

It will probably occur to you to suggest that these difficulties are due solely to 'confusion of thought' which can be overcome by a little mental discipline, and you may think at once of a matriculation course in logic and philosophy as a suitable form of mental drill. Now in so far as 'confusion of thought' can be regarded as inadequate systems of conceptual association in upper (preconscious) mental levels it is probable that formal training could remedy this defect, although the very fact that logical processes work only at this superficial level has manifest advantages, e.g. preoccupations of this kind may cripple our understanding of non-logical processes. But we must remember that 'confusion of thought' has its roots in deeper layers of the mind also, and that to call in logic and philosophy to deal with this difficulty is to call the pot in to cure the kettle of pigmentation.

In the meanwhile: what is this fundamental difficulty inherent in the apparatus? Consider, first of all the case of those who tend to think of 'instinctual energy' (cathexis) as 'substance' or of an 'impulse' as an 'action'. If we come to think of it, all this has a very familiar ring. We know that children behave as if impulses had the same 'guilt value' as actions, as if 'words' were 'things', as if 'painful ideas' were 'outside' them. We know, too, that adult patients often make a significant slip, saying 'Something has come into my mouth' instead of 'Something has come into my mind'. Even more dramatic, from the adult point of view, is the behaviour of the paranoiac. The latter will inform us with every accent of sincerity that some evil-disposed person is projecting against him some dangerous substance, some malignant energy, injurious rays, wireless emanations and so forth. And he may be so convinced of the reality of this system that he takes steps to protect himself from these influences, although onlookers are unable to find any justification for this behaviour. Investigate this state of affairs and you will find that he is activated by 'impulses' directed against the alleged persecuting object: the paranoiac remains unconscious of these subjective tendencies, but apprehends the approach of 'substances' from without. We say that he is suffering from a regression which lights up primitive mechanisms of projection. But we are apt to forget that all individuals pass through the same stages in development and that the core of our organized personalities lies in this primitive nucleus, hence, that in ordinary thinking we all tend to fall back on primitive modes of ideation.

Here then is a perpetual source of difficulty in dealing with theoretical concepts. The relations of ideas to ideas are never – except in the case of particular sublimations and particular psychoses – so highly charged with interest as the associations of direct perceptual experience, and there is a constant tendency to regress from one interest to the other. Our main concern then as psycho-analytical students should be to eliminate all possible pathological stimuli tending to make the path to regression easier or more seductive. Having done so as far as possible (by personal analysis) we can proceed with the finishing touches, viz. various mental disciplines promoting reality (scientific) thinking.

X

SUBLIMATION, SUBSTITUTION AND SOCIAL ANXIETY*

[1931]

The task of defining or re-defining the working terms of psycho-analysis is one that cannot be much longer delayed. Concepts which in their time were in many instances adequate enough require to be amplified in the light of increasing knowledge of the complexity of the unconscious processes they were originally intended to describe. Sometimes, as in the case of the term 'narcissistic phase of development', a much more elaborate distinction of serial phases and nuclear formations is called for: in other instances the original definition of the term is open to a variety of interpretations. When this paper was written, a good deal of confusion existed as to the exact connotations of 'sublimation', and, despite a growing literature on the subject, much of that confusion remains at the present day. It seems worth while, therefore, to reproduce in a considerably abbreviated form, this early attempt to clarify the issue and to relate it to the central problem of anxiety. To the practical-minded psycho-analyst, apt to confuse metapsychology with metaphysics, the presentation may seem a trifle tedious if not superfluous. Yet without close discussion of terms it is impossible to prepare the ground for a systematic theory of psycho-analysis. And without a systematic theory of psycho-analysis, it is impossible either to eliminate clinical error or to control clinical observations, both of which aims are eminently practical. In fact there is scarcely a psycho-analytical term in current use which does not call for detailed examination of this sort. Finally, it is a useful corrective to the glib use of technical terms to remember that however much we may seek to isolate and canonize these by frequent use, mental mechanisms represent merely aspects of a total mental activity, isolated for purposes of convenience in presentation.

To which it may be added that, until psycho-analytical concepts

* First published in *The International Journal of Psycho-Analysis*, Vol. XII, pt. 3, 1931 [here considerably abbreviated].

are more accurately defined, there is little or no possibility of promoting liaison between psycho-analysis and statistical psychology.

Historically the concept of sublimation has passed through two phases of development. Up to the year 1923 interest in sublimation was largely phenomenological. A few generalizations had been advanced concerning the mechanism of sublimation, but pronouncements on dynamic aspects were practically restricted to the relation of sublimation to the 'return of the repressed', ultimately to symptom-formation. From 1923 onwards interest became concentrated on the energies involved and the nature of their modification. It is generally agreed that prior to 1923 a good deal of confusion existed regarding the exact nature of sublimation. Since then it has increased rather than diminished. And there appears to be no doubt that this is due in part to the stress recently laid on dynamic factors. To avoid this source of confusion, therefore, I propose treating the two phases separately.

I. EARLY VIEWS

DEFINITIONS

Summarizing the views of Freud [1] up to 1923, we find the following generalizations: Sublimation is the term applied to a group of unconscious processes which have this in common, that as the result of inner or outer deprivation, the aim of object-libido undergoes a more or less complete deflection, modification or inhibition. In the great majority of instances the new aim is one distinct or remote from sexual satisfaction, i.e. is an asexual or non-sexual aim. In certain instances, however, some degree of gratification of the original sexual impulse can be regarded as sublimation or as an early step towards sublimation provided the greater part of its primitive components and all adult genito-sexual aims are inhibited or deflected, e.g. the aim-inhibited impulses and social relations between individuals of the same sex. A third case not to be distinguished from sublimation, but with closer relation to direct uninhibited aims, is the case of extreme falling in love where the degree of over-estimation of the object cannot be distinguished from devotion to an abstract idea. The new aims are in a large number of instances, especially in the case of the adult, not only non-sexual (although psychically related to sexual aims) but definitely cultural; they are in an ethical sense 'higher', less selfish and socially more valuable than the original aim. Nevertheless some sublimations can be potentially inhibiting to social adaptation, e.g. some sublimations of anal erotism, obstinacy, parsimony, etc. There is in general an anaclitic relationship between sublimated impulses and ego-impulses. This cannot always be distinguished by descriptive study of the new mode, which may appear to be purely an ego-aim, i.e. the psychic relation of the new aim to the original sexual aim may be extremely remote.

Next as to energies: the greater part of the energies in question has its source in the erotogenic zones, i.e. is derived from infantile component sexuality where the object varies from a primary organ-object to a complete secondary external object. These component impulses lend themselves to sublimation owing to the fact that they can act vicariously for one another and change their objects freely. The energies derived from these zonal excitations do not lose their intensity in the process of displacement. Owing partly to the source of sublimated instincts, viz. mainly erotogenic zones, and partly to other constitutional factors, the capacity for sublimation is congenitally variable and is limited by the congenital disposition to fixation, i.e. sublimation proceeds in' direct ratio to the plasticity of the libido. Acquired factors affecting plasticity also affect capacity to sublimate.

Finally as to organization of the process: sublimation is demanded by the same ego-instance that instigates repression, but the amount of sublimation is not necessarily in direct ratio to the strength of the demand. The task of effecting sublimation is, like repression, an ego activity. The general relation of sublimation to repression is one of an auxiliary, in that it satisfies the claims of the ego without involving repression; but it does not loosen existing repression. One form of sublimation shares with repression the mechanism of anti-cathexis.

Considering these views in more detail a number of problems will be seen to emerge.

COMPLEXITY OF MECHANISM

First take the view that sublimation is not a single mechanism but a group of mechanisms. The advantages of this view are the following: it rules out the necessity of producing a short and possibly hampering definition; it indicates the possibility that seeming contradictions may be due to an unjustifiable comparison of components of different mechanisms. The best example here is a seeming contradiction or uncertainty pointed out by Bernfeld [2] and others, viz. that in one of Freud's statements sublimation is regarded as a special example of reaction formation and that, according to a subsequent statement, reaction formation is to be regarded as a special case of sublimation. Thirdly, it affords us breathing space for future research. For instance, increasing knowledge of the workings of the super-ego compels us to consider just how far certain guilt factors play a decisive part in processes of sublimation. In particular, Melanie Klein [3] and Ella F. Sharpe [4] have suggested that certain almost stereotyped 'restitution' phenomena are responsible at the same time for instigating and producing an outlet for creative urges with an ultimately non-sexual aim.

We must not of course rush to conclusions. We should first of all have to consider whether restitution situations are invariably a factor and frequently the only important factor. Even so we should have to decide whether this would justify special nomenclature. Granted that restitutive urges play a decisive part in particular sublimations, artistic, professional and otherwise, it might be considered more convenient to take cognizance of this fact under some system heading, e.g. super-ego factors. Or again we could consider it under the general heading of substitution. Moreover, the sublimation might be labelled by reference to the psychic situation which mainly determined the ultimate presentations of instinct, e.g. expiatory sublimations. We may in fact talk glibly of a number of mechanisms when we ought more economically and therefore more correctly to speak of different components of one main mechanism, as, for instance, a 'substitution' component, or a 'substitution determinant'.

Cultural Valuation

Then as to the cultural valuation of sublimations. On the whole Freud has come down heavily in favour of a social, ethical and cultural valuation of sublimations; but he has left the door open in a minority of instances. Bernfeld [2] in particular has felt uneasy at this state of affairs, and has indicated that the activities of children and adults belong to the same process whether they are concerned with artistic, with scientific or with worthless objects. He recommends the use of the term sublimation for all aim deviation of object libido which takes place without repression and is ego-syntonic. In his view sublimation is a deviation which serves an ego-aim (although the ego-aim may of course have been in existence already). The former view, i.e. definition by relation to repression, does not take sufficient cognizance of the relation, on the one hand, between anti-cathexis and repression, and, on the other, between anti-cathexis and sublimation. The second criterion, viz. the relation to ego-aims, compels us to discriminate between the ego-aims of childhood and those of adult life. It is true that by applying an adult standard to the activities of childhood, many of their sublimations could be made to appear culturally valueless, but we are not entitled to apply these standards. Unless we can establish an appropriate set of ego values for every stage of human development, we must regard the substitution activities of childhood as being either immediately or potentially valuable. On the whole there appears to be no objection to adopting a cultural valuation of sublimations, in so far as sublimated impulses have an anaclitic relation to ego-impulses and in so far as these ego-impulses represent or take cognizance of appropriate external (familial and social) standards. On the other hand, from the point of view of substitution products, there does not appear to be any justification for cultural valuation. And we cannot get away from the fact that Freud has laid the greatest emphasis simply on the deviation from a sexual to a non-sexual aim. We may subsequently proceed to classify substitutions as culturally valuable, neutral, worthless or detrimental respectively, but in that case we must have some exact understanding of the relations between sublimation and symptom formation.

So far we have considered two aspects of the problem, viz. whether sublimation should include a group of mechanisms and whether a cultural valuation is justifiable. A moment's considerawill show that the second issue heightens the importance of the first. For example, it is often argued that the activities of a skilled counterfeiter constitute a lower, socially harmful manifestation, hence that a cultural valuation of sublimation is not universally applicable. From many points of view this argument is unsound. It can be said that the modification of the aim of instinct has already been achieved in the engraver's art, whereas the turning of the art to anti-social ends is a sort of secondary elaboration, involving preconscious processes. Or again, that the instincts gratified in the anti-social activity are unmodified as distinct from the modified instincts gratified by engraving activities. Or again, that these anti-social activities represent an alliance between a real sublimation and an infantile regression. Nevertheless, it might be argued that if we take this point of view, we have no right to claim that 'restitutive' urges of the Sharpe-Klein pattern are *primary* factors in sublimation. They could be regarded as secondary manipulations of processes of sublimation, not as an immediate instigator of sublimation. However that may be, it is evident that some grading of the end results of sublimation is a necessary subject for research.

Sublimation and Object-replacement

In cultural valuations of sublimation, cognizance is inevitably taken of the *object* as well as of the aim of the impulse; and, strictly speaking, this is not in the bargain. I am going to suggest, however, that unless we take a very broad view of 'aims' we cannot avoid paying attention to the objects of sublimated aims. In theory at any rate, the aim of every instinct is gratification, and if we adhere to that view then the change in gratification brought about in sublimation, viz. from a sexual to a non-sexual gratification, permits us to ignore the object. And it is true that in the case of sexual impulses, particularly the component instincts, the object is the most variable characteristic of the instinct. On the other hand, when we think of instinctual aims we are in the habit of thinking behaviouristically, i.e. in terms of the *mode* of gratification. It is in this mode that the degree of psychic relation to the original aim is preserved. Now since we know that sublimation can exert a protective function in mental economy in the sense of giving outlet to quantities of energy and so preventing damming up and conflict, we are bound to consider whether, apart from the absence of sexual gratification in any sublimated activity, the degree of psychical relation preserved in the new mode varies in remoteness *and therefore in protective value*. And there can be no doubt that the degree of psychic remoteness does vary greatly in different accredited sublimations. The impulse of infantile sexual curiosity concerning Oedipus objects, when converted into scientific curiosity as to the sexual habits of adults, has certainly undergone not only deflection of aim but substitution of object. The mode of looking or listening has not, however, been appreciably altered. In the case of scientific curiosity regarding, for instance, the sexual habits of bees, the psychic relation to the original stimulating situation is increasingly remote, not as judged by aim or mode but as judged by replacement of object. Substitute an abstract object, such as curiosity about the concept of sublimation, and the relation becomes still more remote. When anal erotic sublimations take the form of collecting objects, the social and cultural valuation is determined by the nature of the object, not solely by the fact that a component sexual aim has become a non-sexual one. The collecting mode may alter little, but the object may vary from precious first editions, to private collections of pieces of soiled paper or definitions of sublimation. On the other hand, it is to be noted that in three special groups of sublimations (aim-inhibited activities, sublimated homosexuality and devotion to object-idealizations) the degree of psychical remoteness is not so great as in the deviations of component impulses.

SUBSTITUTION AND DISPLACEMENT

Our next step is to consider what is the essential psychic process by which deviation is effected. Since, however, the terms 'substitution' and 'replacement' have so far been used without definition, I think we are justified in shelving further consideration of sublimation until we are clear as to the nature of 'displacement', otherwise it will be difficult to describe the relation of sublimation to 'symbolism', to the 'return of the repressed' and to 'symptom-formation' respectively. To start with displacement, I find that there are about twenty-five terms in use in English translations and original works, all expressing some aspect of the mechanism of displacement, and although these can be grouped under the headings of 'displacement', 'replacement' and 'substitution', there is a good deal of overlapping, the net result of which is that the term substitution becomes rather hazy in meaning.

As the basis of all definitions we fall back on units of instinctual representation, viz. psychic content and charges of psychic energy, of which the latter are in the clinical sense by far the more important; and we are agreed that, in so far as charges are apprehended in consciousness apart from ideational elements, they are termed affects. Bearing this in mind it is evident that the term displacement is the most comprehensive of the three. It implies not only the transposition (movement, release, radiation, diversion, dislocation, transference) of affect (intensity, accent) but the replacement (substitution) of one idea or element by another. The element substituted is more suitable or less unacceptable than the original element or was originally more trivial, indifferent or unimportant, i.e. psychically more remote. Replacement of elements involves transposition of affect, but the terms are not interchangeable. We cannot always use the term replacement in the affective sense. In sublimation, as Ernest Jones [5] has pointed out, sexual energies are not replaced but diverted. On the other hand, although replacement is an accurate term for the dislocation of elements, the term replacement-product is sometimes used in the same sense as substitution-product or substitute-formation. Substitution again, although frequently applied to organized mental formations, is on occasion used (in some definitions of symbolism) in a sense that is already connoted by displacement (or replacement) of elements. It would seem advisable to reserve the term replacement for that aspect of the general mechanism of displacement which concerns ideational elements. This replacement of elements can be observed not only in processes of intercommunication between different psychic systems (dreams, wit, symbolism, etc.), but in communications within one system (allusive forms of verbal (pcs) expression). The term substitution could then be reserved for the relations between organized mental processes (as distinct from elements) in different psychic systems, e.g. the substitution of preconscious ideational *systems* for unconscious phantasy organizations. Freud originally thought of substitution as concerning the ideational representation of instinct after repression. In his view, substitution-formations were similar to but more highly organized than unconscious phantasies. Substitute-formations and symptoms implied the return of the repressed. There were, however, many different forms of substitution and at that time he did not consider that substitution and symptom formation invariably coincided. For example, they did coincide in conversion-hysteria but did not coinci de in obsessional neurosis; in obsessional neurosis, substitution by reaction-formation preceded and differed in content from symptom-formation. Later [6], however, as the result of his re-valuation of the characteristics of mental 'defence', he said that it is better to ascribe to the defensive process what has been said concerning symptom-formation and to regard symptom-formation and substitute-formation as synonymous terms. He would say, for example, that under certain circumstances the replacement of an element (e.g. father by wolf) has claims to be considered as a symptom.

REACTION-FORMATION

The greatest difficulty in establishing a simple relation on the one hand between unrepressed impulse and sublimation and on the other hand between repressed impulse and substitute (or symptom) formation is vagueness concerning the exact meaning of reaction-formation. To make this difficulty clear we must consider the phenomenon of anti-cathexis. We are familiar with anti-cathexis first of all as the mechanism of primal repression. Following psychic situations of an exceptionally grave order (either immediately or potentially traumatic) instinct presentations are denied entry to the system pcs, whilst in the pcs system we find cathexis of ideas to some extent psychically remote from the traumatic group. We also recognize anti-cathexis as one aspect of actual repression. But here it is combined with 'withdrawal of cathexis' from pcs elements. And it is generally held that the *energy of anti-cathexis is derived from the cathexis of repressed elements.* Now should the anti-cathexis involve presentations of a directly antithetical element or interest, we are accustomed to describe this as a 'reaction-formation', although the use of the term formation is not strictly justified except in the case of a system of presentations, or at any rate in relation to a *persisting* anti-cathexis. Judged by the standards of displacement, all anti-cathexes are displacements and reaction-formations are merely a special example of displacement by the opposite.

The problem has been lightened somewhat by Freud's later pronouncement on reaction-formation, viz. that it is to be regarded as a mechanism of defence distinct from repression [6]. But if we are to regard reaction-formation as a mechanism distinct from repression we ought to be able to offer a good metapsychological reason for this change. Is it because we have hitherto included too much under repression and now desire to split off a special aspect, viz. anti-cathexis through antithesis; or is it simply that from the clinical point of view it is more convenient to raise a particular form of anti-cathexis to the status of an independent mechanism? There are some grounds for the latter view. In hysteria we find that *withdrawal* of cathexis is the most striking feature. There are anti-cathexes in hysteria, it is true; these move along lines of displacement but vary in psychic remoteness. On the other hand, in obsessional neurosis we find a *relative incapacity to withdrawal cathexis* together with an extreme exploitation of anti-cathexis, particularly along one definite line of displacement, viz. through antithetical presentations. That is to say, the degree of psychic remoteness is more or less fixed. In one case we have a *mobile* mechanism (exemplified by the changing anti-cathexis of outer stimuli seen in hysteria); in the other we have *organized* anti-cathexis, more or less permanently embedded in the ego. In other words, if reaction-formation is an independent defence mechanism, it must be in the sense of a substitution product having some degree of permanent organization, as distinct from the lability of hysterical anti-cathexis. From this point of view, we are entitled to classify various substitution products in accordance with their depth and the permanence of their relation to ego structure.

SUBLIMATION AND REACTION-FORMATION

In the meantime, let us summarize the possible relations between sublimation and reaction formation in the light of our discussion of displacement. First of all, as regards elements: if reaction-formation is simply a form of anti-cathexis of certain ideational elements, then it is *a priori* a form of displacement and has that much in common with sublimation. But in that case it is difficult to insist that sublimation is solely concerned with un-repressed elements. If, however, reaction-formation is an organized psychic formation, then we may be able to distinguish it from sublimation, provided we are content to regard sublimation simply as a variety of displacement. If, however, we regard sublimations as themselves organized psychic formations, then we can justify the use of a special term, 'sublimation', only provided we can distinguish sublimation from other organized formations, e.g. reaction formations, character formations and symptom formations.

Then as to energies: here the relation to symptom formation is again important. Consider the view that sublimation concerns only unrepressed instinct. If one adheres to this view, then one can

definitely distinguish sublimation from organized reaction-formations because the latter certainly deal with instincts under repression, but in that case the relations of sublimation and character
formation are again obscured. By existing definitions certain
character formations are means whereby an individual can to a
large extent spare himself repressions. And sublimation by itself
will not cover the phenomena of character formation. In any case,
when we talk of an individual sparing himself repressions we mean
actual repression. Perhaps we should do well to avoid this loose
use of the term repression and speak of sublimation phenomena
in quantitative terms: we might say, for example, that a sublimation applied only to the *complete* transfer of an original cathexis to
the replacement element.

Finally, we may recall that Ernest Jones [5] has always drawn a
distinction between these mechanisms. He has stated that sublimation represents the continuation, after modification, of positive
unconscious impulses *only*, whereas reaction-formations include also
certain elements of ego-reaction. He would admit, of course, that
the end product in both cases shows deviation of aim, and the
distinction, as he points out relates essentially to the source of the
instincts concerned. Positive sublimated instincts originally belong
to the appetitive group; reaction-formations contain positive drives
but include also representatives of reactive instincts. By laying
emphasis on the source of instincts and whether they operate
directly or through the ego, he has offered us an apparently simple
solution of the matter. According to this view, deviation of aim
would not be exclusively a characteristic of sublimation.

Tempting as this definition is, there are certain difficulties in the
way. If, as has been suggested, certain creative activities prove to
have been stimulated by restitutive urges, then we have an example
of an apparently positive urge (the impulse to create), functioning
not only in a reactive sense but in a manner which is reminiscent
of the obsessional mechanism of undoing [6]. In obsessional undoing one representative of instinct is followed by another calculated to 'undo' or 'expiate' or 'cancel' it. This suggests that we
may have included and still include under reaction formation,
phenomena which require a separate category.

SUBLIMATION AND SYMPTOM FORMATION

The main feature in the definition of sublimation was, it will be remembered, the fact of change of aim. Now in a large majority of instances a symptom amongst other achievements succeeds in altering the aims of impulses – the substitute product is apparently non-sexual and except in rare instances unaccompanied by sexual gratification. One can try to get out of this difficulty by saying, as Bernfeld does [2], that a sublimation is the opposite of a symptom, that the energies are not conflicting but work together producing increased ego activity. But, unless one combines this with a cultural valuation, one has not discovered a unique characteristic; in certain phases of neuroses, individual activities may be quite excessive. But there is here at any rate *some* point of agreement. We are bound to concede that obsessional energies are expended on trivial activities. Symptoms, as Freud tells us, are either detrimental or useless to life as a whole or may be obnoxious to the individual and involve him in distress or suffering. These remarks do not appear to apply to sublimations which are held to reduce *Unlust* or increase *Lust*. This seems a promising distinction, but one is bound to ask whether it has not been taken too much for granted in the past. It is true that Freud [7] stresses the importance of sublimation as a method of preventing psychic suffering, and in that sense relates it to the operation of the pleasure principle (in its reality aspect); but he was careful to point out in the same essay that we cannot estimate what part in these cultural processes is played by the complete suppression or repression of instinct gratification.

The protest may here be raised that social valuations apart, we have ample means of distinguishing a symptom from a sublimation; in particular it will be said that a symptom is a boundary construction with one foot in the ego and the other in the Id [6]: or to put it another way, that it is a compromise artefact nourished not only by energies proceeding through the ego but by immediate Id energies. Also that it is rejected by the ego. So much may be freely admitted. And we can also agree that many reaction-formations and most sublimations appear to be accepted by the ego without question. But it is equally true that many normal character activities and most neurotic character activities are accepted by the ego without question. Yet neurotic character activities are not generally regarded as sublimations, nor do they have the same structure as symptoms. The fact that neurotic character formations like sublimations are accepted by the ego has been commented on by Ernest Jones [8], who goes on to say, 'it is likely that there is no hard and fast distinction between the two'. He believes, however, that the changes in sublimation are more radical and intrinsic, whereas in neurotic character formations the sexual nature of the impulse is retained, being merely disguised through the contact it has established with the ego. From the point of view of deviation of aim, however, his view can only hold in respect of the degree of *psychical remoteness* achieved by displacement, and is not a completely serviceable distinction for our present purpose.

Sublimation and Inhibition

Perhaps a more fruitful line of approach would be to consider the relations of inhibition in general to sublimation. We know that whereas some inhibitions take part in symptom formation, they can be distinguished from symptom formations in that inhibitions are ego-activities and supplied with energies from within the ego. To use somewhat loose terms, most inhibitions are considered to be the result of excessive erotization of ego-function leading to disturbance of that function (e.g. disturbances of vision): and from the point of view of sexual aims, we might regard sublimations as ego-aggrandizements of certain erotic functions (mainly component).

Apart from that, the relation between sublimation and inhibition brings out a point in the study of instinctual mechanisms which has not yet received sufficient attention, viz. *the chronological order of development of instinct modifications*. For example, we know that inhibitions are the last line of defence in dealing with instinct that has escaped repression, i.e. they are interpolated immediately before motor activity. It might be possible, therefore, to introduce a chronological factor in the estimation of sublimation; the latter may occur at some precise point, probably late in a series of instinctual modifications or defences. It would of course come before inhibition.[1]

A few years ago Melanie Klein [9], considering the relations of

[1] Since writing this I observe that Sterba ('Zür Problematik der Sublimierungslehre', *Int. Z. Psychoanal.*, 1930, 3/4, S.371) stresses the chronological order of mechanisms. Not only does he classify various types of sublimation in order of incidence, but he considers that reaction formation must necessarily be preceded by sublimation in the sense of desexualization.

sublimation and inhibition in some detail, suggested that inhibitions tend to make their appearance where superfluous libido is attached to an existing sublimation. (By sublimation she means the transfer of a libidinal cathexis to an ego activity, the path being determined by sexual-symbolic displacement.) This view emphasizes the importance of chronological order. It is even more important in another respect: it focuses attention on the part played by sublimations as *conductors* for excessive (pathogenic) libidinal cathexes. It was of course already known that in the obsessional neuroses sublimations acted as conductors for symptoms; and it is easy to see that they can play a part as conductors in anti-social constellations (e.g. the activities of a skilled counterfeiter).

SUBLIMATION AND SYMBOLISM

Use of the term 'conductor activity' brings us to what is perhaps the most difficult problem of all, viz. the relation between sublimation and symbolism. For example, it might be said that sublimations do not act as conductors for symptoms but that the element of symbolism does. This is probably true in the sense of presentation, but not as regards energy. Ernest Jones [8] has pointed out in regard to this subject that it is the transfer of psychic energy alone which is the significant feature in sublimation, whereas in symbolism the full significance of the original complex is retained unaltered and merely transferred to a secondary idea. He agrees, however, that sublimated ideas can temporarily regress and sink back to become mere symbols of complexes. From the descriptive standpoint, therefore, the distinction does not help us out of our present difficulties; the result in both cases is displacement or change of aim. It would appear that any fundamental distinction must be effected in terms of energy. Such a view would invalidate completely any form of cultural definition.

The subject has been reconsidered in recent years by Melanie Klein [9]. If I have apprehended her views correctly, the phenomenon of sublimation cannot be understood without constant reference to the related factors of fixation and repression. The stages are as follows: primary identification – sexual-symbolic cathexis – sublimation. Repression can play a decisive part at three points; first, in leading to the distinction between identification and symbolism (fixation here has a retarding effect on all subsequent development), second, in preventing the gradual extension from symbolism to sublimation (here fixation is responsible and the result is symptom formation), and third, in interfering with existing sublimations when these are charged later with excess of libido (here the result is inhibition). These views, however, do not solve the problem of the distinction between sexual symbolic cathexis of ego tendencies and sublimation.

SUMMARY OF EARLY VIEWS

The first and inevitable conclusion must be that the concept of sublimation as originally stated involves a considerable amount of confusion; the second that we have not yet extricated ourselves from this confusion. As regards mechanism, we have produced nothing exclusively characteristic of sublimation. If we reduce sublimation to terms of displacement, there seems no great point in retaining a tautological expression. If we insist on cultural valuations, we cannot be content with a simple definition of 'aim deviation'. We may, if we so desire, introduce a cultural factor, but this implies a complex of mechanisms and we are not in a position to indicate any exact boundary to this complex formation. Moreover, if we include substitution elements in sublimation we have difficulty in distinguishing the latter from other organized substitutions (either characterological or symptomatic). And then we get confused as to the relation of sublimation to repressed and unrepressed instinct.

On the other hand, the degree of psychic remoteness from the original impulse seems to be an important factor in sublimation, but we are unable to estimate this precisely, owing to the element of symbolism present. And if we are to take the remoteness factor seriously, it would appear desirable to exclude mere aim inhibition and object idealization from the category of sublimated processes. As regards the relation to organized psychic formations, a promising line of investigation would appear to be the relation of different formations to the main psychic systems (e.g. super-ego). Also the position of sublimation in a hierarchy (or chronological sequence) of psychic mechanisms seems worth investigating.

As regards energy certain possibilities have presented themselves. A quantitative factor in displacement might permit of a classification in which sublimation would be characterized by complete transfer of cathexes. This naturally suggests the operation (independently or concurrently) of a *qualitative* factor. Indeed, one tends to form the opinion that some qualitative change in energy may prove to be the only valid metapsychological criterion of sublimation. Finally, it is obvious that there is much to be gained by an examination of the sources of instincts involved, particularly the relation between reactive instincts and instincts capable of sublimation.

II. RECENT INVESTIGATIONS

Turning now to recent investigations, we find that these take three obvious directions. The first is clinical, the second a re-examination of psychic structure and the third a qualitative investigation of psychic energies.

TRANSITORY SUBLIMATIONS
(a) Developmental

A good example of direct clinical investigation is that of Bernfeld [2] into transitory sublimations occurring in seemingly normal children and adolescents. He has described two extreme cases, (a) where libido gratification, although ego-syntonic, is *delayed* and the libido is directed towards other ego-syntonic objects of a non-sexual variety; the condition here is that the ego impulses must not (either independently or as the result of libido frustration) be in a state of deprivation: (b) where the libido tends to subserve ego purposes it can be called upon when the ego has insufficient energy to effect an ego-aim. Bernfeld suggests that the amount of sublimation has a definite relation to the strength of the ego, that plasticity of libido is only one factor and that deviation of aim is only one of many aspects of sublimation.

(b) During Illness

A second example of the direct method brings me to part of the clinical material that is responsible for my own interest in sublimation. This concerns transitory sublimations accompanying pathological states. The states, as might be expected, were not neurotic in type but were partly of the unclassified order, alcoholism, drug-addiction, etc., partly in the nature of neurotic character-formations and partly larval psychoses (e.g. apparently normal individuals with paranoidal formations or schizophrenic reactions). A feature of these cases was the *extreme lability* of the sublimation processes. All the patients' energies appeared to be poured in one sublimation and then apparently completely displaced to another sublimation, leaving the original interest like an empty husk. And in each phase there was apparently complete satisfaction. Nevertheless, allowing for the change in idiom (in other words, in the presentation content) the activities invariably showed a common denominator of symbolic expression of unconscious phantasy. But although the processes were extremely labile, and in that way differed from the more usual stable formations of adult life, they could not at first sight have been distinguished from sublimations by the most exacting cultural or æsthetic standards, e.g. they were concerned with singing, painting, sculpture, literature, scientific and historical research, etc. In one case presenting delusional features and a general lack of reality feeling, it could be observed that the delusional mechanism always secured some element of representation in the activities without necessarily interfering seriously with their performance.[1] The patient had mild delusions of reference and in all his sublimated activities, the theme of spying, either in active or in passive form was constantly represented. When, however, owing to some extrinsic cause or some intrinsic factor of guilt any one activity was gradually abandoned, the interval was characterized by restlessness, extreme tension and manifestations of anxiety together with spasmodic outbursts of component sexual activities.

SUBLIMATION AND SEXUAL PERVERSION

A less direct type of observation involves some consideration of sexual perversions. These have always had some theoretical interest for the student of sublimation. For example, the view that in sexual perversion one or more component sexual impulses are retained and accentuated, as the price of complete repression of other components relating to the Oedipus situation, has a certain resemblance to views held concerning aim-inhibition.

On the clinical side the relation of perversion to sublimation is more obvious. In many cases one finds that the perverse activity is more freely exercised where certain æsthetic conditions are ful-

[1] Ella F. Sharpe (op. cit.) says: 'Sublimation springs from the same root as the delusion of persecution.'

filled. For example, an invert with whipping phantasies describes how his erotic activities are inhibited unless the whip conforms to certain æsthetic standards, size, shape, tapering, smoothness, colour, etc. Clothes and shoe fetichists [11] show similar reactions. Underclothes, for example, must conform to certain rigid æsthetic laws of pattern, colour, line and so on. The rigidity of such standards is reminiscent of the severe canons upheld by some critics or exponents of the fine arts. Indeed, if one did not know what was the actual subject matter of association, it would be difficult for the hearer to distinguish some diagnostic discussions of the conditions for perverse sexual gratifications from an æsthetic discussion of the canons of 'good' or 'bad' art.

SUBLIMATION AND AFFECT

Turning to less direct investigations, I think it cannot escape the attention of any analyst that when describing their sublimatory activities, patients very frequently display manifestations of anxiety or guilt either directly or in various reactive forms: anger, irritation, criticism of others, feelings of inferiority and self-depreciation, hopelessness, phantastic ambition of a reassurance variety and so forth. And it cannot escape attention that the attempted analysis not only of these reactions but of components of the sublimation evokes intense resistance. Writing some years ago, on the technical aspects of resistance [12], I pointed out the very high defence value of resistances cloaked by sublimation and remarked that not only was the mechanism of displacement exploited or undermined by Id impulses, but that in this situation the mechanism of rationalization could be exploited to any extraordinary degree as a supplementary defence. These rationalizations are not limited to purely realistic considerations which naturally are a feature of sublimated activities. The patient usually proclaims adherence to a system of absolute values, ethical, æsthetic or scientific; in this way he endeavours to bar any investigation of elements that may appear to the analyst to be thin disguises for repressed impulses. And here we can see one of the main practical difficulties attendant on cultural valuation of sublimation. The analyst who has a strong bias in favour of cultural valuations is liable to be hoist with his own petard during the analysis particularly of such characterological cases. It is almost as if the patient knew that the analyst had given consent to general values and retorted by raising his own values to a series of absolutes. These absolutes are generally held by the patient to be immune from inspection.

Obviously the first step in investigation is to classify the activities in question, next to classify the affective reactions accompanying them and then to compare these with reactions to other social situations in which the element of sublimation is not so stressed. The element of anxiety which, statistically regarded, is a common accompaniment of æsthetic and cultural preoccupations provides us with a link to another group of social-anxiety reactions, viz. social snobbery. Admittedly the value of rationalization would vary in different series, e.g. the standards of social snobbery would gain less universal acceptance than would æsthetic absolutes [13].

Sometimes the anxiety surrounding preoccupation with cultural activities is free floating, sometimes fixed to some specific element of substitution. It is practically a universal analytical experience that patients express open apprehension as to the effect of analysis on their artistic or other creative activities; failing a suitable focus for such anxiety in their own personality, they will propound with great seriousness general problems, e.g. would a great master have produced masterpieces had he been analysed; what would have happened had Christ been analysed; are not neuroses the mainspring of cultural achievement?

Some patients provide the analyst with abundant material of this kind: they will spend days quoting their own researches into the life histories of geniuses, the object being to show that neurotic suffering is an inevitable prerequisite of creative genius.

In addition to anxiety accompaniments of sublimatory activities, one finds frequently a marked association of reactive attitudes. We know that reactive attitudes of hate are a common cover for anxiety states, but the amount of hate and aggression attached to these cultural constellations is so great as to suggest that they provide a more or less direct outlet for destructive impulses. It is interesting to consider in this connection one of the natural polarities of æsthetic or scientific pursuits, viz. creative and critical (destructive) activities. Interpretation is after all simply a compromise between these tendencies. It is no exaggeration to say that a large proportion of critical activities are concerned less with measurement, correlation and orientation than with direct satisfaction of destructive urges. The amount of heat which can be engendered in these fields of æsthetic activity is popularly discounted for three reasons; first, that the indulgence is so common, second that destructive trends are cloaked behind the creative aspect of constructive criticism and thirdly, that particularly in the case of literary criticism, tendencies of wit and recompense of style (technique) help to conceal or extenuate the more primitive interests.

OBSESSIONAL SEQUENCE

In general then there is sufficient evidence of the association of anxiety reactions and aggressive trends with sublimated activities to warrant further investigation. The most natural explanation appears to be that sublimations act as conductors for unconscious impulses and affects. This has already been stated by Freud for the obsessional neuroses. If now we find this conductor system in active operation in the general sphere of sublimations, we are bound to ask whether we have somehow failed to recognize an *obsessional sequence of events*. (The obsessional sequence is: reaction formation – return of the repressed – defence formation.) The direction of this train of thought is obvious; all along we have tried to maintain some clear distinction between sublimation and symptom formation, and now we are faced with the possibility that in many instances sublimations are part of larger psychic formations resembling symptoms.

PHOBIA FORMATION

But it is not only a question of obsessional technique; wherever we find conductors or substitutions plus a certain amount of anxiety we have all the essential ingredients of a phobia formation. Have we any grounds for thinking that sublimations accompanied by anxiety reactions are part of an extended phobia system? You will remember, of course, that the phobias we meet clinically and treat are 'unsuccessful', the measures adopted to prevent affect following the return of the repressed have failed. If we can regard sublimations accompanied by anxiety as extended phobias, it may be that we can establish a criterion for *true* sublimation, viz. that it should be a 'successful phobia', an anxiety-free outlet for repressed energy. But in that case we should have to admit that it is the rarest of human phenomena.

SOCIAL ANXIETY

At this point it is necessary to interpolate some consideration of *social anxiety*. Freud's [6] [7] most recent teaching takes cognizance of primary anxiety states, the phobia formations of early childhood and the classical phobias of adult life. Concentration of interest on adult phobias tends to obscure two important facts; the unassisted dispersal or, spontaneous modification of early phobias, and the distinction between external anxiety and endopsychic (guilt) factors which can be observed in infantile phobias. To put the matter simply, there is a tendency to confuse social anxiety with guilt, and there has been a tendency to easy acceptance of the view that certain anxiety states are spontaneously *resolved* rather than *dispersed* in smaller formations.

We have become accustomed to subdivide the conditions for anxiety in a certain order, starting with those dangers which can be attributed to aggression from without (loss of love, castration anxiety) and ending with a completely endopsychic condition (fear of loss of love on the part of the super-ego). This last form of anxiety gives rise to the affect of guilt experienced directly or in the form of need of punishment, and is regarded as having a special relation to the aggressive impulses. The external factor becomes modified in course of time from anxiety about actual aggression to anxiety regarding external criticism. The internal factor is and remains an anxiety of internal criticism. The anxiety regarding external criticism which is identical with anxiety regarding loss of love is distinguished as social anxiety. A prominent factor in childhood, it is probably grossly under-estimated in adult life. Its relation to internal criticism is, however, very intimate and sharp distinction is difficult. This is to a large extent due to the operation of the mechanism of projection; in the first place the aggression of external authority is exaggerated by projection and in the second the sharpness of internal criticism can be temporarily reduced by displacing it in the form of social anxiety. In the same way introjection processes blur the sharp dividing-line between the two situations. Both are, however, subject to a certain amount of modification in the course of adolescence. Conditions of social anxiety are more precise, and in the same way the most superficial aspects of super-ego criticism begin to merit the term of social or conscious conscience.

RETURN OF DISPERSED PHOBIAS

If now we re-examine the affects and reactions accompanying sublimations, we see that whilst the element of anxiety is in many cases obvious, the reactions appear to present a mixture of social anxiety with displaced guilt. A fair distinction can be drawn between preoccupations that are more or less compulsively followed in order to acquire merit (liquidate guilt) and those in which the desire not to be found out plays an important part. It is not overstating matters to say that many individuals who appear to have spent their lives in cultural pursuits can be found on examination to have been clinging anxiously to a thin façade of cultural preoccupation in order to escape detection and criticism. Doubtless the strength of aggressive components associated with the activity determines whether the reaction falls into one group or the other.

Anyhow we have to consider the possibility that the spontaneously disappearing phobias of earlier life have not in fact disappeared, but have become dispersed and that they tend to reassemble and organize themselves in association with sublimated activities. These formations are of course not so closely knit or condensed as phobias, hence 'hold' anxiety better. At the same time we must ask whether the freedom from manifest obsessional states enjoyed by a large number of people is not due to displacement of obsessional technique to activities which according to cultural valuations are not suspected of being symptomatic.

THE ANXIETY CHARACTER

Now on this point some suggestive work has been published by Ernest Jones in his paper, 'The Anxiety Character'. [8] Basing himself on the view that if defensive reactions to anxiety are localized they are *a priori* phobia formations, he defines an anxiety character as that state where anxiety trends and the defensive reactions are built into the structure of the personality as a whole. They are diffuse and laid down early in the defensive process. He distinguishes three factors in the formation, the amount of libidinal excitation, the development of anxiety and its displacement by absorption into the personality. The individual reacts to social situations wherever they present possibilities of loss or injury of symbolic significance (operations, loss of valued objects) or where they represent minor social deprivations (slights and rebuffs, etc.). Should, nevertheless, the developed anxiety prove objectionable a third component can be distinguished, a concealed anxiety reaction against anxiety. This frequently takes the form of hate reactions, anger and irritability, although here too the relations to guilt reactions are very close. On the whole he has selected social situations in illustration of this condition, but it is easy to see that it could be held to include most of the formations I have already described in reference to cultural activities. Possibly a quantitative factor would help us to distinguish between the anxiety character and sublimations of a phobiac or obsessional type. And I want to suggest that although these latter states are much more diffuse than localized phobia symptom formations, they are, nevertheless, by comparison with the diffuse forms of anxiety described by Jones sufficiently fixed and highly enough charged to deserve a special category.

ANXIETY AND INHIBITION

A third possible view of the relation of anxiety to sublimation is suggested by Klein [9] [10] in her work on the neurotic inhibitions of childhood. According to an earlier paper, there occurs even in successful repression a displacement of affect (in the form of anxiety) from the repressed to ego tendencies; the displacement is effected by identification (later symbolism) and the ego activity in question has in any case some degree of primary libidinal cathexis. The anxiety is not shown directly, but manifests itself in the form of inhibitions. In some cases these can be termed normal inhibitions, but where repression is unsuccessful the amount of displaced anxiety is greater and the inhibitions are of a neurotic type. A complemental relation between repression and sublimation is necessary for a neurotic inhibition. Not only must repression be unsuccessful, but there must also have existed strong sublimatory interests in the ego activity in question. The situation has resemblances to a phobia formation, but differs from it in two ways – first that the anxiety is bound in the inhibition, whereas it is freed in the phobia, and second, that where symptom formation exists fixation has led to repression at an earlier stage, before successful sublimation has been effected.

Melanie Klein's later views (1930) emphasize the fact that owing to anxiety, identification with non-sexual objects is stimulated;

anxiety is then displaced to the appropriate ego interests. This displacement has adaptation value because through identification (symbolism) energies are transferred to ego tendencies. But the degree of anxiety is important; if early anxiety is excessive it inhibits symbolism and therefore capacity to sublimate (i.e. transfer of interest): if, however, the transfer of anxiety is excessive it is liable to end in inhibition of the ego activity (sublimation).

CLASSIFICATION

It is improbable that we can grasp the detailed relations of sublimations and anxiety states so long as we remain content with clinical generalizations. So making due allowance for over-elaboration and overlapping, there would appear to be at least four groups of phenomena to be considered: (*a*) Classical phobia formations (symptoms), which interfere with sublimations in a secondary sense, (*b*) minor, almost occult, phobia formations (Ernest Jones' 'anxiety character' type) which, again secondarily, interfere with sublimations, (*c*) inhibitions which conceal the direct attachment of anxiety to sublimations, and (*d*) anxiety states directly associated with sublimations. The latter, though open anxiety states, are not recognized clinically owing in part to the social sanction given to such reactions or to a social conspiracy of silence (or inattention) on such matters. Other groups could doubtless be added, e.g. (*e*) sublimations which perform a protective function similar to the protective function of an obsessional neurosis, (*f*) sublimations in which a delusional element plays a part.

Summing up these more direct clinical considerations, and taking a broad view of the position, it cannot be said that the outcome of sublimation is invariably to promote *Lust* and diminish *Unlust*. We do in fact find *Unlust* in frequent and close association with sublimated activities. This does not exclude the possibility that there is a type of pure sublimation which has such an effect, but it does suggest that pure sublimation is rather a rare phenomenon. We may indeed inquire whether we have not injected into the concept a subjective and phantastic standard, a kind of omnipotent valuation which detracts from the usefulness of the term in workaday analysis. From this point of view we are thrown back rather on a 'protective' standard in estimating sublimations.

Secondly, observation of the phenomena of transitory sublimations in normal states and of their regression or mobility in pathological states is a useful preliminary to study of processes such as 'desexualization'. The mobility supports the idea of a store of permanently neutral energy which can follow on the heels of unmodified and merely displaced pilot impulses. Regressional changes and reduction of sublimations to symbolisms suggests that the unmodified energy is quantitatively more than a mere pilot impulse, no matter how much neutral energy is in store.

MODIFICATION OF ENERGY

This brings us finally to recent formulations on the *modifications of energy* involved in sublimation. In essence this is a theoretical matter, a matter of Id psychology; our clinical contact is practically limited to a discussion of sources of instincts and to observation of the phenomena connected with reactive instincts. The texts on which all such discussions hang are to be found in the *Ego and the Id* [14]. They are firstly that 'the transformation of object libido into narcissistic libido which thus takes place (when an erotic object-choice is transformed into a modification of the ego) implies an abandonment of sexual aims, a process of desexualization; it is consequently a kind of sublimation'. It is suggested here that perhaps the ego after this transformation has been effected goes on to give the transformed libido another aim. The second suggestion is that there exists in the mind a neutral displaceable energy which can augment the cathexis of an erotic or destructive impulse. This Freud regards as an indispensable concept. This neutral energy 'is probably active alike in the ego and in the Id and presumably proceeds from the narcissistic reservoir of libido', is 'desexualized Eros'. It might also be described as sublimated energy. The third assumption is that the identification with the father from which the super-ego arises is 'in the nature of a desexualization or even of a sublimation'. But it seems 'there occurs at the same time an instinctual defusion'. After sublimation the erotic components cannot 'bind the whole of the destructive elements' and 'these are released in the form of inclination to aggression and destruction'.

If we try to express these ideas in familiar metapsychological terms it will be seen that they can be contained under the heading of deviation of aim. But it is obvious that the 'desexualization' implied is something more fundamental: it implies a permanent neutralization. From this point of view the regression phenomena observed clinically in sublimation activities merit careful consideration. A mere cessation of activities could be attributed simply to withdrawal of this auxiliary energy. But a regression, or if you prefer it, a replacement of sublimations by manifest erotic urges suggests two possibilities. It might imply an excess of displaced but not completely desexualized pilot energy existing in the formation. Or it could be due to the transfer of neutral energy to a previously weakly cathected or strongly repressed erotic trend. Moreover, it is to be noted that the energies are derived from external object cathexis of an advanced type. And this leaves the problem of some earlier component sexual instincts rather in the air. Then as to the view that the erotic component is mainly sublimated after the 'defusion' of withdrawn object cathexes: the simplest explanation of this process would be that the absorption of defused aggressive components by the super-ego provides the additional impetus necessary to initiate sublimations of whatever variety. Another possibility is worth considering; it might be regarded as a rider to the first proposition. It can be stated as follows: is the defusion simply an inevitable result of withdrawal of cathexis and the sublimation simply a necessary fate of the withdrawn erotic component: or is sublimation only possible after defusion has taken place, i.e. after the destructive components have been isolated and bound in super-ego activity?

SUBLIMATION AND AGGRESSIVE IMPULSES

Some points in favour of this view may be suggested here: it is well known that aggressive impulses are more tenacious of aim than sexual impulses. Their objects can be changed and the mode of gratification altered, but the aim remains. And it would appear plausible that this factor must cause difficulty in the displacement of fused impulses. We can see in the case of certain object relations how erotic impulses can light up aggressive tendencies and aggressive tendencies stimulate erotic relations. Returning to our clinical data, it is to be observed that in practically all cases where *Unlust* is associated with sublimation, analysis demonstrated without any difficulty the carry over of some component of unmodified aggression.

MASOCHISM

It has been pointed out that in these recent formulations the study of energy commences at a fairly advanced stage of development, i.e. where incestuous object cathexes are withdrawn. And in the original definition of sublimation we were accustomed to think of the energy being derived mainly from the component impulses, some of which do not necessarily require an external object. Further, as Freud [15] has told us, 'the classical piece of evidence for the existence of "instinctual fusion" is *moral masochism*'. Masochism at the time of his 'Three Contributions' was rated as one of several paired sets of component impulses. Now moral masochism has 'loosened its connection with what we recognize to be sexuality'. We must therefore ask: does the sublimation of impulses apply only to that amount which has gone through a phase of external object attachment and has been withdrawn; and, another problem, is moral masochism a sublimation?

This last is not simply an academic issue: it has frequently to be dealt with in the course of analyses, especially of women. It amounts to this: if masochistic trends are put to a biological purpose in the sexual activities of women and if sublimation implies a deviation of aim (sexual gratification), then the sublimation of masochism must interfere with adult capacities: therefore, according to social valuation of sublimation, moral masochism would not qualify as a true sublimation. According to the older views of sublimation, this could be answered in two ways; first, that whatever the nature of the component instinct, the part sublimated was that which has been directed to an external object, and, second, that sublimation applied only to frustrated object impulses, not to that amount which was ego-syntonic and would therefore be gratified in sexual adaptation.

A more complete explanation is contained in Freud's discrimination between the moral urges due to reinforcement of the super-ego by the sadistic component freed in defusion and the moral masochistic urges due to an increase in the masochism of the ego after defusion. The latter contain a regressional gratification of Oedipus wishes, the former reinforce the repression or defence against Oedipus wishes. This explanation is a satisfying one, but it weakens the original definition, viz. that sublimation simply implies a deviation from the aim of sexual gratification. Descriptively speaking, moral masochism shows deviation from sexual aim, and even if we agree that there is an element of primitive erotogenic masochism behind all moral masochism, it is not openly manifested as such. Freud has appealed to the usages of speech in this matter, and has said that familiar application of the term masochist to those who behave as 'moral masochists' do, connects the behaviour with erotism. That may be true, but this plainly phenomenological usage cripples the equally familiar application of the term sublimation to manifestly non-sexual activities, or, alternatively, detracts from the value of social standards in assessing sublimation.

INSTINCT AND AIM-DEVIATION

Although future investigation of the dynamics of sublimation will be concerned more and more with the relation of destructive to libidinal impulses, it is obvious that, no matter how convenient it would be to use the term solely in a dynamic sense, and no matter how much confusion is introduced by the application of descriptive and social standards, it will never be possible to neglect the factor of aim-deviation. Indeed, a closer study of the lability of instinctual aims will be an important part of future research. It does not require much reflection to see that, judged by the lability of aims, the old Freudian classification of instincts was in some respects more convenient than the recent antithesis of death and life instincts. It is characteristic of certain instincts of self-preservation that they are most refractory of all to repression or modification. It is equally characteristic of sexual impulses that they can be completely repressed and completely modified or, to put it more cautiously, modified beyond recognition.

The facts concerning destructive impulses are interesting. The aims of destructive impulses are refractory to modification. Given a certain association with libidinal impulses they can be repressed or opposed by reaction formations or preceded by expiations. But the modification is only accomplished with great difficulty. Indeed, unless repressed, the aims of aggressive impulses, though capable of change from object to subject, are not much modified. The mode of gratification can be altered. Speech, for example, may sublimate certain erotic components but it does not alter the aim of destructive components. These can only be repressed or held in check or anticipated by the opposite. It is therefore an open question whether the importance of sublimation is primarily that it prevents the damming up of libido by displacing quantities of frustrated energy, or whether its function is to control our surplus of frustrated aggressive impulses; in other words, does sublimation prevent illness by reducing anxiety, or does it prevent illness by liquidating guilt?

III. CONCLUSIONS

It would appear that from the point of view of metapsychology any fundamental conception of sublimation must be expressed in terms of energy (its source and the nature of its modification). The earlier and more descriptive standpoint does not lend itself to the purposes of metapsychology. Nevertheless, the term has considerable descriptive value. It would be much more useful if we could establish a more precise relation between sublimation and symbolism. Pending further research, we are justified in using the term (*a*) for loose descriptive purposes, and (*b*) as a basis of metapsychological investigation of instinct. But we must realize that this double application of the term is liable on occasion to give rise to considerable confusion.

And here I think we can effect a compromise on the vexed question of cultural valuation. From the very outset Freud has emphasized the importance of sublimations in preventing neurotic regression, also the etiological significance of any breakdown of sublimation. On the other hand, introduction of ethical or cultural valuations has so far caused more trouble and confusion than it has been worth. So long as repression exists, the individual valuation of cultural and social sublimations remains an unknown quantity. On the other hand, we are on perfectly safe ground if we maintain that sublimation performs a protective (or defensive) function – operates like a compensating balance. According to the taste of the investigator, this function can be expressed in terms of the pleasure-reality principle, or in terms of illness (which includes secondarily maladaptation to existing social regulations). If we attach a cultural (or any other) fixed form of valuation, we are attributing to the pleasure and reality principles a rigidity of function which would seriously impair their psychological utility, and incidentally we saddle ourselves with the incubus of 'absolute values' without any prospect of adequate remuneration. In other words, a sublimation can be regarded socially as pursuing cultural aims, if and when individual protection from illness takes the form of cultural pursuits. In any case, we must keep a sharp look-out to make sure that the sublimations in question do not run in close association with open anxiety formations or concealed obsessional formations. If such should prove to be the case, we can no longer regard the formation as a true sublimation but as a conductor (substitute) formation, accompanied by or heralding the return of the repressed. And here the factor of symbolism is probably decisive. Should we have any difficulty in arriving at a conclusion as to the significance of any one sublimation, the ultimate appeal must be to analysis. In any case, it is good practice to query the significance of a sublimation, so long as the individual concerned is in any degree incapacitated, unhappy or ill.

BIBLIOGRAPHY

1. FREUD, S.: *Drei Abhandlungen zur Sexualtheorie*, 5te Auf., 1922; 23, 43–4, 100–1 [*Three Essays on the Theory of Sexuality*, Imago Publg. Co., 1949].
   Eine Kindheitserinnerung des Leonardo da Vinci, 1919; 17, 19, 20, 75. [*Leonardo da Vinci*, Routledge & Kegan Paul, 1922].
   C.P. Vol. I, 67; Vol. II, 33, 47–8, 55, 82, 139; Vol. III, 376; Vol.IV, 51, 68–9, 92–3, 116, 123, 127, 132.
   Introductory Lectures on Psycho-Analysis, Allen & Unwin, 1929; 117, 146, 198, 220, 236, 248, 250–3, 259, 290, 293, 301, 306–7, 323, 326, 372, 380.
   Beyond the Pleasure Principle, Hogarth Press, 1923; 52–3, 65.
   Group Psychology and the Analysis of the Ego, Hogarth Press, 1922; 17, 23, 33, 57, 74–5, 118.
2. BERNFELD, S.: 'Bemerkungen über "Sublimierung",' *Imago*, 1922, **8**, 333.
3. KLEIN, M.: 'Infantile Anxiety Situations Reflected in a Work of Art', *Int. J. Psycho-Anal.*, 1929, **10**, 436.
4. SHARPE, E. F.: 'Certain Aspects of Sublimation and Delusion', *Int. J. Psycho-Anal.*, 1930, **11**, 12.
5. JONES, E.: *Papers on Psycho-Analysis*, Baillière, 1923; 20, 34, 50–2, 115–6, 127, 157, 193–8, 209, 216, 247, 257–8, 275, 324–6, 355, 359, 362, 606–7, 657.
6. FREUD, S.: *Hemmung, Symptom und Angst*, 12, 18, 26, 30, 33–4, 39, 41, 44–6, 50–1, 54, 64, 83, 86, 94–5 [*Inhibitions, Symptoms and Anxiety*, Hogarth Press, 1936].
7. FREUD, S.: *Das Unbehagen in der Kultur*, 1930, 30 [*Civilisation and its Discontents*, Hogarth Press, 1930].
8. JONES, E.: 'The Anxiety Character', *Med. Rev. of Rev.*, 1930, **36**, 3, 177.

9. KLEIN, M.: 'Infant Analysis', *Int. J. Psycho-Anal.*, 1926, **7**, 31.
10. 'Importance of Symbol Formation in the Development of the Ego', *Int. J. Psycho-Anal.*, 1930, **11**, 24.
11. GLOVER, J.: 'Notes on an Unusual Form of Perversion', *Int. J. Psycho-Anal.*, 1927, **8**, 10.
12. GLOVER, E.: *The Technique of Psycho-Analysis* [Enlarged edition, Baillière, 1955], 34–5.
13. *See also* EDER, D.: 'A Contribution to the Psychology of Snobbishness', *Int. J. Psycho-Anal.* (Bulletin), 1926, **7**, 128.
    'On the Psychology of Value', *Brit. J. Med. Psychol.*, 1930, **10**, 2.
14. FREUD, S.: *The Ego and the Id*, Hogarth Press, 1927; 38, 63–7.
15. FREUD, S.: 'The Economic Problem in Masochism', *C.P.* Vol. II, 255.

XI

A PSYCHO-ANALYTIC APPROACH TO THE
CLASSIFICATION OF MENTAL DISORDERS*
[1932]

Up to this time the correlation of specific mental disorders with specific phases of mental development was somewhat schematic, including simply the importance of repression and of the infantile genital phase in hysteria, of the anal-sadistic and homosexual phase in obsessional neurosis, and of narcissistic phases in the psychoses. It was clear that a much more elaborate classification was essential and possible. It was also clear that the old generic categories, if too closely applied to clinical disorders, were non-specific. A 'narcissistic' organization could be postulated in all psychoses without any indication of the stage of ego-structure to which any one psychosis regressed. In any case the idea that an early ego or super-ego could have a synthesized form went clean against psycho-biological probability. Hence the formulation of a 'nuclear theory' of ego-development, which would permit the isolation of particular nuclei or combinations of nuclei in particular disorders. The ensuing classification, although useful and indeed essential in the grouping of symptom-formations, fell down when it came to place the sexual perversions and psychopathies, a flaw which was to some extent rectified in the paper on 'Perversion-formation and reality sense' (Chap. XIII).

During a symposium on the psychotherapy of the psychoses held under the auspices of this Section,[1] I took occasion to point out that, owing to the nature of their case material, many psychoanalysts had been forced to undertake this branch of treatment, whether they liked it or not. In the case of psychiatric classification the position is somewhat different. However much the psycho-

* Read before the Royal Society of Medicine (Section of Psychiatry), February 9, 1932, under the title, 'The Principles of Psychiatric Classification', and published in the *Journal of Mental Science*, Oct. 1932.

[1] Glover: 'The Psychotherapy of the Psychoses', *Brit. J. med. Psychol.*, 1930, **10**, No. 3, p. 226.

analyst may choose to procrastinate, he cannot postpone indefinitely the task of correlating psychiatric data with his own systematic formulations on mental development. The more precise and dogmatic these formulations become, the more incumbent it is on the psycho-analyst to test them in the psychiatric field. Already some ventures have been made in this direction, notably in the work of Rickman,[1] Schilder,[2] Stärcke[3] and others. The main justification for a renewal of these attempts lies in the fact that during the past four or five years, appreciable advances have been made in the psycho-analytic understanding of early stages of ego development. A great deal has been achieved by the analysis of small children, and this work has produced reverberations in other directions. I am constrained to make this preliminary explanation in the hope of mitigating an impression which I fear still prevails in some quarters, namely, that in its relations to psychiatry, psychoanalysis displays the dogmatic over-compensation of an ignorant and none-too-welcome parvenu. Indeed, I should like to take this opportunity of stating that psycho-analysis, if even on the barest grounds of economy of effort, looks forward to an increasingly close alliance with pure psychiatry. And I hope to be able to indicate in this paper some problems on which the co-operating energies of the two sciences might well be concentrated.

It may occur to you to ask why psycho-analysts are not content to mould their formulations to existing psychiatric classifications. A satisfactory answer would involve a lengthy digression on the nature of psycho-analytic method and, apart from a few preliminary comments, I can only hope that the reply will be apparent from the nature of the considerations brought forward. It would, of course, be idle to pretend that psycho-analysts do not find some psychiatric classifications unsatisfactory from their point of view, but again I shall refrain from entering upon a lengthy argument on this matter. In any event the onus of criticizing existing classifications has already been shouldered by psychiatrists themselves.

[1] Rickman: *Psycho-analytical Theory of the Psychoses, International Journal of Psycho-analysis, Supplement No. 2,* 1928.

[2] Schilder: *Entwurf zu einer Psychiatrie auf psychoanalytischer Grundlage,* 1925, Vienna [*Introduction to a Psychoanalytic Psychiatry, Nervous and Mental Diseases, Publns.,* 1928].

[3] Stärcke: 'Psycho-analysis and Psychiatry', *Int. J. Psycho-Anal.,* 1921, **2,** p. 361.

Almost all thoughtfully written text-books emphasize the difficulties and confusions of clinical classifications and endeavour to overcome them. This endeavour takes the form either of simplification, which does manifest injustice to clinical detail, or of further elaboration, which is apt to confuse the student. Terminology apart, when one reads of various 'mixed forms' included within the great groupings – schizophrenic, paranoid or melancholic – or when one thinks of complicated transitional groups lying between these main divisions, the ultimate impression is one of matted complexity. Not that complexity of itself is a valid reproach against any classification. It has always been preposterous to suppose that the complications of mental development could be adequately reflected in a simple tripartite division of the psychoses. Serious objection can be taken only when the degree of complexity is in inverse ratio to the fundamental understanding achieved. And the most sympathetic reading of much descriptive psychiatry can scarcely remove the impression that the three most important fragments of the jig-saw puzzle are firmly adherent to all the complementary pieces. Moreover, it appears reasonable to suppose that the rigid interlocking which hampers one system of classification may prove to be the firm groundwork of an unknown grouping. For example, if we find a delusional element common to schizophrenia and paranoia, or an affective system common to schizophrenia and melancholia, it is always possible that the common element should have been the main factor in classification.

Before expounding the principles governing psycho-analytical classifications of the psychoses, we may inquire to what general conditions an adequate system of classification should conform. Presumably it should be sufficiently elastic and skeletal in outline to permit of subsequent modification; it should not crack under the strain of new or awkward data. Not only ought it to leave gaps open, but its very outline should indicate the possibilities of future research. Like the early schemata of atomic weights, it should encourage us to presume the existence of undetected 'elements', or, alternatively, assist us to isolate illuminating 'syndromes' from existing undifferentiated symptom-complexes. Obviously it should present existing data in as comprehensible a light as possible, but there should be no attempt to reduce comprehensibility from fear of refractory exceptions. If, for example, we find it difficult to say what exactly is the *rôle* of a phobia in the psychoses, there is no reason why we should force a square peg into a round hole. The phobia problem can wait.

This is all very plain sailing. Complications arise when we condescend to the details of psychiatric terminology. Should we, for example, be content with a purely clinical and descriptive method? Convenient as such a system may be in the case of organic disease, there is no doubt that it is a dangerous and retrogressive procedure in the case of the psychoses. Owing to the existence of unconscious mental processes, it is unlikely to be either an accurate or even a practical method. We would not trust a cartographer very far if, having told us that all solid objects surrounded by water are islands, he could not say whether the solid object in question was dry land or the dorsum of a whale. As we know, an apparently simple phobia may be a transient neurotic manifestation or the peak of a concealed paranoid construction. The term 'melancholia', too, with its emphasis on the depressed, inhibited and lifeless features of a regression, completely ignores the fact that during this phase, the mind is practically white-hot with excessive charges of hate and aggressive energy. To call the delusions of paranoia a symptom of disease, is as complete a reversal of the psychological truth as to call granulation-tissue an abrasion. It is no more illuminating to talk of catatonia in severe regressions than to use the term 'sleep' in describing uræmic coma. Even in organic medicine it would scarcely promote free exchange of ideas, if we labelled certain cardiac and renal conditions together with cystitis and urethritis under the common heading 'albumen in the urine'. An 'end-product' classification in psychiatry is equally inadequate, and must give way to a more 'functional' approach.

On the other hand, in the absence of general agreement on the etiology of the psychoses, a classification based solely on alleged genetic elements would be a legitimate source of exasperation as well as of confusion. As a temporary measure, therefore, a descriptive factor, even if inadequate, seems unavoidable, and may be laid down as a first factor in classification. The problem arises: can this descriptive factor be combined with criteria which will promote genetic understanding, aid differential diagnosis and prognosis, accentuate the essentially psychotic nature of the psychoses, and yet establish some intelligible relation between the phenomena of psychiatry and the psychological phenomena of everyday life?

This last condition is essential. A classification which cannot relate the psychoses to mental phenomena as a whole has foundered in the dock. In this one respect the term 'melancholia' justifies itself. The man in the street, familiar with his own transient states of depression, is encouraged to assume that he can himself be mad at times. And his assumption is correct. Not only can he be mad at times, but all the time he is a little mad. Still further he passes through a protracted phase of severe madness in his infantile years. Only the consensus of social opinion and valuation entitles him to call his nursery and adult madness normality. This matter can easily be put to the proof. Let anyone maintain a complete system of 'nursery madness' during the period when 'adult madness' only is expected of him; in other words, let any adult adopt the ideology, language and behaviour of an infant of 18 months, and he will promptly be certified by two 'normally mad' doctors. Here we make our second practical contact with the problem of classification. A sound classification must somehow relate the psychoses to normal development. But to do this we must realize just how psychotic normal development is. Converted into systematic terms, a classification of psychoses must be built up in close relation to the historical modifications of ego-structure. And if we do not know all that is to be known of this structure, we must simply leave empty niches in the classification.

In establishing the nature of this second factor, we have at the same time opened the way to discovering a third factor. Granted that we must relate the psychoses to normality, we must not abuse this necessity. Although the community calls on us to diagnose and treat psychoses, it certainly does not want us to call normality madness. So we must check the second factor by a third, representing some specific or almost specific psychotic mechanism. At the risk of neglecting other important specific factors, I shall maintain that loss of reality sense is one of the most striking features of the psychoses, and provides us with an adequate correction for error. We must, of course, lay down some fairly precise definition of this third term. For the moment I shall neglect this obvious precaution; it will be easier to arrive at a definition of reality once we have studied the backbone of the classificatory system, viz., the nature and order of ego modifications.

Doubtless other criteria could be substituted for or added to these three factors. It is partly a matter of convenience, and partly a question of the depth of psychological knowledge and understanding. Obviously we are not debarred from adding alternative labels where this course seems desirable. And in any case the psychiatrist has a long leeway to make up before his psychic systems approach the degree of complexity already regarded as essential in classifications of organic disease. In the meantime let us see what can be done with the three suggested criteria: (*a*) a descriptive, clinical standard, (*b*) a systematic ego standard by which psychiatry can define its relation to other psychological data, and (*c*), a qualitative standard which, by virtue of specific or almost specific relation to the psychoses, acts as a check on the systematic standard.

With regard to the descriptive standard, I have already suggested that owing to differences of academic opinion I am compelled to borrow from existing psychiatric terminology. I shall limit my indebtedness to three or four terms. To begin with, although I have no preference as between the terms 'schizophrenia' and 'dementia præcox', I am bound to borrow one or other in order to suggest a main division characterized by deep and extensive regressive features – a group in which the wholesale detachment of interest from the world of objects is quite unmistakable. In the second place, I would borrow the term 'paranoia' to denote a group in which the relation to the external world is much less limited, but which nevertheless shows a more or less characteristic impairment of reality sense – to wit, the delusional system. Lastly, I would adopt a melancholic group to indicate a regressive system, less extensive than the præcox regressions, associated with a marked degree of inturned psychic scrutiny, together with a characteristic affective state, viz. depression. That there are depressions in other groups is one of the inadequacies of existing descriptive criteria.

With regard to the second criterion, I ought to say that my views on ego organization are derived from purely psychoanalytic sources, in most instances from the writings of Freud. In the simplest terms of structure the ego is regarded by psychoanalysts as an organized system of psychic impressions ultimately expressed in terms of memory-traces. From the dynamic point of view, however, it can be regarded as a psychic organ of adaptation. This organ is, one might say, bounded on one side by perceptual consciousness, and on another by instinctual impulse. Perceptual consciousness is, however, more than a boundary; it is a psychic window system. Using this system the ego not only samples the stimulations of the external world, but, provided unconscious barriers do not interfere with the view, takes measure of an inner world of instinct derivatives. These derivatives are either ideas or affects. The function of the ego as a whole is to effect a compromise between the demands of instinct and the amount of gratification possible in the external world. Strictly speaking, the external world in this sense includes the individual's own body. As, however, only a few component instincts are capable of gratification apart from an external object, we may say roughly that the ego lies between instinct and an external world of objects – in other words, environment. The 'signal' system by means of which the ego tests the success or failure of its manoeuvres is anxiety. If ego manoeuvres are unsuccessful, frustrated instinct will induce anxiety; if in its attempt to gratify instinct the ego attacks the world more than immediate human representatives will endure, an environmental embargo or threat ensues; if the original impulses are exorbitant or impossible of gratification, they frustrate themselves; and if an unconscious guilt system has been established, all impulses counter to the existing unconscious codes of the ego are frustrated from within, and the result is once more anxiety. In 1877 a German psychiatrist said that anxiety was the Alpha and Omega of psychiatry. Psycho-analysis, having traced innumerable indirect signs of anxiety in conscious and unconscious territories, is prepared to say that anxiety is the Alpha and guilt the Omega of human development. Spurred by anxiety the ego makes fresh attempts at adaptation. But there are only three main lines of action possible; (a) inhibition, repression or deflection of instinct, (b) less exorbitant demands on environment (courses which presuppose some tolerance of frustration-anxiety), and (c) a pathological distortion of the ego. This third group is then subdivided into two: cases in which the consequences of ego distortion are roughly limited to the mind or body of the subject (autoplastic), and cases where impairment of reality relations is an outstanding feature. The psychoses represent an extreme example of the third method. The neuroses, too, belong to the third group in so far as a degree of localized ego distortion occurs; but except in some socially unimportant respects, there is in the neuroses no grave interference with 'reality testing'.

Once again this is all very plain sailing; indeed, many psychological schools accept these views without qualification. Disagreement makes its appearance when the psycho-analyst refuses to accept the conscious adult ego as the most important model, and insists on regarding the ego-organizations of the first five years of life as key patterns. Following this line of approach the psycho-analyst first of all inquires what exactly is the nature of instinct in these years, and proceeds to answer his own question with a formulation which at one time aroused either scepticism or disgust or anger in a majority of his hearers. He says in effect that the child is endowed with impulses of a primitive, aggressive and libidinal type, frustration of which produces a vicious circle. The sequence is as follows: Frustration of primitive impulse, anxiety, hate, projection, additional frustration of hate and now guilt; still more frustration of the original impulse and now inhibition; ending once more on a note of frustration. The first mechanism to break the vicious circle is repression, which abolishes *all* representation of the impulses in question. He proceeds then to classify the original libidinal tendencies, and says that the first five years are governed by certain primacies associated with certain erotogenic zones; to wit, an oral libidinal primacy, where the attitude to objects is almost undifferentiated cannibalism; then an excretory libidinal primacy accompanied by intense sadistic attitudes to the world, but with an increase in capacity to master instinct and endure frustration and finally a less sadistic infantile genital primacy of instinct which, though foredoomed to frustration, and therefore to induce a characteristic anxiety (i.e. castration anxiety), can in most cases be successfully repressed, leaving a residue to be deflected into the affectionate family relations of childhood. With regard to the aggressive impulses employed in attitudes of hate, although the ultimate aim of this group is to destroy all sources of tension, and in that sense does not alter, the technique of destruction is to a large extent determined by the libidinal interest governing successive stages.

If we take this view of infantile history, it is obvious that not only the adult ego but the ego of a child of five, however well organized, is essentially a composite. This can be supported by theoretical considerations which I have elaborated elsewhere,[1]

---

[1] 'The Etiology of Drug Addiction', *Int. J. Psycho-Anal.*, **13**. [Chap. XII.]

viz. that any psychic system which (*a*) represents a positive libidinal relation to objects or part objects, (*b*) can discharge reactive tension (i.e. aggression and hate against objects), and (*c*) in one or other of these ways reduces anxiety, is entitled to be called an ego system or ego-nucleus. Thus an oral system gratifies instinct on a part-object (mother's nipple); it can exert aggression towards the nipple (sucking, pulling, biting), and it is able to prevent some degree of anxiety. This is the model or prototype of an independent autonomic primitive ego-nucleus. Applying this system to the conception of a series of primacies, it seems reasonable to conclude that the primitive ego, from at any rate the age of one year onwards, is polynuclear, in the sense of a *series* of comparatively independent organizations; also that the more primitive the ego formation, the more primitive the part objects with which it is concerned.

For a long time psycho-analysis was content with the idea of a consecutive series of fixations, described these mainly in terms of libidinal organization, and applied this system in tracing the etiology of the psychoses. Thus paranoia was related to the early phase of anal-sadistic organizations, and schizophrenia to the oral phase. But I have long felt that the idea of a *consecutive* series of nuclear fixations was applicable only from the anal stage onwards, by which time the ego is more coherent and organized. For one thing melancholias obviously derive their character from the oral phase, thus necessitating etiological differentiation from the schizophrenias. In short, we are driven to conclude that the ego of the five-year-old is not only polynuclear, but that the earliest nucleus is itself a polymorph; or, in other words, that the earliest ego tendencies are derived from numerous scattered instincts and *converge* gradually until, probably about the age of two, a coherent anal-sadistic organization is established. No doubt oral elements dominate what has been called the oral stage, and justify the term 'oral primacy', more particularly since they constitute a model 'autonomic' ego-system. But oral primacy is only relative.

What, then, are the other elements of the first primitive nucleus? The answer is theoretically easy. We have only to collect all the observed and discoverable libidinal relations or erotogenic zones together with all the systems which can be employed to discharge aggression during the first year or eighteen months of life. Any two representative elements which exist in close association could theoretically represent a nuclear formation.[1]

Thus, for example, an oral libidinal system, together with a muscular aggressive system (clawing, tearing, kicking and biting), can be observed in close relation in the child, and could theoretically represent an ego-nucleus. And when we find in schizophrenia that catatonia is sometimes associated with active oral symbolism, the question arises whether this is more than a coincidence. Again, oral incorporation and excretory ejection is a commonplace of the first year, whilst the oral and anal habits and interests of the schizophrenic are not difficult to detect in close association, although frequently anal stereotypies conceal the oral components. Here, at any rate, is a promising field for research. The raw material of possible early ego formations is easy to collect: on the one hand, various erotogenic zones in active function, oral, skin, respiratory, alimentary, excretory and muscular; on the other hand, the reactive systems that discharge aggression. The latter appear to have one element in common, viz. the musculature, but if one thinks more closely it is apparent that the most important erotogenic systems, with the exception of the skin, are also capable of expressing destructive impulses. A small child, for example, can phantasy destroying the world with his urine. I believe it will soon be possible to establish with some exactitude various nuclear combinations of libidinal and aggressive interest which, marshalled under the relative primacy of oral impulse and aggression, give rise to the omnibus fixation-point of schizophrenia. In the meanwhile, one can say with certainty that the fixation-point of melancholia is still essentially an oral fixation-point, one in which oral aggressive function has dominated all other contemporary modes of destruction, has been turned in on itself mainly for purposes of mastery, and has warped the psychic organization in a characteristic way.

To sum up at this point, the primitive structure of the ego might be figured as a kind of skeletal system. At the beginning is a cluster formation of ego-nuclei converging on a consecutive series, the elements of which show an increasing degree of organization. The cluster and the first few nuclei that follow represent the fixation-points of the psychoses; the last organized nuclei represent

---

[1] It need hardly be repeated that the nucleus in question is a psychic nucleus. It represents a closely knit psychic system of impressions, which can not only be reanimated, but can contribute to later ideational processes (unconscious or conscious phantasies).

the fixation-points of the neuroses. The image is of pictorial value only, and expresses a time dimension (see Figs. 1, 2 and 3).

I have said that we have here a promising field for research. I should like to add that in this field psychiatrists have unique opportunities to assist and accelerate psycho-analytical research.

FIG. 1.

ORDER OF LIBIDINAL PRIMACIES
[EARLY VIEWS.]

A. ORAL.

B. ANAL-SADISTIC.

C. { PHALLIC.
     ....
     GENITAL.

FIG. 2.

[ABRAHAM'S SERIES.]

A. ORAL.
　　(1) PREAMBIVALENT.　　[SUCKING.]
　　(2) SADISTIC.　　[BITING.]
B. ANAL-SADISTIC.
　　(1) EXPULSION—DESTRUCTION.
　　(2) RETENTION—MASTERY.
C. GENITAL.
　　(1) PHALLIC.
　　(2) FINAL—POSTAMBIVALENT.

There is ample scope, especially in the case of schizophrenia, and the so-called toxic psychoses, for isolating syndromes, the value of which could be tested by analysis of psychotic and non-psychotic types. In this connection the 'decomposition products' of schizophrenia require the most careful study and grouping; in the case of primitive ego-nuclei the object is invariably a 'part object', and in schizophrenic regression it becomes once more a 'part

FIG. 3.

LIBIDINAL PRIMACIES AND EGO-NUCLEI

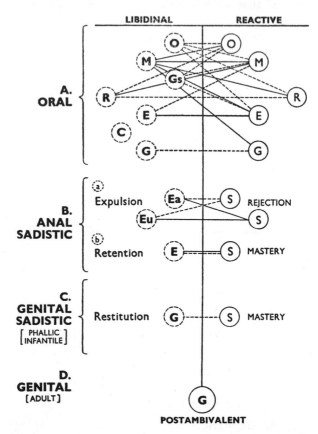

Illustrating the relation of libidinal primacies to ego-formations: A view of ego-development in longitudinal section; ego-nuclei bisected and reflected to show libidinal and reactive constituents; note the relative lack of organization of the oral phase, emphasizing the importance of other zonal components during that stage. Interrelations of different libidinal and reactive zones are indicated by plain and dotted lines.

In stages B, C and D the attitude to the instinctual object (or part-object) is indicated.

Key.—O. Oral. M. Muscular. Gs. Gastric. E. Excretory. Ea. Anal (Excretory). Eu. Urinary (Excretory). R. Respiratory. C. Cutaneous. G. Genital. Oth. Other zonal organizations. S. Sadism.

object'. A prerequisite of any such work would be common understanding of fundamental mechanisms. Without this understanding many syndromes would go undetected. And in the last resort syndrome-hunting is merely a stimulus to etiological research and formulation, not a substitute for it.

We must now turn to the third factor of our classificatory system, viz. the *qualitative* test of reality. Our first task is the definition of reality. Approaching this problem systematically, there are two obvious lines of investigation. The first is the nature of 'objects', and the relations existing between primitive objects and objective reality. The second involves some consideration of the primitive processes of projection and introjection.

Strictly speaking, an 'object' is that on which an instinctual impulse is gratified, and may vary from a nipple in the case of oral impulse, to the idea of the solar system in the case of astrophysical curiosity. But the fact of psychical displacement warns us that even the most abstract objects of metaphysical preoccupation can function as substitutes for more primitive part-objects; in fact, that the whole world can be reacted to as if it were an orange to be squeezed, or a nipple to be sucked. As we know, when certain psychotics withdraw their interest from the world of objects and pile up an unmanageable charge of sadistic libido within their own egos, the resulting damage and destruction is sometimes represented by ideas of world destruction.

Now in the case of auto-erotic activities, the 'object' on which the impulse is gratified is part of the individual's own body – sometimes an organ, sometimes an organic system. So as far as pleasure experiences have some quality in common, there is evidently plenty of scope for confusion as to ego-object boundaries in the earliest phases. Indeed, Freud believes that there is some advantage to be obtained by assuming a state of 'primary identification' between the subject and all instinctual objects. We might say that all the agents contributing to a gratification experience (including the object) are taken to be part of the ego, and secondly, that in so far as gratification experiences at different parts of the body have some psychic quality in common, the contributing agents are liable to be identified. This primitive type of identification is an important element in the process of symbolism.

However this may be, the next steps in the differentiation of ego from 'object' are fairly clear. Experience of mastery of instinct shows the way. An instinct excitation that can be gratified on the individual's own body is *a priori* to some extent manageable. An instinct that requires a true external object, such as the mother's nipple, is unmasterable unless with the collusion of the real object. Hence psychic pain, that immediate consequence of frustration, provides the first great impetus towards the discovery of real external objects. Other experiences contribute to this 'object' system. There are certain painful ego experiences which indicate the existence of a painful 'not-me' – a pin through the diaper, a hard crumb in the mouth, a hot-water bottle against the ribs. When such stimuli are removed the pain stops. So the 'not-me' is gradually reinforced by experience of stimuli which can, as it were, be discarded. But certain 'me' stimuli resemble the pins and crumbs of the 'not-me'. Some colic pains can be eased by the sudden expulsion of wind. So here again we have a source of confusion between the 'me' and the 'not-me'. And here, too, we watch the birth of that great primitive mechanism of projection. If only more enduring colics could be suddenly converted into painful 'not-me's' like crumbs, and violently expelled! At the same time the experiences of mouth, hand and stomach are responsible for building up another psychic tendency, which we dimly try to appreciate by the use of the term 'introjection'. If only the pleasure-producing nipple could be imprisoned in the mouth, the stealing warmth retained in the stomach! Failing these, if we could only make the gesture of holding on with clenched fists, of making pleasurable 'not-me's' part of 'me', how much safer from anxiety the ego would be! Thus, however long the hallucinatory phase of primary identification may last, it gives place to a phase of adaptation which is nevertheless from the adult point of view a phase of confusion confounded. A·pleasure ego that wrongly includes reality objects is set against a painful outer world that wrongly includes parts of the ego. The sequence is therefore acute hallucinatory pan-psychosis, then a part introjection psychosis of the schizo-phrenic, or at any rate melancholic type contrasted with a part projective psychosis of the paranoic type (Figs. 4 and 5).

The concept of a hallucinatory pan-psychosis is a trifle hypo-thetical, although during the earliest infantile stage (sucking) there are hallucinatory phenomena enough and to spare. On the other hand, actual clinical analysis of psychotic children shows that the second main subdivision (introjective and projective psychoses)

FIG. 4.

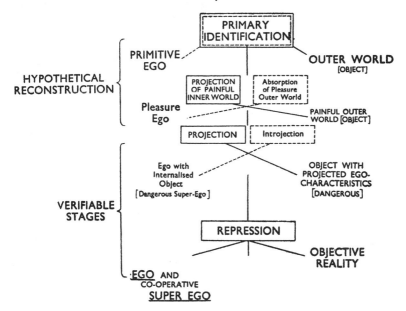

FIG. 5.

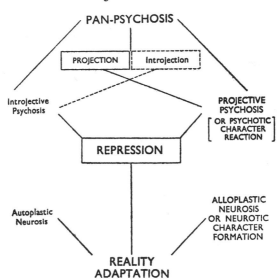

corresponds with the facts. The same general outline can be demonstrated in the adult psychoses, although the system is covered to a varying extent by complicated processes of object restitution. These bizarre attempts take up the foreground of the clinical picture.

In making these correlations between psychotic states and the systems of primitive experience by which ego differentiation is achieved, I have been tempted rather by the illustrative value of these concrete experiences. Because, of course, the introjections and projections that influence reality sense are not simply sensory, but more complicated psychic experiences. The most painful, persistent and unmasterable stimuli are the psychic stimuli of frustrated instinct. They correspond inside the ego to the pins and crumbs of external life, raised in intensity to the nth power.

Now as regards precedence of these mechanisms in the psychic plane, I think it is safe to assume that, in so far as they are not mutually complementary mechanisms, precedence must be awarded to the projective process.[1] After all, the infant's first experience of the world might be regarded as facing massed batteries of excruciating stimuli, and it is clearly important to get these 'outside' as soon as possible. This precedence has fateful consequences. So long as the pleasure-producing nipple was part of the self by primary identification, it was part of the pleasure-ego – a 'good' nipple-self. When it is found to be an external object, only periodically masterable, the painful tension is projected after this vanishing object, which then becomes a painful 'bad' nipple, deserving of hate and destruction. But to destroy it is to kill the goose that lays the golden eggs, i.e. it is a threat to the 'good' (gratifying) nipple as well as to the 'bad' one. This reaction threat to a gratification system involves renewed psychic pain. And the renewed pain, following close on the heels of projected tension, acts as a boomerang. One projects on to the object, hates it, wishes to destroy it, and the object hits back. The experience is already familiar on the sensory plane. Either in course of casual activity or during a rage, the baby hits itself against the bars of the cot. What do the bars do? At precisely the same moment, they strike the child smartly and painfully on the head or hands. A painful,

---

[1] [Note (1955): It should be emphasized that this refers only to the interelations of introjection and projection; in any absolute order priority must be given to the mechanism of regression.]

malignant and remorseless outer world! To this mixed phase of sensory and psychic experience we can ultimately trace the roots of persecutory paranoia. But, of course, the purely psychic structure of the persecutory system develops only when the influence of true introjective processes has played its part in the drama.

Only one part of the ego says 'Kill the goose'. Another part says, 'Swallow the eggs and keep them inside'. But, alas, the eggs are now addled. They have been poisoned by projective hate. In this phase the conflict is terrific. The nearer the child draws to that final termination of nipple mastery which is called weaning, the more necessary it is to retain the nipple psychically. Introjection is essentially a mechanism for dealing with lost or disappearing objects. The more the ego is threatened with loss, the greater the hate; the greater the hate, the greater the projected hate; the greater the projected hate, the more dangerous the world of objects; the more dangerous the world of objects, the more poisonous the effect of introjection.

But if the system has been poisoned, why then continue along the line of introjection? Well, partly because the continued uncertainty of object relations compels it. For a time the ego cannot help itself otherwise. Primitive libidinal need is strong, frustration anxiety intolerable. Partly, too, because swallowing is itself destructive, and is therefore the most natural way of expressing hate of frustrating objects. Moreover, if you really have reason to love an object as well as hate it, perhaps the only way to keep that love alive is to get the object inside. Falling to these additional temptations, the child takes a momentous step; it introjects an object with a persecuting tendency. The immediate result of this manoeuvre is disconcerting. The ego achieves some degree of object mastery, but at the same moment its organization is split almost to the roots. It also preserves an object relation, but at the cost of turning aggressive energies on itself. By short-circuiting the object it can now hate successfully, but it must hate itself. The more the ego rages and struggles, the more powerful the grip of the now internalized persecuting tendency which feeds on the hate tension aroused by continued instinct frustration. Hate rages against hate. The infantile prototype of melancholia has been established.

In this impasse the ego once more turns to the external world with a policy of projection. If you cannot control this sytem you have set up in the mind, eject it. But matters have gone too far; a mental organization once established cannot be summarily ejected. All the ego can do is to continue to project painful impulse. And every projection renders the objects of the external world more dangerous, thereby compelling and at the same time vitiating fresh introjections. For a varying time the ego is in a state of feverish activity, alternating rapidly between policies of introjection and counter-policies of projection. These alternations are reflected in the psychotic 'mixed states'. A vicious circle in ego-economy is now set up. The great primitive mechanism of projection has lost some of its magical power, and introjection paralyses the ego. That the alternating system does not break down completely is due to two factors. The first and most important is the development of an auxiliary mechanism, viz. primal repression, which is supplemented later by secondary or actual repression. The child cannot successfully eject the persecuting instance, but it does achieve a masterly adaptation. By sacrificing (repressing) its primitive instinct it comes to terms with the internal persecutor. And the new institution co-operates by taking on a special function; it acts both as instigator of repression and as detector of dangerous unrepressed impulse. This scrutinizing function justifies a special term. We now call the introjected object the *super-ego*.[1]

The second factor is more important for our present purpose. It is the re-discovery and increased exploitation of reality. Almost from the beginning there is some degree of reality-testing, however faint.[2] This is immensely increased by the tendencies of libidinal impulse and the processes of symbolism and displacement. These make towards an increasing acquaintance with reality. And now comes a dire necessity to establish and cling to a 'real reality',

[1] Although it has been the custom in psycho-analytic literature to reserve the term 'super-ego' for the part of the ego that first instigates repression, there seems to be no logical reason why it should not be applied to earlier, more persecutory differentiations. For descriptive purposes, of course, some such term as 'anti-ego' or even 'alter-ego', would appear more appropriate to the earlier stages, but it would have no other advantage.

[2] [Note (1955): This errs on the side of under-statement. Allowing for the fact that the adult environment goes out of its way to gratify some of the aims of infantile instincts, the reality sense of the infant can be judged by the same standards as apply to the reality sense of the adult, viz. a practical appreciation of the relation of instinct to object. In this sense the reality sense of the infant does not fall much short of that of the adult.

one that is safe from the terrifying elements contributed by projection. Here the actual behaviouristic policies of the parents come into their own. The psychological function of the parents is to act out a reassuring version of external reality, until such time as the child can identify with them more completely and carry on its own reassurance.

The foregoing presentation is inadequate in many respects,[1] but it will assist us to formulate certain generalizations of importance to psychiatry. In the first place we see that from a purely psychiatric point of view the 'normal' infant is in an 'acute psychosis'. But clinical psychiatry cannot be expected to concern itself with such everyday developmental phenomena. The second formulation is of a different order. *Unless the child comes to terms with reality, he remains in a true psychotic state of anxiety.* Exaggerated manifestations of this anxiety are entitled to be called the 'clinical psychoses' of childhood, as distinct from the 'normal psychoses' of childhood. Thirdly, the clinical psychoses of adult life are precipitated by a breakdown in the auxiliary repression system. The individual has maintained a comparatively normal *façade* of reality adaptation by dint of repression, on the breakdown of which he is automatically plunged into a true infantile psychotic state of anxiety. The potential psychotic is one who has come to precarious terms with reality with a narrow margin of effective repression, and who is therefore at the mercy of any severe frustration, either actual or the result of internal (libido) changes.

We are now in a position to define reality. From the psychiatric point of view, adult reality sense represents the capacity to maintain psychic contact with the objects in or through which post-

---

[1] In particular I have done scant justice to the stabilizing influence of introjections of 'friendly' objects. In the phase of primary identification these are simply the result of absorption of gratification experiences. Later they relate to the more obvious attitudes of protection, support and love manifested by the parents. Not only do these 'good' identifications and introjections offset the 'dangerous' introjections by acting as a compensatory system, they put an additional premium on successful repression, and at the same time encourage the ego in its search for 'real' reality. As, however, the 'dangerous' introjections have a more direct relation to anxiety, they act as a more urgent stimulus to instinct modification. They are therefore of greater etiological significance in psychotic exaggerations of normal adaptation.

infantile modified instincts are or can be gratified. This world of objects includes all substitutions or replacements of primary un-modified objects; indeed, a capacity to substitute is a test of normality. The discovery of a real object world is accelerated or retarded in accordance with the amount of anxiety experienced in mastering primitive impulse. Abnormalities in reality sense may be subdivided into (a) shrivelling of this object world due to with-drawal of interest into the ego, and (b) distortions of the world of objects due to projection on it of ego content. Without question, a social (ultimately self-preservative) factor enters into the estima-tions of another person's reality sense. But, roughly speaking, so long as the individual does not attempt to kill his introjected enemies by suicide or his projected enemies by homicide, society is not too exacting in its demands. This is particularly true of remote psychic substitutes for primitive objects. Of course I do not exclude the possibility that normal relations to the world of objects depend on some degree of correspondence between, for example, the projected danger of instinct and the actual danger of environment; but I should imagine that this correspondence is in most cases reduced to the level of unconscious symbolism.

It is clear that the 'reality sense' factor in classification is very closely bound up with the second 'developmental' factor. If you insist on treating a complete object, say, a father surrogate, as if he were a part object, say, the mother's nipple, the result is clinically a 'distortion of reality'; psycho-pathologically it is a 'regression to a stage of part-object relations.'[1] Nevertheless, the reality factor provided us with a control system with which to inhibit any exuberant and unpractical exploitation of systematic views. Taking these two standards together we must now ask whether well-recognized psychotic and neurotic states are capable of orderly presentation. Can we subdivide the main psychoses and neuroses in accordance with ego-object relations? Can we roughly separate out groups characterized by limitation of object relations, by regression to an old ego-system, by processes of introjection, tendencies to retire to primary (hallucinatory) identification? On the other hand, can we distinguish conditions in which the relation-ship to the external world is distorted or vitiated in some important respect, in which the mechanism of projection is constantly

[1] [Note (1955): See footnote on 'part-objects' and 'complete objects', Chap. I, p. 18.]

exploited, in which environment is used as an unrealistic defence against ego excitation? Finally, can we, using the reality sense test, subdivide these two main groups sharply, so that the psychoses will fall into a different category from the neuroses? I am going to suggest that in the case of children we can do so quite simply. An adult classification on these lines would, however, be rather amorphous unless we included a number of characterological and other states, some of which are not considered in standard classifications. Most important in this connection are (a) schizoid or psychotic character types in general, (b) drug addictions, (c) obsessional character formations, (d) anxiety character formations, and (e) mild social inhibitions. An additional advantage of including character states is that we are able to indicate the transitional phases falling between psychotic reactions and so-called normality. And incidentally we are able to grasp the protective possibilities of the neuroses – one might say their potential 'buffer' function.

Some rough idea of the interrelations of these factors I have discussed may be gained from the accompanying diagram (Fig. 6). In the first place the nuclear positions of the ego are arranged in vertical order, commencing with a cluster formation representing the most primitive phase of the ego. To indicate the comparative absence of organization during this first phase, I have duplicated this cluster, the unshaded nuclei representing the introjection and identification aspects, the shaded nuclei the projective aspects of the primitive systems. To avoid complicating the diagram too much I have not filled in all the possible nuclear combinations of this phase; and in any case the formations indicated are of a purely provisional nature. I have not duplicated the later nuclei since, from the phase of excretory primacy onward, ego-organization is much more coherent. I have, however, indicated the introjection and projection aspects of these lower nuclei by variations in the shading. By means of arrows I have attempted to indicate possible fixation factors for different states; here again, in the interests of simplicity, no attempt has been made to indicate more than a few of the factors.

The following points may be singled out for special emphasis:

It will be seen that there is no question of single fixation-points for the psychoses. This is especially true of the dementia præcox group, which has a multiplicity of fixations. These have, however, one feature in common, viz. their primitive order. The same is

Fig. 6.

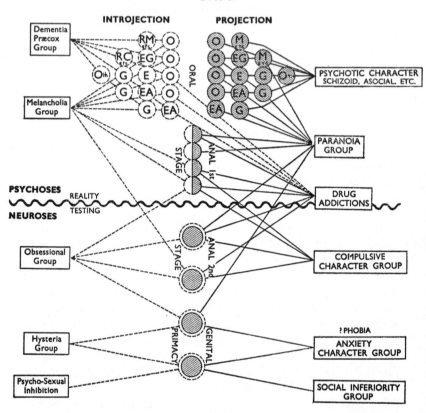

Illustrating the application of three primary factors in classification, (a) descriptive, (b) degree of ego-development, (c) qualitative-reality testing; ego seen in longitudinal section; earlier nuclei bisected and reflected to emphasize (a) lack of organization of oral stages, (b) relatively independent action of processes of introjection and projection. Approximate fixation points indicated by plain and dotted lines.

The oral 'cluster' is represented in five separate layers to suggest a preliminary expansion of ego interest followed by a gradual contraction prior to the establishment of anal-sadistic primacy.

For Key see Fig. 3.

true, but to a less extent, of the melancholias and paranoias. In the case of neuroses the fixation-points are much more localized, although unquestionably earlier developmental experiences are of considerable importance.

We can now arrange a rough parallel series in accordance with the amount of ego absorption of conflict and the extent of environmental (object) exploitation. It is not suggested, of course, that the parallelism is exact; in the early stages progress is much more likely to be zig-zag. I have already said that the schizophrenic fixation is an omnibus fixation, and, of course, from the clinical point of view one might regard some schizophrenic states, particularly the paranoid schizophrenias, and their first cousins, the systematized paraphrenias, as precariously balanced between introjective and projective processes. But in the long run breadth and depth of psychic regression prevail, and it is perhaps better to exaggerate this fact in a diagram. Turning to the terms 'transitional state' and 'mixed states', it will be apparent that from the point of view of nuclear fixations, the first necessity is a closer investigation of the order of progression or regression between different nuclei, and the second an examination of alternating mechanisms. Clinical considerations suggest that the term 'transitional' will in any case justify retention, and theoretically it dovetails with the concept of 'regression'; on the other hand, the term 'mixed states' will give place to a more accurate and detailed terminology once ego-nuclei have been isolated. This will involve a combination of analytic and descriptive (syndromal) methods.

Again, in the case of melancholia and paranoia the main point of contrast lies in their mechanisms. Of course the nuclei from which they are derived are more advanced than in the case of schizophrenia.

Although it is not intended to make this schema comprehensive, or indeed to do more than emphasize a few fundamental considerations, already a significant omission will be noted. In spite of the existence of chronic manias, no attempt has been made to 'place' the maniacal states. Superficially regarded, the impetus towards the object world in many of these states is obvious, but in others maniacal exaltation is accompanied by a disregard of object relations. So the matter is not so simple: and we may well stick to the policy enunciated earlier, i.e. not to force a square peg into a round hole. We are, however, not entirely without some orientation in this problem. It is an old observation, first made by Abraham, that the 'complexes' of mania are the same as those found in melancholia; and clinical psychiatrists have noted that melancholics can have dreams with pleasant affect, also that some manic cases exhibit an undercurrent of depression. According to this view mania is only one phase of an extensive process, and is comparable with the restitution phenomena of schizophrenia. It would therefore be regarded as a spontaneous attempt at cure whether a melancholic phase is manifested openly or not. In this case the 'placing' of mania in a primary classification is not important. Another possibility which I think is worthy of consideration is the following: Mania may relate to a phase of development which follows the phase giving rise to melancholic systems. It would then have etiological factors of a specific kind. These would represent an advance on the melancholic system, and would be exploited as a curative or restitutive system. The more pathogenic aspects of the maniacal system would then be derived from an underlying schizophrenic contribution. This would be in keeping with the view of a zig-zag progression in early pathological states representing a gradual increase in anxiety tolerance. According to this view mania would require a special place in a primary classification. Whichever view one takes, it is necessary to emphasize the fact that in the sense of mechanism there is a more dramatic contrast between melancholia and paranoia than between melancholia and mania.

Considerations of space, to say nothing of caution, exclude for the moment any attempt to 'place' conditions such as epilepsy or some of the so-called organic reaction types. But even a cursory examination of the psychological phenomena of epilepsy show an interesting contrast between the regressions accompanying an attack, and the sometimes stereotyped exploitation of the object-world seen in intermissions (the epileptic character). Similarly, even superficial examination of the psychological formations in many organic reaction types suggests that a more orderly systematization of these phenomena is only a matter of time.

Passing over the transverse line which indicates the 'reality-proving' boundary, we come to the neuroses. Here the contrast between autoplastic neuroses and character states is much more precise, and the fixation-points indicated may be taken as accurate. The main point of interest is the position of the phobia. Conversion hysterias are quite clearly autoplastic in type, but some phobias equally clearly depend on a degree of projection, and in one sense almost caricature the anxiety character type in which there is excessive reaction to all reality sources of danger. Phobias are, of course, more localized constructions. In this connection it is worthy of note that Melanie Klein regards the anxiety phobias of childhood as essentially paranoid in type.

I have given drug addictions a special place in this scheme, not only for clinical reasons, but to bring out some further points in terminology. I have represented the addictions as true 'border-line' states in the sense that they have one foot in the psychoses and the other in the neuroses. They have their roots in paranoid states, although occasionally a melancholic element dominates the picture. Nevertheless, they are sufficiently on the neurotic side of development to preserve a fairly adequate reality relation with the important exception of the relation to drug substances, behind which the paranoid mechanism lies. I find the terms 'borderline' or 'pre'-psychotic, as generally used, unsatisfactory. If a psychotic mechanism is present at all, it should be given a definite label. If we merely suspect the possibility of a breakdown of repression, this can be indicated in the term 'potential' psychotic (more accurately a 'potentially clinical' psychosis). As for larval psychoses, we are all larval psychotics and have been such since the age of two.

I have tried to suggest some of the more fundamental considerations to be taken into account in psychiatric classifications. Before breaking off this tentative study, I would add a few comments on the extension and complication of future classifications. Once the main mechanisms and correlations have been established, subsidiary groupings will depend on some compromise between the claims of different schools, e.g. between clinical and psychopathological standpoints. This is already to some extent necessary even in regard to main groupings. I have tried to suggest the possibility of a terminology based on important mechanisms, but others might well suggest that all psycho-pathological states could be accurately named after specific disturbances in the function of the super-ego. Thus melancholia, whilst essentially an introjective psychosis, might well be called a 'hypertrophy of the oral super-ego', possibly the 'second oral'. In fact Schilder has already made an attempt along these lines. Similarly as to possible sub-groups. The claims of 'isolating' or 'circumscribing' psychic mechanisms are certainly very great, as may be seen in the case of drug addictions and fetichisms. And the same is true of the spreading mechanisms (displacement). But on the other hand, there might be some advantage in arranging sub-groups by reference not only to the instincts involved in the condition, but the degree of completeness of the object. Conceivably also the example of psycho-analysis may be followed in naming certain instincts after the zonal component chiefly concerned. In their characterological studies, for example, psycho-analysts have not hesitated to describe an 'oral', 'anal' or 'genital character', and there are many character states that might be called 'sadistic hyperæmias'. In this matter we have the encouraging example shown by organic medicine. It may be accounted to the older physicians for grace that though they wrote professional treatises in a dead language, they were nothing loath to call a spade a spade.

XII

ON THE ETIOLOGY OF DRUG-ADDICTION*

[1932]

As has been suggested in the case of alcoholism, a systematic approach to drug addiction based solely on the principles laid down for psycho-neurotic symptom-formation is not enough to account for the accompanying psycho-sexual difficulties, whether they are in the nature of inhibition or of perversion, or for the localized defect in reality sense which is covered by the drug habit. This defect helps to link drug-addiction on the one hand to the psychoses, and on the other to the more broadly based psychopathies. With regard to the specific unconscious mental content found in drug-addiction, which, incidentally, varies in accordance with the clinical type and etiological depth of the condition, it seems probable that this is not simply the result of pathogenic regression to various fixation points, but of 'repair activity' such as is found in the 'restitution-products' of the psychoses. Nevertheless, alcoholism and drug addictions have more affinities with the psycho-neuroses than with the psychoses, and although at times interfering gravely with social function can be generally regarded as autoplastic rather than alloplastic in tendency. To place them in relation to the depressions they would have to be designated 'circumscribed narcissistic neuroses'. The basis of these reflections is to be found in the following article.

There are three main sources of psycho-analytic interest in drug-addiction. In the first place its etiology is still obscure; consequently the treatment of drug-addiction lags behind that of the psycho-neuroses. It is true the psycho-analyst is justified in asserting that the only radical approach to drug habits is through psycho-analytic treatment; but he cannot remain content with such a general recommendation. He ought to be in a position to direct his psycho-analytic energies with more precision.

A second source of interest lies in the correlation of drug-

* First published in *The International Journal of Psycho-Analysis*, Vol. XIII, pt. 3, 1932 [here abbreviated].

addiction with various other psychopathological states. Owing to the close connection on the one hand between drug-addiction and the psychoses, and on the other between drug-addiction and social or sublimatory defence-reactions, it is probable that drug states will prove an essential link in the understanding of such different phenomena as paranoia, obsessional neuroses, open-air cults or even an addiction to scented soap.

The third source of interest is mainly domestic. Study of psycho-analytic views concerning alcoholism and other drug-addictions seems to me to illustrate very clearly the different tendencies which from time to time have dominated psycho-analytical research or doctrine. Those whose interest in psycho-analysis is comparatively recent, might be excused for thinking that sadism and the aggressive instincts are new discoveries. In a sense this view is not entirely without justification. Wider historical reading shows, however, that whereas in earlier times the importance of sadism was recognized clinically, its etiological significance was to some extent obscured by a preoccupation with more predominantly libidinal factors.

EARLY VIEWS ON THE RÔLE OF LIBIDO

Now it is interesting to note that the first stage in investigating drug-addiction coincided with a period when the tendencies of psycho-analytical research were more or less convergent. Psycho-analysis bore down on the problem armed with experience of transference neuroses, holding closely to traditions of *libidinal disturbance*, in particular, castration anxiety dating from the phallic phase of libidinal development. The result was a standard reconstruction of psychic events, originally sketched by Abraham[1] in the case of alcoholism and added to piecemeal by later investigators. I need only recall the emphasis laid on fixation of libido at oral or anal levels, on the comparative weakness of adult heterosexual interest, the importance of unconscious homosexuality, the significance of alcohol and other drugs as symbols of the procreative power of the male (father, God), the secondary breakdown of sublimation, and the symbolic castration represented first by impotence and later by physical and mental deterioration.

[1] Abraham: 'The Psychological Relations between Sexuality and Alcolism', in *Selected Papers*, Hogarth Press, 1927.

REGRESSION AND PROGRESSION

Even in this short summary the bias of libidinal interest is unmistakable. But another equally important tendency is liable to escape attention. The approach to drug-addiction was (and still is) profoundly influenced by the concept of *regression*. The opposite view of a *progression* in psychopathological states has never been exploited to the same extent. The idea of progression implies that psychopathological states are exaggerations of 'normal' *stages in the mastering of anxiety* and can be arranged in a rough order of precedence. It is, of course, implicit in Freud's[1] original pronouncement regarding paranoid states: namely, that the symptom is in part an attempt at restitution, i.e. an advance from the unconscious situation it covers. Not only does it restore some link, however inadequate, with reality, it performs also a protective function. The protective and restitutive aspects of other psycho-pathological states have not been given the same attention. For example, we have long known that obsessional mechanisms function comparatively well in the remissions of melancholia: nevertheless we are inclined to look askance at an obsessional neurosis *per se*, as a 'severe regression'. We think and talk of this neurosis as the result of a defensive flight backwards from the anxieties of an infantile genital system of relationships rather than a remarkable impulsion forwards, a striking advance on the discomforts of an unconscious paranoid organization. As a matter of fact, if we study the numerous drug-habits which, owing to absence of dramatic individual or social consequences, are called 'idiosyncrasies' or 'indulgences' rather than addictions, we can see that drug-addiction is frequently a successful manoeuvre. The point is of considerable therapeutic interest. Obviously if we can grasp the progressive relations of psychogenetic states, our therapeutic energies can be directed with greater accuracy. For example, the cure of an addiction or even of a severe obsessional state may depend more on the reduction of an underlying paranoid layer than on the most careful analysis of the recognized habit-formation or obsessional superstructure.

To return to our historical survey, the first discoveries concerning addiction were followed by a phase of stalemate. This deadlock coincided with the realization that what had been

[1] Freud: 'An Autobiographical Account of a Case of Paranoia', *C.P.* Vol. III, 1925.

regarded as almost a specific libidinal factor could no longer be so regarded. The element of unconscious homosexuality had never accounted satisfactorily for variations in the structure of different addictions and it was gradually found to be non-specific. Flight from unconscious homosexuality had already been advanced to account for the systems of paranoia; it was regarded as an important factor in hysteria and the obsessional states; it was discovered to be a source of violent resistance in characterological analyses and it gave considerable trouble in the analysis of normal people. The attempts made to emphasize regressive libidinal aspects of homosexuality, in particular the reassurance obtained by flight from genital anxiety were not satisfactory: reassurance mechanisms alone do not constitute a complete etiology.

SADISM AND AGGRESSION

On the other hand, fresh progress seems to have been made by paying more attention to the associated element of *sadism* and the reactions produced by the *aggressive group of impulses*. These reactions were first of all studied directly in the form of projections, reaction-formations, regressions or inhibitions of psychic and motor activities, and later indirectly by scrutinizing the super-ego apparatus which is responsible for using up certain sadistic quantities. But in spite of the fact that newer concepts of sadism and of the super-ego have been applied in the study of drug-addiction, and have increased our etiological understanding, the amount of progress made has not been entirely satisfactory. And I consider this is due in part to a divergence of views as to the actual significance of sadism. The divergences can be detected not only in papers on drug-addiction, but throughout the field of psycho-analytic research. As I have said, sadism is no new discovery. The concepts of hate, aggression and sadism have always been implicit in the concept of ambivalence and an increasing appreciation of its importance can be detected historically in the emphasis laid on negative transferences. The sadistic factor in transference was obscured for a time by the correlation of the negative transference with the inverted Oedipus situation. But this stage did not last, and there must be few analysts who have studied unconscious homosexuality in recent years without forming the conclusion that the problem of unconscious homosexuality is, roughly speaking, the problem of sadism.

EVIDENCE FROM PARANOIA

This difference in tendency can be brought out by a comparison of earlier with more recent views on *paranoia*, It is true that in Freud's latest paper on paranoia[1] the significance of death-wishes is emphasized, and it is true also, as has been stated, that aggression is implicit in the earlier conception of ambivalence. Nevertheless, in the Schreber paper no direct mention was made of the aggressive impulses and the mechanism of paranoia was described mainly in terms of libidinal conflict and related to repression of the inverted Oedipus situation. Only a few statements in Freud's more recent writings help to modify the earlier emphasis on libidinal factors in paranoia, e.g. that the mechanism of projection depends on ambivalance,[2] or that in cases of homosexuality an exceedingly hostile aggressive attitude has been not only repressed but *transformed* into a love relationship[3]; implying thereby that a homosexual system can function as a defence against hate and aggression.[4] Considering that for the last fifteen years Freud has constantly emphasized the general importance of hate, aggression and destructive impulses in ego-development, it is all the more remarkable that these teachings have not yet been fully reflected in etiological formulations concerning paranoia. Yet such is the fact.

A contrast is afforded by the views of Melanie Klein.[5] She asserts that the fixation-points of the psychoses are pregenital sadistic fixation-points: that the individual experiences paranoidal anxiety in the early anal-sadistic phase: that the fixation-point of paranoia falls in the phase of phantasied attack on the mother's body; that the individual's aggressive tendencies are transferred to the excretory systems, hence that fæces and urine and all associated organs are unconsciously regarded as possessing dan-

[1] Freud: 'Certain Neurotic Mechanisms in Jealousy, Paranoia and Homosexuality', *C.P.* Vol. II, 1924.

[2] Freud: *The Ego and the Id*, Hogarth Press, London, 1927.

[3] Freud: 'Certain Neurotic Mechanisms in Jealousy, Paranoia and Homosexuality', *C.P.* Vol. II, 1924.

[4] Later, in *The Ego and the Id*, Freud takes the view that this transformation does not imply a transformation of hate into love, but is the result of a transfer of neutralized energy to the love aim. This later view does not detract from the defensive significance of the manoeuvre.

[5] Klein: *The Psycho-Analysis of Children*, Hogarth Press, 1932, Chap. IX.

gerous sadistic properties, the projection of which gives rise to anxieties of attack from without; that in particular the fear of poisoning can be related mostly to the individual's original anal and urethral sadism.

CONSTITUTIONAL FACTORS

The same divergence can be demonstrated in the case of drug-addiction. If one studies recent psycho-analytic literature on the subject, it is clear that in spite of copious reference to hate and sadism, early fixations, psychotic components, etc., drug-addictions are ultimately assessed in terms of late genital anxieties. Even where attempts are made to establish deeper roots for the fixations of addiction, the tendency is to look for them in phases of development when psychic structure must be of the most rudimentary order. Thus Radó,[1] although correlating drug-addiction and abstinence with a manic-depressive sequence, looks for the basic fixation in a phase of 'alimentary orgasm' on which a pharmacotoxic orgiastic system is built up. It is true he does not exclude entirely a psychic organization based on this alimentary system, but he has so far attached no specific content to this psychic system. On the other hand, he goes on to say that later guilt systems have no specific relation to drug-addictions: that they play no greater part in these addictions than in other pathological states. Simmel[2] in a recent paper shows both tendencies. He ultimately relates drug-addiction to melancholia but only as a secondary regression following a primary obsessional mechanism. As one might gather from his interest in obsessional factors in addiction, he expresses the anxiety factor mainly in terms of castration anxiety. And he follows Radó in seeking for a fixation factor in a phase ante-dating organized psychic structure, viz. a stage of primal intestinal narcissism. Incidentally, like many other writers, he introduces the 'death instinct' as a factor, a course which always seems to me to beg the question of the actual history of sadistic and destructive impulses. Pre-structural factors of this type can be adequately valued as 'constitutional' or 'predisposing' without employing the term fixation.

[1] Radó: 'The Psychic Effects of Intoxicants', *Int. J. Psycho-Anal.*, 1926, **7**, 396; 'The Problem of Melancholia', ibid., 1928, **9**, 420.
[2] Simmel: 'Zum Problem von Zwang und Sucht', *Bericht über den fünften allgemeinen ärzlichen Kongress für Psychotherapie*, 1930.

SPECIFIC ETIOLOGIES

The opposite tendency, viz. search for a specific etiology of drug-addiction of a kind that is primitive without being pre-structural is hard to find in psycho-analytical literature. Drug-addiction has been treated on the whole as a step-child of the psychoses. I have on previous occasions[1] referred to the mechanism of one type of alcoholism as an 'inverted paranoia' and have said regarding drugs in general that they represent the poisons and elixirs wherewith the sadistic aftermath of early libidinal relations is treated. But the only specific reference I can find in the literature is in the form of a speculative suggestion made by Melitta Schmideberg.[2] Writing on psychotic mechanisms, and in particular on the means whereby dangerous 'introjected' objects (or their substitutes) can be countered, she describes how a dangerous substance can be transmuted into a beneficent substance, also how friendly substances can be used to neutralize or expel malignant substances. She goes on to link this system with medicinal treatment in general and adds: 'Probably this mechanism is at work in morbid cravings, and is 'reinforced by the pharmacological effect of drugs as opposed to medicines that really heal'.

As between the tendencies I have described, recent experience biases me in favour of the second. I agree that interpretations of a nuclear complex existing prior to the mainly genital Oedipus phase are to a certain extent suspect, that they are subject to the charge of being '*rückphantasieren*' products, that they may exploit regression instead of uncovering it. In short, I agree that the onus of proof is on those who attempt to modify existing systematizations. But I cannot find any adequate explanation of drug-addiction which does not assume an active Oedipus situation at a stage when sadistic and libidinal functions overlap considerably and before libidinal systems – chiefly the oral, excretory and early genital systems – have established a stable balance between psychic representation and repression.

[1] Glover: 'The Etiology of Alcoholism', *Proc. R. Soc. Med.*, 1928, **21**, 45 [see Chap. V, this volume]; 'The Prevention and Treatment of Drug-Addiction', ibid., 1931, **24**.

[2] Schmideberg: 'The Rôle of Psychotic Mechanisms in Cultural Development', *Int. J. Psycho-Anal.*, 1930, **11**, 387; 'A Contribution to the Psychology of Persecutory Ideas and Delusions', ibid., 1931, **12**, 331.

THE OEDIPUS COMPLEX IN ADDICTION

The justification for appropriating the term 'Oedipus' in this context would take us too far afield. On the one hand, it enables us to appreciate more fully the amount of conflict existing at a stage when libidinal interests are almost exclusively directed towards mother-imagos and the drive towards father-imagos is limited to one organ-system (real or phantasied). Thus it makes one particular phantasy-system more comprehensible, viz. the phantasy of the 'woman with the (father's) penis'. And it meets the case of the posthumous (fatherless) child where the possibility of actual 'primal scenes' is excluded: the early stages of the child's conflict (including primal scene phantasies) can then be worked out in reference to different maternal organs or zones of gratification and frustration (real or phantasied). The main objection is that it renders the term 'inverted Oedipus complex' less precise than is the case at present. The terminological issue rests on the fact that genital interest exists from the first year of life in both sexes, and is bound to play a part directly or indirectly in all frustrations. In this sense all frustrations have an Oedipus component. If the argument is advanced that in early stages the genital element is quantitatively negligible, there is no objection to the use of some other term, e.g. 'Oedipus prototype', or 'forerunner', 'pre-Oedipus', etc. If we can show that earlier conflicts play a part in the etiology of, say, the psychoses, similar to the part played by the model genital Oedipus situation in hysteria, why not reduce complications by calling all infantile conflict over frustration 'Oedipus' conflict?[1]

NUCLEAR FORMATIONS OF EGO

In supporting these views, I do not intend to suggest that the importance of later and more organized infantile systems can be glossed over in drug-addiction. It is impossible to neglect, for example, the extremely obvious homosexual phantasy-systems observed in, say, cocaine-addictions. It is equally impossible to

[1] Since this was written Freud has made an important pronouncement on the question of terminology ('Female Sexuality', *Int. J. Psycho-Anal.*, 13, p. 281) [*C.P.*, Vol. V, 1950]: he says, *a propos* of pre-Oedipus stages, that there is no objection to attaching a wider significance to the term Oedipus complex; it can be regarded if need be as including all the relations of the infant to both parents.

overlook later 'positive Oedipus' anxieties (i.e. typical castration anxiety); or for that matter the importance of stimuli of a much later date. In one case of cocaine-addiction the final determinant of the habit was without any doubt a fascinated interest in Sherlock Holmes, the publication of whose 'Adventures' coincided with the addict's pubertal phase of masturbation. Incidentally, the patient modified the Sherlock Holmes technique in so far as he injected the drug into the root of the penis. I need not go into all the genital Oedipus determinants of this habit, or enumerate the elements of curiosity, sadism, guilt and punishment represented by identification with a detective. The fact remains that, although interpretation of this familiar type produced signs of anxiety, both in the positive form of discharge and in the negative form of resistance, these reactions could not be compared with the intense resistances shown when a more primitive reading of the situation was given, viz. in terms of sadistic attack on the parents followed by sadistic counter-attack. Only when the situation was reduced to the common ground of a battle between the organs of the parents and the organs of the child, with terrifying excretory substances as weapons, was any adequate response evoked. Only then did an existing compulsive system of inventive and creative work – which had hitherto been singularly unsuccessful and by means of which the patient frittered away time and money – begin to lose some of its compulsive power and at the same time become more effective. Observations of this kind suggest that we are not justified in sticking rigidly to the idea of a *fixed* nuclear system. There is some reason to assume that what in the case of the neuroses has been called the 'nuclear complex' could be more usefully described as a 'polymorphonuclear' complex. My impression is that in drug-addiction we can detect, perhaps more clearly than in well-defined neuroses or psychotic states, the existence of a *series* of nuclear 'Oedipus' situations, to each one of which there is an appropriate symptomatic or para-symptomatic (social) response. In general the changes in the series may be attributed to two factors, (1) a quantitative factor relating to the charge of aggressive impulses carried, and (2) a qualitative factor contributed from erotogenic sources. At different levels one seems to find not only varying confluences of genital with pregenital libido, but different fusions of each libidinal component with aggression. Moreover, the different varieties of drug-addiction seem to suggest that the earliest nuclear formations are not arranged simply in a *consecutive* series but rather in a *cluster* formation. This cluster formation represents a group of component interests and develops into a consecutive series only after what we call the anal-sadistic phase has been established. To express the same idea in terms of anxiety and frustration we might say that drug-addictions are a caricature of the normal processes whereby a number of earlier infantile psychotic anxiety states are carried over into and submerged by social adaptations of an 'ingestion' order (reading, taking medicines, etc.).

THEORETICAL IMPLICATIONS

Like all other systematizations, the foregoing has to be judged mainly in terms of descriptive convenience; in other words, the aptness of what Freud has called 'the metaphorical expressions peculiar to psychology . . . of the deeper layers'. There are, however, certain theoretical consequences to be considered. Acceptance of an early polymorphous ego-organization involves some recasting of existing rather rigid descriptive views of narcissism; or at least some distinction of the problem of narcissistic *energies* from (*a*) the problem of narcissistic *topography*, and (*b*) the clinical problems of narcissistic *feeling* or reaction. For example, a good deal of what has hitherto been considered as belonging to a narcissistic organization would have to be relegated to a system of object-relations. The term 'part-object' though to some extent helpful seems to me to beg the question of the narcissistic boundary. On the other hand, the term 'fixation' would require to be used with more precision. To say that a person has an 'oral fixation' is much too vague and throws too much emphasis on the constitutional factor. It would be much more helpful to be able to say that owing to instinctual urges and frustration (occurring at a time to be estimated for each individual) a person is fixated to one or more of a series of nuclear positions. But we must be careful in the use of the term series. It seems to me that difficulties in establishing the fixation-points of psychoses are due in part to a bias in favour of a consecutive series. The complex clinical picture of dementia præcox itself suggests a possible combination of nuclear fixations. And, as I have said, the same appears to be true of drug-addictions.

The following case illustrates some of the points already discussed:

CLINICAL ILLUSTRATIONS

A woman came for treatment who appeared at first sight to be suffering from a severe obsessional neurosis with some accompanying anxiety-hysteria and some conversion symptoms mainly affecting the alimentary tract. Preliminary analysis did not alter this diagnosis, although it was noteworthy that the obsessional system seemed to have effected less distortion of ideational content than usual: the ceremonial systems were as to one part almost unmodified homosexual representations, in which however a phantasy element of hermaphroditism was introduced, e.g. obsessional pictures of possessing a penis, sometimes of fantastic shape, by means of which contact was made either with a female figure having a fantastic penis or with a male figure with a fantastic vagina. These pictures provoked typical obsessional ceremonials. Outside the range of obsessional systems there was no manifest homosexual interest. It soon became apparent that, under cover of sedative medicinal treatment, she had established a strong drug-addiction of the paraldehyde type. She had been treated by various doctors for several years previously, all of whom had either initiated some medicinal treatment or sanctioned existing hypnotics. One naturally rescrutinized the history for evidence of earlier addiction tendencies, and found that evidence not only in the form of medicine-taking but in various social habits concerning eating. A hunt for paranoidal mechanisms was not successful. Tracing all these elements separately in the subsequent analysis, it became possible to reconstruct the symptomatic course of events as follows: an active phase of neurosis formation could be established between the age of 2 and $3\frac{1}{2}$. This corresponded to the period between the birth of the first rival sister and the first rival brother. Infantile anxiety reactions and tantrum scenes in which the beating of animals or inanimate objects played a part were followed by a stage in which it was not clear whether anxiety phobia-formations or obsessional mechanisms would obtain the upper hand. Eventually obsessional technique won the day; animal phobias gave place to obsessional fears, and by the age of three the child was practically an adult obsessional neurotic with obsessional fears of contamination and attack together with obsessional precautions affecting thought, speech and action. For a short period at about the age of 5, hysterical conversion symptoms dominated the picture and recurred occasionally in later years. It was clear that the later alternations corresponded to fluctuations in unconscious homosexual and conscious heterosexual interest, stimulation and frustration. But only for a few months, at about 25, after an important change in work, emotional relations and social surroundings, was the neurotic activity effectively suspended. The rest of the time obsessional systems and defences were constantly increasing, one contamination fear giving place to another with always an increasing element of psycho-sexual preoccupation or cover (e.g. masochistic pregnancy-phantasies). At puberty some organic illnesses obscured the picture but, on the emergence of faint homosexual interests and more intense reactive brooding over the problem of homosexuality in general, the obsessional systems became more extensive. An alarming cannibalistic element entered into them at about 18, and from then on to the forties the ego was almost completely absorbed by acute obsessional systems, ringing every possible change on a disguised sadistic contamination theme together with a manifest infantile homosexual theme. As regards the addiction system, the earliest compulsive interest uncovered was concerned with the taste of the first rival baby's bottle feed; that was at the age of 2. Later (at about 8) a phobia of tea made its appearance. Still later (at 10) an anxiety-free ceremonial concerning reading and eating developed, but was soon linked up with contamination-affect concerning teeth and tartar. Still later (at 15) the obsessional hermaphroditic systems became attached to the mouth. Pressure of upper on lower teeth, or of teeth on gums or of tongue on teeth could function as substitutes for more manifest sexual content. Contamination anxiety then spread to anæsthetics. At 18, as has been noted, cannibalistic fears attacked the eating process, and at about 26 the first sedative was given by the father. For some years afterwards, the fears were associated with impulses to take medicine of all sorts in order to combat infections and the patient veered between physical illness requiring medicine and hysterical vomiting. During the first years of addiction, a reduction of the acuteness of ingestion fears coincided with a spread of complicated ceremonial to eating in restaurants.

Applying clinical standards to this case, it could be said that there were no paranoidal formations, although study of the phobia systems both early and late showed significant reactions; first, the involvement of 'pursuing' animals in the phobias and later a tendency to expand obsessional phobias to cosmic dimensions, together with a sense of personal doom in relation to any natural disturbances.

During the course of analysis, but particularly in its later phases, the patient voluntarily undertook courses of abstinence which were mostly abortive. Complete reduction of a lesser bromide habit was ultimately effected, but at the cost of great anxiety and followed by an increase of obsessional activity, particularly of the more manifestly sexual ceremonials and defences. At this stage it was clear that the original strength of the addiction was due in part to the fact that the drugs were officially prescribed (i.e. benign substances). An increase in the paraldehyde habit then occurred. This developed to such an extent that a formal deprivation course became essential. The deprivation phase was accompanied by the usual hallucinatory manifestations. When these died down, two facts emerged; that the patient had a slight paranoidal system in operation and that *the obsessional neurosis had for the time disappeared*. As the paranoidal system slowly vanished, the obsessional system returned in full swing. The paraldehyde deprivation was complete, but on occasions of acute anxiety the patient was allowed small doses of non-habit-forming hypnotics. These she herself supplemented with doses of sal volatile. Of the various changes observed I will note here just one. The drugs had previously always been employed in a ceremonial way, not as a direct hypnotic. Now they were used less obsessionally as sedatives and more for their hypnotic effect, but the same drug was definitely regarded as a 'good' or 'bad' drug depending on whether the amount conformed to or exceeded the prescribed amount. The amount over the prescribed dose was a bad, evil, dangerous substance. The same differentiation applied to the person of the prescriber. Increases sanctioned by the physician who had regulated the deprivation were good; those sanctioned in emergency by myself were dangerous. A pseudo-paranoid mechanism had made its appearance in the drug system. Incidentally the phase following deparaldehyding showed an immediate transference alteration in which I became more dangerous; first of all the lessened defence to sadistic phantasies increased reactions of anxiety during any absence on my part, and in the sexual part of the obsessional phantasies I was made to play a more direct rôle.

Casting back to the open paranoid features that were manifested immediately after deprivation, it became clear that the mechanism was not purely paranoic. At first sight they had appeared to be pure delusions of reference, but that was not quite accurate. The jeering voices and hostile reproaches, or attacks, which were supposed to damage the patient and at the same time to remove something from her were linked on to a conspiracy system. For example, certain hostile individuals were conspiring to take away some good substance from a clergyman. There was, however, a hint that the patient herself might somehow be in the conspiracy – or at least that she was being used by others as a tool in order to effect their designs. But by dint of identifying herself with the clergyman she could restore the damage provided she took drugs. The clergyman was a not very effectively disguised mother-figure. This system of identification was on ordinary occasions concealed by the manifest homosexual content of the obsessions, e.g. active or passive contamination or destruction effected by the 'fantastic penis' systems.

Here was a case that showed historically a gradual crescendo of symptoms rising to a paranoid crisis, but including elements of reaction to every stage of development from primitive oral reaction down to infantile genital and adult genital anxiety systems. In the next place the most dramatic and permanent feature, the severe obsessional system, appeared in the rôle of a defence formation, guarding against anxiety of a paranoid type. The homosexual system which had played an obvious part in the obsessional formation was still present in the early hallucinatory phase of deprivation, but gave place to more direct phantasies of incestuous attack by the father; this suddenly gave place to the delusions of persecution. The homosexual element thus showed its 'regressive' aspect in relation to the incest phantasies and its 'progressive' aspect in relation to paranoid fear of the mother. Moreover, in the phase prior to actual deprivation the increase in drug-addiction corresponded directly with an increase in the destructive aspects of obsessional thinking and ceremonial; after the deprivation there was a more manifest connection between ceremonial habit and destructive impulse.

A similar compromise-mechanism could be detected in the Sherlock Holmes case I have mentioned. The castration elements appeared to be mostly concerned with later genital systems. The homosexual organization was kept under effective repression and there was no clinical sign of paranoid reaction; nor was there any notable paranoid reaction after deprivation. The melancholic element in the case was, however, extremely obvious. There was a constant recurrence of manifest depressed oral reactions, and phases of injection of massive doses of cocaine which were practically unsuccessful attempts at suicide. But even in the most acute stages the melancholic mechanisms were not actually pure. The drug habit represented sufficient of a projective system to prevent deeper regression. And after final deprivation it was maintained in the modified form of medicinal drugging for which justification had to be found in every possible source of organic disturbance. For example, a heavy meal would be taken in order to justify all sorts of alimentary medicine drinking. The reduction in projected sadistic charge allowed a substitution of mainly 'good' drugs for 'bad'. Nevertheless, the good drugs, by upsetting the patient's internal economy, carried on the work of bad drugs, although in a milder degree. Even the 'injection' element was maintained for a time under the guise of vaccine therapy.

Reviewing the paraldehyde case briefly, it could be said that, in spite of the obvious importance of later infantile genital systems (the model Oedipus nucleus), the drug element attached to the obsessional neurosis related to a more primitive Oedipus conflict occurring at the age of 2, and coinciding with the birth of the rival sister. It was an attempt to deal with sadistic charges only slightly more tolerable than those dealt with by purely paranoid mechanisms. It came into action because the later and more developed Oedipus relations (inverted and positive) still maintained a high sadistic charge. No adult derivative from these later systems could be permitted to act as a reassuring system of relations, hence every ordinary fluctuation in libido or aggressive tendency laid the patient at the mercy of an older anxiety system.

TRANSITIONAL STATES

While, therefore, I agree with the tendency of recent attempts to compare drug-addiction with melancholia and obsessional neurosis, I feel that the emphasis laid on the latest Oedipus phase and on early constitutional factors has obscured not only an equally close relation to paranoia, but the possibility of establishing a *specific* mechanism for drug-addiction. This specific reaction represents a *transition* between the more primitive psychotic phase and the later psycho-neurotic phase of development. I imagine that different types of drug-addiction represent variations in the amount of original erotogenic sources of libido (and consequently different fusions of sadism): hence that they represent variations not only in the structure of the primitive ego, but in the type of mechanism employed to control excitation. When Simmel claims that drug-addiction is closely connected with both obsessional neurosis and melancholia,[1] I have no objection to offer, except that

[1] Simmel, op. cit.

this applies only to some cases and that it neglects the relation of other cases to paranoia. But in spite of many correspondences of mechanism I cannot confirm his view that the state belongs essentially to the obsessional group, acquiring a melancholic character as a result of regression. Nor do I agree with his general statement that in the first stages the addiction represents a pleasure-toned obsessional state. This description, in my opinion, applies with more accuracy to the medicinal and food idiosyncrasies seen in neurotic-character cases, and particularly to various social habits of normal individuals, e.g. food indulgences and dietetic systems, habits of bodily inunction and inhalation, routine medicinal habit, fresh-air apostledom, and so forth.

PHANTASY FORMATIONS

A word here about the question of *specific phantasies* in drug-addiction. In my experience the main phantasy of drug-addictions represents a condensation of two primary systems, one in which the child attacks (later restores) organs in the mother's body, and one in which the mother attacks (later restores) organs in the child's body. These phantasies are also represented in masturbation systems and are still present in later, genital object-relations. In this paper I have not stressed the question of specific phantasies: it is always possible that the main element in any psychopatho-logical state is not so much the actual unconscious phantasy-system as the degree of localization or mastery of anxiety achieved. In any case we cannot estimate the significance of such stereotyped phantasies until we know what organ-substance is represented by the drug.

PROVISIONAL CONCLUSIONS

(1) Drug-addiction implies fixation to a transitional Oedipus system – a system lying between the more primitive Oedipus nuclei that produce paranoid (or melancholic) anxieties and the Oedipus nucleus that is responsible for later obsessional reactions.

(2) Its defensive function is to control sadistic charges, which, though less violent than those associated with paranoia, are more severe than the sadistic charges met with in obsessional formations. (An alternative formulation would be that the libidinal components found in drug-addiction are stronger and contain more genital

elements than those associated with the psychoses, but weaker than those associated with the transference neuroses.)

(3) Drug-addiction acts as a protection against psychotic re-action in states of regression.

(4) Unconscious homosexual phantasy-systems are not a direct etiological factor, but represent a restitutive or defensive system; on account of their stronger libidinal cathexis (both narcissistic and genital), homosexual systems act as a protection against anxie-ties of the addiction type. Hence the close association of homo-sexual interests with drug-addiction implies either the persistence of a defensive system or the ruins of a defensive system.

ADDICTION AND SOCIAL HABIT

The next step is to consider what relation exists between drug-addiction and neurotic habits or social usages, in particular habits and customs belonging to an 'ingestion' group. Most processes of incorporation, e.g. the processes of eating and reading, are subject to modifications of a more or less pathological stamp. These habits must be correlated with the usual drug-addictions. We must know, for example, why noxious drugs are chosen in certain addictions in preference to less harmful or harmless substances and whether the fixations and defensive systems are identical. Why does an individual swallow, inhale or inject cocaine instead of smoking cigarettes or sucking chlorodyne lozenges or eating ice-cream or drinking almond emulsions or taking nutrient enemata or rubbing in lanoline ointment or chewing bus tickets?

The answer originally given by psycho-analysis was perfectly simple. Study of clinical data confirmed what was already apparent to the student of mythology and anthropology. The drug repre-sented the phallus or semen of the father (God) and the breast – nipple – milk of the mother (Goddess). Less obvious at first – possibly because less attention was paid to this aspect – was the fact that drugs represented other bodily substances of an excretory nature, urine, fæces, etc. Soon it was held that all bodily 'ejecta' – breath, sweat, spit, urine, fæces, blood, semen, milk, could be represented by the drug. It was nevertheless believed that the phallic (seminal) symbolism was the most important, and that, through this link, drug-addiction could be traced to the genital Oedipus situation. The other elements were regarded as contributions to genital interest from earlier erotogenic zones (oral, anal, etc.); or simply as disguised displacements of genital interest. The inverted (homosexual) Oedipus aspect was thought to account for the predominance in some cases of anal symbolism.

More careful clinical investigation showed that this apparently water-tight system was inadequate. It had always been known that under conditions of suggestive *rapport*, a comparatively inert substance (injections of salt water, tablets of aspirin, chewing-gum, etc.) could function as a drug-substitute. True, in many cases it was felt to be inadequate but it would tide over phases of deprivation. A more striking observation was to follow.

There is now no doubt that the pharmacotoxic effects of drugs do not play such a specific part in dangerous drug-addictions as is supposed in extra-psychological circles. In certain addiction-cases where a harmless substitute was established (in one case sugar was used in this way), I have observed the same slavish compulsion attach itself to the substitute. And deprivation of the substitute loosened massive charges of anxiety. On the other hand, during the analysis of psycho-neurotics and of neurotic (or psychotic) character abnormalities, I have discovered idiosyncrasies which had the same subjective sense of compulsion and aroused the same anxiety on deprivation as standard drug-habits. These are some-times connected with food, e.g. a compulsion to eat stewed meat with a highly seasoned ketchup added to the gravy. Compulsive habits of 'taking medicine' are even more common. I recall in this connection an addiction to white purgative emulsions, attempts to abandon which invariably induced severe anxiety. In another case the 'addiction' was to hot water. Moreover in actual drug-depriva-tions it is well known that the last and most diluted drop of an addiction substance is as significant to the addict as the last and most trivial ceremonial is to a severe case of obsessional neurosis. In one recent case, consuming steak-pie, beer, and reading a newspaper shared equally in an 'ingestion' compulsion, by means of which an intolerable state of boredom and depression was periodically relieved. The evidence in other directions is over-whelming. For every contamination-phobia, there is a corre-sponding compulsion, either social, fetichistic or 'perverted'. For every cleansing ceremonial there is a corresponding ingestion habit. This fact escapes attention owing to the number of com-promise-formations. When a washing maniac must use 'scented' soap or an ointment reeking of antiseptic, or when the fresh-air addict with a 'fog' phobia insists on living in a pinewood, the mixture of phobia and 'counter-addiction' usually escapes notice.

'PSYCHIC' ADDICTIONS

The substitution of psychic 'substances' for concrete is not difficult to demonstrate. The activity of reading is perhaps the simplest example and it is clear that systems of 'good' and 'bad' reading have some resemblance to addictions. In the paraldehyde case I have described the only guilt-free ceremonial was as follows: having drawn the blinds in a particular room the patient removed all objects from the pockets which were then filled with biscuits; she then sat exactly opposite the centre of the fireplace with legs apart and feet raised and proceeded to read 'good' books, at the same time munching biscuits. Here again compromise-formations abound: e.g. compulsive reading of 'elevating' or 'good' books, particularly theosophical literature, during the process of defæcation. Perhaps the most interesting group is that where psychoneurotic processes and psycho-therapeutic activities function as 'drugs'. It is easy to observe that obsessional psychic constructions and the affects accompanying melancholia are felt and described in terms of 'substance'. The obsessional feels that if his neurosis were cured he would be left with a 'hole' or 'gap' in his mind, and the depressed case very frequently expresses the state of endopsychic conflict and affect in terms of 'weights' and 'masses' in his 'inside'. I have recently studied a case in which a very definite drug-addiction was suddenly and spontaneously abandoned in favour of an obsessional neurosis. The patient then reacted to the idea of cure of the neurosis precisely as a drug-addict reacts to the idea of abstinence. She 'must have' the neurosis; she 'could not give it up', and so forth. The change was not due solely to an alteration in methods of defence; the obsessional psychic construction with its accompanying affect provided a suitable drug 'substance'. The immediate stimulus to substitution was the establishment of friendly relations with a mothering type of male admirer. A similar valuation of psychotherapeutic activities was suggested by Janet[1] in the case of hypnosis: he pointed out that the stage of somnambulic passion is comparable to the craving of a

---

[1] Janet: Névroses et idées fixes, 1898, Paris, p. 429.

morphine addict. Ernest Jones,[1] commenting on this observation, linked it up to similar manifestations exhibited in alcoholism. And it is common psycho-analytic experience that patients react to interpretations as if they were either hostile foreign bodies or friendly substances. In short, there is every reason to think (a) that given suitable psychic conditions *any* substance can function as a 'drug', (b) that 'psychic substances' can function as replacements for ideas of concrete substances, (c) that both types of substance can be subdivided into good or bad, innocent or guilty, beneficent or malignant, restorative or destructive.

'NOXIOUS' AND 'BENIGN' ADDICTIONS

It is difficult to resist the conclusion that, however varied may be the contributions to drug-addiction from erotogenic sources, one special interest is represented by all drug-substances, viz. repressed aggressive or sadistic interest. Admittedly it is hard to isolate this interest and therefore to claim that drug-addiction is solely and simply a reaction to sadism. Quite apart from the indisputable importance of libidinal components in drug-symbolisms, there are certain attributes of drugs which represent a combination of libidinal and aggressive components. Thus it is clear that the good and bad elements in some addictions depend on the impregnating and abortifacient powers unconsciously attributed to the drug. Nevertheless, it might be inquired whether by accentuating the sadistic element we could establish a specific factor operative in the 'noxious' as compared with socially 'benign' addictions.

The first step in this investigation is to compare the actual properties of 'noxious' with those of 'benign' drugs. It is evident that noxious drugs possess certain injurious and destructive properties. And although many non-noxious foods, if eaten regardless of consequences, produce equally disintegrating effects (as in the case of a patient who refuses to follow a prescribed diet), the distinction appears to have some general validity. This would suggest that in the choice of a noxious habit the element of sadism is decisive. The drug would then be a substance with sadistic properties which can exist both in the outer world and within the body, but which exercises its sadistic powers only when inside.

[1] Ernest Jones: 'The Action of Suggestion in Psychotherapy', in *Papers on Psycho-Analysis,* 3rd Edition, Baillière, 1923.

The situation would represent a transition between the menacing externalized sadism of a paranoid system and the actual internalized sadism of a melancholic system. The addiction would represent a peculiar compound of psychic danger and reassurance. Doubtless the melancholic (internalized) aspects would be increased by an attempt to deal with the externalized menace (drugs) by swallowing, and the fact that drugs actually exist 'outside' (in chemists' shops) would encourage a move towards abstinence during the dangers of the exacerbated melancholic phase.

The second group of properties of noxious drugs presents a more difficult problem. These substances have the capacity to produce effects that are usually described in a compromise terminology, partly psychological, partly physiological. They are called stimulants, depressants, hypnotics, narcotics, analgesics, sedatives, intoxicants, etc., and various sensory and psychic disturbances are described in the same terminology. Clinical experience of melancholia, hypochondria and conversion-hysteria warns us, however, that this semi-physiological approach is not only inadequate but misleading; that subjective sensory and affective experiences cannot be understood apart from the existence of conflict between psychic institutions. For example, in one of my cases, the effect of strong doses of a hypnotic was to produce a 'tottery' feeling as if the legs were 'cut off'. Incidentally, the hypnotic was rarely taken at the most appropriate time, i.e. at bedtime. As a rule it was swallowed just before the patient was about to go for a walk. A few associations connected the idea with weakness in the mother's legs. At this time the patient's mother was unable to get about owing to a debilitating illness. So the patient not only carried out a form of self-punishment, but repeated the crime of cutting off the mother's legs. In this case drug-taking was frequently followed by a feeling of 'sanity' in the upper parts of the body. This system was illuminated by the discovery that, during obsessional preoccupation with the idea of possessing a penis, one of the ways of ridding herself of this dangerous organ was to imagine it stowed away in one or other of the lower limbs. Evidently not only the legs but the concealed penis were destroyed by taking the drug. The same patient was clear that the compulsion to take a 'dose' frequently coincided with worry over the mental images of some person. She felt they were 'in her head', and that the drug could 'kill them inside her'. It could also 'dull' (kill) the intensity of

certain obsessional 'pictures' (organs, persons). Here again there
was admittedly a masochistic element: when she was stupified,
'little enemies' could steal a march on her, a system which had
more obvious representation in conscious rape and pregnancy
phantasies.

In this type of case the relief following drug-taking depends to a
large extent on the exploitation of sadism to cure sadism, although
undoubtedly there is a strong factor of masochistic gratification.
In other cases where the immediate effect of the drug appears to be
entirely alleviating and gratifying and where no secondary deterioration is apparent, punishment and masochistic aspects are gratified in the abstinence period. This is in keeping with the views of
Simmel[1] and many others, viz. that abstinence phases are essential
parts of an organized addiction. On the whole the evidence seems
to suggest that the narcotic and noxious properties of certain drugs
put them in a clinical class by themselves, in so far as they are
excellently adapted to the purposes of sadistic expression. The
necessary formula appears to be that the individual's own hate
impulses, together with identifications with objects towards whom
he is ambivalent, constitute a dangerous psychic state. This state
is symbolized as an internal concrete substance. The drug is then
in the last resort an external counter-substance which cures by
destruction. In this sense drug-addiction might be considered an
improvement on paranoia: the paranoidal element is limited to the
drug-substance which is then used as a therapeutic agent to deal
with intrapsychic conflict of a melancholic pattern. In the sense
of *localizing* paranoid anxiety and enabling external adaptation to
proceed, this may be one of the specific functions of drug-
addiction.

On the other hand, there are some considerations which suggest
that we should not push this view to extremes. In the first place we
find that patients at different times regard the same drug as 'good'
as well as 'bad'. Secondly, obsessional neurotics without any
manifest addiction tendencies are prone to use food images in
'cleansing' as well as in 'contamination' systems. Moreover, some
drug-addicts exhibit a distinctly obsessional tendency in their
dosage and timing of noxious drugs (e.g. taking them when their
thoughts are 'bad'), thereby suggesting more friendly exploitation

[1] Simmel, op. cit.

of the drug-system. Again, in some noxious addictions the sedative and restorative effects are a prominent feature. On the other hand, in a great majority of 'benign' addictions, the restorative and life-giving properties of the substance are clearly manifest. Finally, however important unconscious paranoid and melancholic factors in drug-addiction may be, the clinical fact remains that throughout the greater part of many severe addictions there are no manifest symptoms of this kind. Even allowing for disturbances occurring under the influence of drugs (e.g. intoxication), and for impairment of psychic function during comparative abstinence (e.g. retrograde amnesia), the patient's reality sense is not grossly and obviously distorted. Moreover, as I have indicated, some drug addictions show an actual refractoriness to paranoid regression.

Analytic support for the benign aspect of drug-substances is based almost entirely on three groups of observation: (a) the close connection between drug-substances and erotogenic interests, (b) the exploitation of later and more predominantly genital libidinal development as a reassurance against earlier more sadistic phases, (c) the existence of 'cancellation' and 'restitution' mechanisms.

There is no need to recall the extensive evidence in support of a *symbolic relation between drugs and erotogenic interests*. The symbolism in many cases requires no interpretation. And there is a good deal to be said for Radó's conception of 'meta-erotism',[1] in the sense of a system of drug-excitation which short-circuits the zonal components of infantile sexuality. I am unable, however, to confirm his assumption of a decisive 'alimentary orgasm' based on alimentary erotism. That alimentary erotism is an important factor in most cases I have no doubt. It is in my experience most obvious in addictions of the chlorodyne type. But in still other addictions, e.g. chloroform, ether, etc., it is obvious that nasal and respiratory erotism is picked out. Again, in certain cases of alcoholism it is clear, not only from the symbolism but from actual reports of the patient, that urinary erotism is picked out in preference to the alimentary element. In one instance the first mouthful of white wine, whisky, sherry or beer produced immediate erotic sensations in the bladder which were then referred to the tip of the penis. In any case, whether the important mechanism is 'short-circuiting' or a process of direct selection, the guilt or anxiety system involved

[1] Radó, op. cit.

is not simply a reaction to excitation of one zone. In the alcohol instance just mentioned, although urinary erotism was obviously the important factor, it was important because the ego-object relations as a whole were expressed in urinary-sadistic terms. Thus wine was a dangerous poison: it could only be cured by taking in more wine; it was an impregnating substance; it was an abortifacient, etc. And ultimately it was a loving and curative substance.[1]

This brings us to the second point, viz. exploitation of later and more genital elements as a *reassurance against earlier anxieties* of menacing external substances. This aspect of drug-addiction has been emphasized by Simmel and later by Schmideberg. The closer the identification with a comparatively friendly 'semen-penis-child' system the more compulsive the benign aspects of addiction. The friendliness is of course only comparative, because in the stage of infantile genital interest a sadistic component is still important, and can be measured by the amount of castration-anxiety.

The third point is also concerned with reassurance. It involves the idea that a good substance can either neutralize a bad substance or can make good any injury caused by an existing bad substance. These mechanisms have now been shown to play a large part in obsessional neuroses[2] and in many apparently normal activities, e.g. sublimations.[3] So far as my experience goes it is difficult to exclude these factors in drug-addiction. The main difficulty is that, owing to the confused state of identifications of self with object, what appears to be a pure object-restitution is condensed on a system of restitution of the self by the object.

ADDICTION AND FETICHISM

An interesting aspect of this problem of benign elements in addiction is presented by the companion problem of *fetichism*. The

[1] Although there is general agreement as to the importance of oral, excretory and genital interests in the etiology of drug-addiction, we are not yet entitled to make any final pronouncement on their relative importance. No deep analyses of 'respiratory (inhalation) addictions' have yet been published, and until this has been done an open-minded attitude seems indicated.

[2] Freud: *Hemmung, Symptom und Angst*, Wien [*Inhibitions, Symptoms and Anxiety*, Hogarth Press, 1936].

[3] Sharpe: 'Certain Aspects of Sublimation and Delusion', *Int. J. Psycho-Anal.*, 1930, **11**, 12.

relation between fetichism and some forms of drug-addiction, particularly alcoholism, is well known. But the negative aspects of fetichism have had less attention paid to them, for the reason that they are usually regarded as obsessional phobias of the contamination type. I have observed on several occasions that, after a more than usually anxious phase of abstinence, a type of obsessional phobia makes its appearance which is of this negative fetichistic type. Also that after a more spontaneous abstinence phase the return of the addiction seemed to be delayed by a more positive fetichistic interest, with or without genital masturbation. In the case of the positive fetichistic activities, a feature of the situation was that the interest also obtained narcissistic representation. In one case excitement over the idea of stockings of others could be expressed also by a lesser degree of excitement over the individual's own stockings and shoes. On the other hand, in her phobia system, fears which had originally been attached to contamination ideas concerning the clothes of others later took the form of acute anxiety concerning the destructive powers of the patient's own clothes. Two types of fear-localization could be detected: fear in which the organ-interest was displaced from the genital-abdominal area to stockings and legs, collar and neck, etc., and secondly, fear attached to clothing having close contact with the genital and abdominal area, underclothes, corsets, etc. The amount of anxiety provoked seemed to depend on whether an early paranoidal system or a later genital system of phantasy predominated. Fear lest part of the patient's knickers should 'get into' gluteal or genital folds, and effect some disastrous change, varied in intensity in accordance with the 'goodness' or 'badness' of the drugs taken. If the drugs were bad, the 'getting in' of clothing had no more anxiety than one might expect to accompany a masochistic genital phantasy. When, however, the drugs were reduced or good, the underclothing fear was almost paranoidal in intensity.

Space does not permit more detailed investigation of this subject here. But perhaps two rough formulations are permissible: (1) that in the transition between paranoidal systems and a normal re-action to reality, drug-addiction (and later on fetichism) represent not only continuations of the anxiety system within a contracted range, but the beginnings of an expanding reassurance system. The reassurance is due to contributions from later libidinal stages in infancy which contain a decreasing amount of sadism. (2) That

clothing in general is, after food, the next line of defence in overcoming paranoidal reactions to reality. It appears reasonable to
suppose that the first paranoid systems of the child attach themselves to food, that these anxieties are modified not only by the
appearance of less sadistic impulse but by a determined effort at
displacement of anxiety. In this displacement clothes play their
part. When subsequently displacement leads to reactions to the
clothes of external objects, the foundation of the classical fetish is
laid. So that when anxiety is excessive the result is either a typical
sexual fetish or the negative form, viz. a contamination phobia. I
would suggest that the association of fetichism and alcoholism
implies a combined effort to establish friendly relations with
external dangerous objects which, at an earlier stage, are thought
of as existing within the patient's body, e.g. the sadistic penis of
the father which the child has stolen from the mother. *A propos*,
the most successful exploitation of a fetichistic principle is to be
seen in the mild forms which accompany or merge with the
fore-pleasure of adult genital primacy.

To sum up the position of noxious drug-habits as compared
with benign habits: there appears to be no question that noxious
addictions represent the reaction to a more acute state of anxiety;
that the destructive properties of drugs lend themselves to symbolic and actual expression of sadism, nevertheless that the restitutive and neutralizing effect even of noxious drugs cannot be
excluded. In the benign addictions the substance still represents a
vehicle of sadism, but the sadism is less heavily charged, and
connected with less archaic phantasies. Hence anxiety both as to
the state of the body and the dangers of the external world is
reduced. Reality has taken on a more friendly aspect, consequently
non-injurious foods or their substitutes can function in these
milder addictions. With regard to the corporeal element represented by the drug, I have already indicated that we are not in a
position to speak with finality on this subject. One or two modifications of earlier ideas are, however, already justifiable. The obvious
emphasis laid by drug-addicts on phallic elements must be to some
extent discounted. And although in the past I have stressed the
importance of oral elements, I have come to realize that particularly in the case of noxious drugs, these are sometimes emphasized
for defensive purposes. Admittedly in the melancholic types oral

elements are the most important, but, taking the average run of noxious addiction, I have the impression that the drug symbolizes excretory substances which in turn represent a primitive and almost uncontrollable form of excretory sadism.

Super-Ego Factors

So far I have deliberately avoided using the term *super-ego*. My main aim is to draw attention to the significance of drug-addiction as representing a compromise between projective and introjective processes. And owing to lack of agreement as to early phases of super-ego formation it is advisable to keep to these more general terms. Nevertheless I feel convinced that when Radó says guilt-processes do not play a specific part in drug-addiction, he has in mind the guilt associated with the late Oedipus phase of super-ego formation. Theoretically speaking, however, a super-ego formation can be presumed as soon as an introjective process is sufficiently organized to attach to itself energy which would otherwise strive for more direct discharge on objects. And the whole point about drug-addiction is that it represents a phase of development when primitive-objects are introjected and absorb psychic energy, but before projection of a massive type has been finally abandoned. It has always been difficult to conceive how the *physiological* effects of alcohol could have a specific effect on *psychic* institutions, e.g. the super-ego. The answer is now apparent: the drug has no more *direct* effect on guilt than a stunning blow on the head. The effect is produced by virtue of a psychological and mainly symbolic manœuvre, to which the physiological action of drugs adds an element of realism. The physiological action of drugs is exploited by the addict because it saves expenditure of psychic energy. The same system is seen to operate in the psychoses and neuroses. The remissions of melancholia observed during intercurrent organic illness represent a saving of melancholic energies; and a conversion-hysteric obviously makes the most of any casual organic disturbance, thereby reducing the labour of symptom-formation.

I do not underrate what the physiologist would call the selective action of drugs on or through the nervous system. On the other hand, I maintain that the phenomena of *psychic* inhibition (or relief from inhibition) accompanying drug-addiction cannot be explained along purely *physiological* lines. My view is that the addict *exploits* the 'action' of the drug in terms of an infantile system of thinking. In the earliest stages endopsychic appreciation of instinctual stimuli corresponds closely to sensory experience of disturbances in the bodily organs, or, more generally, of disturbing substances in the body. The same is true of the earliest experiences of the operation of primitive psychic institutions (e.g. super-ego conflict leading to frustration). So that when an infant psychically incorporates objects (or important organs of objects) and when a primitive form of guilt ensues, this guilt can be dealt with, as it were, along physiological lines. From this point of view the significance of addiction can be described as follows. By 'cutting off' the body (i.e. sensory perceptions) the drug appears to have obliterated instinctual tension or frustration: it can also kill, cure, punish or indulge not only psychic 'objects' in the body but the body as 'self'. By 'cutting off' the external world, the drug can obliterate not only actual instinctual stimuli from without but stumuli due to projected instinct. By the same obliteration it can kill or punish external objects with or without projected characteristics: it can also rescue them by keeping them at a distance. This 'double action' accounts for the extreme sense of compulsion associated with addiction. It is specially marked in cases where both 'self' and 'introjected objects' are felt to be bad and dangerous, and the only chance of preserving a good self lies in isolating it in the external world in the form of a good object.

RESEARCH AND TERMINOLOGY

In conclusion, we must inquire what bearing the foregoing discussion of addiction has on the tendencies of psycho-analytic research and in particular on terminological usage. I can imagine that recent emphasis laid on 'sadistic' factors might give rise to an undervaluation of libidinal factors, or to a degree of misuse of terms. The phrase 'oral-sadistic fixation', for example, is just as inadequate as its fellow, 'oral libidinal fixation', or 'narcissistic fixation'. And its use might foster the tendency to think of a hypothetical 'pure sadistic' (aggressive) fixation. It must be repeated that the 'complexion' of sadism is contributed mainly by its libidinal fusion, whether primary or secondary. And in drug-addiction particularly it can be observed that although positive libidinal constructions are used as a cover for and reassurances against earlier more sadistically-charged situations, this very fact gives rise to a compulsive emphasis on libidinal components which is indistinguishable from a fixation effect. In short, there is a great deal to be said for the retention of the term 'ambivalence' in etiological essays, provided due emphasis is laid on the primitive and rudimentary nature of the objects towards which the ambivalence is directed, and provided a series of characteristic expressions of ambivalence can be isolated.

XIII

THE RELATION OF PERVERSION-FORMATION
TO THE DEVELOPMENT OF REALITY-SENSE*
[1932]

The power of the sexual impulses to affect and often to disturb reality sense is attested by a great variety of manifestations both normal and abnormal: as can be easily seen by studying in series the influence of unconscious sexual phantasy on idealizations, illusions, hallucinations, delusions, and other end-products that affect object estimations. It would seem natural, therefore, to suppose that, reversing this line of approach, we might arrive at useful conclusions regarding the development of reality sense by studying the developmental order of perversion formations and their relation to different types of anxiety and guilt. It is also reasonable to enquire how far the perversions serve to promote or preserve reality-sense by localizing and erotizing unconscious conflict regarding displaced infantile objects. Admittedly one of the difficulties of this approach is that sexual disorders cannot be so easily arranged in developmental series as symptom-formations, e.g. that some inhibitions and perversions may be found in association either with a fairly normal ego or with quite definite forms of psychosis. But the same can be said of certain functional or neurotic anxiety symptoms; and in any case there seems no good reason to be intimidated by overlaps in classification.

The term 'reality-sense' and 'reality-testing' are frequently used in psycho-analytic literature, but very seldom defined. As a rule there is no serious objection to this practice, but where the terms are themselves the subject of investigation, some preliminary definition seems unavoidable. At the risk, therefore, of begging the question, I propose to define them provisionally as follows:

(1) *Reality-sense is a faculty the existence of which we infer by examining the processes of reality-testing.*

* Expanded from a paper delivered before the Twelfth Internationa Psycho-Analytical Congress, Wiesbaden, September 7, 1932, and published in *The International Journal of Psycho-Analysis*, Vol. XIV, pt. 4, 1933 [here slightly abbreviated].

(2) *Efficient reality-testing, for any subject who has passed the age of puberty, is the capacity to retain psychic contact with the objects that promote gratification of instinct, including here both modified and residual infantile impulse.*

(3) *Objectivity is the capacity to assess correctly the relation of instinctual impulse to instinctual object, whether or not the aims of the impulse are, can be or will be gratified.*

The nature of reality-sense has so far been investigated from three different points of view. The first of these can be studied in Ferenczi's classical paper on the subject [1]. This was based on inferences drawn from (*a*) a *behaviouristic* study of infants, and (*b*) knowledge of mental mechanisms observed during the analysis of *adults*. The conclusions he arrived at are too familiar to require recapitulation, but it is to be noted that from the systematic point of view his presentation was incomplete in the following respects. With the exception of the 'stage of unconditioned omnipotence', which he related to the 'oral' phase of development, no precise indication was given of the nature or complexity of the *wish* systems involved. Again, he described a series of *relations* (mostly reactions), to the object-world, but gave no corresponding description of the *nature* of the instinctual *objects* concerned. This omission was partly rectified later by Abraham, who described a developmental series of libidinal objects including a number of 'part-objects'.[1] Since then no systematic correlation has been attempted.

From the point of view of the present investigation it is interesting to note that Ferenczi endeavoured to correlate his stages in reality-sense with adult psycho-pathological phenomena. In particular he associated certain obsessional manfestations with 'magical phases' of ego-development. The theoretical importance of this correlation was quite considerable. It implied a marked disparity between the ego-regression and the libidinal regression in obsessional neuroses. In other words, the ego of the obsessional neurotic reacted as in the very earliest stages of ego-development, while, according to then accepted views, the libidinal fixation of the obsessional neurotic was of a much later (anal-sadistic) type. Moreover, obsessional neuroses were then held to be of com-

[1] [Note (1955): See Note on 'part-objects' and 'complete objects', Chap. I, p. 18.]

paratively late onset. If the order of reality stages suggested by Ferenczi was accurate, then strictly speaking one ought to have found neuroses during early childhood. Even so, the phase of 'magical reaction' which Ferenczi described as corresponding to obsessional technique must also exist in the oral and first anal stages when so far as I know obsessional reactions are seldom observed. Ferenczi himself was evidently aware of the discrepancy because he suggested that the obsessional case makes a *part-regression* to this early ego-phase. I do not regard this view as very plausible. I have never been able to observe any case of striking ego regression which did not activate unconsciously the libidinal system appropriate to the phase of ego development.[1]

The second line of investigation is that associated with the name of Federn [2]. By means of a careful analysis of subjective as well as reported introspections, in particular, various degrees of depersonalization, alienation, etc., he endeavoured to delimit narcissistic ego boundaries. From this we can to some extent deduce the order of object-recognition and assessment. For example, he regarded variation of corporeal ego-feeling as an ascertainable symptom of ego regression and he attempted some correlation of ego boundaries in transference neuroses, psychoses and dreams. More detailed study of these ego boundaries and regressions would certainly help us to arrive at some idea of the reality systems in vogue at different phases of development. The main difficulty appears to be the somewhat rigid concept of narcissism generally accepted by psycho-analysts. This term really begs the question of ego-object boundaries.

The third and most recent approach is that made by Melanie Klein [3] in her work on *child analysis*. Here again we have to deal with inferences. She emphasizes (*a*) the importance of early mechanisms of introjection and projection, (*b*) the importance of anxiety as an instigator of defence, (*c*) the importance of sadistic impulses in instigating anxiety, and (*d*) the gradual expansion of reality-sense and of a capacity for objectivity as the result of

[1] [Note (1955): The converse of this proposition does not hold quite so firmly. It is a clinical commonplace that manifest sexual regressions can occur without any manifest ego-disorder. Analytical investigation, it is true, does show that profound sexual regressions tend to light up earlier ego-reactions, but these ego changes are not so extensive as the sexual regressions activated in ego-regression.]

conflict between an arbitrary Id and an almost equally unrealistic super-ego.

Taking this and other recent work [4] into account, it becomes clear that stages in the development of reality-sense should not be considered solely in terms of *impulse* or *object*, but should be related to *stages in the mastery of anxiety*, in which the rôle of libidinal and destructive impulse is alternating. In the long run, of course, the definition of reality-testing must be in the simplest terms of instincts and their objects. And I have already formulated such a definition. But the *demarcation of stages* cannot be achieved without an accurate understanding of the earliest phantasy systems and of the mechanisms for dealing with the anxieties these systems arouse.[1] From the adult point of view the 'reality' systems of infants and children are predominantly[2] phantastic, and this in turn is a necessary consequence of the type of mental mechanism predominating during these infantile stages, e.g. introjection, projection, etc.

Secondly, whatever the analysis of children may establish concerning the mental content from which we can infer stages in development of reality-sense, *this must have an intelligible relation to the order of perceptual experience of the external world*. And this involves not only a greater number of child analyses but *an entirely new behaviouristic study of infancy*. In particular, a more detailed investigation is needed of the nature, order and 'scatter' of early anxiety formations. And by this term I do not mean those commonly described 'primary infantile phobias' (e.g. fear of the dark, of strangers, or of being alone), to which, owing no doubt to our preoccupation with the antecedents of castration anxiety, our attention hitherto has been rather exclusively directed. Above all, the *minor* phobias require systematization. These are signalized not so much by glaring anxiety reactions, but by less obtrusive manœuvres, e.g. transitory immobilization, turning away attention, sudden drowsiness, decreased play-activity, or on the other hand by concentration of attention combined with slight restlessness, increased play and so forth. As I have suggested, the earliest displacements of interest from immediate instinctual objects are

---

[1] [Note (1955): This is not very happily expressed. Early unconscious phantasy systems *reflect* anxiety as much as they *activate* it.

[2] [Note (1955): See qualifying footnote on 'reality', Chap. XI, p. 178.]

stimulated by anxiety of whatever sort. Moreover, these displacements are governed by symbolism, a process which is in part
responsible for their apparently illogical order. Nevertheless, there
is every reason to believe that the frequency and order of presentation of external perceptions plays a part in the *focusing* of infantile
anxieties as it does in the formation of adult phobias. The more
an adult phobia is attached to 'unusual' objects or situations the
more successful it is: e.g. it is more advantageous to suffer from a
tiger-phobia in London than in an Indian jungle. What we already
know of infantile instinct would lead us to suppose that, symbolic
factors apart, the child's interest should radiate out from its own
body (in particular oral, glottal, gastric and respiratory zones, in
other words, inner things) to food, food organs and appurtenances;
from skin (and in particular zonal promontories and invaginations)
to its own clothes and the clothes of external objects; from excretory zones, organs and content (again almost exclusively inner
things) to excretory paraphernalia and the excretory areas of
external objects, ultimately to non-excretory contacts, smells,
colours, noises and tastes; from body and clothes in general to cot,
bed, room, furniture, curtains, hangings, shadows; from the presence or anchorage of 'instinctual' objects to intermittent absence,
disappearance or detachability of certain 'concrete objects'. Thus
experience of the presence or absence of the nipple (breast, body,
mother), establishes a criterion of interest in all moving or movable
objects coming within sensory range of the child in its cot (clothes,
toys, flies, etc.). And not only concrete objects but moving
shadows on the wall, beams of sunlight, recurrent noises and
smells. In this sense perceptual experiences are classified by
instinctual experiences, but the factor of recurrence (familiarity)
cannot be ignored. Sporadic stimuli may be, doubtless are,
ignored unless their intensity is such as to provoke anxiety. But
recurring impressions provide the earliest avenues of displacement.
In other words, *we may infer that stages in the sense of reality
will combine an instinctual order, an order of anxiety-defence, an
apparently illogical but actually symbolic order and a natural
preceptual order [of a series of object-relationships]*. The apparently
illogical order of infantile interest is, however, not due solely
to the fact that repression has converted a primary interest or
displacement of interest into a symbolism. All-important as
symbolism is, we must not neglect the ignorance, blindness, lack

of *Einfühlung* and unconscious anxiety of the behaviouristic observer, as the result of which an *adult order of perceptual interest is imposed on the natural order of the child, and is erroneously regarded as normal for the child.*[1]

But pending more precise analytic and behaviouristic investigations of children, we may with advantage review the possibilities of *adult* research. It has to be admitted that our interest in adult psycho-pathology has been too specialized and circumscribed. We have been so exclusively concerned with the etiology of individual neuroses and psychoses that the relations of these to other social or sexual abnormalities have been by comparison neglected. It is not difficult to imagine that pathological data could be so arranged as to give a distorted reflection of normal development. But this involves a more detailed and systematic classification than has hitherto been attempted. Some time ago I endeavoured to outline such a classification [6]. By including a number of characterological abnormalities it was possible to arrange parallel developmental

---

[1] This interest in a new behaviouristic study is not based solely on the need for additional clinical data. It would prepare the ground for a fresh discussion of the old controversy regarding endopsychic and external factors in development or in illness. Modern tendencies in psychoanalysis have swung away from theories of traumatic environmental experiences and it would appear that the recent contributions of child analysts reinforce these conclusions very strongly. In a sense that is true: ideas of traumatic genito-sexual experiences in childhood have been so recast that they are now regarded as on occasion exercising a favourable influence on development. But their place has been taken by others. The significance of enema experiences as representing a violent attack by the real mother on the actual body of the child has now been more adequately valued. But investigation cannot stop here. To the infant with reinforced respiratory erotism and sadism, violent expulsion of breath is a sadistic attack [5]. Hence it follows that when its parents or nurses cough or sneeze they are attacking or seducing the child. When the child envelops its enemies with destructive darkness by the simple expedient of shutting its eyes, it is only natural that the drawing of nursery curtains by the mother should be regarded as a counter attack. There is no difficulty in observing that infants do react with fear to such current events. And the same argument can be applied to primal scene hypotheses. If the parents can be thought of as copulating with their breath, [respiratory impregnation], the conversation of parents may under certain circumstances be a primal scene. In short, we have not yet solved the problem of endopsychic and external stimuli. We have merely laid ourselves under the obligation to investigate it at an earlier level and in more primitive terms.

series in accordance with the predominance respectively of primitive introjection and primitive projection mechanisms. It was also possible to narrow the gulf between the psychoses and the neuroses by the interpolation, not of 'borderline psychoses' but of 'transitional states' such as drug addiction. Thus I would place the average drug addiction as transitional between the paranoias and obsessional character formations, the reason being that in drug addictions the projection mechanisms are more localized and disguised than in the paranoias, yet stronger than in obsessional disorders. In drug addictions the projection mechanisms are focused (localized) on the noxious drugs: in obsessional states the need for projection is lessened by the existence of restitutive reaction-formations.

But although these correlations were of necessity rather sketchy, one point emerged from a study of transitional formations, such as drug addiction [7]. It became clear that by localizing his paranoid systems on the noxious drug, the drug addict is able *to preserve his reality-sense from gross psychotic disturbance*. Owing to the fact that we have as yet no adequate terminology for describing reality stages, it is difficult to express this more precisely. Borrowing, however, the over-simple and one-sided terminology of libidinal primacies, we can state the position as follows: whereas the paranoiac regresses to an *oral-anal reality system*, the drug addict regresses to the point where the infant is *emerging* from this oral-anal reality system. In other words, up to this point the external world has represented a combination of a butcher's shop, a public lavatory under shell-fire, and a post-mortem room. And the drug addict converts this into a more reassuring and fascinating chemist's shop, in which, however, the poison cupboard is left unlocked. Having to this extent reduced the paranoid dangers of the immediate world the infant (or addict) gains breathing space in which to look out of the window (assess objective reality).

It was this observation that first directed my attention to *the possibility of reconstructing the development of reality-sense from adult psycho-pathological data alone.*

In the first place it was obvious that even amongst drug addictions there was an apparent order of complexity, which together with prognostic differences suggested a definite order of regression. If then there was a definite order of regression within the addiction group, presumably the stages in development of reality-sense corresponding to addictions were equally complicated. There can be no doubt about the structural differences in drug habits. Not only are there addictions of a melancholic as well as of a paranoid type, but it is clear from examination of the phantasy material that the different component instincts are responsible for some of the clinical variations. There seems no alternative but to consider the possibility of a natural order amongst the component impulses similar to, possibly bound up with, the order of primacy of erotogenic zones.

Study of drug addictions brought out another problem in classification which has also some bearing on the development of reality-sense, viz.: the significance of perversion formations and fetichistic phenomena so commonly accompanying drug habits. Biased no doubt by Freud's pronouncements on the subject, in particular his view that the neurosis is the negative of the perversion, I had already had difficulty in 'placing' the perversions in a systematic classification of psycho-pathological states. I was inclined at first to arrange the psychoses and neuroses in a single developmental series, and then to interpolate the perversions at different points in the main sequence. Thus starting with the psychoses, I took drug addictions as a transitional type, introduced thereafter the more primitive polymorphous perversions, continued with the obsessional neuroses, introduced here the fetiches and homosexual perversions, and ended with the hysterias, sexual inhibitions and social anxieties. But there were many reasons why this order could not be maintained. In particular, experience of the analysis of homosexual perversions, obsessional neuroses and psychotic states showed both direct and indirect evidence of a much more complicated regressional or developmental order. It can frequently be observed that during psychotic crises occurring in some analyses patients develop *transitory* perversion formations of a standard type. During the analysis of a schizoid state to the superficial layers of which was attached an active homosexual perversion, one of my patients was subjected to a severe heterosexual love trauma. The immediate result was not only a strengthening of schizophrenic features, but a regression of the active homosexual formation first of all to a passive phase and then to a polymorphous excretory ceremonial with both active and passive components, but without any tactile experience. The obvious feature in this regression was the weakening of true object relations in favour of 'part' object relations. In the excretory ceremonial the 'complete object' was never seen, much less touched. Less obvious at first was the fact that these ceremonials acted as a protection against anxieties liable to induce schizophrenic systems. In other words, *they assisted in maintaining the patient's reality-sense to some degree.* The perversion ceremonials were not constant: they *alternated* with phases of schizophrenic depression. Between ceremonials he became markedly schizophrenic: his reality-sense suffered extreme diminution.

Some additional details may illustrate this point more clearly. The patient's heterosexual advances included some playful strangling gestures: his standardized form of homosexual interest concentrated mainly on the buttock area and included a very high degree of idealization particularly of the anal ring.[1] The sudden regression involved visiting a lavatory (especially after having had a lonely meal) and there carrying out with mixed feelings of anxiety and guilt, yet with fascination and great temporary re-assurance a complicated series of active and passive anal exposures through a hole in the partition. Contact was strictly limited to the passing of suggestive notes of invitation through the spyhole; the person in question was never recognized. Moreover, the slightest suspicion of aggression broke the spell. For example, to pass pieces of stained or wet toilet paper through the hole or over the partition induced an immediate and terrified flight reaction. This cubicle ceremonial followed a brief phase in which urinary exposures were practised. The urinary ritual was abandoned because of the degree of contact with recognizable objects and the presence of a number of other neutral (potentially suspicious) onlookers in public lavatories.

These are not in themselves uncommon forms of ritual: their special interest lies in the fact that the ceremonial functioned as a regression to a previously unfamiliar or unknown technique. In other cases the more primitive form of ritual is already apparent or practised in a modified way as part of a more advanced homosexual

---

[1] I have been greatly impressed by the combined re-assurance and screening function of idealization in this and many other cases. It seems to me to be much less than we have thought, a simple derivative of aim-inhibited impulse exaggerated for purposes of defence. The most urgent forms of idealization (mostly in symbolic form) occur in psychotic characters; schizoid and cyclothymic. [See Chap. XVIII.]

relation with complete objects, but becomes accentuated by regression. One patient divided his homosexual relations into a friendly group with or without genito-anal connection and an extremely erotic group characterized by violent hostile feeling and violent erotic action towards the object *who was thought of simply as one or more organs held together by an indifferent mass of connective tissue – the body.* When the regression occurred the more advanced homosexual relations disappeared for the time being, and gave place to a complete lavatory ceremonial. In this case also the spyhole system reduced the object's body to the dimensions of a part object. Should a hat or other part of the ordinary external clothing be seen, the spell was immediately broken. This was obviously determined by the symbolism of the clothes, but the patient's rationalization was interesting, viz.: that it was 'too much like a real person'. These cubicle systems bear some resemblance to certain types of masturbation, for example, where the subject visits a museum and has orgasm without erection on contemplating fragments of statuary, the torso, head or hands. In other melancholic and schizoid cases I have frequently noted that relief of depression with corresponding increase of reality-sense was preceded by an uprush of primitive sado-masochistic phantasy. Frequently attempts are made by such patients to sidetrack their phantasies into adult genito-sexual relations. But as a rule the attempts fail or are unsatisfactory, in which case there is a notable drive towards perversion-formation. This may take an alloerotic or autoerotic form. As an example of the latter I would cite a depressed case who passed through a transitory phase of going to a lavatory where she stripped, defæcated and urinated into the hand basin and played with the substances with a mixed feeling of anxiety and adoration. During this phase the actual depression disappeared. In short, although I have long held that the ordinary systematized homosexual relations constitute a defensive and restitutive system protecting against earlier anxieties as well as against later purely genito-sexual anxieties, I believe that in most cases the link is not direct, that there is a deeper 'perverted' system (repressed and therefore not featuring directly as a perversion), which corresponds more accurately with the original anxiety system. And this I believe must be uncovered before adequate contact can be made with the repressed anxiety system. From the therapeutic point of view I believe however that this tendency to regression in perversion-formation should not exceed a transitory formation, and if possible should be short circuited by interpretation of repressed perversion phantasies.

Even more curious is the stablization of reality relations which can be effected by transitory fetichistic interests. I have previously reported a case [7] in which an obsessional neurotic passed through a phase of drug addiction, the termination of which was signalized by a transitory paranoid regression. During the recovery from the paranoid phase, a temporary fetich-formation was observed. This evidently functioned as a substitute for the paranoid reaction to reality. Having localized the anxiety on a neutral yet symbolic set of body organs (legs), and having counteracted it by a process of libidinization (fetich-formation), the patient was able to recover reality relations.

Taking these facts into consideration, the problem of relating perversions to psychoses, neuroses and other social and sexual abnormalities is to some extent simplified. *It appears likely not only that perversions show an orderly series of differentiations as regards both aim and completeness of object, but that this developmental order runs parallel to the developmental order of psychoses, transitional states, neuroses and social inhibitions.* This obviates the necessity of *interpolating* perversions in any classificatory series of psychoses and neuroses. It is merely necessary to recognize or discover the elements of a *parallel series.* Following these ideas further it would appear plausible that waves of libidinization and true symptom formation are both exaggerations of normal modes of overcoming anxiety, having moreover a compensatory or protective interconnection or alternation. The main problem could then be formulated thus: Do perversions form a developmental series reflecting stages of overcoming anxiety of the individual's own body or of external objects by excessive libidinization? And as a corollary do they not only help to preserve reality sense in other departments of the psyche but *indicate the order in which reality sense develops?*

The arguments in favour of attempted reassurance by excessive libidinization are not very seriously in dispute (see, for example, Freud's [8] remarks on the etiological relation of hate to homosexuality). The arguments against a developmental series are mainly (*a*) the 'polymorphous' conception of infantile sexuality, (*b*) the generalization that the *neurosis* is the negative of the perversion. As regards the first point I have already indicated that the term 'polymorphous' although accurate enough in a general descriptive sense and by comparison with genital. impulse is too vague for present-day purposes. We are already more fully informed as to the orderly development of infantile impulse during the first years, and as research on children becomes more precise, the term will become superfluous. As for the second point: this generalization, viz. that the neurosis is the negative of the perversion, is still profoundly true but in a strictly limited sense. It is completely accurate for those perversions and fetiches which run parallel to their appropriate neuroses, e.g. a glove fetich and an antiseptic handwashing mania. But we must now add that certain perversions are the negative of certain psychotic formations and certain others the negative of transitional psychoses. Indeed, following Ferenczi [9] and considering the mixed clinical pictures of psychosis, perversion and neurosis one so frequently observes, it is worth inquiring whether a perversion is not in many cases a *symptomatic formation in obverse* or the sequela or antecedent of a symptom as the case may be – a prophylactic or a curative device?

A further difficulty lies in the earlier pronouncement of Freud [10] that perversions are not formed directly from component impulses, but that the components in question must first have been refracted through an Oedipus phase. So long as this pronouncement referred to a stereotyped Oedipus phase occurring between three to five years of age, it practically paralysed etiological differentiation, as witness Fenichel's textbook [11], in which the etiology of perversions is somewhat monotonously described in terms of castration anxiety. But since Freud [12] has sanctioned a broader use of the term 'Oedipus', we are quite free to consider a chronological element in perversion-formation. Even so, the idea of layering in perversion-formation has always been hinted at. Sachs [13] advanced this view on the grounds that repression was a serial process. Rank [14] too considered that the perversion group had different layers of evolution relating to corresponding psychic systems or localities, but he narrowed his generalization by stating that the pervert remains fixated to the stage before the wish for a child, suggesting that the pervert's inhibition is directed specifically against 'generative libido'. Both writers regard the determining factor as libidinal, and the accompanying anxiety as castration anxiety. The only serious objection to classifying perversions has been made by Fenichel. He does not believe that it is practicable to produce a classification corresponding to that of the neuroses, i.e. in accordance with the depth of regression and the nature of object relations. This, he says, is due to the absence in perversions of the element of *distortion* which characterizes neuroses and renders them amenable to classification. Clinically speaking, this is an unsatisfactory state of affairs. I would suggest that difficulties in classification are due rather to the incomplete nature of our researches. In any case clinical differences in perversions are quite as striking as differences in neurotic distortion.

Now it appears to me that Rank was nearer to the solution of the problem when he said that sadism, in so far as it excluded guilt, was the true type of perversion. I would suggest that in the history of sadism or rather the aggressive and destructive impulses we have a sounder guide to the etiology and order of perversion-formation. Libidinal history, it is true, gives the positive and manifest content of the formation. But apart from this the main function of the libidinal contribution is a protective one. Sachs himself pointed out the relation of perversions to phobia formations: but he did not apply this view logically to the whole of infantile history. He restricted himself to castration phobias, neglecting thereby the more primitive infantile phobias. The importance of the study of perversions in relation to reality-sense is that perversions represent periodic attempts to protect against current introjection and projection anxieties by a process of excessive libidinization. In some cases the libidinization is directed towards those parts of the body (either of subject or of object) which are threatened in the unconscious phantasy system: in others the mechanism of displacement introduces an additional element of defence and disguise. In others again it is the mode of gratification that is libidinized rather than the objects believed to be in danger in the phantasy. In all cases, however, there is some degree of interference with adult genito-sexual function. In other words, *perversions assist in preserving the amount of reality-sense already achieved by what in the long run represents a sacrifice of freedom in adult libidinal function*, whereas the neuroses often allow a degree of freedom of adult libidinal function at the cost of some inhibition of reality relations, and the psychoses frequently show an apparent freedom of adult libidinal function accompanied by gross disturbances of reality-sense.

To sum up: We are justified in postulating a constantly changing (developmental) series of anxiety situations which, should they become overcharged, give rise to a phase either of symptom-formation or of perversion-formation. This generalization can then be turned to advantage in the study of reality-sense and its development. As Klein has pointed out, stable reality relations cannot be established so long as primitive anxieties have not been mastered. This is all the more true of the faculty of objectivity. In other words, reality-sense depends upon the *emancipation* of systems of bodily and environmental perception from excessive interference through projection and introjection mechanisms. And this emancipation occurs in a definite order which I suggest provisionally to be corporeal zones or organs, food, clothes and ejecta, whether belonging to the self or to instinctual objects.

The course of events can be described somewhat as follows: As a result of alternating processes of projection and introjection, brought about by frustration of instinct, the child's relation to what the adult observer would call objective reality, becomes distorted and unreal. Nevertheless, the child during this phase has some primitive objective reality of its own. In the first place it has psychic contact not only with objects catering for crude self-preservative instincts, but with objects actually threatening self-preservation (real external dangers, injury and aggression): secondly, it has contact with that part of reality which does gratify some love needs. This enclave of infantile objective reality is swamped by the distorted products of fear. One of the primitive cures for this distortion is the process of libidinization. Libidinization cancels or holds in suspense some of the unreal fear systems and it does so by neutralizing sadism. This process is soon reinforced by some form of repression. The result is that the original nucleus of infantile reality can be *extricated* from the mass of unreal reactions. This libidinizing system is never really abandoned, although its most dramatic effects are to be observed just before repression becomes really massive. Adult objective reality is a by-product of this process. Once rescued, infantile objective reality expands through the auxiliary devices of displacement and sublimation to the limits of adult necessity or interest. Only when sadism is adequately neutralized can sublimation proceed and, following the track of symbolism, add to our reality contacts. *Adult objective reality, self-preservation apart, is not so much some-*

thing we come to recognize, as an inheritance from infancy, something we maintain possession of and expand after it has passed through screens of fear, libidinization and sublimation. In some respects it is a residue, a view which is in keeping with the fact that in many ways adults are less objective than children. This expanded inheritance or residue functions to a large extent as a guarantee of the absence of fear. It is manifestly limited in accordance with the range of individual interest plus the range of interest of individuals we either love or hate.

When, for whatever cause, some form of infantile anxiety is re-animated or exacerbated in adult life, one of many ways of dealing with this crisis is the reinforcement of primitive libidinization systems. *This gives rise to what we call a perversion.* I agree with Searl [4] that sublimation can be successful only provided reality is not too highly libidinized, which means in turn, provided the problem of sadism has been solved. Nevertheless, this does not contradict the view that a *localized* excessive libidinization (i.e. a perversion) may, by sacrificing *some* relations to reality, *some* sublimations and *some* adult genital function, preserve a reality relation over a wide area. Perversions help to patch over flaws in the development of reality-sense. For this reason the more primitive perversions are in some respects more compulsive than advanced homosexual perversions. They are more appropriate cures for old anxieties. The drawback of primitive perversions is that they are nearer to the source of anxiety, i.e. *too* appropriate. Ordinary homosexuality reassures mainly in respect of *complete objects, not of primitive 'part' objects.* The apparent gradual increase in the capacity of libido to reassure is to my mind more apparent than real. Or perhaps it would be more accurate to say a concern with real love objects, though undoubtedly a great source of reassurance is a less appropriate cure for primitive anxieties than is a primitive love of part objects. Here we have a theoretical justification for the view put forward by Melanie Klein [3] that under favourable circumstances infantile sexual experiences may promote reality development. But we must accept also the conclusion that such experiences, whether of active or passive nature, accidental or sought-after, promote reality development only in so far as they function as infantile perversions.

I have indicated the lines along which adult psycho-pathological material may be investigated in order to discover the stages of development of reality-sense. Apart from this particular interest I believe the attempt is worth making if only to reduce existing confusions regarding the classification of mental disorders. It remains to indicate what are the most profitable lines of research and what are the most serious obstacles to progress. As regards immediate lines of approach, I am to some extent biased by the accidental circumstance that my own material came within the group of transitional states, perversions and obsessional neuroses. And although I am bound to agree that analytical study of, for example, the stereotypies of schizophrenia, to say nothing of so-called hysterical phobias, will prove invaluable in this connection, I am inclined to believe that a better sense of perspective will be obtained by starting at the point where transitional psychoses, perversions and obsessional neuroses meet. Indeed I have the impression that one of the most profitable approaches to the study of reality-sense lies in the study of fetishism, including here *narcissistic fetiches* in which parts of the patient's own body or clothes provide sexual gratification. There is in fetishism a degree of localization of interest and stereotyping of displacement which promises to give more exact information of early anxiety systems than does the average ramifying perversion. Freud [15] himself has pointed out that the denial of anxiety effected by fetishism is similar to the psychotic denial of reality.

I have used the term narcissistic fetich with reluctance. On the one hand I believe that what we call 'erotic narcissism' is a compound of true autoerotic activities and concealed alloerotic relations with 'part' objects. Again the term masturbation is notoriously unsatisfactory. And the same applies to descriptive terms such as transvestitism. Many of the phenomena I have observed would be regarded descriptively as half-way between transvestitism and masturbation. Yet I hold they are fetishistic in principle, just as many other of the so-called spontaneous sexual activities of childhood are already – in principle – perversions.

Compare, for example, the following two systems observed in one case. The individual in question had a simple piano fetich, that is to say, contact with a piano of a certain type (i.e. with a new and shiny case) induced sexual excitement and orgasm, with or without manual manipulation. Thereafter the same piano gradually lost its stimulating effect. A scratched or faded or worm-eaten piano case was taboo. On the other hand, whenever the patient put on new articles of clothing, in particular when he purchased a new suit, he developed an erection lasting twelve hours at least, and ending sometimes in orgasm. During this period he was in a state of extreme happiness. Another case combined a motor car fetich, which lost effect as soon as the car was splashed with mud or the upholstery spotted with grease, with masturbatory excitement over his own shoes when they were new and so long as the original shine was preserved intact. In both these cases the apparently autoerotic manifestation corresponded closely to the object-system.

The examples I have given may serve to illustrate one of the many obstacles to research on this subject: viz.: the fact that terms such as 'narcissism', 'auto-erotism', 'component impulse', 'poly-morphous perverse', etc., have to some extent outworn their usefulness.

A second difficulty is also brought out by the study of fetichism, viz.: the fact that obsessional neuroses are inadequately subdivided or classified. I have already described an obsessional case in which a transitory fetich interest helped to promote convalescence from a paranoid phase. And I have frequently observed that cases of drug addiction develop (during abstinence) transitory obsessional symptoms rather localized in action. So much so that I have described some of these obsessional reactions as 'negative feti-chistic phenomena'. Many localized contamination phobias with or without washing-manias are of this type, and can be observed to alternate with erotic interest in the same parts of the body.

Referring in an earlier paper to the etiology of fetichism I wrote [7]: 'perhaps two rough formulations are permissible: (1) that in the transition between paranoidal systems and a normal reaction to reality, drug-addiction (and later on fetichism) represent not only continuations of the anxiety system within a contracted range, but the beginnings of an expanding reassurance system. The reassur-ance is due to contributions from later libidinal stages in infancy which contain a decreasing amount of sadism. (2) That clothing in general is, after food, the next line of defence in overcoming paranoidal reactions to reality. It apears reasonable to suppose that the first paranoid systems of the child attach themselves to food, that these anxieties are modified not only by the appear-ance of less sadistic impulse but by a determined effort at displacement of anxiety. In this displacement clothes play their part. When subsequently displacement leads to reactions to the clothes of external objects, the foundation of the classical fetich is laid. So that when anxiety is excessive the result is either a typical sexual fetich or the negative form, viz.: a contamination phobia'.

Finally, study of the etiology of fetichism brings out what is perhaps one of the most important immediate obstacles to the understanding of reality development, viz.: the lack of systematized information as to the exact nature of the oral phase of development. The first etiological formulations concerning fetichism singled out phallic, scopophilic and sadistic factors: later the importance of the imagined phallus of the mother was increasingly emphasized. Still more recently the significance of other elements has been stressed. Freud had himself remarked that the fetich chosen may not necessarily be a common penis symbol, and we now know from the work of Ella Sharpe [16] and others that this is due to the contribution of pregenital elements, e.g. oral sadism. But the more universal such factors are found to be, the less helpful they are in etiological differentiation. Without making one single analytical observation one might safely assume from behaviouristic data that the first phase of infantile development must be predominantly oral. Even the existence of a phallic interest during the oral phase might well have been inferred without analysis. The more analysis confirms the importance of these early interests the more urgent it becomes to sub-divide the oral stages and to consider the part played during what we now call the first oral stage by other important erotogenic zones and by component impulses, in particular respiratory, gastric, muscle, anal and urinary erotism. It is not enough to establish the outlines of development in terms of phases. More detailed differentiation is needed before we can provide these etiological formulæ which the existence of clinical variations in mental disorder demands.

BIBLIOGRAPHY

1. FERENCZI: 'Stages in the Development of the Sense of Reality'. *Contributions to Psycho-Analysis*, Badger-Boston, 1916.

2. FEDERN: 'Some Variations in Ego-feeling', *Int. J. Psycho-Anal.*, 1926, 7, 434; 'Narcissism in the Structure of the Ego'; ibid., 1928, 9, 401; 'Das Ich als Subjekt und Objekt im Narzissmus', *Int. Z. Psychoanal.*, 1929, 15, S. 393; 'Das Ichgefühl im Traume'; ibid., 1932, 18, S. 145 [in *Ego Psychology and the Pychoses*, Imago Pub. Co., 1953].

3. KLEIN: *The Psycho-Analysis of Children*, Hogarth Press, 1932.

4. SCHMIDEBERG: 'The Rôle of Psychotic Mechanisms in Cultural Development', *Int. J. Psycho-Anal.*, 1930, **9**, p. 387; 'The Psychology of Persecutory Ideas and Delusions'; ibid., 1931, **12**, p. 331; 'Zur Psychoanalyse asozialer Kinder und Jugendlicher', *Int. Z. Psychoanal.*, 1932, **18**, S. 474; also SEARL: 'The Flight to Reality', *Int. J. Psycho-Anal.*, 1929, **10**, p. 280; 'Danger Situations of the Immature Ego'; ibid., 1929, **10**, p. 423; 'The Rôles of Ego and Libido in Development'; ibid., 1930, **11**, p. 125; 'A Note on Depersonalisation'; ibid., 1932, **13**, p. 329.

5. SEARL: 'The Psychology of Screaming', *Int. J. Psycho-Anal.*, 1933, **14**, p. 193.

6. GLOVER: 'A Psycho-Analytic approach to the Classification of Mental Disorders', *Brit. J. Ment. Sci.*, October, 1932 [Chap. XI, this volume].

7. GLOVER. 'On the Etiology of Drug Addiction', *Int. J. Psycho-Anal.*, 1932, **13** [Chap. XII, this volume].

8. FREUD: 'Certain Neurotic Mechanisms in Jealousy, Paranoia and Homosexuality', [*C.P.* Vol. II, 1923].

9. FERENCZI: 'The Nosology of Male Homosexuality', *Contributions to Psycho-Analysis*, Boston, 1916.

10. FREUD: 'A Child is Being Beaten', [*C.P.* Vol. II, 1923]. See also *Introductory Lectures on Psycho-analysis*, Allen & Unwin, 1929.

11. FENICHEL: *Perversionen, Psychosen, Charakterstörungen*, I.P.V., 1931.

12. FREUD: 'Female Sexuality', *Int. J. Psycho-Anal.*, 1932, **13**, p. 281, [*C.P.* Vol. V, 1950].

13. SACHS: 'Zur Genese der Perversionen', *Int. Z. Psychoanal.*, 1923, **9**, S. 173.

14. RANK: 'Perversion und Neurose', *Int. Z. Psychoanal.*, 1922, **8**, S. 397.

15. FREUD: 'Fetichism', *Int. J. Psycho-Anal.*, 1928, **9**, p. 161 [*C.P.* Vol. V].

16. SHARPE: Lecture on 'Fetichism and Art', British Psycho-Analytical Society, November 18, 1931. [See also 'Similar and Divergent Unconscious Determinants Underlying Sublimations of Pure Art and Pure Science', *Int. J. Psycho-Anal.*, **16**, 186-202, April, 1935.]

XIV

MEDICO-PSYCHOLOGICAL ASPECTS OF NORMALITY*

[1932]

It is now a psycho-analytical commonplace to say that the 'normal' mind is more difficult to understand and to explain than the 'abnormal' or 'disordered' mind. This is borne out by the fact that analysts themselves are more at loggerheads regarding such concepts as 'ego-strength' than they are about 'ego-weakness'. Obviously, however, if we take the liberty of speaking of 'disorder' or 'abnormality', we cannot escape the task of describing 'order' or 'normality', however much the task may expose us to the risks of wandering from metapsychology into metaphysics. Certainly there is no competent psycho-analytical consultant but makes use of working standards of 'normality' or 'normal adaptability'; yet his theoretical definitions may vary widely from those of his clinical colleagues. The following paper constitutes an early attempt to define the nature and range of normality. It should be read in conjunction with the papers on 'The Psychology of the Psycho-Therapeutist' (Chap. VI) and 'The Concept of Dissociation' (Chap. XX).

I. HISTORICAL: THE INTRODUCTION OF PSYCHOLOGICAL STANDARDS

Alongside the immunities conferred on medical practitioners by Act of Parliament, there run certain unwritten privileges of a unique order. Perhaps the most important of these is the right of each practitioner to establish a standard of normality for his patients. Had this been restricted to the sphere of organic medicine, to distinguishing between physiological and pathological function, the privilege might well have gone unchallenged. What ultimately undermined the doctor's authority was the invasion of his consulting room by an expectant file of psycho-neurotics; these made the most convincing show of organic illness, yet remained in many cases refractory to every nostrum. In face of this reduction of

* Delivered before the British Psychological Society, Feb. 29th, 1932, and published in *The British Journal of Psychology*, Vol. XXIII, pt. 2, Oct. 1932.

authority and laceration of professional pride, the physician was quick to take steps to repel the invasion. He had two alternative plans of campaign, one conscious, the other unconscious. The unconscious plan consisted in falling in with the patient's belief in his own illness and exacting revenge by a series of painful and sometimes humiliating retaliations. He drew the dyspeptic spinster's teeth, removed the unconscious homosexual's appendix, scoured the conversion hysteric's uterus, purged the latent paranoid hypochondriac's bowels and injected all and sundry with vaccines or glandular extracts. The alternative and conscious plan was to oppose the patient's view that he was sick, convince him of this palpable untruth and return him to his friends rejoicing or lamenting, as the case might be. Both of these methods are essentially suggestive in nature.

But in this neurotic combat, the doctor's victory was never very secure; it was gradually turned into a partial defeat by the superior enlightenment of the lay public. Modern psychotherapy owes a great deal of its authority to the fact that in psychological respects, patients are more up-to-date than their doctors. Anyhow, for good or ill, psychological medicine became a speciality, and with the formation of this new branch it was no longer necessary to eject psychological cases on to the pavements of Harley Street in a state of suppressed fury and disappointment. But by the same token *the old organic standards of normality went by the board*. Their disappearance was accelerated by the increasing demands made by the lay public. The obsessional neurotic with his peculiar mental constructions had followed in the footsteps of the hysteric, the borderline psychotic had followed the obsessional, but now the unhappy and the maladapted, dejected husbands and dissatisfied wives, and every sort of idiosyncratic character type, all crowded into the consulting room demanding attention.

In the face of this fresh invasion, the courage of the new medico-psychological specialist failed him; and he began to copy the tactics of his predecessors. Unhappy and incapacitated cases who could not produce a respectable psychological symptom narrowly escaped being called social malingerers. And once more Harley Street resounded with a hum of admonition punctuated by firm slamming of doors. In course of time some of these therapeutic outcasts were treated by psycho-analysis, a method that had already been found useful in hysteria and obsessional neuroses.

The results of these early experiments were patchy. Some remarkable successes were offset by minimal improvement in many other cases, in spite of years of patient work. Nevertheless, the amount of success was such that *it was no longer possible to exclude a capacity for personal happiness and peace of mind from the professional categories of normality.*

II. WORKING PSYCHO-ANALYTICAL DEFINITION:

DIFFICULTIES AND OBJECTIONS

To round off this compressed history; the psycho-analyst has found himself compelled, owing to the nature of his case material, to include amongst the standards of *abnormality* not only bodily symptoms and psychic symptom constructions, but various social inhibitions and degrees of maladjustment in work and love. He stipulates, however, that these maladjustments should be accompanied by sufficient affective discomfort to drive the patient to consultation. In so doing he has committed himself to a tentative definition of *normality*. As I expressed it once 'a normal individual is anyone who is free from symptoms, unhampered by mental conflict and who shows satisfactory working capacity': to complete this definition I would now add 'and who is able to love someone apart from himself'.

Now the flaw in this system of definition is obvious: I cannot add the rider that anyone who does *not* come to consultation is sufficiently happy and well adapted to be called normal. There are innumerable social occasions when casual observation compels us to recognize the apprehensions, eccentricities, inhibitions and symptom formations permeating everyday life. Perhaps the most impressive example is that organized 'health movement', which seeks to canonize anxiety reactions as part of a praiseworthy hygienic system. It is not simply that our advertisement columns encourage intestinal hypochondria by the terrifying caption 'Constipation', or that we are exhorted to purify the blood, to kill flies, to wear soft collars, expand the chest and breathe pure air, use carbolic soap or drink hot water: the fact is we are encouraged to invest every round of waking activity with a typical neurotic or psychotic anxiety charge. And the man in the street enters into this fearsome conspiracy with feelings that range from intimidated acquiescence to almost religious enthusiasm. I shall not labour the point further, merely asserting that this inculcation and expression of mass anxiety can be tracked down to individual anxieties, in fact that within the range of socially accepted normality, we can detect reactions which, were they manifested during an analysis, would be regarded as 'abnormal'.

Now even if the man in the street agreed that some of his emotional phases might be regarded clinically as exceeding a normal standard, he would doubtless repudiate with warmth the suggestion that many of his most cherished habits are simply unlabelled symptoms. He would suspect and with good reason that the sanctuary of his private character was threatened. To any such protest the medical psychologist's reply would be purely professional, viz. that the character of the man in the street is quite safe from professional inspection so long as the man remains in the street. The mere fact, however, that such acute differences of opinion might arise, compels us to examine carefully all professional standards of normality.

Curiously enough a more urgent reason for investigation seems to have escaped the notice of the people most concerned. Possibly theologists, metaphysicians and sociologists are too busy with their routine work to observe that the frontiers of their sciences have been violated. Yet the appearance of the medical psychologist with his inquisitive tendency to measure happiness and peace of mind, his preoccupation with conscience and crime, his concern with categorical urges, inhibitions and the phenomena of 'will', is at the least something of a portent. And it is incumbent on the medical psychologist to justify his intrusion.

To a certain extent he has already done so; but his favourite method has usually been regarded as begging the question. He has naturally been concerned with the patently abnormal and has applied his discoveries in this field to the problem of alleged normality. For example; when the theologian has said that human guilt and original sin belong to his particular province, that happiness and misery are essentially theological measures, the medical psychologist has usually responded by producing a sheaf of case notes. Fortified by his most recent interviews with a case of melancholia or mania or manic depressive insanity, he has pointed out that the melancholiac feels and appears the incarnation of misery, that the expansive hypomanic greets us with the sunny smile of happiness. He may go further and claim that the manic depressive psychosis is essentially a conscience phenomenon, an alternating hypertrophy and atrophy of unconscious conscience. Some of these facts are not denied by lay psychologists and are accepted even by enlightened laymen; yet any attempt to apply them to normal affective states is liable to be regarded as a *non sequitur*.

III. SYSTEMATIC APPROACH

(a) Clinical

Starting with the descriptive aspects of human normality, it may be of interest that the most difficult person in the world to analyse completely is the ordinary so-called 'normal' person. Nor is this surprising observation to be explained by mere perversity. The 'normal' person resists all affective examination of his stability for a very natural if no longer justifiable reason. He resists it because his 'normality' represents a victory over an original state of madness. We no longer regard the psychoses and neuroses of adult life as spontaneous pathological disruptions and distortions of a normal life. One of the earliest and, at the time, almost incredible psychoanalytic formulations was that which ran, 'no adult neurosis without an infantile neurosis'. Already that has become a mere platitude compared with the newer and more far-reaching conclusion, 'no adult normality without an infantile "psychosis".' The formulation is not entirely original: it has been put forward at various times by the more intuitive of our writers. To quote a recent example: the author of *High Wind in Jamaica* in a curiously technical digression remarks concerning the minds of children that they 'are not just more ignorant and stupider than ours, but differ in kind of thinking (are *mad*, in fact)'. He goes on to say regarding the mentality of infants, 'one can no more think like a baby, in the smallest respect, than one can think like a bee'. And although this second pronouncement is completely wide of the mark, the former is a sound intuition. The professional psychoanalyst has reduced these and similar intuitions of naïve psychologists to an orderly systematization. Every child in the first year of life is from the adult psychiatric point of view in a state of panpsychosis always acute and very largely hallucinatory. Between the ages of 1 and $2\frac{1}{2}$ his mentality alternates between an introjective psychotic pattern (schizophrenic type with or without melancholiac elements) and a projective psychotic pattern (paranoid type). Assuming successful struggle with this phase, he emerges between 2½ and 4 with patterns of an infantile obsessional type and this phase overlaps a little with a phase of infantile hysterical reaction and phobia formation between the ages of 3 and 5. These may be regarded as the *normal psychoses* and *normal neuroses* of childhood, but any accentuation of the anxiety appropriate to one state may bring about a *clinical* infantile psychosis or neurosis; and naturally any persistence in later infancy of characteristics more appropriate to an earlier stage is also to be regarded as pathological for the later stage. There are three main reasons why these earlier psychotic patterns have not been recognized. The most superficial is that we naïvely expect the 'psychotic' reactions of a child to be identical with the clinical psychotic reactions of an adult: actually adult psychoses show certain repair aspects which are developed in response to a highly specialized environment. The second reason is more interesting to us. We ignore the 'psychotic reactions' of childhood because it would be intolerable to reanimate stages we have ourselves passed through and overcome. So we term them the 'normal reactions' of a child, even when they are plainly of a psychotic pattern. If a child rushes into our arms because it is suddenly terrified of a bundle of clothes, we are unperturbed. If an adult does the same, we gravely consider his 'certification'. The third reason is as comprehensible as the second if a little less flattering to our self-esteem. Having brought the infant into the world, we find its claims on our adult endurance too persistent and exorbitant, and are only too glad when it appears to change from a red-faced brat squalling in ectoparasitic need, to an angel face of two or three displaying endurance that entitles it to enter the Kingdom of Heaven. So we are not too ready to recognize the fact, if and when this sudden pallor of character indicates an internal drenching psychic hæmorrhage.[1]

[1] In such a brief survey, a certain amount of over-emphasis may be permitted. It is only fair to add, however, that during these 'normally psychotic phases' the average child develops a degree of adult organization with which it is seldom credited. The latter enables us to distinguish between the 'normally psychotic' and the 'clinically psychotic' child. Interesting parallel observations may be made in the field of anthropology. The 'normal' primitive tribesman combines a remarkable degree of reality organization with systems of a frankly psychotic and neurotic type, e.g. paranoid fears (animism) and obsessional systems (magic).

To return to the child of five: from then on to puberty there is apparently a lull. And in so far as it is a true lull, implying a reduction in the intensity of primitive infantile instinct, it is a well-earned rest from the anxieties and unconscious guilts of childhood. But the respite is largely a matter of surface calm. Actually the child is busy consolidating the barriers it has already thrown up against the intolerable anxiety of frustrated instinctual drives. Day after day it seeks to entrench itself in a more reassuring reality, supporting itself the while on affectionate relations with its family, the aim-inhibited residue of more tempestuous claims. And there is not too much time to lose. The child's defensive rampart will soon have to weather the last great thrust of instinct which approaches with puberty. It is not difficult to imagine the possible course of events after the first shock of puberty. If the defences break down, two possibilities are open. One individual may sooner or later develop a neurosis or a psychosis: in other words by sacrificing certain ego functions, a degree of normal relation to reality is preserved (except, of course, in the case of total regression). Another may escape open neurosis and psychosis, but he does so at the cost of a sub-acute inflammation of all his relations to reality, particularly his social contacts. We then say for purposes of description that he has developed a major characterological defect.

Should, however, the defences hold, all we can detect is a phase of volatile emotional reaction corresponding with the years of adolescence; this is followed by more or less permanent stability, only occasionally shaken by adult events of psychic importance: births, marriages and deaths, or successes and failures in career. In other words under the immediate internal impact of adult genital primacy, the ramparts of child defence, although violently shaken, remain intact and apparently solid.

Now we might say that for the adult this stable rampart system represents normality; that apart from a little cultural French polishing, *adult normality is the end-product of child defence.* But if we test this general formulation by clinical inspection of the population at large, we are once more brought up short by the number of idiosyncrasies of habit, minor symptoms of an anxiety and obsessional type to be detected in so-called normal people. And that is not all. There are times when the ramparts are so hard and enclosing that they appear to function as a mausoleum. The individual is entombed within his rigid character. The voluntary celibate, the sterile but compulsive work fiend, the shilly-shally, the miser, and the compulsive criminal, may be cited as illustrative types. Even a quantitative standard does not solve our difficulty. We might say that so long as the mausoleum type is not a nuisance to himself or to other people and neither comes nor is driven to consultation, he can be called normal. But that is only to say that socially it is not our business to interfere. If we permit ourselves the lesser interference of thinking about human behaviour, we may pass the self-appointed bachelor or spinster or even the work maniac and the doubter without comment, but we can scarcely label the miser normal without further investigation.

(b) Structural

It will be apparent that a purely descriptive approach does not allow us sufficient elbow room for measurement, so we must turn our attention to the structure and function of the ego as a whole. Making use of spatial conventions, the psycho-analyst tries to express his views of the ego by calling it a psychic organ, and still further a surface psychic organ. He fixes it in psychic space by reference to perceptual consciousness. The ego is developed round perceptual consciousness. It is a surface organ with at least two facets, one turned towards the external stimuli of the outer world, and the other turned towards the instinctual stimuli of the inner world. The instincts are represented by derivatives, either in ideational form or in the form of affects. The primary function of the ego is to assist in the reduction of psychic stimulation; and this in effect means that the ego must cater for the gratification of inner needs in so far as these can or may be gratified in the external world. If instinct cannot or may not be gratified in the external world or on the person's own body, the ego must undertake the task of mastering instinct. This mastery can be achieved in numerous ways. One is the way of repression, which if successful prevents ideational representation in consciousness and prevents the development of affect. Another way is the way of reaction formation. This is a kind of counter-charge, wherewith tendencies are reinforced which nullify or inhibit the tendencies of primitive impulse. Still another is the mechanism of sublimation whereby primitive energies are deflected from their original aim and gratified in other directions. There are many others, but taking the three I have mentioned it is to be noted that repression is silent, invisible and incalculable; reaction formation is noisily obvious; and sublimation, though obvious in end results, is much less obtrusive in operation. Now if we are going to judge normality solely by the noisier reaction mechanisms (that is to say, apply mainly characterological standards), we neglect the fact that none of these mechanisms can master instinct independently. We neglect the compensating and balancing tendency of the ego and in particular we do less than justice to the factor of repression. From this point of view our miser, though open to the charge of abnormality in a characterological respect, might plead that in the sense of ego function he was perfectly normal, that he felt perfectly comfortable in his adaptation, and finally that it was none of our business. And unless his miserliness took a form that justified social interference – such as collecting dangerous micro-organisms or high explosives without adequate precautions – we would be compelled to apologize and beat a retreat.

In passing we learn something here of the animus behind characterological studies. Fundamentally we are interested in character for self-preservative reasons: it pays to be able to estimate quickly the instinctual tendencies of our neighbours. Characterology provides us with a quick 'spotting' system for this purpose. But 'good' or 'bad' categories apart, we have a special reason for being suspicious of the terms 'normal' or 'stable' character. If we find that our neighbour is not dangerous, we are apt, partly from relief and partly on the principle of 'live and let live', to turn a blind eye upon his peculiarities. In short, *the concept of character is a legacy from naïve, conscious, self-preservative psychology for which there is little use in metapsychology.* Some years ago I endeavoured to define it as an organized series of behaviour reactions promoting a stable equilibrium between instinct tendencies and reality gratification, adding that these reactions produce a more or less harmonized adaptation through the mechanism of displacement. I believe this definition may still be of service in estimating normal aspects of character, but it must be admitted that characterology is one of the most lop-sided of psychological pursuits.

The argument so far amounts to this. Descriptive standards of normality, taken from behaviouristic psychology, are too narrow. An examination of the structure of the ego is a little more satisfactory, because it gives us a better grasp of the individual aspect of normality, viz. *a psychic organ in successful function.*

(c) Economic

It has been indicated that the function of the ego is to reduce psychic tension to an optimum level: that whatever instinct barriers are erected for this purpose, they should not impede the ego in legitimate adaptation. We can express this in another way by saying that the psyche is developed to deal with quantities of excitation, and that it does so by virtue of its conscious and unconscious appreciation of certain other quantities, viz. quantities of anxiety. For purposes of simplification, I shall include in the term anxiety that special form which by reason of its endopsychic conditioning is thought of as guilt. *The pleasure-pain principle then is seen to be the most primitive measure of normal reaction for the infant; but it cannot become an adult measure until it has undergone that slow process of modification during childhood which converts it into the reality principle.* So far the prospects of accurate definition appear rosy. But the question arises: can we regard the establishment of the reality principle as an absolute measure of adult normality? Presumably we ought to stop at this point in order to define reality: I propose, however, to approach this definition in a roundabout way. For the moment I shall simply state the conclusion that *in the present state of Western civilization we have no grounds for assuming that normality and complete reality adaptation are identical.* As the sole criterion of adaptation, the adult reality principle is inadequate: the adult must have a certain capacity for exploitation of earlier pleasure systems. But that exploitation must not induce an intolerable charge of anxiety. In other words, the two systems must not act in complete opposition. They must be mutually complementary: the pleasure system must learn to be content with the exploitation afforded by adult reality, and adult organization must be sufficiently porous to permit the safe expansion and discharge of infantile vapours.

Now in the course of examining the most primitive mechanisms set in motion by the 'pleasure-pain' principle, we make an astonishing discovery: a discovery that has considerable bearing on definitions of 'normality', to say nothing of definitions of 'reality'. Earlier in this presentation I described the first phases of childhood in terms of psychotic reaction and indicated a developmental series of 'normal' psychoses and 'normal' neuroses preceding the 'normality' of later childhood. And it may have occurred to the reader that unless this description is altogether fantastic, there must be many grades of reality differentiation. This inference can be supported by the psycho-analysis of children, normal adults and psychotics. The child sets out on its developmental journey equipped with an intolerance of anxiety which it proceeds to turn to biological advantage. When, for example, an infant suddenly turns puce, alarmed onlookers hunt for a crumb or a pin or a wet napkin: when it yells, those within earshot run to its assistance. Failing all help, the child tends to pass quickly into exhaustion and, if really deserted, would whimper its way to sleep and ultimately die. But the spirit of the age is on the whole against infanticide by neglect. The external world frantically conspires to make environment approximate to the child's demands for immediate relief. And the child responds by loving the most ready part of environment. To cut a long story short the result of these experiences is to bring about a confusion of the external and internal world. The child tends to regard the pleasure-producing environment as part of itself and tries to treat internal pain as a foreign body. But the main source of psychic tension and 'pain' is frustrated instinct and in particular frustrated aggressive instinct. When, therefore, the child tries to rid itself of this painful stimulus, it employs the most primitive mental mechanism of projection. It projects its painful instincts into the external world, which in turn is felt to be dangerous and painful. Admittedly the outer world is dangerous and painful in many respects. But it is seldom dangerous in the projected respects. A father may be cruel and stern, but he is not as a rule a dangerous homicide. A mother may be vexatious or severe, but she is not a devouring animal. Yet phobia after phobia proves that parents are so regarded in the unconscious layers of their children's minds. Out of the frying pan into the fire: projection tends to defeat its own ends and so a vicious circle is established. The more frustration, the more hate: the more hate, the more dangerous the external world: the more dangerous the external world, the more inhibition: the more inhibition, the more frustration. And so it goes on. This vicious circle is broken in two ways: first, by the auxiliary mechanism of primal repression and secondly, and this is what concerns us now, by an exploitation of 'real reality'. The more terrifying the phantasy external world, the more reassuring the actual outer world. So the hunt for reality commences. In place of the phantasied dangers, there is in some cases a positive welcoming of reality dangers and in most cases a fuller exploitation of the actual love, affection and protection afforded by family environment. Whether the original projected system is ever completely abandoned is questionable. So far analysis of the normal adult shows that his psychotic mechanisms still exist but with such a weak charge as to be negligible.

Turning once more to the task of definition, we are compelled to conclude that at present, at any rate, it is not within the scope of metapsychology to give a definition of 'absolute reality'. In spite of this we are able to attach a precise significance to the term 'reality-testing'. The metapsychological definition of 'reality-testing' is based on the view that the ego is a sampling apparatus as well as an organ for reducing instinctual excitation. *Reality-testing then, from the medical psychologists' point of view, is the capacity to maintain psychic contact with the objects which promote gratification of the modified impulses of adult life. And adult normality is a state in which infantile 'psychotic' views concerning the external world have been so reduced that they do not interfere with possibilities of adult gratification; in other words it is a state in which the psychotic estimate of the object world coincides with an objective estimate in two main respects, (a) the amount of love that can be satisfied and (b) the amount of danger to the ego that is present.*

IV. Adaptation Factors: Real and Unreal Anxiety

Once again, however, our hopes of an absolute definition of normality are dashed. Examination of our now familiar friend in the street shows that on many occasions it is difficult to distinguish between real and neurotic anxiety. Run a foot plank along a pavement and most people will walk it with ease and pleasure: run it across a shallow stream and not a few adults will baulk: run it across a deep crevasse and except in situations of extreme urgency baulking will be regarded as common sense, that is to say, a normal reaction.

It is sometimes equally difficult to distinguish between real anxiety and psychotic anxiety. I have already hinted that some 'modern' health movements are in many respects manifestations of psychotic reaction. Systematic examination would doubtless uncover many others. When, after looking at a landscape, an individual experiences surpassing peace of mind and a deep sense of communion, our investigations are rather hampered by preconceptions of æsthetics. But when another develops a deep feeling of depression and sense of guilt at the sight of a rain cloud in a distant sky, we are entitled to suspend æsthetic judgment and enquire whether this is not an occult paranoia. The list might be continued indefinitely. How much of the peace of mind of seemingly well-adjusted individuals is due to their symbolic preoccupations and satisfactions? How much primitive fetichism is represented by the 'hotis' and 'netsukis' of the collector's cabinet, the china dogs of a nineteenth-century kitchen mantelpiece, the treasured editions of the bibliophile, the favourite conceptual preoccupations of the metaphysician or the record vegetable marrows of the allotment holder?

Anyhow, the fact cannot be concealed that with every attempt to establish an absolute standard of normality, we encounter the same difficulty, viz. that there is no sharp edge to the definition. It is invariably blurred by a number of obvious exceptions. There is, however, one point to be noted about the exceptions: the individuals in question rarely come to medico-psychological consultation. And this implies either that the activities are playing a part in the balance of individual adaptations, or that the amount of associated tension and anxiety has not become unbearable. Besides, if we find that the exceptions to a number of standards are invariably of the same type, there appears to be no reason why we should not overcome this difficulty by incorporating the exceptions in a fresh definition. In short *the exceptions to individual standards compel us to introduce into the definition a crude factor of social adaptation.*

V. Summary of Definitions

We are now in a position to assemble some rough generalizations concerning the medico-psychological aspects of normality. From the descriptive point of view the most superficial estimation of normality is made by reference to the presence or absence of symptoms, characterological defects and maladaptations. Taking a broader view, normality can be subdivided into a number of reaction systems, each of which is appropriate to a particular phase of instinct mastery. These systems are in the first place 'psychotic', later 'neurotic' and in adult life 'characterological'.

They represent ramparts created under the stimulus of anxiety. The most obvious normal rampart is adult character. Character is a series of behaviour reactions promoting a stable equilibrium between instinctual demands and gratification in reality, using for this purpose mainly the mechanism of displacement. This particular standard of normality is inadequate, (a) because character is mainly a (pre)conscious end-product, (b) because it is itself liable to deep pathological changes which may go undetected. Taking a wider view of the ego, normality implies simultaneous yet harmonious function of a number of mechanisms, (a) for controlling instinct and (b) for securing direct (or substitute) instinct gratifications. The ego normally acts as a compensating balance. The most incalculable and elastic factor in this aspect of normality is the mechanism of repression. A still broader view of normality is that it represents a harmonious confluence of the reality principle with the primitive pleasure principle. At this point a more cautious definition is necessary: normality is possibly an approximate overlapping of 'psychotic' and 'objective' reality-testing. An alternative view is that normally the anxiety precautions evoked by reality are sufficient to cope with coexisting 'psychotic' and 'neurotic' (unreal) anxiety systems.

This last formulation is perhaps the most important of those I have put forward and it may be well to underline it by additional illustration. It is true that when the ordinary man catches a bus we do not call for his certification as a lunatic. Nor do we certify the hysteric when, dashing into the traffic, she narrowly escapes being run over. The poet may sing of Phoebus Apollo with complete immunity: and the artist, if he chooses, is safe to paint the wheel of life in tartan colours or with eccentric axle-hubs. But we *do* certify the melancholiac when she threatens to throw herself under a real bus; we do certify the paranoiac when, having affirmed that all busmen are trying to run him down, he attempts to set depôts on fire; and we certify the schizophrenic when he begins to see Juggernaut coming down Bond Street. Nevertheless, the ordinary man may owe his freedom from incarceration to a happy merging in time and space of real and lunatic interest in omnibuses. To repeat: *normality may be a form of 'madness' which goes unrecognized because it happens to be a good adaptation to reality.*

The task remains of reconciling these more or less absolute standards with the fact already stressed, namely, that, judged by all of them excepting possibly the last, normality is non-existent. I have already suggested that we can get over this difficulty by introducing a crude social factor, viz. *a social standard of adequate adaptation*. By so doing we can artificially increase the normal range of characterological and emotional reactions and at the same time sanction the exploitation of minor symptom formations, provided the latter are not disruptive in individual respects or offensive in conventional (social) respects. As a matter of fact such a standard is not so crude and artificial as it appears. It corresponds to an individual factor which we might call the *factor of elasticity*. An elasticity factor takes cognizance of variations in constitutional predisposition, e.g. an innate sensitiveness to the stimulation of particular instincts or their components. Perhaps the most practical way of expressing this constitutional factor in terms of elasticity is to say that *a normal person must show some capacity for anxiety tolerance*.[1] No matter how stable anyone may appear, the term 'normal' cannot be applied if, during the familiar crises of life, he is swept off his balance into major symptom formation or into prolonged and exaggerated emotional states.

VI. The Illusion of Absolute Normality: Its Significance

If, however, exception be taken to these corrections of absolute normality for social adaptation and individual elasticity, we are not yet at the end of our tether. Taking a leaf out of the first book of Euclid, we can preface all discussions of normality with the following postulate: 'The introduction of the term absolute in discussions of normality is itself a proof of abnormality.' The expedient may suggest sharp practice, yet I maintain that it can be justified on good scientific grounds. Not only does it take due cognizance of the fact that normality standards cannot be relentlessly applied to the man in the street; it throws some light on the functions of one special group of mental mechanisms and illustrates a particular compulsive habit. One of the main functions of the mechanism of

---

[1] Since writing this I have had an opportunity of reading an address by Ernest Jones on 'The Concept of a Normal Mind'. Although deprecating any attempt to establish standards of normality, he points out that in the long run the nearest attainable criterion is *fearlessness*, thereby stressing the importance of anxiety systems in psychic development. What I have called 'a capacity for anxiety tolerance' represents a clinical modification of this more fundamental standard.

rationalization is to help us not to recognize a number of our own personal maladaptations. Rationalization varnishes over the cracks in the egg-shell of character formation. Indeed, if we are in a good mood, that is to say, if we are free from anxiety and guilt, we may even go so far as to daub a little of the varnish on our next-door neighbour's carapace. But that is not an invariable practice. On many occasions we derive more satisfaction from innocently inserting a finger nail in the weak places. A second mechanism is really derived from the repression group. We have an unlimited capacity for turning a blind eye to any idiosyncrasies, examination of which would make ourselves uncomfortable. When these two mechanisms run harmoniously together in consciousness, the end result is for all practical purposes a lie. And there is a good deal to be said for the view that the concept of absolute normality is one of those comforting lies with which we beguile our sense of inferiority.

In any case interest in an absolute standard illustrates one of many seemingly normal mental compulsions. Even apparently healthy egoists seldom refrain from maintaining absolute standards for others; but, apart from this, there is a form of endopsychic anxiety which appears to be assuaged by unswerving allegiance to standards of perfection. There is a certain harshness in the quality of these absolutes which is manifested by intolerance of any deviation from their sharply outlined categories. Indeed, one is inclined to believe that, but for the saving humour of common folk, normality might have taken its place alongside other theistic substitutes as an abstract object for adoration. A similar harshness can be detected in many reform movements. And since psycho-therapy might be regarded as a variety of reformist activity, it behoves the physician to eliminate as far as possible from his scientific standards any suggestion of private psychological gain. One is tempted to add that the same policy might well be followed by the man in the street: that he should cultivate a greater degree of tolerance of other people's humours and vapours. But that would take us deeply into the motivation of individual and social reform. I have no desire to evade these issues, but my original object was to discuss normality as viewed from the medical psycho-. logist's consulting room; and although I may appear to have trespassed a good deal, I feel entitled to retire within this sanctuary at the end. I do maintain, however, that in return for the privileges and immunities bestowed on him, the medical psychologist is under two definite obligations. He should himself take whatever steps are necessary to eliminate infantile omnipotence and anxiety during business hours at least. And he should never exploit his professional views of life in social relations.

XV

THE APPLICATION OF PSYCHO-ANALYTIC PRINCIPLES IN PSYCHIATRY*

[1935]

Up to the time this paper was written the term 'psychiatry' had, retained its close association in this country with the supervision of the certifiable psychoses. The term 'medical psychologist', more rarely 'clinical psychologist', still served to distinguish those who by inclination and opportunity were more concerned with the broader fields of mental disorder, the psycho-neuroses, the character abnormalities and sexual disorders. Between the two main groups a gulf still existed which has only recently been formally bridged by extending the term psychiatry to connote an interest in the whole field of 'abnormal psychology'. But although the 'medical psychologist' has disappeared for the time being and although there has been a marginal infiltration of the new psychiatry by psycho-analysis, there is no sign that psycho-analysts have attained in this country the psychiatric authority they acquired in the United States. Such rapprochement as has developed in Britain has been more than off-set by the increasing popularity of 'neuro-psychiatric' methods of treatment, medicinal, electrical and surgical; in other words by the increasing influence of neuro-physiology and pathology. In any case the gap between descriptive and dynamic psychology cannot be closed by terminological sutures: in the absence of common principles which take cognizance of unconscious factors there can never be any effective alliance between psychiatry and psycho-analysis. For these among other reasons it may be of some interest to reproduce one of the earlier psycho-analytical attempts to proselytize in the fields of formal psychiatry.

The science of psychiatry has always been subject to a certain amount of moral intimidation. On the one hand it is subject to constant pressure from the physical sciences. Neurologists carrying

* An address delivered before the Psychiatric Section of the *Royal Society of Medicine*, and published in the *Proceedings*, Vol. XXVIII (Section of Psychiatry, pp. 13–22, 1935) [here slightly abbreviated].

the banners of organic etiologies are just as ready to ambush research parties seeking tentatively towards mental origins as are the most case-hardened materialists. On the other hand the forces of academic psychology have commenced what promises to be a strenuous battle for the right to aid psychiatry. And they have the moral advantage of claiming to represent the true science, psychology. Threatened on both sides by these friends; psychiatry has but one main source of independence – the fact that till now it has enjoyed almost exclusive approach to its own wealth of clinical material. At this juncture psycho-analysis, secure in its conviction that the essence of pure psychology is *clinical* psychology, is more than ready to put at the disposal of psychiatry these weapons of research which it has found of service in the clinical fields it has so far been free to investigate.

As will naturally be suspected, the offer is not entirely disinterested. Psycho-analysts have never concealed the view that they have much to learn from psychiatry. Nevertheless it is to be regretted that in psychiatric quarters psycho-analysis is too frequently thought of simply as a more or less questionable therapeutic procedure, neglecting the fact that the greatest of psycho-analytic contributions to mental science consists of certain fundamental formulations concerning the *psychic apparatus*, its differentiated parts, the mechanisms it puts in operation, and the developmental order of these mental organs and functions.

It may provide a suitable approach to this conception of a psychic apparatus to refer again to the subject of normal (academic) psychology, to consider why this body of science, which openly professed its right to adjudicate on psychological affairs, should have contributed so little to abnormal psychology. In the first place it is only fair to recognize that the dice were rather loaded against the normal psychologist. He was restricted to the study of normal people. He never had what the psychiatrist has always enjoyed, namely, free access to those disintegration products from which at any rate a caricature of normal mental structure and function might have been outlined. The common criticism of learning about normal from pathological mental function is completely beside the point. The fact is that normality is characterized by a certain quality of resistance to disintegration which makes it practically impossible for psychologists to learn anything about it save its descriptive features. What is most

astonishing in the history of psychiatry is the fact that psychiatrists
– possessing, as they did, first-hand acquaintance with the distorted
elements of broken normality – did not capture the whole science
of psychology and pontificate on human motivation for all time.

Now academic psychology could not help psychiatry, for
precisely the same reason that psychiatry came to neglect an
unprecedented opportunity of leading the psychological thought
of the world. What stood in the way of both sciences was a fundamental over-estimation of conscious processes, the unquestioning
acceptance of what was in fact a shibboleth. It was practically
never questioned that the terms 'conscious' and 'mental' had the
same significance. Yet in their everyday speech both parties would
use such phrases as 'the innermost recesses of the mind', would
talk of ideas 'coming into' the mind, unaware that with every
phrase they used they were expounding a system of psychic
topography.

But there is this to be said for the normal psychologist, that, as
a rule, however much he intended to take flight into physiology,
he did cling to the method of introspection as a means of assemb-
ling data. In so doing he gave tacit recognition to the fact that our
sole access to mental processes is through consciousness. It was
when he came actually to assemble the data that the formal
psychologist drove a coach-and-four through every canon of
objective observation, and ended by rediscovering in consciousness
the whole coach-load of preconceptions as to its content with
which he set out. Admittedly the difficulties were unique. The
histologist, after all, clips a slide on the stage of his microscope
and proceeds without contortions to point a system of lenses at his
section. The introspectionist is compelled to a most extraordinary
contortion, he is compelled to turn the psychological nose-piece on
the interior of the microscope barrel, he has to turn lenses on
themselves, he inspects consciousness with the instrument of
consciousness. It is small wonder that the key to the riddle of mind
slipped unrecognized from his grasp. Failing to recognize that
primary mental process which in its conscious form is described
as 'free association', he continued to work through his introspective data guided either by arm-chair logic or by the mensuration
tables which he had set up in his barely disguised physiological
laboratories. And to this day he is caught in the tentacles of the
physiological octopus.

Indeed, it is curious that with all this physiological preoccupation the formal psychologist did not grope towards the idea of a mental apparatus. For no one, outside of physiological textbooks, had made such free use of conventional diagrams representing the reflex arc. Looking back on the history of psycho-analytic discovery it is easy to see how some of the most revolutionary changes were effected. The outline of a mental apparatus was the result of years of research by the inspired founder of psycho-analysis, yet its conceptual forerunner was nothing more or less than the idea of a simple reflex arc. And the application of this formulation to a chaotic mass of conscious descriptive data consisted simply in the localization of this apparatus. Naturally, by localization no sort of anatomical localization is implied. The idea is more easily grasped by thinking of a sequence of events, and then interpolating at some point in that sequence a set of mechanisms performing certain mental functions. For some people the mental apparatus is better fixed in time than localized in concepts of space.

It is to be remembered that in one important respect what we call bodily processes do not differ from what we call mental processes, in that the individual himself knows of them only through the medium of consciousness, which one is justified therefore in calling a psychic perceptual organ. A brief examination of consciousness discloses (1) the existence of certain ideational content together with (2) a mental tendency to do something in order to modify (3) certain qualitative states which we call affects. Further examination shows that both ideational presentations and affects are linked at some point with an awareness of certain bodily processes, i.e. with involuntary body changes and what we call behaviour. In other words, ideational systems include awareness of body behaviour and an affect when analysed always includes some degree of awareness of bodily change. If one studies this awareness still further it begins to be clear that inner perceptions of bodily processes can be related to their position in a sequence of events. Some are associated with stimulation and others with mental discharge. Similarly with regard to affects. Some are experienced early in the state of stimulation and others represent various phases in a process of affective discharge. And the assumption is made that what is called ideational thinking has also some relation to mental stimulation, its distribution and discharge. One is then able to indicate boundaries to this mental apparatus and at the same time to delimit the spheres of influence of physiology and psychology respectively. The first frontier line is indicated by the use of the term instinct, i.e. the stimulation-end of the mental apparatus. On one side of this boundary physiologists and pathologists examine body-processes and record their relations. On the other side of the same boundary the psychologist examines the various states of instinct excitation existing in the deepest unconscious layers of the psychic apparatus. At this stimulation boundary the spheres of influence of psychology and physiology can be more or less accurately determined. But the same cannot be said of the other end of the psychic apparatus, viz. the discharge end. At this frontier the psychologist becomes something of a busybody. In spite of the fact that affective and motor discharge are also very intimately concerned with bodily processes, the psychologist resists strongly any attempt on the part of the physiologist to regard these as his exclusive concern. There is a huge gap between the two frontiers, represented by the psychic apparatus, or, if the idea is preferred, an intermission during which psychic manipulation occurs. The gap has not yet been fully explored. The analyst has never pretended a full knowledge of unconscious processes. Nevertheless, at this discharge-frontier the psychologist claims prior rights over the physiologist, insisting above all that a new terminology is necessary – that one must no longer talk simply of motor and sensory discharge, but of behaviour, thought, and feeling.

It is necessary to emphasize these preliminary considerations, because although the formulations themselves are now over thirty-five years old, they still serve to separate the psychologist and pure psychiatrist from the neurologist. But it must be made clear that if the psychiatrist admits the concept of the mental apparatus it will prove the most fateful admission of his professional life. It involves a more or less formal repudiation of the authority of organic medicine on all matters concerning psychogenetic states (neuroses and pure psychoses). And it involves a material shrinking of the same authority concerning the mental symptoms of *all organic states* whatsoever. One cannot admit the existence of an essential link in a chain of events and then say 'Of course, in such and such a disease this link should be ignored.' Equally impossible is it to make immediate causal connections between, let us say, oral and intestinal sepsis and psychic depression or confusional states.

The metabolist or endocrinologist or toxicologist or neurocytologist or electro-physiologist is entitled to full respect in his own field, namely the farther side of instinctual excitation, the frontier of bodily stimulation, but he may not cut across country to apply his findings unmodified to discharge phenomena. And he has always to bargain with the fact that after the first few years of life, when the mental apparatus is for all practical purposes complete, even his own legitimate territory is liable to invasion. The mental apparatus has acquired an awkward knack of striking back at bodily processes, and in this way modifying the rhythms of bodily stimulation which it was originally intended to subserve. It can also dragoon bodily organs into some sort of behaviour. Even the jealously guarded preserve of parasitic disease is not immune from interference. The psychic representation of internal parasitic disturbance cannot be neglected. Indeed we cannot indulge in the simplest forms of external parasitism, such as being eaten by a tiger, without bringing into operation vital psychological factors. Having discovered the mind we must forever bargain with it.

Omitting now those stages of research which consisted in adding to our knowledge of unconscious mental content, impulse and affect, we find that during the past fifteen years psycho-analysis has been busily engaged building up its own psychological formulations into a system of depth psychology. It is this system in particular that deserves the attention of psychiatrists. The central concept of the mental apparatus remains unchanged. Depth psychology consists in the expression of this central concept in three different sets of terms, the topographic (the layers, subdivisions and differentiations of mind), the dynamic (the instinctual forces driving the apparatus), the economic (the mechanisms of distribution of energy within the apparatus). To this is added a fourth approach, that of developmental order. There is no way of avoiding this apparent complication. Indeed it is fair to say that metapsychology is not complicated enough; it is at the moment too simple to explain adequately the variety of compli-cated disorders with which it is concerned.

It may perhaps give some idea of the possible application of these principles to psychiatric data to say that if the clinical condi-tion known as schizophrenia had not existed, it would have been necessary to invent it. By this is meant that the elementary divisions of the ego up to the middle of the second year of life, the nature

of ideational content, the affective reactions and the types of mental mechanism prevailing during that period constitute the raw
material from which a psychiatrist of imagination might easily
reconstruct the picture of an adult psychosis. And the same is true
of the paranoid and depressive states respectively. I do not,
however, wish to repeat here the views put before this section
some years ago,[1] but rather to dwell on some more general considerations which might tempt you to take an active interest in the
psycho-analytical approach.

To begin with, the very name schizophrenia is a venture in
psychic topography, the term depression an essay on psychic
affect, hallucinatory psychosis an ideational caption, dementia a
restatement of the principle of regression. And so throughout
psychiatric nosology, it is impossible, unless we wilfully use code
words, to avoid classifying our clinical data otherwise than in
accordance with the most fundamental of mental phenomena, or
the fundamental divisions of the mind. But it has to be admitted
that the original application of these descriptive labels was mainly
in terms of conscious psychology and therefore did not permit of
developmental correlations. When the analyst thinks of psychic
topography, he thinks in terms of superimposed layers, and when
he thinks of the earliest of these layers he has in mind the possibility of loosely-knit systems of ego formations. Similarly with
affect, the analyst has in mind certain primary affects which in
course of development become modified, fused, and interwoven.
Mechanism he thinks of as a sort of hierarchy beginning with the
processes of regression, projection, introjection, repression, and
reaction-formation down to the most elaborate and refined forms
of displacement. And he combines these various approaches in a
developmental sequence which in turn involves accepting the view
that every mental illness is a form of regression. These formulations have been built up mostly from analysis of normal and
neurotic adults and children. But in the long run they depend on
inferences. It is well to be clear about this fact. However far back
we may push the frontiers of observation, we come sooner or
later to a barrier which can only be overcome by plausible inference and hypothetical reconstruction. Recent analytic observations on infants hardly out of the suckling period suggest that a

[1] 'A Psycho-Analytical Approach to the Classification of Mental Disorders', *J. Ment. Science*, 1932, 78, 819 [Chap. XI, this volume].

degree of mental organization exists at that period which some years ago would have been thought quite inconceivable. Naturally, therefore, in our reconstructions of the earliest stages of development, it is difficult to be certain about the exact degree of importance to be attributed to any one layer, or nucleus or ego-system or affect. At this point there is no doubt that psychiatry can be of the greatest assistance to analysis. To give a simple example. If we had no psychiatric information on the subject, our understanding of coprophagia would, apart from anthropological data and some scanty observations of the habits of certain children, be limited to inferences made by interpreting unconscious phantasies in normal and neurotic persons. Psychiatric observations as to the habits of schizophrenics and other dements not only show that these interpretations are correct, but provide a clinical measure of their importance. They help to confirm the analytical postulate of, in this case, an 'anal ego-system'. If now one can be fairly certain of the existence of such early ego-systems, it is only logical to re-scrutinize psychiatric material, to see whether the new idea enables us to subdivide the group phenomena of schizophrenia. What has been said of ego-structure applies also to primitive affects and mental mechanisms. There can be no doubt that when subdivisions of all psychoses are attempted along these lines, problems of diagnosis, etiology, and prognosis will be greatly simplified.

The importance of schizophrenia has been emphasized because the stereotypes observed in this disorder provide a specially rich field for observation. Even such apparently banal observations as that a schizophrenic may habitually lie on the same bench, or stand in the same corner, or try to take refuge from the morning round by bolting into a lavatory, are full of significance for the research student. Next in order of significance come the rhythmical flights of the maniac's imagination. Depressives, too, have much to say that is of interest, but the degree of mental organization exhibited in the depressive product is much more advanced. In a way, of course, the behaviour and ideational products of the G.P.I. are the most interesting of all. There is something about the orderly regressive withdrawal of the general paralytic which is specially worthy of study from the developmental point of view.

It has been suggested that the systematic, developmental psychology built up by psycho-analysis can be of service to psychiatrists in their diagnostic and etiological work (for the moment no attempt has been made to draw therapeutic parallels). It is equally clear that, in return, psychiatry has much to offer psycho-analysis – in particular a classified arrangement of the huge amount of clinical material at its disposal. But although there is no question that this material is invaluable, there is equally little doubt that in its raw state it is of considerably less value. In some cases indeed it may be no more or less than a collection of undeciphered hieroglyphs. In short the psychiatrist has to face the fact that, however fascinating his descriptive observations may be, their significance cannot be assessed without *interpretation*. At this point the conventional psychiatrist usually begins to shake his head. He feels that he is being asked to abandon all pretence of scientific procedure, and wonders whether perhaps it would not be better to trust the electrodes and recording tambours of the experimental psychologist. This apparently praiseworthy attitude is really profoundly unscientific. There is only one instrument capable of examining the human mind and that is the mind itself. And one must learn the languages of the mind before one can hope to read its records. A dozen stenographers, an Alexandrian library of case-histories, gramophone, dictaphone, and moving-picture records are useful up to a point, but beyond that point they are no more use than a differential blood-count. Analysts have already made that discovery, anthropologists are beginning to make it. There is a point in the approach to the waking life of infants, savage or civilized adults, sane or insane, when the same technique must be applied which is essential in translating the dream. The stock criticism that the art of interpretation varies with the observer and with the observer's preconceptions is not so reasonable as it appears. It is only one more proof of the fact that there are a number of superimposed layers in both unconscious and pre-conscious mental systems. The real scientific safeguard in this region is essentially empirical. Let us not quarrel about the alleged laxity of control in interpretation, but see that the interpretations are adequately tested by their plausibility and usefulness, not incidentally their therapeutic utility, but their etiological and diagnostic value.

As a matter of fact, despite apparently wide differences in the depth to which interpretation is exercised there exists a remarkable degree of accuracy in the interpretations made by different observers in any one level.[1] And even although from time to time quite irreconcilable differences appear between interpreters from different schools, this is no argument against the science and art of interpretation. The fact is that the right to interpret has already been won for clinical psychology by analysts and there is no justification for its neglect in any branch of mental science. It is, again, a matter for wonder that the language of symbolism was an analytical discovery rather than a psychiatric one. And there is still time for psychiatry to contribute materially to this most obscure of mental phenomena. But the psychiatrist must be ready to sink his distrust of such methods, and not only to sink his distrust, but to learn somewhat laboriously the language. Some individuals, it is true, have a remarkable flair for the interpretation of symbols, and most psychologists are able to translate a few unaided. But all observers must learn the details systematically, just as an anthropologist must learn a tribal dialect before he commences field-work with the tribe. And there is no doubt that when the psychiatrist equipped with a proper knowledge of symbolism and armed with some knowledge of the procedure of interpretation, comes to investigate the disintegration products of schizophrenia he will be able to tell analysts a good deal more of the structure and content of the infant's mind than they know at present.

So far the gifts offered by psycho-analysis may appear to be unsubstantial, merely the stimulus of ideas which may or may not be correct. Something of a more immediately practical nature may be desired. It will no doubt be agreed that the system of psychiatric case-recording is an essentially practical problem. For what, after all, is a case-history? It is the orderly arrangement of descriptive and introspective data, from which the observer usually seeks to

---

[1] [Note (1955): This argument is not quite so cogent as it was at that time. The intervening development of wide differences of opinion regarding the validity of hypothetical reconstructions of early mental life has given rise to equally wide differences in the interpretation of unconscious mental content. So much so that some modern interpretations cannot but be regarded as a form of 'wild analysis' – a term formerly reserved by trained analysts for the extravagances of untrained analysts. It is true, however, that such differences do not constitute an argument against the science of interpretation; they merely emphasize the necessity of applying with greater care the available scientific criteria of interpretation (see also Chap. XXVI, 'Research Methods in Psycho-analysis')].

relate cause and effect. It is an exercise in descriptive psychology ending in an analysis of surface phenomena. Provided one recognizes the fact that in taking a case-history one is examining a psychic surface, the method is legitimate and sometimes even of therapeutic value. Moreover, in the quest for precipitating or immediate causes, in the valuation of traumatic factors, particularly environmental factors, the statistical analysis of proper case-histories may contribute valuable information. But what is a proper case-history? Studying some of the history sheets of modern psychiatric institutions, one is forced to the conclusion that they are for the most part useless. It is indeed a melancholy reflection that so much enthusiasm for detail, so much ardour for statistical correlation, should have been rendered ineffective for lack of systematic approach. For the fact is not simply that a conventional case-history is a sampling method (that, in itself, is not a drawback), but a sampling that is partly haphazard and partly hampered by emotional considerations. How many case-histories will inform the reader about such essential points as these: Whether the patient was suckled at long or short intervals, allowed to cry in the night, given enemas or soap pills, dragooned into excretory observances, had his hands tied for infantile masturbation, was beaten for breaking things or for being untidy, played with spit, was afraid of shadows or feathers, disliked smuts on the skin, kicked his mother, slept with his mother, played with toys, or could not play with them, was irritated by noises, went to sleep too quickly or too slowly, regurgitated his food or refused it – and so on? If one is going to investigate the instinctual factors in a psychotic case, the least one can do is to inquire about childhood manifestations of impulse-life (self-preservative, sexual, or aggressive); if one wishes to know about adult anxiety-states or guilt, one must inquire closely into the minor phobias or inhibitions by means of which they are distributed in childhood; if one is concerned with paranoid, depressive, or schizophrenia mechanisms, it is necessary to know about the mental mechanisms prevailing in childhood. If again a patient's reality sense is under scrutiny, one must certainly know about his childhood capacity to play and to day-dream; one must know what his recurrent dream-life was like. If one is faced with a disease of the emotions such as a depression, it is essential to discover such simple facts as whether the child was usually aggrieved, frequently hurt, mortified, or ridiculed. The information required for proper statistical investigation of psychoses is almost endless, and in practice it becomes necessary to select. The selection should, however, be representative; it should represent fairly the factors of instinct, ideation, affect, mental mechanism and discharge (i.e. affective behaviour).

The method of history-taking brings out another problem in approach, viz. whether the adult psychoses should be regarded as clinical entities or as a phase (temporary or permanent) in a life-history. For the analyst a case-history is much less an investigation of apparent causes than an abbreviated life-history, obvious gaps in which must be filled in later by study of the unconscious content. In the case of the psychoses the task can be simplified by a general formulation: No adult psychosis without an infantile psychosis. A diagnosis of psychosis is inadequate unless at the same time the mental reactions prevailing at all important periods in the patient's life are established. These are not only essential for diagnosis, but often invaluable in prognosis.

Consider a parallel case taken from ordinary analytic practice:

A patient complaining of working incapacity together with a tendency to exaggerated unhappiness in social life showed the following features after a simple investigation of previous history – a slight asocial tendency during early childhood and some obsessional symptoms just about the age of puberty. A more complete examination under analysis filled in the gaps as follows. The early antisocial phase was prolonged and severe, but had been preceded by a still earlier phase of acute phobia formation. It was followed by a distinctly paranoid phase in the latency period, which gave place, as it so often does, to an obsessional system. The obsessional system was followed by a retarded and depressed phase. Having weathered puberty the patient embarked on a series of social symptoms mostly involving his love-life – at first a slight hysterical period of homosexual attachment and later a series of unsuccessful heterosexual relations culminating in a mixed paranoid and depressive phase. None of these features was obvious to ordinary examination. Clinically he would have passed as a normal intelligent individual suffering from weakness of will and lack of initiative. A board of psychiatrists would certainly have passed him on these terms. Yet, analytically speaking, he was, on the whole, of the depressive type with an unsatisfactory prognosis. Had he been filed under the heading of 'lack of working capacity', without regard to his life-history, the case would simply have gone to swell the inaccurate statistical totals from which untrustworthy scientific conclusions are drawn.

But that is not all. It must be admitted that fundamental differences as to etiology or deep antagonisms regarding the relations of body and mind are liable to be transferred to the therapeutic field. And very naturally too, because in the therapeutic field there is ampler scope for the interplay of anxiety and moral factors. The most extreme, and certainly the most pointless, recriminations take the following forms: On the psychiatrist's side, raising the bogey that analysis is a dangerous weapon in any case, but that it is tantamount to malpraxis to recommend it in the psychoses, or alternatively that analysis being such an ineffective instrument its recommendation is an unethical exploitation. If the analyst is given to the pleasures of repartee he may reply that it is absence of reasonable skill to treat the psychotic with pills and potions, to hedge in his mind with banalities, platitudes and exhortations, or in the last resort, having thrown a bundle of raffia grass into the ward, to turn a Chubb key on his patient's conflicts. Such vituperation defeats itself. More difficult to deal with is a sober shaking of the head, an ominous frown at the suggestion of psycho-analysing a manic-depressive case, an outspoken scepticism as to the possibility of an analytic approach in paranoia.

Now it should be remembered that no one has been more cautious and conservative in these matters than Freud himself. Nevertheless, psycho-analytic handling of the psychoses has been thrust on the analyst. And for three reasons: first, that the patients themselves frequently come to demand treatment; second, that the work so far done in this direction has been encouraging; and third, that it is against all the traditions of medicine to be intimidated by the very obvious difficulties psychotic material presents.

One of the general assumptions underlying the opposition seems to imply that fools rush in where angels fear to tread. Yet consider the case of paranoia, obviously one of the hardest of therapeutic nuts to crack. In the whole field of clinical psychology no one has more experience in dealing with (paranoid) projection mechanisms than the psycho-analyst. Child analysts are dealing with these daily, adult analysts spend at least one-third of their time tracking them down in their daily routine. The more opportunity I have of studying paranoid mechanisms the more convinced I am that a conventional attitude of pessimism based on institutional observations is scientifically defeatist. For one thing the diagnosis of paranoia is in the same condition nowadays as the diagnosis of consumption was in the middle of last century, when so-called 'early' cases were in fact in the latest stages of the disease. Moreover, the significance of paranoid phobias in childhood together with the curative influence of an obsessional neurosis on paranoid mechanisms, suggests that, given sufficient skill and knowledge applied at the right time (*preferably not later than puberty*), the outlook is not so black as it is painted at present.

In the case of depressive disorders the position of the analyst is naturally much more secure and there is much less hesitation nowadays in handling selected cases, again with suitable precautions.

When one comes to examine this situation more closely, it seems probable that both extra-analytical opposition and analytical timidity owe a good deal to that phobia of insanity or fear of being driven insane which is present to some degree in all adults, and in a more primitive form in all children. And the analyst is after all just one adult among others. There is no doubt that he is unduly intimidated by the constant suggestion of danger, and he knows perfectly well that should a nervous relative insist on calling in a general consultant in the midst of a crisis the case will soon be out of his hands, and one more mark scored up against psychoanalysis in the smoke-rooms of medical societies. At this point the psychiatrist could render not only psycho-analysis but the cause of mental science inestimable service, and this without having to endure trespass on his professional preserves. On the contrary, if the psychiatrist were to co-operate in this procedure, if he were to organize and adequately staff homes for the psychological handling of suitable cases of psychosis, he would have established a psychiatric unit to the expansion of which there is no limit. It is not suggested that such friendly co-operation does not exist. I personally owe a great deal more than I can express to the patient and timely co-operation of psychiatrists and sometimes of neurological colleagues. Nevertheless, such experiences are regrettably infrequent and the absence of an effective liaison service does much to retard the progress of both sciences.

One other consideration may be brought forward. It is fair to say that throughout its development psychiatry has been hampered to some extent by the numerous restrictions of a social, legal, and administrative kind imposed upon professional work. It is interesting to consider why secular authorities have succeeded in maintaining such a tight hold over a branch of medicine. Making due allowance for all the common-sense social arguments in favour of this course, something may be attributed to the fact that restriction of some sort has consistently held its place as a therapeutic principle in psychiatry. Society, jealous for the rights of the individual, has stepped in with counter-restrictions aimed at the therapeutist. The result is that those persons coming between normal groups and groups of the certifiably insane are subject to considerable hardship and even neglect in the therapeutic sense. One is inclined to believe that this counter-restriction is in part due to scepticism and lack of faith on the part of society, and that only when psychiatry has established a claim to more complete trust, only when it comes out boldly to show that its approach to mental disease is primarily psychological, will it gain sufficient prestige to guide the secular arm of the law, not be controlled by it. In this process of establishing prestige it is my sincere conviction that psycho-analysis will play its part.

XVI

A DEVELOPMENTAL STUDY OF THE OBSESSIONAL NEUROSES*

[1935]

The theories that adult psycho-neuroses can be traced to a pre-disposition established through the interaction of endopsychic and environmental factors during the latter half of the infantile period (0–5) and that the adult neurotic has already experienced during childhood a similar type of neurosis, have many corollaries; e.g. that adult mental disorders can be arranged in a developmental series and that the infantile neuroses shed light on the phases of normal mental development. It is for this reason that 'transitional' disorders lying between the neuroses and psychoses, although comparatively rare in incidence, throw even more light on mental development than do the great psycho-neurotic and psychotic groups. Nevertheless, much can be learned about mental development from a study of the obsessional neuroses, which have obvious connections with 'normal' character formations, with some types of alcoholism, with some delinquent reactions, with certain forms of sexual perversion, in particular homosexuality and the fetichisms, and, through the depressive states, with the psychoses. In the case of hysteria, the connection with obsessional neuroses although statistically obvious is by no means obvious in the sense of mental content and mechanism.

The fact, however, that the obsessional neuroses seem to lead to a pathological degree of control of affect offers us a fresh approach, provided of course we believe that the control of affective stresses is as much the aim of symptom-formation as it is of character-formation. Following this line of thought we can conceive of various mental disorders not simply as the products of regression to a fixation point but also as ramparts against regression beyond that point. This, roughly, is the thesis of the following paper.

* Read before the Thirteenth International Psycho-Analytical Congress, Lucerne, 1934, first published in a slightly amplified form in *The International Journal of Psycho-Analysis*, Vol. XVI, pt. 2, p. 131, April 1935.

Progress in understanding the obsessional neuroses has been considerably hampered by the very natural tendency of the clinician to concentrate his energies on characteristic clinical features of the disease. By so doing he limits the scope of his etiological investigations. Study of various transitional or mixed types shows that the real significance of obsessions cannot be appreciated until the relations of the disease on the one hand to hysteria, and on the other to the psychoses, have been established. The tendency to treat the obsessional neuroses as an isolated clinical entity has been fostered by the peculiarities and complexities of the symptom picture. Freud has himself commented on this complexity and regretted the absence of a synthesis of symptom-variations. Actually the degree of ramification of a neurosis is itself significant. The more extensively a symptom-construction is spread over or penetrates ego-structure the more likely it is to correspond to a phase of ego-development. In other words, the complexity of the obsessional neurosis is a tribute to the scope, vigour and elasticity of its defensive functions. The obsessional neurosis is indeed the most elastic of all neuroses. And it is well that it should be so. For the task of the obsessional neurosis is an important and difficult one. It is to permit a regressive flight from the anxieties induced by advancing development, and at the same time to stem that regression. It is not, of course, the first or only line of defence. We have some reason to believe that in the case of the adult a more immediate buffer of repression and conversion absorbs to some extent the anxieties precipitated by the onset of adult sexuality and adult conditions of life. But clinical examination shows how frequently behind the constructions of anxiety-hysteria there appear layers of obsessional organization. When the hysterical defence fails to stem regression this obsessional layer is ready to take up the additional burden.

What is true of the obsessional symptom as observed in the adult is all the more true of that phase of 'obsessional primacy' which I would put roughly between the ages of eighteen months and three to three and a half years. Whereas the obsessional neurosis serves to conceal the fact that, but for its help in instinctual crises, there would be no stopping-place for the patient short of the psychoses, the 'obsessional phase' of infancy serves to conceal the fact that but for its activities there would never be any advance for any child out of the 'normal pan-psychosis' of the first year.

EARLIER ETIOLOGIES

Before proceeding to elaborate this thesis of the developmental and defensive functions of obsessional mechanisms and symptoms, it is necessary to put forward some more general considerations. These concern the nature of symptoms and the methods by which they can be examined to best advantage. Analytic research is still enormously influenced by the fact that the earliest investigations disclosed the existence of a kernel Oedipus-situation. This manifestation, characteristic (as it then appeared) of children from three to five years old, was found to be common to all psycho-pathological states, and ever since it has been the custom of analysts to range their etiological systems round this nucleus. Developmental factors were at first thought of exclusively in terms of phases of libidinal development, allowing, of course, for the influence of constitutional predispositions. Using these basic factors psycho-analysts proceeded to build up tentative etiological systems. And for a time all went well. This or that neurosis formed naturally round the kernel complex, but owed its special features to certain fixation levels. These fixation levels were determined by a regular order of instinctual primacies, together with special instinctual crises arising as the child passed through these primacies. The obsessional neurosis, for example, stimulated by the common factor of castration anxiety, owed its distinctive clinical features partly to constitutional factors, partly to precocious ego-development, to special experience of anal-sadistic ambivalence, to defusion of instinct on frustration, and to a marked quality of regression. But gradually, as researches expanded, this etiological system threatened to become sterile and unilluminating. The same factors could be observed, for instance, in drug addictions and perversions, and, in any case, precocious ego-development, defusion and regression are general rather than specific influences. Study of the psychoses at first gave promise of a more accurate etiology, in so far as it disclosed wide *variations* in development during the earliest infancy which might be responsible for clinical differences. But simultaneous research on normal development and on the pathology of character showed that in principle at any rate there was little the psychotic could teach the normal person about abnormality.

So it came to this, that whatever the clinical manifestations of the case, the same phantasy-content, the same types of mechanism, the same concealed psychopathological constructions could be demonstrated by every analyst. In this way the older etiologies lost both their vitality and their interest. However much symptom-formations may overlap, however many transitional forms of neuroses and psychoses exist, the fact remains that characteristic differences both as to form and as to prognosis do exist. And these specific forms show a refractoriness to treatment which suggests a degree of stability in the underlying determinants. This stability must be accounted for in any satisfactory etiology. Constitutional factors are generally assumed to be variable. A number of environmental influences are no doubt common to all infantile development, but obviously a larger number are subject to wide variation: characteristic clinical entities can scarcely be attributed to casual combinations of sporadic and highly individual factors. On the other hand, psycho-analysts tend to be too easily satisfied with the discovery of striking environmental stimuli. Fixation experiences, previously regarded as specific, have lost a good deal of specificity in recent years, and some of them (e.g. observation of parental coitus) can no longer be regarded as of universal occurrence. Typical neuroses have been demonstrated in the absence of any such stimuli. One is tempted therefore to look for specific factors in two directions, (a) certain more or less stable *combinations* of endopsychic factors and (b) environmental stimuli, if any, associated *exclusively* with the particular form of neurosis under investigation.[1]

PSYCHO-PATHOLOGICAL CRITERIA

It is apparent then that more comprehensive investigations of analytic data are necessary to establish the significance of symptom-

[1] [Note (1955): A propos the etiological rating of the Oedipus complex as a 'kernel' factor in all mental disorder and the relative importance in etiology of endopsychic and of environmental factors, it is interesting to note a recent tendency to devalue the Oedipus factor and to emphasize environmental influences which has developed since the Second World War. Stimulated no doubt by observation of the traumatic neuroses of children consequent on war-time evacuation, the concept of the 'broken home' has gained currency even in psycho-analytical circles and has been supported by studies of so-called 'separation anxiety' in infancy. While no doubt a useful corrective to theories which postulate organized Oedipus reactions in the earliest months of life, this recent tendency ignores the fact that the effect of such early environmental situations depends on later endopsychic reactions to the Oedipus situation.]

formations. The search for isolated factors is no longer justified by results. Of course, whatever methods of approach are employed there is bound to be a good deal of overlapping, but, broadly speaking, we cannot go far wrong if we adopt any of the following methods:

(1) Trying to discover what specific forms of *affect* or *combinations of affect* are defended against by the symptoms. This involves a quantitative and qualitative estimation of the instincts concerned. Incidentally, we must consider not only the question of specific fusions and defusions of instinct but specific fusions and defusions of affect.

(2) Trying to discover what specific *mechanisms* or combinations of mechanisms are exploited in particular symptom-formations.

(3) Trying to discover what *developmental phases* are reflected or caricatured by the symptom-construction. This last method is by far the most comprehensive, and to some extent includes the problems of characteristic affects and mechanisms, but it has a specially close connection with psychic structure, differentiations and layers.

The Function of Displacement

It may be said at once that the obsessional neuroses respond readily to investigation by all of these methods. This is particularly true of the study of mechanisms. Indeed, it is interesting to reflect that Freud's early discoveries regarding the importance of *displacement* were largely stimulated by observation of obsessional cases. This is only natural because, owing to peculiarities in the functioning of repression in this neurosis, there are many more surface-products to be examined than, say, in the case of anxiety-hysteria. It is perhaps unfortunate that this original line of investigation was not more closely pursued in later times. Studying the clinical features of various obsessions, it is easy to draw a working distinction between ideational, speech and behaviouristic end-products. These products can then be subdivided quite elaborately in accordance with the amount of *psychic distance* interposed between instinct-derivatives and their possible expression in action. Strictly speaking, two sets of observations should be given here, those made solely from the study of true obsessional neuroses in the clinical sense, and those made by studying minor obsessional manifestations accompanying other neuroses or appearing in apparently normal people. But, speaking broadly, the content of ideational obsessions can be arranged in an ascending series: viz. aggressive images, sexual images, images concerning matters of social importance to the individual, images concerning social matters of a trivial order and more or less nonsensical images. That is to say, however much an apparently nonsensical obsession may give indirect expression to instinct through the processes of symbolism, condensation and distortion, the practical fact remains that direct expression is minimal. The obsession is a widely displaced derivative. In the ritual (behaviouristic) obsessions a similar arrangement can be detected. Nonsensical or trivial compulsions are most frequent, whilst social rituals, in the sense of compulsive sexual or aggressive acts, are least frequent. Comparing these two types it is evident that much more direct expression of instinct is permitted in the ideational obsession than in the obsessional action. Word obsessions are not so easy to classify, but are, nevertheless, capable of subdivision along the lines indicated. More latitude, however, appears to be allowed to obscene and aggressive words than is the case with the two other types described.

Returning to the main subdivisions, it is to be noted that each of them has a positive and negative phase. The ideational obsession is accompanied or alternates with phases of doubt and rumination; obsessional actions are associated with fluctuating phases of aboulia (indecision), whilst word obsessions are frequently accompanied by difficulty in verbal expression.

Affective Obsessions

It is easy to see that these complicated processes of displacement and substitution serve the purposes of instinctual defence, more particularly when they are accompanied by the inhibition-phenomena of doubt, rumination and aboulia. But they do not account very satisfactorily for some of the disturbances of affect noted in some obsessional states. These disturbances are, broadly speaking, of three types: reactions of guilt associated with 'forbidden' thoughts and actions; reactions of anxiety or panic when expiatory or protective rituals are neglected; and a degree of emotional impoverishment. This impoverishment sometimes gives rise to the impression that the aim of the rituals is to master affect. This is only true if we say that the aim of the obsessional neurosis *as a whole* is to master or prevent the emergence of painful affect. In point of fact the conspicuous nature of ideational and ritual obsessions has deflected our attention from the root-problem of affect. Some recent clinical observations have led me to the conclusion that what we usually term clinical obsessional neuroses, with their elaborate thought, speech and action rituals, are really in the neurotic sense highly sophisticated end-products. *The primary obsessional state is essentially an affective state or rather a sequence of alternating affects having very simple unconscious ideational content.* The reason such cases are not more frequently recognized or reported is that in consciousness there may be no ideational content of an obsessional type whatever, and that ritual actions may be disguised in the form of social symbolisms, e.g. alternately staying in town and country. There being no obvious hallmarks of obsessional reaction; such individuals tend to be regarded as psychotic in type and are generally included amongst the mild depressions. In the cases I have observed the affective sequence is one of depression and elation, or put in another way the rapid experience of *good* and *bad* affects, which by the way is common enough in everyday life. A good state of mind *must* be followed by a bad state. A transient improvement (corresponding to a feeling of ordinariness) is sometimes experienced; but although this is much sought after it is seldom achieved, and some degree of indifference and depression leading in severe cases to various intensities of depersonalization is the more common outcome. Where the affective obsession is accompanied in consciousness by ideational or ritual obsessions, one generally observes that the compulsive element must be thought of or acted out first of all whilst feeling in a good state, and immediately after repeated in a bad state. Some of these symptoms are, of course, to be detected in operation throughout the most conventional obsessional neuroses, as when a good state of mind is regarded as dangerous or where the enjoyment of an obsessional idea is guilty and must be expiated by repetition of the idea in a state of remorse. In all these affective obsessions there is a tendency to introduce complications by reversals or overlappings. For example, instead of a sudden swing from 'it is bad to feel good' to 'it is good to feel bad' some such sequence as the following may occur. 'It is bad to feel good' changes into 'it is good to feel good'. This apparently natural feeling is, however, felt to be unnatural and changes into 'it is bad to be good to feel good'. This in turn becomes 'it is good to feel bad'. But this is again felt to be unnatural (presumably by the reality-ego) and turns into 'it is bad to be good to feel bad' and finally once more 'it is bad to feel good'. This affective play may go on endlessly and with infinite variation. Nevertheless, shorn of their complications these emotional obsessions have one feature in common: *a drive to rapid alternation of 'good' and 'bad' affective states.*

Subject-Object Relations

Returning for a moment to what I have called the more sophisticated forms of obsessional neurosis, it is to be observed that they are also capable of subdivision in terms of *subject-object relations*. This is not so obvious where the clinical complications are due to an elaborate displacement, e.g. where a contamination phobia spreads rapidly from one object to another. In some cases, however, it is clear that the displacement is not simply from one object to another but from subject to object. I have observed, for example, a patient pass consecutively through a series of touching obsessions concerning parts of her own body, a series of washing rituals concerning her own clothes, a series of contamination and touching rituals involving the clothes of external objects and finally a series of touching rituals concerning the exposed parts of the bodies of others. Having followed this order the patient then reversed the process starting with object obsessions and ending with subject obsessions. As a rule this pendulum swing was gradual in type, but on occasions of special anxiety a more violent swing could be observed, e.g. a jump would be made from a subject-touching ritual carried out secretly in a closed room to an object ritual carried out in streets or buses. In other words, the patient played backwards and forwards on an ego-object scale of obsessions, and if need be could deal with more acute attacks of anxiety regarding the ego by a sudden spring into object obsessions, and vice versa.

Developmental Aspects

Summing up these observations we see that apparently complicated rituals have the same object in view, viz. *to provide an ever more complicated meshwork of conceptual systems through which affect may pass in a finely divided state.* When for some reason or other these rituals are interfered with we observe once more the existence of massive affects. In the purely affective obsessions I have described, we can see a more primitive attempt to change or substitute qualities or intensities of affect. It is apparent also that behind this obsessional system must lie some significant system of ego-object relations, one obviously which does not subscribe to the ordinary rules of reality-testing. Admittedly, we have not so far produced a specific etiological formula, but we have sufficient information to justify what I have called the developmental approach. This approach is based on the following general assumptions: (1) that those larger symptom-constructions which we unearth during the analysis of all cases of whatever clinical type are crystallized residues of mal-function contributed to by every phase of development: (2) that what contributes the characteristic features of each disease is more what we might call 'a primacy of developmental phases and mechanisms' than a simple 'primacy of instincts' as we are accustomed to think when speaking of fixations: (3) that the mechanism of regression has a number of positive as well as negative functions; that is to say, it is not simply a defensive flight. Regression has indeed always been a key mechanism in psycho-pathology, but it has in the past been thought of too much in terms of flow of energy. Regression is, in my view, largely a *strategic withdrawal to an earlier psychic level*: having by this withdrawal secured the mental rights, privileges and methods of defence peculiar to that earlier level, the individual once more advances on life with these reinforced but antiquated methods. The resultant peculiarities in adaptation constitute most of the symptom picture. When we say that the danger of regression is that it may proceed too far, we imply also that each phase of development must have offered a sanctuary from the dangers of the preceding stage. If a flight to obsessional mechanisms can be shown on some occasions to drive the patient back into paranoid or melancholic activities it is only fair to assume that the primacy of obsessional mechanisms was and is a reaction to the paranoid and melancholiac phases of development.

There is, of course, nothing very new in all this. Freud said, a long time ago, of the neuroses that these are not simply episodes in development, but that every phase of development seems to have a type of anxiety peculiar to it. And it was Freud himself who about twenty years ago laid the foundations of all subsequent developmental etiologies, when in a few masterly sentences he made a hypothetical reconstruction of primitive reality-development. He first advised us of the part played by projection, primary identification and (or) introjection in establishing ego-object boundaries. These early views have been considerably expanded. At any rate we can now indicate roughly some of the peculiar states of mind, phantasy-systems and reality-systems in vogue in the first three years.

We have to recognize, however, that owing to the lack of organization of the ego (and I think myself the fact that the early ego is multilocular), the child is during this period at the mercy of violent fluctuations in affect, which in turn induce a violent pendulum-swing between introjective and projective processes. Just how violent and urgent these affects are can be conjectured from the painful affects associated with melancholiac and paranoid states respectively. These so-called pathological states have already helped to modify the more catastrophic dangers with which the child feels itself to be threatened in the earliest months of life. They have helped, but at a price. The infant, hounded by the threat of overwhelming affect, alternately clings to and lets go its cherished mechanisms of introjection and projection. It is this confused, bewildered and agonized state of psychic affairs which the obsessional phase sets out to overcome. And it does so in a very simple and effective way: viz. by splitting up the too isolated phases of introjection and projection – interweaving them, as it were – reducing the time interval between them. These processes are reinforced by the exploitation of displacement mechanisms, which, coinciding with the development of conceptual thought and speech, broaden the path to reality. The infant not only produces more rapid alternations but smaller doses of anxiety attached to less important ideational systems. It compounds affects, and in that way reduces the necessity for excessive anxiety or guilt feeling. It compounds them so closely, indeed, that the subject soon gives an appearance of lack of emotional feeling.

This is the supreme virtue of the obsessional technique. Repression, of course, helps from the beginning, but repression has the defect of being an all-or-none reaction. The more elastic mechanism of substitution comes into its own in the obsessional phase. And from the point of view of reality it is infinitely superior to that older, more haphazard and anxiety-provoking system which we call symbolic thinking.

UNCONSCIOUS CONTENT

Having justified stepping outside the clinical boundaries of the obsessional neurosis, the next step is to consider the unconscious phantasy-systems which can be discovered in children and in various adult pathological states. A good starting-point is the group of child phantasies which bridge to some extent the gap between Freud's *theory* of the primitive ego and his *clinical* analysis of three to five year old children. The main features of these phantasies are as follows: the child regards itself (its body) as a kind of playground for warring and (or) loving organs (both inside and outside the body) and it regards external objects (parents) in the same way. They, too, are bundles of warring and loving organs. The two systems are also interrelated: parts of the child can represent outside objects; parts of the outside objects can represent the self. Life consists of a series of encounters (battles, alliances, etc.) between these compound egos and compound objects, and the fortunes of war depend on the extent to which loving (good) parts prevail over hating (bad) parts. This depends in turn on the nature of the child's primitive impulses, and the extent to which they are mastered (in the main) by processes of introjection and projection. In course of describing these phantasies all sorts of terms have been used, e.g. 'introjected penis', 'good' or 'bad' parent, etc., which require more disciplined definition. There is a tendency to confuse phantasy products with dynamic mechanisms. But that is a matter which can be dealt with later. The main objection which might be advanced is also one which time no doubt will remedy. The phantasy-systems have been described too rigorously in terms of older (and much more schematic) systems of 'primacy', e.g. oral and oral-sadistic phantasies. It is true that these primacies have been amplified by including phases of sadistic development as well as purely libidinal phases. *But there is not yet sufficient subdivision of these phases in terms of a more elaborate primitive ego: that is to say a body-ego in which a considerable number of component factors combine to produce a loosely organized whole.* It is evident also that in the attempt to reconcile these earlier phantasies with what might now be called the classical Oedipus situation a certain timidity in reconstruction has made itself felt. The next stage in research is to distinguish between those phantasies which give rise to affects (anxiety and guilt) secondarily and those which are due to an attempt on the part of the mind to bind existing affects, i.e. to lessen states of tension by building up appropriate explanations, using for the purpose existing (conscious and unconscious) ideations, e.g. symbolic thinking. In the meantime we can safely use the terms 'introjection'- and 'projection-anxieties' and 'body-phantasies' (injuries, restorations or renewals of the body of subject and object).

CLINICAL RELATIONS

My interest in the developmental significance of these systems was roused by observations on one or two cases of transitional disorder of the drug-addiction type. Not only could one observe the same systems of body-phantasy, but it was apparent that as affective tensions increased the mind fell back on more violent forms of introjection and projection. I have reported a case in which I observed a patient proceed from an obsessional phase to build up a drug-addiction and then develop a paranoid crisis on abstinence. When the anxiety was reduced the symptom-series was reversed. This brought me to a conception of the relation of drug-addiction to paranoia. I thought of drug-addictions as a transitional manifestation in which the projection mechanisms were localized on the drug-system, thus freeing the reality-ego from more widespread interference. Certain clinical considerations gave rise to difficulty at this point. Obviously many addictions are built up on a melancholic basis. Some obsessional neuroses, too, have a melancholic side (cf. Abraham on the obsessional character found in the intermissions of melancholia), whilst in others a schizophrenic layer can be detected. These clinical relations could be confirmed by analysis. The inference was obvious: just as there are paranoid and melancholic obsessional addictions, so there must be paranoid and melancholic obsessional types. Here the customary clinical picture of the obsessional neuroses proved rather a stumbling-block. It is rare to see obsessional neuroses in which the paranoid (or melancholic) features dominate the clinical picture. The picture is usually mixed.

INTROJECTION AND PROJECTION

At this point I was able to observe some cases of paranoia in which obsessional mechanisms were still active and helped to preserve some reality-relation inside the delusional system. The main feature in such cases is the existence of 'good' as well as 'bad' persecutors.[1] In addition I was able to study analytically some cases which I have described earlier in this paper, viz. obsessional neuroses in which the technique applied only or mainly to affective experiences. These had originally been diagnosed as mild depressions. Now behind these 'emotional obsessions' I was able to detect simple and well-defined anxieties about the body, its integrity and its relation to the bodies of objects, in short, the now familiar systems of body-phantasy. The conclusion was obvious: *the main function of the obsessional system must be to combine and consolidate the advantages of introjection and projection mechanisms and at the same time to eliminate as far as possible the disadvantages of depending too exclusively on any one mechanism.* These disadvantages are apparent in the affective disturbances of melancholia and paranoia respectively and in the affective difficulties of melancholiac and paranoid drug addictions. It is assumed that a state in which mainly 'bad' objects are introjected threatens panic, and that the opposite tendency to project 'badness' on to objects is just as dangerous in its own way. Study of obsessions in which subject-object relations are important proves that this assumption is correct. In the contamination case I mentioned earlier, the swing between introjection and projection dangers could be easily observed. When bad internal objects threatened the ego, the patient developed gradually a 'projection' system of obsessions (contamination rituals in streets and buses) affecting real external objects, thereby denying and swinging away from 'introjection' dangers. When the 'projection' system aroused too much panic, a swing back to 'introjection' patterns of obsession took place (touching rituals carried out in a closed room). We see then that the function of the obsessional neurosis is not only to split up mental tensions before they reach the stage of producing panic and to allow a more rapid swing between introjection and projection affects, but *by expanding the mechanism of displacement*

---

[1] I have recently seen another of these cases in consultation. The patient had on occasion some insight into the possible delusional nature of his ideas. He was under the influence of good and bad systems of external interference. The good system was a system of 'good observation' and 'control' intended to bring him up as a world-Saviour. But when it pressed too hard (i.e. interfered) this 'good' system became 'bad', and the patient reacted as in the ordinary delusions of persecution, i.e. with violent rage. The good and bad systems had preserved an obsessional character.

to develop the first stable relation between the ego and its objects.[1] In other words, obsessional mechanisms soften the sharpness of introjections, prevent irrevocable projections and, by their flexible range of intercommunication, bind the ego to the object.

OBSESSIONS AND PHOBIAS

Having considered the factors giving rise to obsessional phases of development, it is only logical to inquire what is the relation of obsessional symptoms to anxiety-phobias. The latter are usually supposed to belong to a more advanced state of development and have been credited with a quite characteristic set of mechanisms. Here again there are some clinical obstacles to overcome. On the one hand, according to Klein, Schmideberg and others, so-called anxiety-phobias may be modified residues of original paranoid fears. And, on the other hand, there has always been some uncertainty as to the relation of anxiety-phobias to obsessional fears. Some observers are in the habit of speaking of 'obsessional phobias', whilst others feel that the phrase is a contradiction in terms. Of course, it can always be argued that, whether anxiety-phobias are primary or whether they are derived from earlier paranoid fears, there is no need to suggest that they have any close connection with obsessional systems or phases. I do not find this view very satisfying. I certainly agree that many anxiety-phobias

[1] In a recent discussion in the British Psycho-Analytical Society some confusion arose as to the exact meaning to be attached to the terms 'ambivalence', 'pre-ambivalent', etc. It is clear from recent work that Abraham's idea of a pre-ambivalent phase existing prior to the dentition period does not take into account the violent fluctuations of affect that occur in the first six to nine months of life. On the other hand, the original discovery that obsessional neurotics exhibit a high degree of ambivalence is undoubtedly accurate. It is in keeping with the view that from the ages of at least $1\frac{1}{2}$ to $3\frac{1}{2}$ years the child does suffer from simultaneous feelings of love and hate towards any one object. In short, it has consolidated subject-object relations, combined affective attitudes to objects and achieved some balance of mechanisms. In the formal sense therefore it may be right to talk of a pre-ambivalent stage, i.e. in the sense of ego-object organization. But the fluctuations of affect occurring before this period are certainly more violent and painful; ambivalence, painful as it is, is a more stable state. It is an advance on the uncertainties and despairs which go with an uncontrolled swing in affect. Gratification-affects no doubt help towards acquiring a sense of safety. But for a long time their influence is bound to be transient.

cover a quite considerable residue of paranoid fear; although in
other cases the residue is so small that the anxiety state is for all
practical purposes primary, being mainly a defence against genital
anxieties. But experience of clinical forms seems to me to make it
impossible to exclude obsessional influences. There are so many
cases in which hysterical anxiety is combined with obsessional
manifestations. And even where this connection is not obvious,
one is occasionally able to uncover in analysis an obsessional
system originally interposed between a hysterical anxiety and a
primitive projection anxiety. *In such cases it would appear that the
hysterical phobia constitutes an isolated fragment of an obsessional
system.* A simple example is that of a woman with a phobia of
oilcloth of a certain colour. It was impossible for her to pass a
furnishing shop without experiencing anxiety to the point of
nausea. In analysis this appeared to be the tail-end of a series of
obsessional substitutions. The original compulsive idea was found
to be the familiar one of having caused a baby to be thrown out of
a pram and killed. The oilcloth was the same colour as the pram
cover. Behind the obsessional system there existed a considerable
degree of 'body-anxiety', which resolved itself into a fear of her
mother who during the patient's early childhood wore clothes of a
similar colour. Allowing for an inevitable amount of over-determi-
nation, such cases suggest that the connection between anxiety-
phobias, obsessions and fears of a projection type is much closer
than the clinical features suggest. In the early days of psycho-
analysis Freud was faced with the necessity of re-classifying
existing clinical data. Having provisionally established some order
in the relations of various '*Aktual-neurosen*' to the anxiety states,
he was able to clarify his etiological formulas. But since that time
little has been done in the way of more systematic classification
either of neuroses or of psychoses. It seems that the time is now
ripe for further efforts along these lines.

In the foregoing account no mention has been made of cases in
which there is an obvious overlap between sexual perversions or
phantasies, on the one hand, and compulsive sexual thinking or
action on the other. It is interesting to observe that amongst the
clinical perversions, there are some well-defined types showing
the same tendency (disguised, of course, by sexual activity) to
combine and consolidate the mechanisms of introjection and

projection. Until these various relations are worked out, it would be premature to attempt laying down detailed etiological formulas. The object of this paper is to indicate that the most fruitful line of etiological research is the developmental one. When we know enough about the early manifestations of the ego, the interrelations and combinations of various mechanisms in different stages and the relation of these combinations to specific affects, we may look forward to a more effective subdivision of clinical syndromes and a more exact statement of etiological factors in any one instance.

XVII

UNCONSCIOUS FUNCTIONS OF EDUCATION*

[1937]

Up to this time the pre-occupation of psycho-analysts with the disturbing (pathogenic) influence of unconscious or preconscious systems had led to a certain neglect of those pre-conscious methods of instinctual control that are ostensibly brought into operation after the close of the infantile period. In particular little work had been done on the carry-over of certain defence mechanisms into the pre-conscious system. In fact the then existing arbitrary distinction between 'formal' and 'infantile' education was too readily accepted at face value. The object of the following communication to a symposium on the subject was to stress the continuity of certain unconscious and preconscious systems of defence. Followed to its logical conclusion this view would necessitate a re-examination of the interrelation of unconscious 'educational' aims with those of inhibition, sublimation, super-ego activity and other recognized systems of unconscious defence. The suggestion in the concluding paragraph, that psycho-analysis itself may operate at deeper levels as a form of pedagogy, has been borne out in recent times by the direct importation of ego-education as a preliminary to some forms of child-analysis. I have carried this idea farther in a recent suggestion that the earliest forms of subject-object relation give rise during analysis to 'unanalysable' transferences which, in all but the pure 'transference-neuroses' influence the ultimate 'accessibility' of the case to treatment.[1]

It is good scientific practice to open a symposium with a simple definition of terms. Unfortunately in the case of education there can be no such definition. It is bound to vary in accordance with

* Introduction to a symposium on 'Psycho-Analysis and Education' held by the British Psycho-Analytical Society, May 8, 1935, and first published in *The International Journal of Psycho-Analysis*, Vol. XVIII, pt. 2–3, p. 190, 1937.

[1] See 'Therapeutic Criteria of Psycho-analysis', *The Technique of Psycho-Analysis*, Baillière, Tindall & Cox, London, 1955.

the psychological views of the symposiast. For example, the definitions accepted by most academic bodies are partly descriptive and partly psychological. But the psychology concerned is a conscious, almost academic, psychology. When psycho-analysts come to consider the problem of education these definitions are quite inadequate. Before defining the term they must subject it to a process of decomposition (in other words, analyse it): and in the last resort they must be ready to *interpret* it. They must interpret the various components of the process, and on the basis of these interpretations attempt to characterize the total activity.

This is only another way of saying that while psycho-analysis is entitled to take over the term 'education' (indeed, *must* recognize it as a form of mental mechanism or group of mental mechanisms) it is bound to attach a deeper significance to it. This deepening process is amply illustrated throughout the history of psycho-analytic terminology. Take the case of 'repression'. Originally borrowed from common language, because of its conscious (topographic and dynamic) implications, the word was given a scientific twist by means of which it could be used to represent an unconscious mental mechanism. The same is true of terms such as 'projection', 'displacement', etc. But in all these instances analysts and, although to a lesser extent, non-analysts are aware of the special usage. In the case of 'education' even psycho-analysts are not fully aware that the term although applicable to a conscious volitional process is also a ready-made label for an unconscious mental mechanism, or, as the case may be, a combination of unconscious mental mechanisms. Confusion must inevitably arise from this special usage, just as it arose in the case of the term 'sublimation'. But that cannot be helped. The comparison with sublimation is also apt in that sublimation, too, includes a number of unconscious component mechanisms which have become fused to give the impression of unitary function.

Now it has frequently been remarked, more particularly by analysts, that education seems in many instances to be a form of open inhibition. The evidence in favour of this view is indeed overwhelming. From first to last the 'Don't' of education is as emphatic as the 'Do'. Yet as I have suggested, even amongst analysts the view that education is an *unconscious* mechanism (or mechanisms) serving amongst other purposes the purpose of *unconscious instinct inhibition* is rarely emphasized. This is due I think to the fact that analysts have not yet assessed exactly the inter-relations of endopsychic (central) and environmental factors in mental development. Having established the extreme import- ance of unconscious factors in, for example, symptom formation they have a natural anxiety lest the traumatic effect of a bad early environment or the prophylactic effect of a loving environment should be over-emphasized. The result is that they tend to isolate environmental influences, i.e. distinguish them sharply from endopsychic influences. Education being obviously environmental, they are disinclined to think that it can be anything else. Yet even if it were purely environmental it could still be manipulated (exploited) by unconscious mechanisms. This has been demon- strated amply in the case of projection mechanisms. In the case of projection, the child seizes on true environmental conditions and exaggerates them in some way to suit its own unconscious pur- poses. Indeed, we might say that since the unconscious conflicts of the educator and those of the child are partly identical and partly complementary, the educational policies of the former must be a constant temptation to the child. They cry out for manipula- tion.

The curious situation then arises that analysts, in their anxiety over environmental factors, may come to neglect one of their own important discoveries, viz. that concurrently with the application of environmental influences in education, the individual is, to put it quite simply, unconsciously educating himself. Education from without can act as a displacement or projection of unconscious self-education and ends by becoming a screen for it. The distrust of conscious self-education exhibited by the educator is a measure of this screening function. There is some reason to believe that most problems in infantile conduct can be solved by refraining from pointed attempts to educate the infant, i.e. by leaving it to the child. The best example is undoubtedly the unnecessary system of training in cleanliness.

To approach the problem of education more systematically it is necessary to enquire what in fact is being educated. At this point individual preferences begin to assert themselves. Some have a preference for thinking that education is directed at the ego (including here, for the moment, the super-ego). Others prefer to think that education is a process directed at instincts. Strictly speaking, a satisfactory approach involves combining these different points of view. Yet it is convenient to deal with them separately.

If we consider education from the point of view of instincts, it is clear that we must distinguish between the methods used for different instincts. Accepting the customary subdivison of self-preservative, sexual and aggressive impulse, it seems obvious that from the first, education makes a good show of training self-preservative impulse. In so doing it harnesses the mechanism of displacement in order to provide more immediate and effective adaptation. Reading, writing and arithmetic serve useful purposes in checking the grocer's bill, and so expand the range of simpler nutritional drives. In the case of aggressive impulse the mechanisms of displacement and substitution are also brought into play, but from the earliest phases they are reinforced by other mechanisms. Every variety of prohibition or inhibition or precipitation of guilt feeling is employed by the educator to stem aggressive urges. The same may be said of primitive sexual impulses. The educator makes strenuous efforts to achieve their displacement, but at the same time subjects them to extreme forms of inhibition. It is to be noted, however, that the plan of encouraging displacement of sexual impulse in the sense of promoting sublimations is not quite so deliberate and open as in the case of aggressive impulse. It is often admitted by the educationist that he encourages physical and intellectual activities not merely for adaptation's sake, but to use up what he might call 'animal spirits'. But except in the case of pubertal education he rarely admits that his quarry is sexuality. And in fact except at puberty he seldom realizes the aim of his educational thrust. At this point it is easy to see what is actually the unconscious function of education. As practised and preached it is to a very large extent an inhibitory process covered by systems of rationalization. Like all systems of rationalization it offers a part truth to conceal a whole truth. It stresses the adaptation value of its processes to conceal their unconscious inhibitory intent.[1] From the beginning, aggressive and sexual impulses have been modified by a series of unconscious mechanisms, projection, introjection, repression, displacement, reaction-formation, sublimation. This

[1] In this respect education shows an affinity with repression. The efficiency of repression depends on anticathexis: i.e. '*this* is what you are concerned with, not *that* (repressed) idea'. The educator says, 'we are teaching you to do *this*', but omits to add 'we don't want you to do *that* (repressed)'.

constitutes self-education. From the beginning education affords a good deal of 'cover' for these defences, at the same time acting as an auxiliary to them. At the school age it steps boldly into the foreground, substituting extra-familial for parental rationalizations.

Having roughly distinguished the educative procedures with different instincts, we must note that conscious education of one instinct may contribute to the unconscious control of another. The displacements necessary to develop self-preservative impulse, for example, act to some extent as a counterpoise to the anxieties caused by projection of aggressive impulse on external reality, and to that extent allow a constant amount of projection which is in effect anxiety-free. They do this by increasing our experience of true external reality. The more we know of practical botany and of bacteriology, the better the quality of our salads and the less likely we are to contract typhoid fever by eating them. But the safer we are in this respect the more easily can we indulge mild 'poison phantasies' due to the projection of unconscious aggressive impulse. Similarly the displacements effected by sublimation of sexual impulse, aided and abetted by processes of education, act as a reinforcement of self-preservative impulse by increasing our range of knowledge. Our infantile sexual interest in the 'primal scene' may become partly sublimated in an interest in the growth of plants or bacteria. And this concern with practical botany and bacteriology will no doubt improve the quality and increase the wholesomeness of our salads. Even more interesting are the situations where owing to the variety of instincts concerned the *unconscious* aims of education *defeat* the *conscious* aims. Perhaps the best example is that of the impulses of sexual curiosity. Here the unconscious aim of the educative process might almost be called hypocritical, viz. to aid in stemming curiosity by the offer of substitute information. As we know, the effect of this manœuvre in some cases is not only to stem direct forms of sexual curiosity, but to inhibit the substitute forms of aimless questioning to such an extent that the individual is unable to exploit the ordinary self-preservative aims of curiosity.

The view that education is an unconscious mental mechanism brings with it certain responsibilities. Education is easy game for the critic. It is the habit for each generation to pillory its inadequacies, and critics are rarely mollified by the moral and biological rationalizations of the pedagogue. The fact is, however, that, in the sense of mental defence, effective education is no more to be criticized than effective repression. It is unsuccessful repression and unsuccessful education that call not so much for moral criticism as professional attention.

And here we come to what I imagine is an issue worthy of discussion, viz. whether psycho-analysts are in a position to say what constitutes unsuccessful education, or for that part successful education, or whether they must fall back on a purely empirical (professional) valuation. Other cognate issues are: whether if they do know, they are able to communicate this knowledge to pedagogues in an effective form: or again whether it would make much difference to the outcome of individual upbringing if they did know and could communicate the knowledge. To be able to answer these questions we must have a fairly exact measure of our powers of directing impulse, of substituting one mechanism for another, and of the effect, favourable or otherwise, produced by such efforts. And it seems to me that in order to decide these points we must have a good deal more information than we already possess.

The second or ego aspect of education requires equally close discussion, but as this has been given more attention than the instinctual aspect I do not propose to do more than refer to a few main points. First of all we have to consider the basic identifications or introjections which render the ego amenable to educative processes of whatever sort. An adequate discussion of this point would involve summarizing the whole of our recent researches into ego structure, particularly those ego differentiations occurring during the first two to three years of life. Even so, it would scarcely be complete without a parallel assessment of the educative function of projective systems in the ego. The next step is more within our present scope: to consider the type of energy which best promotes the formation of educable identifications. There seems to be good reason for assuming that libidinal energies are pre-eminently suitable in this respect. This is only another way of saying that education through love (either because of its direct effect or through reduction of anxiety) is the most suitable system. For many years now we have recognized that the process of 'libidinization' helps to counter crude anxieties. But we are much slower to observe how much and how unobtrusively it oils the wheels of existence. We cannot escape from the conclusion that particularly during the earliest years the actual amount of (non-ambivalent) love afforded the child by parents and substitutes determines to a large extent the infant's amenability to the more painful and inevitable varieties of education (i.e. instinct modification.

Finally, we have to consider the subdivision of identifications in accordance with their reality and moral aspects respectively. This brings us to the central problem of the super-ego. Around this central problem cluster all those issues about psycho-analysis and education with which we have been made familiar in the past, e.g. how far moral drives persist in psychotherapy and pedagogy respectively. I would only add here one general consideration. The old issue of endopsychic *versus* environmental factors in super-ego formation is by no means a settled one. It is true that for some time in this country the environmentalists have had to hide their diminished heads. But as I have pointed out before, this is only a swing of the pendulum. Further researches will almost certainly produce a swing in the opposite direction although the age-period at which these researches will be directed will be a much earlier one than heretofore. In this one respect I am rather pessimistic about the outcome of present-day discussions on education. I personally believe that our researches on child development are still in their infancy, that the degree of merging of true endopsychic and environmental influences in super-ego and ego formation has not been ascertained. But I suspect that for many reasons this merging will be found to be very extensive. Until this transitional phase has been examined thoroughly and its realistic and unrealistic components isolated, I fail to see how we can be very dogmatic about the relations of psycho-analysis to education. *I can well imagine that we may discover an early phase of development the characteristics of which will blunt very considerably those sharp distinctions between the processes of psycho-analysis and pedagogy which we have been in the habit of making.* It will help us to maintain some perspective in the matter if we keep in mind that education (however rationalized) is itself one of a series of unconscious mental mechanisms.

XVIII
A NOTE ON IDEALIZATION*
[1938]

The following short communication continues the process of re-examining standard psycho-analytical concepts which was applied in some detail in the paper Sublimation, Substitution and Social Anxiety (*Chap. X*)*, and, although in a more cursory manner in the note on* Unconscious Functions of Education (*Chap. XVII*)*. In contrast to the then generally accepted view, it is maintained that many mechanisms attributed to preconscious activity (secondary processes) and commonly regarded as characteristic of the latency period, are already in operation during the infantile phase; and that, although their earlier manifestations may fall before repression, their unconscious function is continuous from infancy to adult life. Although the uses of aim-inhibition, sublimation and idealization as means of overcoming anxiety is stressed, it is not to be thought that the anxiety factor accounts fully for these processes. That would be to confuse positive manifestations of instinctual activity (however inhibited their aim) with reactive products of anti-cathexis, and would lead to the further error of assuming that defences against unmodified libido are more creative in effect than derivatives of modified libido – a view which, in spite of its psycho-biological improbability, seems to have gained currency in recent years.*

In recent years we have been compelled to recast our ideas about early stages of mental development. Already the discovery of the early onset of the Oedipus complex has brought about recognition of an early form of super-ego. The effect of these clinical discoveries on psycho-analytical theories is far reaching. As I have pointed out on several occasions, an early super-ego based on relations of the infant with so-called 'part-objects'[1] completely alters our views

* Read before the British Psycho-Analytical Society, Wednesday, November 1, 1933, and first published in *The International Journal of Psycho-Analysis*, Vol. XIX, pt. 1, Jan. 1938.

[1] [Note (1954): See footnote on 'part-objects' and 'complete' objects. Chap. I, p. 8.]

on narcissism, to say nothing of more dynamic concepts such as 'autoerotism' and 'polymorphous-perverse' impulses. Once this work of re-definition is begun there seems no reason to limit it to the structure of the ego or the stages of instinct modification. Logically we must apply it also to the nature of mental mechanisms. In particular we must enquire whether some unconscious mechanisms do not begin to function much earlier than has hitherto been supposed.

During the observations of sexual perversions occurring in certain psychotic types, I have been struck with the fact that despite the early origin of the symptoms in question most of these patients made constant use of the process of idealization. Now according to accepted views idealization is a process which commences in late childhood and adolescence. It seemed difficult to reconcile this view with the fact that all these cases showed evident signs of regression of both ego and libido to very early stages of development.

Before considering this problem further we may summarize briefly what the accepted views are. Discussing the effect of repression on the sexual impulses of the five-year-old child, Freud points out[1] that the child afterwards remains tied to the parents by aim-inhibited impulses, his emotions towards love objects being characterized as 'tender'. At puberty these tender feelings may in unfavourable cases remain separate from the sensual current. A striking feature of being in love is presented by the phenomenon of over-estimation. If the sensual tendencies are set aside 'the *illusion* (writer's italics) is produced that the object has come to be sensually loved on account of its spiritual merits'. 'The tendency which falsifies judgment in this respect is that of *idealization*.' The object is being treated like the ego: it has attracted a considerable amount of narcissistic libido, and so functions as a substitute for some unattained ego-ideal. If this process increases the object may become more and more precious until it 'has, so to speak, consumed the ego'. This devotion of the ego to the object 'is no longer to be distinguished from a sublimated devotion to an abstract idea'. Re-emphasizing the fact that tender feelings are derived from earlier infantile sensual feelings Freud points out that these diverted or aim-inhibited instincts always preserve a few of their original sexual aims and adds, 'If we choose we may recognize in

[1] *Group Psychology and the Analysis of the Ego.*' Hogarth Press, 1922.

this diversion of aims a beginning of the *sublimation* of the sexual instincts.' Further, 'the inhibited instincts are capable of any degree of admixture with the uninhibited, they can be transformed back into them just as they arose out of them.' Although purposeless in aim they provide 'a much frequented pathway to sexual object-choice'. Finally, they arise as a consequence of 'repression during the period of latency'.

It is clear from the above that there is a close relation between the concepts of aim-inhibition, idealization and sublimation,[1] a fact which present-day observations fully confirm. Secondly, it is implied that aim-inhibition occurs in the latency period, idealization not earlier than the pubertal phase. This no longer seems to tally with clinical experience. On the contrary, I would maintain that all these processes take effect in the pre-latency period, indeed, that the process of idealization is more active in the pre-latency period than in any other. This does not affect the view that idealization depends on the nature of super-ego conflict and the degree to which psychic relations with objects can resolve conflict. On the other hand explanation of idealization solely in terms of repression of infantile sensual components seems incomplete. Freud's own remark on the element of *illusion* in idealization itself suggests different probabilities, viz. that the rôle of repression is a secondary one, that idealization is in principle closely related to the *delusional* defences of the psychoses and that it is bound up with the operation of projection and introjection defences. This would suggest that the ego, as a result of introjection and projection phantasies invests parts of the self and true external objects with anxiety and is therefore compelled to idealize (libidinize) them in order to reduce this anxiety. Further, it seems probable that the regression to sensual origins that can sometimes be observed in aim inhibition, in idealization and in sublimation is determined not simply by the break through of inadequately repressed sensual elements, but by the fact that regression permits a more extensive libidinization of pathogenic anxieties.

Clinical evidence in support of these contentions can be gathered from a number of fields, in particular from the study of early infancy, of sexual perversions in the adult and of those borderline psychoses in which a degree of perversion-formation occurs.

[1] [Note (1955): For a full discussion of these concepts see Chap. X on *Sublimation, Substitution and Social Anxiety*.]

In the case of infants up to the ages of eighteen months or two years it is of course difficult to check the inferences (or interpretations) made on the strength of observations. Yet although it is never difficult to establish the existence of sensual currents during that early stage, it seems that we are inclined to neglect the existence of tender currents. At the very least there are obvious indications of sexual over-estimation in the attitude or behaviour of infants towards accessible parts of their own bodies. This is perhaps easiest to observe in the case of hands and arms. The child can be observed in lengthy contemplation of these organs which are doubtless conceived of as objects. And although the pleasure is no doubt in the main sensual in nature it suggests a degree of wonderment and adoration which is a constant feature of adult sexual over-estimation and which is closely combined with tenderness towards the object. The same reaction can be observed in relation to many inanimate external objects, e.g. dangling pieces of coloured glass. These inferences are confirmed when through increasing age and the development of speech we are informed by the growing child what exactly is its attitude to parts of its own body and to real external objects animate and inanimate. Characteristically these attitudes are more fully expressed in the case of inanimate substitute objects (toys, etc.) than in the case of animate objects (parents, etc.). An attitude is adopted towards favourite toys which can scarcely be distinguished from the idealization of the object. The same attitude can sometimes be detected in the child's word-play, an activity which is extremely pronounced in adult idealization. Studying these early manifestations one is compelled to reassess the relation of repression to idealization systems. One can say, of course, that since repression itself occurs earlier than has hitherto been supposed the relation of idealization to repression as originally described by Freud is still valid. But there is no reason to suppose that the original tender current towards objects does not exist in a primitive and rudimentary form which is at the same time or perhaps later reinforced as the result of repression.

Evidence from study of the perversions is even more striking. Apart from marked sexual overestimation of part-objects and their immediate substitutes, many cases exhibit an attitude of extreme idealization of these objects however primitive they may be. With this almost sexual variety of idealization goes a general tendency to idealize not adult objects but more remote abstract objects and interests. These are indistinguishable from sublimatory idealizations. Yet the language used is identical with that used for the most primitive sexual objects. This is a common characteristic of the sexual pervert. However devoid of idealization of adult relations he may be, his geese are usually regarded by him as swans. The sexual part-objects treated with this combination of sexual over-estimation and idealization vary with the individual, but my experience seems to indicate that these reactions are more common in the case of objects of anal and urethral sexuality. Next to these come those fetichistic idealizations behind which lies a good deal of sadistic interest. In a typical case the anal ring was phantasied as a kind of halo suspended in the sky. It was then contemplated, adored and idealized. The qualities attributed to it were mystical and the whole attitude of the patient was religious in type. A fetichist arranged his extensive collection of women's shoes in a bookcase in such a manner that the soles of the shoes looked like the backs of books. Of these, one pair with high-pointed heels was singled out for special reverence and idealized as if it were a highly superior being. As the analysis progressed the sadistic attributes of this special pair of shoes came to the surface, and incidentally as the construction loosened the patient altered his previous policy of illiteracy, and became an extensive reader and collector of books.

Although the first case quoted might appear to belong to a schizoid group such manifestations are not uncommon in people who both clinically and as tested by after history are not psychotic. In schizoid types the process is naturally more obvious. Sexual over-estimation and idealization extends to every variety of part-object, food, fæces, urine, sexual zones, etc. They have attributed to them every variety of concrete and abstract virtue. At the same time these patients tend to excessive idealization of their natural surroundings, the sun or sunshine, woods, flower gardens, cliffs, valleys, the sea. In their relations with adult objects however, idealization is rare. Depressive cases in my experience do not show the same forms of sexual over-estimation of part-objects but they do tend to idealization of certain natural surroundings obviously selected in accordance with a 'good and bad' system. The best example is also the commonest, viz. idealization of sunlit as opposed to shady spaces or streets. The one is associated with goodness, safety, life and God, the other with baɑness, danger, death and evil. Still other cases reverse this valuation, idealizing dark places and fearing or avoiding the almost persecutory glare of open sunlight.

It might be argued that none of this evidence is valid; that however primitive the unconscious content may be, nevertheless idealizations need not be of the same date. They might well be pubertal deviations of sexual impulse which act as late anticathexes reinforcing the repression of primitive drives. Study of psychotic types seems to me to dispose of this argument quite effectively. In the analysis of such cases one is in a position to observe regression during which the developmental relation of idealization systems to unconscious content becomes quite clear. During their more stable phases many schizoids and mild depressives complain of the shallow nature of their contact with adult objects. Even if they don't complain, it is easy to see that in those relations (either sexual or social) there is very little idealization of the adult object. It is all the more significant therefore that when they go through a phase of regression culminating in an outbreak of perverse phantasy or behaviour the most extreme forms of idealization are exhibited. These, however, show no signs of being deviated towards adult objects but are directly concerned with primitive objects or with natural surroundings which symbolize them.

Still more interesting is the fact that during this phase of idealization of natural surroundings, the patient alternates rapidly between a sense of being in security and an apprehension of great danger together with a feeling of isolation which may develop into a sense of alienation. This suggests that one of the aims of the regression is to seek for and secure the comforts of an idealized relation with primitive objects. The fact that this aim is not achieved or achieved only in part and at the cost of still greater anxieties does not invalidate this conclusion. It is characteristic of symptom formation that on the balance it does not succeed in its aim of securing peace of mind.

Summing up these impressions I would suggest that the pubertal idealizations we encounter are contributed from two sources. They can be traced indirectly through the paths of aim-inhibition back to the repression of infantile sensual components. This is the commonly accepted view. All we need to add to it is that repression operates in the earliest years when the impulses are directed mainly towards part-objects, and that true idealizations occur already in that early phase. The second component is derived from a primitive form of idealization, a tender attitude to part-objects which is not directly incited by repression but is gradually modified in expression as object relations develop. These primitive idealizations have in my opinion a specially close relation to anal-sadism, a relation which renders them subject to part repression. If early relations with objects are on the balance unsatisfactory these early idealizations may be completely repressed, so that when they re-appear later (? latency or puberty) they give the impression of being primary rather than derived. Finally, these early idealizations have a considerable reassurance value and can take part in the process of 'libidinizing' anxiety objects. It is this last factor which puts an additional premium on regression when later on in life the patient is faced with some fresh instinctual stress, and in consequence is threatened with breakdown.

XIX

THE PSYCHO-ANALYSIS OF AFFECTS*

[1938]

One of the first and most obvious consequences of Freud's discovery of unconscious mental function was the realization that the organized and synthesized products of adult mental activity, both normal and abnormal, are 'end-products', the various antecedents of which can be traced to their separate roots in unconscious layers of the mind. To this extent descriptive psychology both normal and clinical proved to be a stumbling block rather than an aid to psychological understanding. But in two respects at least psycho-analysts failed to apply logically the analytic doctrines they had so painfully established. Perhaps under the impression that psychotic manifestations, instead of being end-products, are somehow 'nearer' to the unconscious, they tended to look for and consequently to 'recognize' adult psychotic reactions in early childhood. And they have looked for and made bold to discover adult affects in the earliest stages of mental development. This flies in the face of all psycho-biological probability. The truth is that the psychoanalyst, deprived of the mental content by which he recognizes stages in mental development, is very much at sea about all but very simple reactive affects such as anxiety; and even there the influence of mechanisms such as repression serves to confuse the trail. Under these circumstances the best course seems to be to apply the tests of metapsychological probability to the problem of affects; and to check in the clinical field the various working hypotheses arrived at, such, for example, as the 'fusion' of different affective components to form new but specific 'secondary' affects. In the following paper an attempt has been made to isolate and describe one of the early 'tension-affects' by applying the metapsychological concept of a 'tension-discharge sequence' to a number of clinical observations.

As time goes on it becomes clearer that the recent fallow period in the development of psycho-analysis is due to a comparative neglect

* First published in *The International Journal of Psycho-Analysis*, Vol. XX, pts. 3 and 4, p. 299, July–Oct. 1939.

of the problem of affect. The obscurity surrounding early stages of ego organization or the nature of early ideational content is as nothing compared with the obscurity that clouds the understanding of primary affects and their vicissitudes. And this for a number of reasons. Not only is ideational content easier to grasp than the more labile and impermanent expressions of affect, but the exploration of affect tends to arouse greater subjective resistances. Moreover, clinical observers naturally focus their attention rather exclusively on those affective reactions that are most frequently and most obviously responsible for pathological states. Thus the constant reference made during recent clinical discussions to the factor of 'anxiety' (either manifest or latent) tends to give the impression that analysts regard this state and its immediate sequelæ, hate and guilt, as the only affective responses of early childhood and therefore as the mainsprings of neurotic or psychotic reaction. Similarly, a recent recrudescence of interest in transference is justified by its sponsors on the ground that the latent anxiety content of these transferences has not been duly appreciated. Although praiseworthy enough this over-emphasis is not without its dangers. Therapeutically regarded the essence of transference is the displacement of affect, and undue concentration on the 'anxiety-hate-guilt' group is likely to impede understanding of other important affective reactions.

Yet another factor in the comparative neglect of affects is the tendency to be too exclusively interested in ideational derivatives of instinct (e.g. in the more stereotyped forms of primitive unconscious phantasy); or again, to consider such unconscious phantasies solely in terms of the specific instinct from which they are felt to be derived. By so doing the observer is liable to gloss over the fact that the driving power of instincts cannot be properly appreciated without some measure of the affects they engender. In other words the boundary concept of instinct is of clinical value in two directions only: in so far as it promotes an adequate classification of phenomena, and in so far as the concept of continuous flow of energy makes it easier to understand the existence of periodic stresses and of regressions. It is to the *actual derivatives of instinct-stress* that we must look for an explanation of mental behaviour. And amongst the primary derivatives of and responses to instinct-stress, affective reactions are by far the most powerful.

A fresh investigation of affect therefore requires not only more careful analysis of affective experiences but a plausible reconstruction of the affective states occurring during early phases of infancy, when analytic observation cannot be checked by examination of ideational derivatives, when, in fact one can do little more than draw inferences either from behaviouristic data or from analytic observations made on other and older subjects.

As far as reconstruction is concerned, it is appropriate to recall that one of the most successful efforts in this direction lies to the credit of Ernest Jones. In his paper on 'Fear, Guilt and Hate'[1] he set himself the task of describing systematically some early 'layerings' of affective states, if one may use a mixed dynamic-topographic expression. These views were a logical development of the author's earlier interest in the relations of instinct to morbid anxiety, and although they do not claim to be a complete reconstruction of the vicissitudes of affect in infancy they provide an instructive example of the method by which more comprehensive reconstructions can be made. It is clear that adequate understanding of affective problems cannot be achieved unless the subject is approached from a number of angles. Freud has already shown that no mental event can be understood unless it is examined metapsychologically. And affective phenomena call for a greater variety of approaches than any other mental manifestation. This is borne out by the fact that affects can be classified in a great variety of ways. They can be described in crude qualitative terms, e.g. of subjective pleasure or 'pain', or labelled descriptively according to the predominant ideational system associated with them in consciousness. They can be classified by reference to the instinct or component instinct from which they are derived, or they can be considered as either 'fixed' or 'labile'. They can be divided into primary affects and secondary affects, more precisely into 'positive' and 'reactive' affects, or they can be considered as tension and discharge phenomena. Finally, they can be grouped as simple or compound ('mixed' and/or 'fused') affects.

Generally speaking, the simpler the classification the less value it has. In this respect the pleasure-pain criterion is not very satisfactory. Similarly, the approach by reference to instinct requires considerable expansion before it can be of much service. Study of the affective reactions following frustration of different com-

[1] *Int. J. Psycho-Anal.*, **10**, 1929.

ponent impulses provides a valuable line of inquiry. Variations in the distribution of libido or of aggressive charges throughout the different body organs or zones are responsible for characteristic affective experiences. And no doubt these could be traced back to differences in the nature of sensory excitation and of stimulation of the sympathetic system. For example, the contribution of gastric, intestinal, skin and muscle erotism (sadism or agression) to the characteristic states that go to make up 'oral depressive' affect is certainly worthy of investigation. Similarly, the psychic displacement of libido from one zone to another, e.g. from the genitals to the extremities is responsible for a good deal of complication in subjective feeling. In short, the more complicated the relation of affective states the more necessary it becomes to distinguish clearly between simple and compound affects. The concept of *fusion* of affects has to be distinguished from that of 'mixed' affect, or again from simultaneous experience of affects of different origin. To take a simple example, the phenomenon of ambivalence is ill-described as a rapid alternation of love and hate affects or as a simultaneous experience of love and hate attitudes towards one and the same object. It is much better understood by extending the concept of fusion of instinct (which has been so abundantly justified in the case of sadism or masochism), and postulating an actual fusion of affect. The refractoriness of ambivalence to analysis and the fact that its partial disappearance during analysis involves a series of defusions and refusions of instinct is convincing evidence in this direction. The compelling and sometimes disruptive force of ambivalence is more comprehensible if it is regarded from the affective rather than from the ideational standpoint. This view is borne out by study of more complicated states of 'mixed' affect, such as are encountered occasionally in cases of perversion, where frustration affects are associated with gratification affects, or again in cases where compulsive sexual activity arises as a response to anxiety.

Moreover, in the case of affects that have proved pathogenic it is easy to demonstrate that many of these, although apparently simple, are actually compound or fused. They disappear only after a number of distinct affective elements (whose existence is proved by the presence of characteristic unconscious phantasies) have been analysed. Several writers, in particular Joan Riviere,[1] have

[1] 'Jealousy as a Mechanism of Defence', *Int. J. Psycho-Anal.*, **13**, 1932.

pointed out that jealousy formations are by no means simple: that they comprise a *number* of psychic situations. But clinically regarded the significance of jealousy depends on the fact that it is an extremely disturbing affect reducible on analysis to simpler elements of grief, anger, and fear. Perhaps the best example of an affect which although apparently primary is actually exceedingly complicated is that of depression. Some states of depression are certainly simpler and more primitive than others, compare e.g. the relatively simpler manifestations occurring in schizophrenia with those of 'depressive states'. The later depressions are, however, extremely elaborate. The simplest examination of ideational content shows that they combine a feeling of impoverishment due to internal loss of love, a feeling of deadness due to the action of internal anger directed against the love-object (with which the ego is partly identified) together with reactions of anxiety, guilt and remorse. These different reactions are bound together by what might be called an 'affective matrix', in this case an overwhelming feeling of hurt, the ultimate expression of frustration. The feelings of depression experienced in hysteria although similar in constitution are much less closely fused, and overlap more with other affects. They also conceal a deep jealousy reaction which induces a greater sense of active stress and therefore counteracts to some extent the 'stone-dead' feelings occurring in true depression. Hysterical depressives, despite their 'dead' feelings, are notoriously hyperactive. In any case, these more stereotyped ('fixed') components by no means exhaust the analysis of depressive affects. As has been suggested, these include also a variety of emotional reactions contributed specifically by disturbed or overcharged components of infantile instinct. And at this point the difficulty arises of discriminating between purely psychic experience and corporeal sensations of a hypochondriacal kind (e.g. mental and physical feelings of 'weight').

These findings suggest that it is to the lesser known components of any emotional cluster that one must turn in order to elucidate the early history of affect. And in this connection the most useful classification of affects seems to be that into tension affects and discharge affects. Freud himself indicated the importance of this approach when he called attention to the fact that the effects of excitation should not be regarded solely from the quantitative point of view. Rise and fall in excitation, he suggested, is important because there are definite qualities associated with different quantities of the same instinct excitation. So that presumably there are qualitatively different affective responses to frustrations of different quantities of instinct. And since there is no exact correlation between tension and 'pain', or between discharge and pleasure, there seems no alternative to investigating a large mass of clinical material in order to isolate and identify *specific tension affects*. The following clinical considerations may serve to illustrate how one of the tension affects can be isolated.

Those accustomed to analyse acute anxiety states must have observed that the more distressing forms of panic occur during periods of instinctual stress. The nature of the stress can be gathered by studying the efflorescence of unconscious phantasies (e.g. of sadistic intercourse) that ensues. The accompanying tension is experienced both physically and mentally. The physical forms include a variety of muscular innervations and organ sensations; the most familiar psychic reaction is best described as a feeling of mental 'bursting' which usually induces a lively apprehension of 'being disrupted', 'flying into fragments' or 'going mad'. Similarly, in depressive cases, when the feeling of internal weight begins to give way to active suicidal feelings, it is not hard to detect an increase in unconscious sadistic tensions which can no longer be immobilized. In this phase the depression affect frequently disappears to be replaced by a vaguely described but compelling 'intolerable feeling', comparable to bursting. Unlike the hysteric, the depressive case does not exhibit any panic on experiencing these explosive tensions. He simply takes it for granted that the feeling justifies any action calculated to relieve it. Where the hysteric would be content with fits of screaming or jumping up and down, the depressive is ready to commit suicide. These are, of course, outstanding examples. In milder conditions the bursting feelings are less constant and require for their periodic release some external justification. Thus, in some cases of frigidity, increase in the fear of penetration can be shown to accompany increase in unconscious sexual tension and phantasy. The actual bursting feeling is due to an overcharge of sado-masochistic energies, and the genital penetration is thought of as pricking an inflated balloon. In mixed cases of anxiety hysteria and obsessional neurosis the feelings are much more localized. If, as is frequently the case, they are given physical expression this usually takes the form of intolerable tension on the bridge of the nose, hands or feet, forearms or shoulder girdle. The mental forms readily pass over into a 'letting go' of obsessional ideas not unlike a maniacal 'flight', although much more organized and accompanied by actual dread. During the analysis of hysterical phobias, particularly phobias of insanity, it can frequently be observed that the mutilation ideas present are stimulated by an explosive feeling following an unconscious sadistic tension. A similar situation can sometimes be uncovered in phobias of pregnancy. Anxiety of bursting is a common accompaniment of neurotic disturbances of sexual function, particularly in those cases of impotence where there is a strong unconscious homosexual organization oscillating between active and passive phantasies. In such cases there is usually no outlet for adult sexuality except perhaps a residual and rather abortive type of masturbation; social activities are restricted to a sort of hermit-like existence, and sublimatory outlets are heavily curtailed. In less severe cases of conditional impotence, the anxiety of bursting is sometimes represented by a marked repugnance to growing fat. Marjorie Brierley[1] has observed a similar reaction in women and regards it as due to 'homosexual' tension. It is more marked where outlets for masculinity are missing or impeded, e.g. in talented women who cannot find or sustain any relieving activity or else cannot work at their chosen career. Finally, one might mention that in the later stages of some organic disorders (e.g. cardio-vascular, liver and kidney diseases) the appearance of acute œdema or ascites may produce a frenzied reaction quickly followed by a phase of despair.

Whatever may be the state of mind common to these various reactions, its unconscious ideational expression evidently depends on the level of mental organization and instinctual conflict existing at any given stage of development. And obviously the analytical interpretation would vary either according to the clinical picture or according to the theoretical predilections of the analyst. Thus it could be described as a typical Oedipus reaction exhibiting the usual fears of orgasm and penetration: or it could be regarded as a form of unconscious homosexual tension. Between these two forms there lies a strong pregnancy fear associated with infantile theories of impregnation, e.g. delivery by bursting through the abdominal wall. Its anal components are not difficult to detect, in particular

[1] Personal communication.

the fear of anal retention. This retention is not the usual passive form, but an active inhibition of a powerful drive towards expulsion. In both anal and urethral aspects the fear of incontinence (i.e. of the phantasy significance of incontinence) is indisputably a factor of the first importance. Incidentally bursting sensations are probably more urgent in urethral than in any other forms of experience.

The feeling can also be interpreted in the usual topographical terms. The part played by the super-ego (using this term in the customary sense) is quite clear. Not only does the fear increase with any rise of sadistic Id-tension, but there seem grounds for assuming that the total psychic tension is increased by active interference on the part of a maternal type of severe super-ego. Brierley has observed this in particular in cases of frustrated unconscious homosexuality. At deeper levels the influence of early ego development is obvious. Melitta Schmideberg has pointed out that the infant projects its love and hate feeling to various parts of its own body and consequently fears conflict between these independent parts. The pleasure parts are good and narcissistically loved, the 'pain' parts are hated and feared. She believes that anxiety of hostile parts of the body fighting each other gives rise to a fear of disruption. It is stimulated by unpleasant physical sensations (including reactions to clothes), frustration or pain, and is increased by identification of parts of the body with dangerous introjected objects. It is, in her opinion, counteracted by achieving control over the body through muscular activity. Finally, observations of the painful anxieties exhibited by infants when subjected to increasing stimulation either mental or physical (e.g. screaming reactions on being tickled, or later, fears of bursting during explosive laughter) indicate that the feelings of psychic disruption follow sudden rise of libidinal excitation. The important point is, however, that this excitation owes its peculiar disruptive quality to simultaneous rise of sadistic tension. Not just simply to accompanying hate, rivalry or aggression, but to a characteristic quality of sadistic over-excitation. *Psychic feeling of disruption is thus a typical and very early tension affect, which in course of development may become fixed in different forms ('canalized' by association with phantasy systems) according to the experiences and unconscious ideations of different developmental periods.*

If this view be accepted certain conclusions follow of both

theoretical and practical interest. It would seem desirable to investigate more closely the earlier psychic forms of fear that previously have been regarded rather from a theoretical standpoint. Here again Ernest Jones[1] has opened a path by describing the dread of what he calls *aphanisis*. Aphanisis, in his view, is essentially a tension reaction due to the unavoidable absence of efferent discharge of erotic excitation. Owing to the existence of sadistic components this tension becomes intolerable and a dread develops of 'total annihilation of the capacity for sexual gratification, direct or indirect'. The most familiar clinical manifestation of the dread of aphanisis is, he believes, the castration complex. Although there is much in common between his views and those of the present writer, the fact that Jones stresses the element of destruction and mutilation distinguishes the dread of aphanisis from the dread of disruption or bursting. From the writer's point of view aphanisis is a slightly more organized fear which develops later than the fear of disruption. The former is no doubt reinforced when the full force of projected sadism is reflected on the self. Fear of aphanisis occurs at a point nearer to 'discharge' (motility). This is in keeping with theoretical views of the development of affects at different points in an 'excitation-discharge' sequence. No doubt these affects overlap with each other or merge to some extent. Undoubtedly there is fear of disruption in aphanisis, and fear of aphanisis contributes to the fear of disruption. Nevertheless, until further investigations are made there seems good clinical ground for distinguishing between these two forms. In aphanisis the excitation travels to a point near to motility. It threatens to break into destructive action (directed outwards and therefore threatening destruction in return). The consequent reflection of this excitation back to the central psychic system gives rise to the characteristic affect. In the case of 'bursting' affect the excitation is freer (more mobile). It, too, stimulates the central psychic system and sets up its characteristic affect. But there is some reason to suppose that the backward flow of excitation causes increased stasis in the afferent system. This increased stasis sets up intolerable tension, and, the avenues to motility remaining blocked, a variety of physical sensations ensue. These take the form of sensory disturbances

---

[1] 'The Early Development of Female Sexuality', *Int. J. Psycho-Anal.*, **8**, 1927 [In *Papers on Psycho-Analysis*, Baillière, 1938].

and/or muscular tensions, i.e. an 'ineffective' form of 'internal' behaviour.

Explanations of this sort are of necessity extremely tentative. It might be argued, for instance, that bursting tensions occur nearer to motility than the tensions inducing dread of aphanisis. Or again, that differences between the two states are due to the fact that dread of aphanisis is fostered by introjective tendencies, whereas the bursting affect has a closer relation to projective tendencies of the mind. One is tempted to add that these dynamic relations between excitation, affect and behaviouristic discharge may throw some light on the manic-depressive affective sequence. It seems likely, for example, that the bursting feelings accompanying depression represent an abortive manic phase, in which excitation is arrested short of activity, but cannot be completely inhibited. However this may be there seems reasonable prospect that the application of metapsychological criteria to clinical observations will lead to a more comprehensive understanding of primary affects. There is certainly ample scope for investigation since it is, at any rate, plausible that there are as many primitive affects as there are primitive ego-nuclei.

XX

THE CONCEPT OF DISSOCIATION*

[1943]

Of most psycho-analytical symposia it may be observed that they deal with matters concerning which a minimum of agreement exists and that their results are uniformly inconclusive; which latter observation is in no way surprising, since the answer to most disagreements is further research. The concepts of 'ego-strength' and 'ego-weakness' are no exception. Having isolated the various factors that contribute to mental function or malfunction, we are thrown back on the over-all factors of 'organization' (synthesis) and 'elasticity' of function. Even so we have to correct both these factors for excess (rigidity and low threshold of sensitivity).

But although synthesis and elasticity of function point to 'dissociation' as being the major factor in ego-weakness, further researches are hampered by two circumstances; first, that the standards of dissociation are clinical rather than theoretical; and, second, that the functional organization of the mental apparatus, described by Freud in the theoretical part of his 'Interpretation of Dreams', has received little or no attention since that date. Apart from a few generalizations about 'free' and 'bound' energy we have no adequate understanding of the contrast between the functionally 'dissociated' systems of the unconscious and the high degree of synthesis found in the pre-conscious system. And we know little or nothing of the 'approaches' to perceptual-consciousness (pcpt-cs).

The following article combines a number of distinct aims. Starting as an exercise in metapsychological definition, it seeks to extend the 'nuclear theory of ego formation' (outlined in Chaps. XI, XII and XIII) and to correlate this theory with a purely psycho-analytical conception of 'dissociation', which in turn is correlated with the interaction of 'psychic systems' and with a

*This is the original draft of a contribution to a symposium on 'Ego Strength and Ego Weakness' held during the Fifteenth International Psycho-Analytical Congress, Paris, 1938. Owing to considerations of time, it was then given in an abridged form. First published in the *International Journal of Psycho-Analysis*, Vol. XXIV, 1943, pt. 1–2.

*variety of clinical data. The conclusion takes the form of a re-
definition of 'normality' which may be compared with that given in
'Medico-psychological Aspects of Normality' (Chap. XIV). It is
clear however that these studies cannot be carried farther, until
more attention is paid to the structure of the deeper layers of the pre-
conscious and to the suggestion originally made by Freud that
between the repression barrier and the system perceptual consciousness a number of subsidiary censorships may exist. It seems likely
that we have taken the phrase 'approaches to perceptual consciousness' in too literal (diagrammatic) a fashion, and that a more
dynamic approach would suit our clinical purposes better, e.g. the
canalization of excitation through a 'nuclear series'.*

It would be a mistake to infer from the title of this symposium
that the subject is one of purely theoretical interest. Actually the
issues bear closely on the development of 'clinical' psycho-analysis.
To give but one instance: progress in the application of psycho-
analytic findings to the diagnosis and prognosis of mental disorder
has been increasingly hampered by the adoption of clinical
criteria borrowed from more conventional (psychiatric) fields.
Quite apart from the fact that standard psychiatric classifications
of neuroses and psychoses are too schematic and at the same time
too rigid to meet the requirements of the clinical psycho-analyst,
it is obvious that they cannot be applied to the multitude of
characterological and psycho-sexual disorders that constitute a
large proportion of the analyst's practice. Indeed the attempt to
combine psychiatric diagnosis with psycho-analytical standards is
responsible for a considerable variation in the criteria used by
analysts in their consulting work. Although there is general agreement on the differentiation of neuroses and psychoses and comparative unanimity about their prognosis, considerable confusion
exists as to the diagnostic and prognostic significance of pathological character changes, inhibitions, perversions and social
difficulties. Sometimes analysts fail to discriminate between manifest psychotic reactions and psychotic mechanisms or even
episodes the existence of which is inferred on purely analytical
(interpretative) grounds. This lack of discrimination may be due
in part to inadequate psychiatric experience, but it is certainly
increased by the fact that a knowledge of unconscious psycho-
genetic factors tends to disturb the analyst's appraisal of manifest

symptoms. This is reflected in a lack of uniformity in therapeutic recommendations, and in the long run gives rise to misapprehensions as to the therapeutic effect of psycho-analysis. Thus the failure to discriminate between evidence of excessive (unconscious) projection and a paranoid character or a state of mild paranoia will sooner or later end in the discomfiture of the analytical therapeutist, if indeed it does not damage his reputation for sound clinical judgment. Many of these difficulties would disappear if we faced the fact that psycho-analytical practice calls for purely psycho-analytical criteria, and set about the task not only of re-classifying mental disorders but of establishing analytical criteria whereby they can be suitably appraised. It is my view that recognition of the signs of ego strength or weakness will prove to be one of the first steps in this direction. We must, however, be able to establish not merely theoretical but clinical distinctions between strength of the ego and ego weakness.

This problem is of course as old as psycho-analytical characterology. Although it has sometimes been held that under the spur of unconscious anxiety or guilt some neurotic individuals may have a more effective working drive than many normal persons, it has always been agreed that psycho-neuroses and psychoses constitute weaknesses of the ego. On the other hand, psycho-analytical opinion has always been divided as to the strength or weakness of character-formations. This applies to normal as well as to abnormal character-formations. For although it may be assumed that a normal character is on balance a sign of ego strength there is no certainty as to which particular features of a normal character we are to regard as strong and which as weak. And when in the long run even normal character came to be regarded as a sort of honeycomb of minor (some would nowadays go so far as to say major) peculiarities, it became obvious that conventional analytical views of ego strength were seriously threatened. Nevertheless, it is useful to look back on earlier researches on psycho-analytical characterology and assess the value of these contributions to our present subject.

The first of these advances was made by examining the influence of repressed sexual impulses on adult character. Study of so-called 'libidinal character' – e.g. oral, anal and genital character – showed that libidinal components contribute to the strength of the normal ego in two ways: first, by providing more or less permanent ego-syntonic substitute gratifications (sublimations) of infantile impulses, and, second, by setting up useful reaction-formations against ego-dystonic gratifications. On the other hand, it was made perfectly clear that both positive substitutions and reaction-formations could be exaggerated or inhibited or distorted. They could obstruct adult energies and activities and at the same time give disguised discharge to ego-dystonic infantile energies. Although not regarded as symptom-formations in the strict psycho-analytical sense of the term such disorders of character were held to function as substitutes for symptoms and in any case proved to be of considerable value in diagnosis and prognosis. The second step followed inevitably. Abnormal character-formations began to be named after the clinical states with which they had closest affinity – e.g. hysterical, obsessional, cyclo-thymic or paranoid characters. This classification into neurotic and psychotic character groups was based exclusively on concepts of ego weakness. The weakness might lie in gross accentuation or gross inhibition of certain mental *mechanisms*, or it might lie in the scatter of *minor* (neurotic or psychotic) *symptom-formations* throughout the ego. This classification really begs the question of ego strength and is vitiated by the fact that what is in one case a source of strength may be a source of weakness in another. The drawback is most obvious in the case of the so-called compulsive or obsessional character. Here a prominent psychic disposition or mechanism is singled out and its relation established to current ego function, to sexual and social life and to possible neurotic and psychotic symptoms. Examined by these criteria few normal characters would stand up to inspection. True obsessional characters apart, the compulsive character is a clinical jumble in which the concepts of weakness and strength are so confused as to be valueless.

Inconclusive as these early researches were, it must be conceded that the approach was sound. Libido-characterology singles out the factor of *instinct*; classifications based on clinical resemblances to symptoms pay attention to *structure* and *mechanisms*. The approach was on the right lines but it was not comprehensive enough. It is curious to reflect that although metapsychology is the main contribution of psycho-analysis to psychology, psycho-analysts themselves frequently neglect to apply the threefold criteria of metapsychology in the clinical field. No mental event can be described in terms of instinct alone, of ego-structure alone, or of functional mechanism alone. Even together these three angles of approach are insufficient. Each event should be estimated also in terms of its *developmental* or regressional significance, and in the last resort should be assessed in relation to environmental factors past and present. The last of these criteria, namely *the relation of the total ego to its environment*, is the most promising of all. It suggests that the most practical (clinical) criterion of weakness or strength should be in terms of *adaptation*. Even so it would be difficult to work out different degrees of weakness or strength without taking into consideration those instinctual, structural and functional factors that either promote or hinder adaptation. For example: using the criterion of adaptation, the old controversy as to whether some neurotic compulsions may or may not contribute to the effective drive of the individual becomes irrelevant. The question becomes one of the *balance of adaptation*. Similarly the significance of emotional discharges of the type of grief or mourning is essentially a problem of discharge and adaptation value.

From these introductory considerations it will be clear that a satisfactory examination of the concepts of ego strength or weakness must involve a systematic approach in terms of the factors indicated above.

(A) Dynamic Criteria

It is convenient to consider criteria of weakness and strength in the first place in terms of *instincts* and of the *affects* which constitute their most important representatives. Here the most obvious standard is that of *mastery of instinct*. By this of course is not meant conscious control, but unconscious mastery of such primitive instincts as disturb development. Now development is disturbed when any primitive instinct prevents either internal adaptation or adaptation to external reality, that is to say, interferes with freedom of mental function, or with freedom of relation to the external objects of ego-syntonic instincts. In this ideal sense, mastery of instinct is obviously a source of strength. Yet mastery of primitive instinct may result in the building up of over-rigid defences and so lead to over-inhibition of adult instinct, and to interference with adaptation. In such cases it is a source of weakness. This is far from being a purely theoretical consideration. Repression of instinct can paralyse memory, the anti-cathexis of

reaction-formation can become an obsessional compulsion, introversion of instinct can end in depressive inhibition, projection of
instinct derivatives can produce the over-activities of paranoia,
mania or delinquency. Clinically regarded, the criterion of instinct
mastery is not very helpful, and is constantly vitiated by powerful
and incalculable factors such as the quantity of masochistic
impulse present in the psyche. A good deal of apparent mastery is
due to masochistic renunciation.

As with the mastery of instinct, so there can be no doubt that
the *mastery of affect* is in some respects a sign of strength. Again
not control of the expression of consciously experienced affect,
but unconscious control of primitive affects. Owing to lack of
knowledge we cannot subdivide these affects with any accuracy.
Many primitive affects are already compounded and fused before
they are experienced as depressions, elations, envies, jealousies,
etc., and the simplest anger affect is not so simple as it feels. Yet
we can safely distinguish those affects that are *expressions* (psychic
representatives) of different stages of instinct-tension[1] from affects,
such as anxiety, guilt, etc., that are *reactions* to different stages of
instinct-tension. It seems to be agreed that mastery of certain
reaction-affects, e.g. of unrealistic anxiety and of unconscious
guilt, is one of the most profound sources of strength in adaptation.
Yet here again the statement requires qualification. The apparently
guilt-free states observed in delinquency and in some sexual
perversions are extremely misleading. Again, the mastery of some
affective responses by anti-cathexis, for example, the mastery of
hate by reinforcement of infantile love, can if excessive cripple the
personality. Over-inhibition, for whatever reason, of infantile love
affects, can cripple adult sexual adaptation. So mastery of affect
can prove a source of weakness. On the other hand, it is not possible
to trust to an apparent *affective balance*. In the obsessional type of
character we find a balance of affect which so long as it is not too
pronounced suggests a healthy equanimity. This equanimity may
be misleading; it may be only a sign of emotional impoverishment.

The only provisional conclusions we can arrive at about instinct-
criteria are, first, that psychic strength depends on a (non-obses-
sional) affective balance, together with an elastic response (adaptation) to the demands of instinct – in other words freedom of
relation to objects – and second, that the soundest affective

[1] See 'The Psycho-analysis of Affect' (Chap. XIX.)

criterion of strength is an optimum freedom from anxiety and guilt. One ought perhaps to include also depressive affects, although this is by no means a purely reactive affect. If these conditions are fulfilled, the ego will prove strong, however peculiar it may look. I mention this last point because, where there is considerable freedom from guilt and anxiety in any situation in which guilt and anxiety reactions are customary, the behaviour of the individual may appear so unconventional as to suggest abnormality.

(B) Economic Criteria

The second line of approach is through study of unconscious mental mechanisms. Every mechanism has no doubt an optimum function, excess or deficiency of which gives rise, in theory at any rate, to some degree of weakness. But clinically this view is subject to considerable correction: in many instances excess of function gives a misleading appearance of strength. Perhaps the best example of this false strength is to be observed in the reaction-formations of obsessional cases, where an appearance of stability is found on examination to be mere rigidity accompanying a paralysis of affective drive. Similarly, the paranoid character with its active aggressive façade proves to be a projective defence against inner weakness and anxiety. On the other hand, study of masochistic characters and of certain depressive types shows that an appearance of weakness can also be misleading. Many of these types are in fact extremely egocentric, obstinate and aggrandizing, stopping at nothing to gain their own ends, so that over-emphasis of introjection mechanisms is not a sure criterion of weakness. And it is notorious that the activity of the hysterical type is episodic and unstable to a degree, depending as it does on periodic defences against a phobic reaction to external relations.

On the other hand, even making due allowances for spurious strength and weakness, it is by no means easy to say which mechanisms contribute most to actual strength or weakness. Analysts with a bias in favour of introjection defences are usually extremely suspicious of projection characteristics and regard them as weaknesses. This is quite unjustified. Projection is an instrument of adaptation without which man would lose almost a third of his capacity for *rapport*. The mistake here is to regard mechanisms as pathogenic in themselves. The *reductio ad absurdum* of this view can be observed in a suggestion that has gained currency in some quarters, viz. that much so-called normal conduct and activity is a defence against an underlying (kernel) depressive position. I doubt if this is even theoretically true: it is certainly unsound clinically. Normality may be a compound of every variety of mechanism, and its variations may be due to emphasis on particular combinations, but each variety has as much right to assessment as a state-in-itself as depression, mania or paranoia have to be regarded as clinical entities. In any case there is a serious and inevitable flaw in all such discussions. It is due to the difficulty in assessing the *rôle of repression*. Being an unobtrusive mechanism, repression exerts an incalculable influence. All we know is that it is important (advantageous) for the anticathexes of repression to have some discharge value. Following this idea we arrive at the familiar conclusion that next to repression the sublimatory varieties of *displacement* contribute more than any other mechanism to ego strength. Within reasonable limits, the wider the range of displacements and the more diversified they are, the stronger the ego. Exceptions to this rule are where the displacements are so scattered as to be trivial and ineffective or where they are so highly charged as to deplete the ego. To be sure elasticity in displacement is called for where changes in environment are frequent. A passionate attachment to a hobby is often an effective displacement, but the psychic situation is not without risk. In short I do not believe it is possible to lay down standards of ego strength and weakness in terms of unconscious mental mechanisms. We can infer from certain pathological states (which are in theory signs of weakness) that certain mechanisms are overworked or understressed, but that in itself proves nothing about the mechanism, which may after all be overworked or understressed as a means of spontaneous cure for underlying conflict.

(C) STRUCTURAL CRITERIA

This brings us to the third and apparently most promising factor in assessment, viz. the structure of the ego. Actually, the title of this symposium is misleading: it should have been called 'Psychic Strength and *Psychic* Weakness'. The ego is after all only a part or aspect of the total Psyche, and, as we have seen, the problem of strength or weakness cannot be divorced from dynamic concepts of instinctual and affective energy. Yet it is difficult to *measure* the strength of drives unless we observe their effect on the structure of mind both in its internal and in its external aspects. The strength of existing pathogenic drives is inferred from the presence of autoplastic symptoms or of character peculiarities which obtain alloplastic expression. If study of the ego cannot provide us with criteria of strength or weakness, the search for such criteria is well-nigh hopeless.

It is not my intention to repeat here the well-worn views on this subject arising out of a primary division of the psyche into ego, super-ego and Id. It is obvious that if we take the Id as in the main an instinctual and constitutional factor, we can speak of *fixation* as primarily an Id phenomenon, and add that herein lies one of the handicaps of the ego. We can also say that a rigid super-ego structure jutting into the pcs. system of the mind is a source of weakness, e.g. that over-conscientiousness or hypercriticism is a sign of weakness. Indeed, we might go further and say that weakness or strength never lies in the ego and that the ego reacts to life either with difficulty or freely to the extent that it is or is not encroached on by Id or super-ego. But I do not feel that such generalizations, however valid and interesting they may be, are of much clinical value. For many years now I have suggested that the idea of a simple conflict between super-ego and ego, or between ego and Id, loses clinical significance the farther back we trace these institutions. And I have also maintained that so far as the first two years of life are concerned, the old *serial* views of development by phases and their more recent modifications, viz. concepts of *serial positions* and defences against serial positions, are no longer either theoretically plausible or clinically sound.

Rather briefly condensed, my views on early psychic structure are as follows. From the earliest weeks of life the primitive psyche (I use this term to avoid the confusion arising from the phrase Primitive Total Ego) experiences a variety of primitive urges. As a consequence of partial or sometimes total frustration of these urges, it is forced to exploit a number of psychic reactions and tendencies which are sooner or later perfected as unconscious mechanisms. As, however, many of the instincts with which the primitive psyche has to deal are component instincts (no doubt various combinations of components also exist) arising from different body zones and organ centres each one of which has an optimum importance and, despite the theory of primacy of certain instincts, a specific intensity, it follows, in my opinion, that primitive ego-structure is best described as *multi-nuclear* or multi-locular. The instincts are of course both appetitive (libidinal[1]) and reactive (instincts of mastery or aggression or flight[1]). In the most general terms, these psychic nuclei represent a precipitate of the reactions between the primitive psyche and the objects of its instincts, wherever these objects may lie and irrespective of whether the actual object is recognized as such: for it seems likely that the aims of the instinct are appreciated before exact ego-object boundaries are realized. Precipitates of experience are represented in memory traces which are organized in Ψ-systems as described by Freud. It is from these systems of memory traces built up from summations of different instinctual experiences and reactions, that ego nuclei are formed. Each nucleus is concerned with both appetitive and reactive responses to whichever instinct is concerned, and is soon expanded when with the help of primitive mechanisms experiences of anxiety are reduced or avoided. For convenience in description we may regard them as miniature egos. How soon these nuclei show signs of inner differentiation it is impossible to say, but it is safe to assume that, when the instincts they represent are gradually mastered, displaced or abandoned, a rudimentary division occurs. According to this view, these ego differentiations, which have generally been described as fore-runners of the super-ego, are not at first organized divisions of the total ego but appear in each ego nucleus, and merge only when the ego itself is synthesized. As has been admitted, no exact period can be stated at which this differentiation takes place since there is no direct evidence during the earliest months of life from which definite conclusions can be drawn. In any case these rudimentary formations in the psyche must be clearly distinguished from more complex and highly organized mental institutions: for example, the super-ego which we have been accustomed to regard as a differentiation of the Total Ego occurring when infantile instinct has reached its final development. Ego-nuclei can best be described in terms of their dynamic function. Theoretically an ego-nucleus can be defined as a psychic organization which (*a*) represents a positive relation to the objects of any important instinct, (*b*) secures the discharge of reactive tension consequent

[1] Including of course in both cases the components previously isolated as 'self-preservative' drives or reactions.

on frustration by objects of that instinct, (c) promotes the relation to reality through gratifying impulses of self-preservation, and (d) in one or other of these ways reduces anxiety within the psyche. Rudimentary differentiations within the nucleus can be presumed when, in the case of any given instinct, primitive forms of introjection are sufficiently advanced to absorb energy that would otherwise strive for gratification on external objects. The function of these differentiations is similar to that of later fully synthesized differentiations, viz. to reduce the quantity of instinct excitation by distributing it. But this is unlikely to occur until earlier modes of dealing with frustration (e.g. the hallucinatory tendencies of the psychic apparatus) have shipwrecked on the reality principle. Then no doubt they play a part in reinforcing introjections. We must also presume that the earliest phantasies derived from any given instinct are cathected in the appropriate nucleus.

The point I wish to stress at present is that although these nuclei have a good deal in common, *they have in the earliest phases a partial autonomy*. They share a common relation to reality (in effect to the real objects of their instincts) which is due at first to the strength of self-preservative drives, and such libidinal and mastery drives as are capable of satisfaction and have similar objects. Their autonomy is due in the first place to the fact that not all self-preservative drives have the same object, in the second to gross differences between various libidinal and aggressive drives, particularly as regards their somatic source, and in the third to factors of frustration and fixation which set up regressive activities within the nucleus, thus preventing it from merging with others.[1] *According to the strength of its instinctual endowment,*

---

[1] The concept of nuclear *autonomy* has to be distinguished clearly from concepts such as *auto-erotism* where instincts or their components are gratified without the interposition of an external object. It goes without saying that in primitive stages of development when auto-erotic activities help to maintain the balance of instinct gratification, these activities will also contribute to the formation of ego-nuclei. This is most obvious in the case of oral impulses where auto-erotic activities have the same zonal centre as object impulses. But the main contribution of auto-erotism to nuclear formations is probably more economic than structural: it adds to the libidinal cathexis of the nucleus, and so promotes fixation and subsequent regression. Structural differentiation arises more readily from variations in the conditions of frustration of object impulses.

to the severity of frustration, the degree of fixation, and the richness of its phantasy products, a nucleus can attempt, as it were, to seize the psychic apparatus and occupy the approaches to perceptual-consciousness (Pcpt.-cs.). Clinically such attempts are easiest to observe in the comparatively sudden regressions that occur in alcoholism and drug addiction. Owing to the suddenness of the regression, the ego is less able to disguise or distort it. Particularly in melancholic types of drug addiction can we observe that the personality becomes for the time being an oral ego: sexual regression impoverishes genital libido and oral types of satisfaction take its place; masturbation gives place to oral manipulations in which a violent element of face-scratching can frequently be observed. The emotional tone varies between a loquacious euphoria and a maudlin reaction to imagined hurts. But I shall not attempt to give here the numerous clinical and analytic observations on which I have based this view of the early ego; they are derived mainly from study of transitional types of psychosis in which the relations of schizophrenia, paranoia, mania and depression can be observed.

However fragmented the early ego, there is from the first a synthetic function of the psyche, which operates with gradually increasing strength. As development proceeds, the nuclei merge more or less (it is always a case of more or less with ego-synthesis) and a coherent and complicated ego structure appears. From study of the nature of the object in early homosexual perversions I am inclined to put the first signs of effective synthesis about the period of Abraham's second anal-sadistic phase. Similarly the constituent parts of each nucleus (the rudimentary divisions I have described) tend to merge and organize, and prepare the way for those more massive institutions which are set up during the final Oedipus conflict and which, I assert, we are too ready to regard as massive from the first. But, given conditions of emotional stress, causing acute or chronic regression, the ego tends to split again, and to permit a pathological amount of expression to those nuclei which for reasons of early conflict and fixation are ready to occupy the approaches to consciousness. In short, I maintain that this nuclear theory of the ego has considerable advantages over both the earlier conception of serial phases and over more recent concepts of serial positions and defences.[1] To my mind it is much more

[1] The term 'ego-nucleus' is a logical extension to the structural aspects of the normal mind of the concept of an unconscious 'complex'

elastic, and gives a more adequate etiological basis for the complex interrelations of the basic psychoses.[1] It also brings us nearer to the possibility of a combined theoretical and clinical definition such as we are seeking in this symposium. Put in the most general terms, *the original state of nucleation of the ego is fateful for its later strength or weakness.*

But the term *nucleation* is obviously not a satisfactory clinical term. And in thinking over this problem I came to the conclusion that the time is ripe for analysts to take over the term *dissociation*, provided always they give it a more precise meaning, one more in keeping with psycho-analytical concepts, than it has hitherto enjoyed. I am well aware that the history of the term dissociation is a chequered one, starting with Janet's use of the atomistic association-theory by which dissociation is a falling away of groups of atoms from the aggregate of consciousness, and ending in such recent attempts as that of McDougall to establish the relation between dissociation and repression. McDougall wishes to co-ordinate the neural and the mental facts of disordered states. And his 'dissociation', which is a cerebral phenomenon, is distinguished from 'disintegration' of a hierarchy of moral or mental elements having perhaps no neural equivalents. This approach is at the same time too wide and too narrow; for although he endeavours to relate repression and dissociation factors in any case of conflict, his psychology has little in common with the metapsychology of Freud. But despite this unpromising start, I believe the term could be conveniently brought into metapsychological usage. And to begin with, I believe that its greatest value would be in the topographical field. It would of course need to conform to certain

which proved convenient in the description of pathological function. The essential difference is of course that a nucleus has preconscious as well as dynamically unconscious aspects. The more organized the preconscious aspects, the greater the likelihood that under conditions of stress the system Pcpt.-cs. will be encroached on by the nucleus. Using this term, it is possible to give a more satisfying description of certain clinical manifestations, e.g. those conditions of obsessional organization where, according to earlier descriptions, the ego was compressed and/or im-poverished by the expanding symptom. This can be understood better by estimating the degree to which the obsessional formation proliferates in the Pcs. and occupies the approaches to consciousness.

[1] [Note (1955): The idea of a nuclear system occupying the approaches to consciousness is strikingly illustrated in the case of those masked paraphrenias which can be observed over a prolonged period. The

standards, that is to say, not be regarded simply as a by-product of repression, but refer to the (comparative) isolation of nuclear elements occupying the approach to consciousness and modifying other mental elements of instinctual representation as they pass through these approaches. In this respect the term is more satisfactory than the more vague word 'splitting', which usually begs the question of what is split.

But as well as being useful in the structural sense, the term dissociation is also valid in the *dynamic* and *affective* sense. Dissociation of affect is most easily studied in the manic-depressive sequence, where, although there is an externalization of instinct energy, there is not by any means a complete transmuting of energies or affects. The depressive or, as the case may be, the manic affects are dissociated. In the next place, both structural and dynamic aspects are accentuated by the selective action of mechanisms. Thus repression favours both structural and dynamic dissociation. This is seen especially in hysteria. Reaction-formation also favours the isolation of special nuclei. This is observed most clearly in the localized reaction-formations of hysteria, and the more extensive reaction-formations of obsessional neurosis. I suggest that the more we study a variety of mental phenomena which are by general consent regarded as signs of weakness, or more accurately as signs of conflict (I would instance here such symptoms as alienation, depersonalization, fugues, split personality, etc.) the more important it would seem to commence our study of weakness from the point of view of nuclear development of the ego.

To sum up briefly at this point my views on ego strength and weakness, the conclusions I wish to present are as follows:

(1) From the dynamic and affective standpoints psychic strength depends on (*a*) affective balance, (*b*) an elastic adaptation to the

seemingly sporadic 'episodes', although apparently separated by sometimes prolonged periods of apparent 'normality', represent out-croppings of a system which is never far from the surface, as is shown by the fact that the normal phases on closer examination are frequently disturbed by transient manifestations of 'peculiarity', also by the nature of dream material. When the series of nuclei through which pathogenic excitation is canalized begins to 'organize', the latent formation emerges in consciousness and gives rise to an 'episode' during which 'reality estimations' are governed by phantasies belonging to the fixation period.

demands of instinct, including freedom of relation with the objects of those instincts, (c) an optimum freedom from the reactive affects of anxiety and guilt – possibly also of depression.

(2) Although it is impossible to characterize strength or weakness in terms of unconscious mechanisms, it may be said that excess or restriction of these functions contributes to weakness of the ego. Alterations of this sort are, however, highly individual and cannot be made the basis of generalizations. On the other hand, it is very probable that harmonious adaptation to the total (ego-syntonic) requirements of instinct depends to a very large extent on the mechanism of displacement. A capacity for harmonious adaptation through displacement is therefore a sign of strength.

(3) Structurally, the strength of the ego depends on the degree of integration of various early nuclear components. I do not suggest that fusion is necessary – merely integration. The weakness of the ego depends on the degree to which early nuclei retain energy and are capable of a degree of autonomic function – in this way preventing mental energies from being distributed amongst more integrated layers. Energy can be withdrawn or absorbed from more integrated layers in two main ways: (a) regression to, and re-activation of primitive interest; (b) absorption of energy by direct conflict in the more integrated layers themselves. This conflict is in its turn exacerbated where there exists already an excessive amount of active primitive interest. (I suggest the use of the term *dissociation* to describe this clinically.)

(D) Developmental and Adaptation Factors

In the introduction to this paper I pointed out that, in addition to these three approaches, one ought to take into account the highly individual factors of *development* and of the *relation of the total ego to its immediate and potential environment*. I have suggested that the old analytical conception of a single or central series of instinctual primacies or serial positions can no longer be regarded as adequate, and have suggested that the ego develops from a cluster of primitive islets until about the end of the second year it becomes definitely unified. I would only add that from this time onwards the concept of fixation can be extended from its customary instinctual reference to include fixation of the total ego to any one period of development. Until our knowledge is more complete it is inadvisable to label these phases, and we must be content for the time being to relate them to particular age periods. Closer study of many transitional forms of psychoses and of psychotic episodes, which psychiatrists are content to label as 'mixed' in type, shows that the psychotic regression activates reactions which are typical of some particular year of infantile development. In this sense the concepts of fixation and regression have a broader significance and can be included amongst the criteria of ego-weakness. There is, however, one important qualification to this general statement. It is not true that all regressions are a sign of weakness – nor is progression always a sign of strength. It is notorious that what we call precocious progression or development can function as a defence against conflict. It, too, can be a sign of weakness. But this is only to repeat that however close we come to absolute standards of strength and weakness, it is essential to check these by a clinical assessment of the total psychic function of each individual – i.e. his capacity to adapt to life as he finds it. Potential strength is a readiness to adapt to life as he is likely to experience it.

Here we reach the final criterion of ego strength or weakness, viz. the relation of the total ego to environmental stresses, past and present. The capacity to withstand earlier stresses is clinically of considerable value in estimating current strength or weakness, but before we can, strictly speaking, speak of ego strength, the margin of safety must be sufficient to meet oncoming stresses. This is essentially a *traumatic criterion*, and is subject to the disadvantage that we cannot anticipate with certainty any but the usual 'critical phases' of adult instinctual life and work. But so far as 'previous history' is concerned it provides a useful check on the standards of strength or weakness already detailed.

Space does not permit a systematic account of the clinical indications by which any of the foregoing standards can be applied. Speaking in the most general clinical terms we can say, however, that where the ego is strong the individual will not present outstanding peculiarities of a symptomatic type (major neuroses, psychoses, sexual perversions, inhibitions or character disorders). He will be elastic in adaptation, labile in mood but with a capacity for happiness or at least tranquillity. He will be comparatively free from the usual signs of unconscious anxiety or guilt and show good working capacity with an elastic response to working stresses. His regressional activities will be regulated by the necessity for psychic recuperation, and not anchored to past phases of development in such a way that his total personality is dominated by a single facet of it. He will be able to make social contacts of a friendly type and to fall in love with an object other than himself, without, however, exhausting his store of self-appreciation. And, subject to the reasonable claims of society, he will be able to exploit his instincts of mastery and aggression in order to supplement his self-preservation and allo-erotic impulses, to support his familial responsibilities and, if he should so desire, to give expression to his social idealizations. If it should be argued that an individual possessing *all* these qualities would be something of a monstrosity, my answer is that the remedy lies in the common sense of the consultant, who will be amply satisfied with a safe margin of ego strength over ego weaknesses.

XXI

PSYCHOLOGY AND THE PUBLIC*

[1945]

If space permitted, a volume of selected papers might well carry an appendix comprising selected reviews, or at any rate a selection of the theoretical or clinical comments provoked in course of random reviewing. The following critical notice is included here, not because of the importance of the book reviewed, which was only of ephemeral interest, but because it puts on record some impression not only of public reactions to psychology about the middle of the Century, but of the state of clinical psychology at that time. The rapid expansion of 'eclectic' psychology described in this review has in fact continued without remission during the subsequent ten years and threatens to provide the basis for a 'unified' psychology, which may blanket research for a considerable time ahead. As a matter of interest the publication of this review led to a further commission, namely, to survey Jung's psychological works and to establish the theoretical and practical differences between Jungian and Freudian psychology. The results of this survey were published a few years later in a volume entitled Freud or Jung.[1]

For some time past the popular attitude to psychology has become increasingly complacent. This change in reaction is the more remarkable in that it cannot be attributed to increased understanding on the part of the general public. Man has always been afraid of his mind or, as we would now say more accurately, afraid of his unconscious mind. Hence he has reacted to the study of psychology with a superstitious dread which is often thinly concealed by contempt or indignation. The reaction has been enhanced by three circumstances. As organic medicine began to free itself from obscurantist traditions and became a more respectable 'science', fears of the mysteries of the body were transferred

---

* Being a 'selected notice' of *The Lady of the Hare*: a study in the healing power of Dreams, by John Layard: London, Faber & Faber, first published in *Horizon*, Vol. XI, No. 63, March 1945.

[1] *Freud or Jung*, by Edward Glover, Allen & Unwin, London, 1950.

to and augmented existing fears of the mysteries of the mind. The other and more important factors were the discovery by Freud of the unconscious mind and the development of psycho-analysis which owes its existence to that discovery. Ancient fears of magic and mesmerism were promptly displaced to the new science. Indeed a good deal of the early abuse of psycho-analysis was due not so much to its supposedly pan-sexual views – a myth, by the way, which is still extremely tenacious of life – as to the fact that study of the unconscious mind was identified in the popular imagination with dabbling in the occult.

A similar explanation may be given of the lively though un-instructed interest at one time taken in the defection from psycho-analysis of some of Freud's early adherents, in particular Jung and Adler. Their repudiation of fundamental Freudian principles must have been a comfort to all who had been shocked by the, usually garbled, accounts they had heard or read of Freudian psychology. To this day it is a comfort to academic psychologists to point to the existence of warring 'schools' of clinical psychology; and well-meaning general physicians vie with less well-meaning psychiatrists to draw the preposterous conclusion that because Jung and Adler disagreed with Freud, the monumental structure of Freud's unconscious psychology must rest on shaky foundations. So when it appears that 'psychology' itself is being accepted as 'respectable' we may reasonably suspect either that the public has developed fresh misconceptions on the subject or that the psychology they now come in contact with has in fact become more 'respectable', that is to say less realistic. Actually there is some truth in both surmises.

If we ask ourselves what 'psychology' is generally supposed to mean the answer is that in the great majority of cases no supposi-tion at all exists. Setting these cases aside, we conjecture that 'psychology' is popularly identified with 'psycho-analysis' and 'psycho-analysis' with 'Freud', but a rectified Freud, unobjection-able and even salutary when administered in a highly diluted form by some non-Freudian 'specialist'. No doubt there are some in whose imagination 'psychology' is pictured as a sort of hyphenated monster answering to the name of 'Freud-Jung-Adler'. This mis-conception was strengthened when, not long before the present war, 'psychiatry' awoke from its non-psychological slumbers in mental hospitals to find that it had been invested with psychological attributes overnight. And with the expansion of army psychiatric services, whose personnel is largely recruited from asylum officers, a rapid deterioration of psychological science has in fact set in. War is a bad time for 'depth' psychology and it will take anything from 20 to 50 years to recover the ground lost by pitchforking psychologically untrained psychiatrists into the field of mental science.

But whereas we may hope that sooner or later this misfortune will be overcome, the same cannot be said of the Eclectic Psychologist who, it is to be feared, we shall always have with us. The term denotes not any coherent school of thought, but merely a class of unclassifiables having in common a perhaps excessive disregard for the claims of logical consistency. For although it is possible to take a little bit of Freud, a little bit of Jung and a little bit of Adler, the bits are, even for practical purposes, extremely small. In matters of principle, Freud and Jung are poles apart while Adler inhabits an entirely distinct and not very important planet. Among the eclectics are many very useful persons, aiming at, and in favourable cases obtaining quick therapeutic results; or, at worst, intervening between the sufferer on one hand and on the other the massed misunderstandings and moral indignation of his family, his family doctor and himself.

Besides this practical and pedestrian kind of eclectic we have a sublimer race of beings whose only discernible object is to astound. These very often affect a sort of super-Freudianism mixed up with anything else they fancy. A favourite dodge is to pity and revile Freud for his initial errors with the implication that these errors were ultimately corrected not by Freud but by the triumphant super-Freudian and his allies. The typical eclectic has often an instinctive tendency to edge away from the deep (Freudian) unconscious, preferring (superstitiously) the term subconscious, which has the advantage of meaning anything or nothing. Sometimes he seems to have no suspicion of any distinction of meaning between the two terms.

Omitting many interesting varieties of eclectic psychologist, we are now obliged to introduce the Crank: one whose main interest is a fad or good intention of some sort accidentally linked up with something supposed to be of a psychological nature, perhaps merely a small but ill-chosen vocabulary, perhaps a fairly ambitious system (of nonsense) based on a fairly complete misunderstanding of Freudian, Jungian, or some other psychological doctrine. For the crank's purpose Freud has the advantage of notoriety, but combines less readily with pure mush than do some of his competitors. Jung has obvious attractions, chiefly his turn for uplift, also perhaps his curious fairy-tale symbolism so readily transformed by ignorance into a mythology. Adler too has his appeal, having fathered a simple one-way system to counter the complexities of mental life, but on the other hand his barren simplicity does not lend itself to the mystical afforestations of the crank.

Mr. Layard, author of the book now before us, has chosen to attach himself to the skirts of the Jungians. Not unwisely: feeling perhaps that 'his nonsense suits their nonsense'. The result is more *palpable* nonsense than he could probably have produced alone. The Jungian collective unconscious (or his notion thereof) does give him something to muddle himself about. Without some such 'framework' he must have wallowed indefinitely in the foamy seas of his own revivalistic emotions and might perhaps never have become a psychologist. It was, significantly enough, a country parson who had the idea of prescribing 'psychology' for the troubles of a young parishioner, 'Margaret Wright', and 'psychology' was luckily forthcoming in the shape of Mr. Layard, who readily consented to try what he could do. Margaret, however, who was mentally defective to begin with, was in such a state of internal tension as to be inaccessible to a direct approach; so Mr. Layard decided to tackle the problem from an environmental angle. Not at all a bad idea either. It is well over twenty-five years since Abraham pointed out that the neuroses of mothers can, via the unconscious, stimulate the formation of neuroses in their children. And for a long time now child-psychologists of all brands have sought to bring influence to bear on their patients by contacting (and sometimes by analysing) the parents. It is equally well known that defective children are even more sensitive to unconscious anxieties than neurotic children, although the muted exterior of their minds has even less chance of expressing such fears. And since defective children are almost invariably handled with unwisdom, they naturally respond by retreating into their lonely interiors, from which it takes a good deal of love and reassurance to entice and rescue them.

It is all the more curious therefore that Mr. Layard should have passed over the claims of an unlucky neurotic 'Aunt Bertha' (who, living in the 'Wright' household, was the bane of Margaret's life as Margaret was of hers) to attack the problem via the girl's mother 'Mrs. Wright', the predestined Lady of the Hare. In her he discerned rare and lofty qualities (of intuition and so forth) under the simple exterior of an elderly countrywoman unspoiled by so-called education, a midwife by trade, a Northern Irish-woman by birth, by early upbringing a Presbyterian. The presentation is not unlifelike: we are able to develop from what we are told certain further qualities: particularly an obliging readiness to flatter and be flattered, and a censorious attitude towards the female part of humanity, together with a tolerable conceit of herself. This was the human instrument Mr. Layard now sought to temper by the enlightening and at the same time curative or, to adopt his terminology, redemptive process of Dream Analysis.

Here we should note that dreams (according to Mr. Layard) may be taken as being 'of God' if we know how to read and profit by the messages they contain, but 'equally of the devil' if we do not. This, if it made sense, might seem alarming: but Mr. Layard, rightly undismayed, proceeds to make a somewhat arbitrary mess of the very few old dreams and visions which are all 'Mrs. Wright' has to show for a lifetime of fifty-four years. They are fortunately sufficient to prove that there is something askew in 'Mrs. Wright's' inner life: she is not entirely faultless. Like Mr. Darcy, however, she has chosen her faults well: a little over-righteousness, an excessive purity, and (very naturally) a little pride. To all this, and to the subsequent discovery that she has for a long time been inadvertently *exercising a maleficent influence on*, or in the simpler tongue of our forefathers, bewitching her daughter, the patient reacts with modest equanimity.

Meanwhile the dreams have become numerous and of the most redemptive sort. Visionary Blood Sacrifices, notably that of the Hare, symbolize and promote the transformation of the dreamer's 'instincts' into 'spiritual power'. 'Instincts', we are told, 'desire' to be so transmuted. Behind this statement there lie unplumbed depths of psychological confusion. A clearer head than Mr. Layard's might have perceived the advantages of always holding fast to symbolism: the idea of a hare bent on 'transformation' (self-immolation) is silly enough but not actually inconceivable. This numinous beast, the Self-Immolating Hare, first appears in modest circumstances. 'Mrs. Wright' dreams that she finds him occupying

a bowl in the kitchen of a cousin's house in Ireland; she is required
to kill him, and does so rather incompetently with a kitchen knife.
The hare manifests no concern in the proceedings: 'The hare never
moved and did not seem to mind'.

Mr. Layard, however, minded greatly. In 'Mrs. Wright's' accom-
modating memory the nonchalance of the hare is retrospectively
improved into a 'look of extreme satisfaction and trust'. (This
occurs in connection with the dream sacrifice of a local tradesman,
a handsome young Jew.) But the self-immolating hare becomes the
hero of the book, though it was not until a couple of years later
that Mr. Layard discovered him in Buddhist mythology; all that
is most ancient and archetypical. The creature likewise, we are
told, immolates himself to this day in the fields of County Armagh,
Northern Ireland; which might be thought to abate the wonder
of his appearance in the consciousness of 'Mrs. Wright', but Mr.
Layard seems not to notice this. The *ancient archetypical* of her
dream is somehow combined with the discovery and cure of the
negative *participation mystique* exercised by the lady on her child.
And Mythical Hares of all kinds romp freely through the last and
much the longest section of the book (pp. 100–227).

Returning to 'Mrs. Wright', we find her passing from ritual
symbolism to 'intellectual' instruction. After some talk of a dream
featuring a Black Pony drawing a load of three-leaved clover we
hear Mr. Layard saying to his patient, 'What is it that is against
God? . . . Well, God is light, isn't He? Then evil is dark, that
means, what we don't know' . . . 'God can be a Destroyer as well
as a Creator, for all things are possible to Him. He rules over the
night as well as the day. But if we say He rules only over the day,
what happens to the night? . . .' (Of the Black Pony) 'He is the
hidden fourth Power representing, like all animals, the instinctive
reactions that we in our present civilization have tended to lose
through our too great concentration on the light side of the god-
head, thereby neglecting the dark . . .' (Instinct was represented
by the Pony and) 'it was to the Pony that the Teacher' (a dream-
figure) 'referred as being "the one higher than God", meaning not
that he *was* higher than God, for as we have seen, the two should
be equal and married, but that he must for the moment be *represented* as higher because our instincts had been too much
neglected' . . .

Mr. Layard's divinity has perhaps delighted us long enough. It remains to inquire what the therapeutic results have been. Reports are up to a point reassuring: 'Mrs. Wright' herself, who seems never to have had anything much the matter with her, has gained in stability and diffuses blessedness. The neurotic aunt is more or less cured through the merits of her sister of (seasonal) swooning and of quarrelling with 'Margaret'. From the same cause, or perhaps because of the removal of her mother's aforementioned maleficent influences (negative *participation mystique*) 'Margaret' has learned to speak up nicely, take an interest in her clothes, and love her Aunt Bertha. Apparently too, she has lost her addiction to miscellaneous reading, formerly much and adversely commented upon. Further news arrived about two years after the end of the mother's formal analysis: 'Margaret' (by her mother's account) had continued to improve. A phase of daylight visions developed into 'second sight'. Visionary perceptions of a long-deceased grandfather became merged with the traditional figure of Bonnie Prince Charlie – whom Mr. Layard regards as a probable 'legendary hero' for a 'loyal Northern Irish family'; strangely, we think, however Scottish their descent. This Royal 'concept', however, 'merged into or was replaced by a higher concept still, that of the Heavenly Father, under whose direct guidance she now believes herself to be'. It is almost needless to add that she is developing a 'power for spiritual healing', happily protected by her 'so-called mental deficiency' from the illusory belief that disease of the body is anything other than a disguised disease of the soul.

Further volumes are to be devoted to all these matters. But we need not wait for their appearance to say roundly that neither the validity of Jung's psychology, nor any of the controversies between followers of different 'schools' can be affected by any part of this book. Nor is this judgment altered one whit by the fact that Mr. Layard has padded out his essay with a collection of myth and folklore regarding the Hare. By itself and shorn of the interpretations which Mr. Layard freely interpolates, this part would make a useful addition to an anthropologist's collection of pamphlets. As a background to Mr. Layard's theses it is of no value, for the theses depend on Mr. Layard's arbitrary interpretations, and the nature and function of myth cannot be determined by a brand of interpretation for all the world like the marginal comments on the Song of Solomon to be found in the Authorized Version. Had 'Mrs. Wright's' Ninth Dream concerned the gutting of a herring, it would have been equally possible to produce a volume entitled 'The Lady of the Herring', containing abundant references to the mythology of the Fish, including even polite allusion to its universal employment as a phallic symbol.

But in that case, it may be asked, why bother to give Mr. Layard more than a three-line reference? There are I think, two good reasons for bothering. In the first place informed reviewers can exercise a considerable and beneficent influence by spreading objective information about psychology. If they are not well informed they can, even if inadvertently, do their readers a disservice by suggesting that any new book of arty format and precious title represents a milestone in psychological progress. Having forgotten or never having heard of the earlier stages of psychological controversy, they may hail as new and potent wine some heady brand of ginger beer that has been poured into old wine bottles.

The second reason is even more important. As I have said, the eclectics we shall always have with us; and as they grow in numbers, the impression will no doubt be created that the old controversies between Freudians, Jungians and Adlerians have given place to a happy eclectic concert. Now to a certain extent it is true that the controversies have died down, but that is largely because a newer generation of adherents are too busy with their own practices to bother about the said old controversies. In a sense, of course, they are well advised because they will seldom or never succeed in influencing their opponents. Nevertheless, the issues remain and cannot be burked or glossed over. The Freudian will continue to maintain that you cannot abandon the libido theory, the theory of repression and the dynamics of transference, and remain a Freudian. He will never accept the picturesque Jungian concept of the collective unconscious and all it connotes in place of Freud's orderly conception of the relation of the Id to the various structures and institutions to be found in the unconscious mind. Although aware that the earliest phases of mental development are still for the greatest part *terra incognita*, the Freudian holds that this lack of knowledge cannot be compensated by a vague concept which is incapable of expression in terms of mental structure, economy and dynamics. Until he knows more he will cling to the basic formulations regarding the mental apparatus which were laid down by Freud and which have served to this day to keep our heads clear when faced with the complicated problems of mental research.

Apart from this it has to be borne in mind that Jung and Adler, although the best known, were not the only dissidents from Freudian psychology. They were followed by Rank seeking to develop in his Birth Trauma theory a monistic explanation of mental development and disorder. Even at the present time the urge to reconstruct early stages of development has, in this country at any rate, led to a split in psycho-analytical circles. Already the Klein theory, which, although not strictly speaking monistic, attributes an overwhelming preponderance to the developmental significance of the instincts of aggression, has given rise to a 'reconstruction' of a so-called 'depressive position' existing at the third month of life due to the infant's sense of overwhelming loss arising from the imagined destruction inside itself of the all-loving mother. Orthodox Freudians have already challenged this as a mystical deviation. And no doubt from time to time other deviations will arise and will require to be challenged with equal vigour. The fact is that the issues of modern clinical psychology are not simply therapeutic issues to be settled by some kind of gentleman's agreement. No clinical issue will be determined by therapeutic results alone. Many patients would get quite well if only a golliwog were put in the psychologist's chair having some mechanical contrivance capable of saying from time to time 'what does that bring to your mind'? or 'you must become more aware of your redemptive process'. The psycho-analysis of Freud is not simply a psycho-therapeutic process; it lays down certain fundamental conceptions which are and will remain the test of all future progress in mental science.

XXII
THE FUTURE DEVELOPMENT OF
PSYCHO-ANALYSIS*

[1948]

The fact that psycho-analysis commenced by investigating clinical symptoms and subsequently developed as a special therapeutic method has fostered the tradition amongst psycho-analysts that research is largely a matter of establishing etiological formulae for different disorders and so adding point and efficiency to therapeutic endeavour. This is far from being the case. The main concern of psycho-analytic research is to establish the nature and order of mental development. In this task the role of clinical observation is twofold, first, to check theoretical surmises, and, second, by tracing the developmental sequence of different disorders, to encourage dependable reconstructions of early phases of normal mental development which are not accessible to direct analysis.

For these reasons alone it is important to check and countercheck the alleged 'discoveries' made by enthusiastic analysts in the clinical field. From the therapeutic point of view it would not matter a great deal how prodigally they turned out uncontrolled interpretations of clinical phenomena. For even if their surmises ran counter to psychobiological probability, they might well have an excellent therapeutic effect, such is the force of transference rapport. From the point of view of extending the range of analytical theory, however, the exercise of uncontrolled imagination in the clinical field can be nothing short of disastrous. There is so far no fool-proof system of training psycho-analysts which would prevent the persistence, through 'training-transferences', of faulty theory. And, as is indicated in the following paper, it is only too easy for Freudian theories to be transmuted, into, for example, Jungian and other non-Freudian formulae.

For the rest the paper outlines in systematic form some of the directions which psycho-analytical research must pursue if its main task is to be achieved.

* Address to the Dutch Psycho-Analytical Society, delivered at Amsterdam, Nov. 1948.

This is not intended as an essay in prophesy. Obviously anyone who could predict with reasonable accuracy the progress of psycho-analysis would be too busy making discoveries to write papers foretelling its future. My intention is quite otherwise. It is to examine some existing psycho-analytical principles, theories or methods with four distinct objects in view: first, to establish the *tendency* of new theories; second, and more specifically, to recognize such tendencies and methods as are inherently bound to *obstruct* or delay analytical progress; third, to indicate the more promising *lines of advance*; and fourth, to estimate the *research potential of the methods* employed.

In psycho-analysis more than in any other medical science it is true that discoveries cannot be made by examination of data selected at random from random practice. One must know what one is looking for and where to look for it. This explains why the usual methods of statistical approach and control, favoured by natural scientists, are, in the case of psycho-analysis, so un-promising. The analytical investigator who does not know what he is looking for is likely at best to establish negative findings, at second best to re-discover what he already knows and at worst to waste his time.

Historically, the only exception to this rule was provided by Freud himself when, starting from consciousness, he discovered the unconscious. Indeed a survey of so-called progress in psycho-analysis during the past twenty years shows conclusively that it still consists for the most part of giving body to the skeletal structure set up by Freud. The directions for future research had already been indicated by Freud, sometimes in considerable detail, sometimes only in a suggestive sentence or footnote. All the investigators had to do was to follow these suggestions and collect the material necessary to corroborate them. And this is practically all they did do. But Freud is no longer with us to direct, advise on, and criticize our researches and theories: or perhaps it would be better to say provide us with theories. The time to break new ground cannot be much longer delayed. And with the prospective development of new ideas, it is all the more essential to sharpen our instruments of research and to establish even more exacting disciplines whereby we may avoid blunders.

The outline of a survey such as this must obviously be deter-mined in the first instance by metapsychological considerations;

by discussing in turn the advances that can be made along, respectively, *structural, dynamic, economic,* and *developmental* lines. To these should be added some reflections on *analytical methods* together with an assessment of their most suitable *point of application,* in other words; the option of fields of research.

RESEARCH ON EGO-STRUCTURE

It is appropriate that we should start with a *structural approach.* For not only did Freud start with a study of perceptual-consciousness from which he deduced the existence of the unconscious, but it is precisely in this field that the most dramatic forms of resistance to psycho-analysis still operate. Study of various schismatic movements makes this abundantly clear. It is true that deviations from analytical principles can occur at many other points. Rank, for example, gambled on a mono-traumatic theory of neurosogenesis, thereby eliminating the theory of unconscious conflict. Others have boggled at infantile sexuality and at repression; but the main stumbling block still remains the existence of the true dynamic unconscious and of the primary processes that govern its activities.

During the past few years I have made an extensive study of the psychology of Jung,[1] in order to determine the theoretical basis of his repudiation of his former enthusiastic allegiance to psycho-analysis. And it was not difficult to establish that Jung, starting from pre-Freudian views of mind (consciousness) finally retreated to his pre-Freudian position, covering this retreat, however, with a smokescreen calculated to mislead the undiscerning. There are, of course, two ways to disintegrate the concept of the unconscious; one, by transposing unconscious functions to the field of consciousness, when concepts, such as the 'self' and 'will', regain their pristine *metaphysical* status; and the other by converting the unconscious into a constitutional factor. Jung adopted both plans. Having claimed, or rather re-affirmed, the priority in mental affairs of his 'ego-consciousness' and having reduced the Freudian unconscious to a shallow pre-conscious system which he labelled 'Personal Unconscious', he disguised what was then left of the Freudian unconscious as a constitutional element – the so-called Collective Unconscious. In so doing he was bound to jettison the primary processes, repression, dream-

---

[1] *Freud or Jung,* by Edward Glover, Allen & Unwin, London, 1950.

work and such other mechanisms as can only be understood with the aid of these fundamental Freudian concepts. Having, however, postulated a still more unconscious unconscious, Jung was bound to equip this with psychic content and energy. Hence the Jungian archetype with its alleged incomparable powers of wisdom, prognostication and guidance, to say nothing of its powers of disruption. Hence, also, his postulation of the unmodified, monistic life-force he called libido. The fact is that Jung is an arch-projector determined to abolish the Freudian unconscious either by projecting it forwards into consciousness or backwards into the realm of constitutional factors. What he could not explain in terms of consciousness he thus put beyond the reach of understanding by insisting that it was racial in origin.

Apart from this the real flaw in Jung's system was due to a neglect of psychological thinking. Whatever your views of racial inheritance, you must nevertheless express them in terms of a mental system or part of a mental apparatus. Freud's boundary concept of instinct and his later concept of the Id provided, as it were, a base line from which one could investigate the mind – in other words, an endopsychic frontier or limit to mind. Whoever oversteps this frontier steps out of psychology altogether and becomes either a physiologist or a transcendentalist, a natural or moral philosopher or a priest.

And here I should like to refer to a system which during recent years I have criticized to the point of tedium; and which would be of little moment were it not for the fact that its exponents have for the time being gained administrative and training authority in psycho-analytical circles in Britain and in South America. One of my original criticisms of the Klein system of child psychology was that its founder followed the error of Rank in postulating a traumatic situation occurring not indeed at birth, as in the case of Rank, but within a few months after birth, a system which, it is claimed, modifies and regulates all subsequent development both normal and abnormal. I also pointed out, however, that Klein had 'broken through the limitations of psychology to postulate a bio-religious system which depends on faith rather than on science', adding: 'In my considered opinion the concept of a three-months-old love-trauma, due to the infant's imagined greedy destruction of a real loving mother whom it really loves, is merely a matriarchal variant of the doctrine of Original Sin'. Since then study of Jung's psychology has made it clear to me that Melanie Klein is essentially a neo-Jungian, who believes in neo-Jungian archetypes of the neo-Jungian Collective Unconscious, disguising her beliefs, however, in Freudian terminology from which she has excluded Freudian meaning.[1]

Now it is interesting to study the subsequent development of these theoretical tendencies. In my essay on the Klein system I pointed out that the accredited followers of Klein exhibited much less caution in expanding her theories than did their originator; and I have frequently maintained that this state of affairs would give rise to endless confusion. Two recent contributions from Kleinian sources have provided confirmation of this simple conjecture. In a recent clinical paper[2] Winnicott describes a case he analysed during which transference regressions occurred and were frequently repeated. These regressions, Winnicott maintained, went back to prenatal life. The birth process was relived: every detail of the birth experience had been memorized and catalogued in the exact sequence of the original experience: all this was re-enacted in the transference. The case is cited by Winnicott in illustration of his view that in the beginning the individual is just a body: psyche and soma are not be be distinguished. Psyche is here defined as 'the imaginative elaboration of somatic parts, feelings and functions'. These 'two aspects of the same thing', psyche and soma, then become interrelated to form the 'psyche-soma' which subsequently forms the basis for the 'imaginative self'. The development to this stage can become 'fairly complete by the time the baby has been born a few days'. If the psyche-soma develops satisfactorily, i.e. is not too much disturbed, mind does not exist as an entity but as 'a special case of the functioning of the psyche-soma'. If disturbances are severe, memorizing or cataloguing can become the 'enemy of the psyche-soma' because it

---

[1] 'To establish the Kleinian system it must be proved *inter alia* 'that the original Freudian unconscious system has at its core a central system or enclave as distinct from the rest of the unconscious as the Freudian unconscious is distinct from the Freudian pre-conscious' (p. 19).

In Edward Glover: 'An Examination of the Klein System of Child Psychology', *The Psycho-analytic Study of the Child*, Vol. I, Imago Publishing Co., London, 1945: also published separately as a monograph, London, 1945.

[2] D. W. Winnicott: 'Mind and its Relation to the Psyche-soma', *B. J. med. Psychol.*, 27, pt. 4, 1954.

is associated with environmental persecution: on the other hand, failure in catalogueing can give rise to mental confusion and defect. Mind in the normal child is something which makes the good enough environment or mother into the perfect environment or mother, 'perfection being absolutely needed by the psyche-soma at the beginning'. Mind is not directly related to the soma.

In an earlier paper by Scott,[1] we can find 'theoretical' formulations which are in keeping with these wild Rankian surmises. Scott describes a so-called 'body scheme' which is apparently intended to be synonymous with the psycho-analytical concept of a 'real ego'; and defines it as 'that conscious and unconscious integrate of sensations, perceptions, conceptions, affects, memories and images of the body from its surface to its depths and from its surface to the limits of space and time'. 'In other words', Scott continues, 'part of the body scheme is a continually changing world scheme – the extended limits of which have to deal with what can only be called the limits of space and time.' 'For', says Scott, 'we believe that there is a relationship between the unconscious forces in the discoverer and the discoveries which are made of forces in the world.' All this alchemistic philosophy[2] is regarded by its author as a new orientation regarding the relation between the Id and the ego, and, in his opinion, calls for co-operative research amongst embryologists, neurologists, psychiatrists and psycho-analysts.

Time does not permit a detailed discussion of this curious and confused document. It is perhaps sufficient to say that the author equates the 'body' with the 'body-ego'; that in his view the roots of the body-scheme lie in pre-natal life; that one of the earliest splits in the ego- or body-scheme is a split between '(1) all that becomes consciously integrated to form the body or body-ego, and (2) the mind – the psychic reality – the inner world – the psyche as opposed to the soma'. Scott is apparently impressed by the difficulties that arise when we try 'to clarify a relationship between the psychic-ego and the bodily-ego'. These difficulties, which incidentally are entirely artificial, for no analyst regards

---

[1] W. C. M. Scott: 'Some embryological, neurological, psychiatric and psycho-analytical implications of the "body scheme",' *Int. J. Psycho-Anal*, 29, pt. 3, 1948; see also 'The "body scheme" in psychotherapy', *B. J. med. Psychol*, 22, p. 139, 1949.

[2] This is undiluted Jung: see Glover, op. cit.

mind as a 'thing', or as anything else but a working concept, he feels he can overcome by substituting the term 'body' or 'bodily' for 'mind' or 'psychic'. The word 'scheme', of course, simply means functional organization.

Now apart from the fact that in using the term 'ego' at all, Scott is employing a simple psychic concept which eliminates any confusion arising from the implications of the term body; in other words, apart from the fact that Scott does not understand the empirical uses of psychic postulates, the whole tendency of this thinking is purely Jungian. Presumably fretting at the restrictions imposed by the basic concept of the Id, he adopts the Jungian and Kleinian device of projecting parts of the unconscious ego into the Id, and, by equating the Id with body, the Id body ends by projecting itself out of psychology into embryology and neurology. Moreover, the psychology of instincts and their objects gives place to a body 'scheme' and by way of compensation for this loss we are offered an extension of the Kleinian concept of 'internal objects' – itself a confused idea. The invisible but palpable breath, both inside and outside the mouth, nose, chest is, for example, one of the earliest objects, subject immediately to introjective and projective processes.[1] Winnicott's objects are much earlier and foetal.

I have singled out these examples of tendency to illustrate how an original dogmatic error proliferates rapidly in the minds of disciples. I need only add that this issue has an important bearing on the teaching of psycho-analysis. Jung, it is true, is no longer a member of a psycho-analytical society, but the latest views of the neo-Jungians may soon be taught as official psycho-analytical theory, in Britain at any rate.[2]

[1] This idea seems to have some affinity with Fenichel's concept of 'respiratory introjection', but refers to an earlier period.

[2] [Note (1955): In the 1920s it was the habit of analysts to protect themselves from the interpretations and other techniques of 'untrained' practitioners by describing their activities as 'wild analysis'. It would seem that a similar defensive measure might well be employed in the case of theoretical speculations of 'trained' analysts. It was Jung who once maintained that Freudian views of neurosis were supported to a limited extent by the fact that Freud himself illustrated their operation in his personal neurosis. And of course it can always be argued that the wildest interpretation or theory can be supported by the fact that its sponsor has excogitated it. The fact remains however that, however valuable the

Turning now to the more positive aspects of this survey, and examining the present state of *psycho-analytical topography*, it is evident that for some time to come our energies can still be best spent filling out the gaps in structural psycho-analysis. To make this point clear we may consider the concept of the super-ego. As a convenient descriptive term for a special ego-institution or differentiation, the term super-ego requires no elaboration. Nor need we add much to the view that in both racial and individual aspects, the super-ego is an internalized (i.e. psychically organized) system of incestuous taboo. But in the dynamic sense its development represents a *phase of instinctual regulation*; and as such requires to be correlated with its antecedents. Moreover, as the primacy of genital impulse in childhood is only relative, the super-ego concept requires detailed structural subdivision in terms of component impulses, and their appropriate reactive responses. The isolation of various types of reactive libidinal character is itself a proof of the fact that super-ego structure is composite and must be differentiated. And I need not repeat that the history of each differentiation must be traced back to the period, however short, when the component in question itself enjoyed relative primacy. As a step in this direction I have advanced a theory of the 'nuclear development' of the ego (and super-ego) which, I believe, gives us more elbow room to investigate the early stages of mental development than does the concept of an early synthesized ego.[1]

A more elaborate differentiation of super-ego structure will, however, involve a closer study of the *relation of different ego systems to consciousness*. A number of observations indicate this necessity, e.g. the fact that under certain circumstances ego and super-ego structures are automatically unified, that in other instances (in the depressions, for example) unconscious super-ego organization occupies the approaches to consciousness to the exclusion and detriment of the reality-ego. In this connection it may be remembered that Freud was prepared to postulate the existence of a

exercise of the imagination can be in research, it is in the long run essential to distinguish between the 'psychic reality of phantasy' and the occasional combination of phantasy with reality thinking which contributes to the formation of a sound theory. Once the 'criteria of interpretation' have been established, the task remains to lay down the 'criteria of theory'.]

[1] See Chaps. XI, XII, XIII and XX.

series of censorships lying between the repression barrier and perceptual-consciousness, that is to say, operating at different levels of the preconscious system up to and including the margins of consciousness. The suggestion has not been seriously pursued owing in part to the predominating importance attached to the repression barrier and partly to the discovery of deeper levels of the unconscious ego. But certainly we ought to be in a position to say exactly by what means the reality ego is deprived of effective function in certain psycho-pathological states. For the spontaneous remissions and recoveries occurring in even advanced psychoses indicate that in these cases the function of reality-proving is not destroyed or even impaired by the psychotic process. The explanation that returning reality sense is nothing more than the reinvestment of real objects with libido is not entirely satisfying. An explanation in structural terms is called for. *The existence of a series of censorships would give some plausibility to the view that in certain symptom-formations the increased charges at the disposal of the super-ego permit a forward extension of unconscious super-ego elements along the series of intermediary censorships to the point where they can overrun perceptual consciousness.*

Needless to say, investigations of this sort would involve collateral investigations of the *deeper layers of the preconscious system.* Experience gained during actual analyses, in particular of the relation of dream symbolism to symbolic behaviour in waking· life (e.g. symptomatic acts), suggests what is in any case inherently probable, namely, that a transitional period exists between the phase when primary processes predominate and the phase when secondary processes succeed in establishing effectively their binding function. In many cases of obsessional neuroses it would seem that earlier preconscious layers exist in a state of loose repression, which can be reduced during analysis without any effective discharge of the pathogenic content of the repressed. Here lies possibly one of the causes of the frequent stalemate occurring in the analysis of obsessional cases.

Economic Researches

To turn for the moment from structural to *economic considerations* – and admittedly it is impossible to study structure apart from function – a scrutiny of mental mechanisms suggests that we should pay much more attention, first, to their *interrelations* and, second, to the serial *order of primacy* of mechanisms. When psycho-analysis was concerned almost exclusively with the nature of repression, it was natural that the observer should tend to isolate and circumscribe the concept. Further observations suggested, however, that *in repression we have to deal with a* PROGRESSIVE SERIES *of tendencies concerned with variations in distribution of cathexis* – e.g. anticathexis, hypercathexis and the like; that in fact we have to deal with a *group* of tendencies having different end-results. The best example, of course, was given by Freud in his description of the relation of repression to negation and denial. Following this line of thought it is desirable to think of the mechanisms that have so far been isolated as representing only the final forms, derived from a group of tendencies which exert their maximum influence during particular *phases* of development.

Similarly *the interrelations* of different groups of mechanism requires detailed scrutiny. It may be assumed, I think, that throughout the greater part of early mental development, the existence of repression is essential for the effective operation of all mental mechanisms, and I think that clinical investigation will enable us to isolate particular combinations which have influenced development. So far the simplest example studied is that of the combination of regression and reaction formation observed in the obsessional neuroses, but I believe that in transitional states such as alcoholism and drug addiction, we can observe, in some cases, a curious interplay between repression and introjection and in others between repression and projection. *If this be the case we ought to be able to establish the original transitional phases of mental development during which these combinations first operated.*

It is scarcely necessary to add that such investigations call not only for careful analytical observation but extremely disciplined thinking. Indeed, the time has come to review the whole field of mental economics as much to determine which terms we can discard or replace as to find which conceptions require to be expanded. And in the first instance we must agree on standards of definition. Should a mechanism be described or valued or placed in a developmental series in terms of its end-result or in terms of its function or in terms of the part of the mind specially involved, or in terms of the clinical symptoms with which it is mainly associated or in terms of its relation respectively to primary or secondary processes? The term *undoing*, for example, was isolated on the strength of its end result. Repression is by contrast a functional term. Undoing is part of a symptom process, as in the obsessional neurosis; it is a super-ego derivative; like the rest of the reaction formation group to which it belongs, it is in the nature of a secondary mental process bolstering up faults in repression, and it can be descriptively classified as a system of magical thought (originally action). Indeed, if we study the operation of undoing in children it is clear that it can be placed at that stage of development of the pre-conscious when conceptual thinking is still under the influence of primary symbolisms. Even so, undoing is very far from a primary process.

A similar comment can be made regarding the mechanism of *isolation* in which the associations and emotional significance of traumatic events not only disappear, but spatial or temporal intervals are interposed between the event and its association or emotional content. The emotion can in some cases be discharged through displacement. It has even been suggested that the infantile dichotomy of libido into erotic and tender components is an example of isolation, although it would seem that the processes of aim-inhibition and displacement provide a more satisfactory explanation. However that may be, it is undeniable that a tendency exists to regard secondary and highly elaborate defence-mechanisms as having the same status or value as a primary mechanism. And in the case of isolation, it is evident that the root mechanisms on which it is based are repression and displacement. Indeed, the whole subject of dissociation is involved in this type of investigation. And with dissociation we are brought back once more to the relation of structural elements to consciousness.

This is even more evident in the case of the mechanism described by Laforgue as *scotomization*. As far as one can grasp the author's idea, this seems to be a combination of a primary and a secondary defence mechanism. Even so it is possible that we may have to reduce it to the level of a clinical end-product: i.e. not a mechanism *per se* but the result of a combination of mechanisms.

And here I should like to draw attention to a tendency in psychoanalytical literature which is to say the least of it extremely unscientific. Once an alleged new mechanism or alleged clinical discovery has, so to speak, caught the psycho-analytical eye, and provided it is referred to frequently enough by its author or his followers, there exists a tendency on the part of less biased but equally suggestible observers to write as if it were an accepted part of psycho-analytical theory. And so in the case of scotomization, for example, we find it included almost as a matter of course in lists of mechanisms by writers who would be hard put to it to give a plain definition of the term. It is for this reason that I favour the formation of a standing psycho-analytical research commission in all countries, recruited from research analysts, whose duties should comprise *inter alia* the re-definition of accepted analytical concepts and the critical examination and correlation of such new concepts as may be advanced from time to time.

THE ANALYSIS OF AFFECT

To turn now to the *dynamic aspects* of psycho-analytic theory, it is not difficult to indicate the direction in which exhaustive research is called for. It lies in the field of the *affects and emotions*,[1] those instinctual derivatives which spring from the Id and yet are potentially so close to behaviour and consciousness, indeed give an urgent impetus to behaviour. Historically, psycho-analysis was concerned in the first place with establishing the relation of specific instinctual stresses to emotion, secondly, with the action of repression in preventing the emergence of potential affects, and thirdly with inhibitions which paralyse the emotions. Here again the classical examples were provided by analysis of the obsessional neuroses and the depressions. By comparison the emotional set of the paranoias was relatively neglected. It is clear, however, that those positive and negative aspects of the problem were understood first because they are by far the simplest aspects to investigate. But affects being derivatives of instinct must reflect the fate of instincts. Instinct excitations are not simply discharged unmodified, repressed, inhibited or sublimated, they are also actively distributed within the mental apparatus: and they are also fused. One would expect, therefore, to find that some degree of fusion must occur during the development of affect. This is all the more probable, in that one and the same variety of discharge can satisfy different varieties of instinct, e.g. weeping can serve to discharge anger as well as grief. Moreover, as I have pointed out on previous occasions, the disappearance of depressive affect

[1] See 'The Psycho-analysis of Affects' (Chap. XIX).

during analysis is due not simply to analysis of the underlying traumas but to the ventilation in memory or transference of the various affective elements of which the depressive state is compounded. Admittedly, the analysis of affect can never be so precise or informative as the analysis of ideational content. But now that we know more of the relation of some unconscious content to some affects, e.g. of repressed libidinal phantasy to anxiety and of repressed hostility to guilt, it should be possible to advance the analysis of the more complex emotions. Indeed it is essential to do so if we are to proceed with the investigation of early infancy without importing concepts that are valid only for late infancy and childhood. The all too common confusion between the adult affect of depression, the affective accompaniments of a clinical depressive state and the prototypes or components of depressive types of affect in infancy and childhood illustrates the danger of identifying affects without adequate examination, or alternatively of presuming adult affects in infancy or again, assuming for the sake of argument that the affects are identical, of taking for granted that they have identical unconscious content, or indeed that they invariably have content. *The real history of mental development must surely lie in the history of affect.*

It goes without saying that the problems discussed above are merely samples selected from an extensive field of research. Even so it must be realized that before they can be approached effectively a great deal of preliminary spade-work is necessary to clear the ground of a *terminology* that has become, if not cumbersome, at least an obstacle to progress. The super-ego, as I have said, is a useful generic term, but must be divided into a number of developmental components each calling for description of specific characteristics. Similarly with terms such as narcissism. It is some years now since I indicated that such terms had to a certain extent outworn their usefulness, that, for example, in the case of a narcissistic phase, the developmental range of this system called for some contraction and for a more specific description of the object systems in vogue during early ego-centric stages. The task of *re-defining and extending psycho-analytical terms* is a laborious one, and in any case calls for certain qualities and training which are not too conspicuous in psycho-analytical groups.

METHODOLOGY

We must now consider the problem of *methods and techniques of research*. Here again the main issue is not hard to indicate. It is whether a psycho-analysis carried out primarily for purposes of research can arrive at scientifically reliable conclusions. We already know that it is hard enough to arrive at reliable conclusions in a therapeutic analysis, also that it requires an effective 'will to recovery' on the part of the patient as well as effective handling of the transference neurosis on the part of the analyst to uncover the unconscious nexus of phantasies and original environmental traumata responsible for the fault in repression. *The question is whether in analyses not carried out for therapeutic purposes we do more than rediscover our own preconceived assessment of the situation.* This incidentally is a source of difficulty in the analysis of such psycho-analytical candidates as do not suffer from neurotic symptoms or characterological disorders, and have no particular 'will to recover from normality'. In any case as I have indicated we are not likely to make successful researches unless we know roughly what we are looking for and where to look for it. How then are we to conduct researches, avoiding the obvious danger of projecting into the unconscious of the patient our own ideas or intuitions which may be right or on the other hand may be completely wide of the mark.

This methodological issue has acquired additional point since the development of therapeutic techniques such as the 'vector' analysis of Alexander and the 'sector' therapy described by Deutsch. Both are based on psycho-analytical principles and employed by psycho-analytically trained psychiatrists. The sector therapy of Deutsch[1] was developed from what he called 'associative anamnesis' and depends on making a selective use of the technique of free association; i.e. guiding the chains of association so that the material is 'centred around certain symptoms or certain conscious and unconscious conflicts' thereby keeping the therapeutic approach 'within certain strata of the personality'. Although maintaining that his therapy is not strictly speaking psycho-analysis, Deutsch nevertheless describes it as a form of 'active' or 'applied' analysis, having the aim of 'goal-limited adjustment'.

'Vector' analysis, although apparently a more extensive pro-

[1] Felix Deutsch: Applied Psycho-Analysis, New York, Grune Stratton, 1949.

cedure, and combining a variety of techniques, such as 'supportive' therapy, 'relationship' therapy and 'expressive' therapy, has a similar guiding rule, namely, to confine analytic processes to that aspect of the patient's mind that bears on his most important difficulties or symptom-precipitants. Although sometimes described as 'psycho-analytically oriented therapy' or 'brief psychotherapy' (the duration seems to vary, as in Deutsch's cases, from a few sessions, to a few weeks' or months' treatment) it is at other times clearly regarded by its sponsors as psycho-analysis. In fact despite superficial differences in the respective techniques and in the descriptions of the rationale of 'sector' and 'vector' therapy, there seems little difference in principle between these two forms of short-term therapy.

Now let us agree that, owing to transference factors, any kind of modified or shortened or circumscribed analysis, which incidentally might well be described as 'focal' or 'selective' analysis, can effect 'cures' or major alleviations of symptoms, even in the brief course of a diagnostic anamnesis. Let us agree further that, as a therapeutic agent, 'focal' analysis is suited to the need for mass-psychotherapy. Nevertheless, we should never blind ourselves to the fact that terms like 'sector' or 'vector' are mainly polite descriptions of 'complex-hunting' or 'symptom-analysis'. It would appear that in this respect some analysts have completed a historical cycle by returning to their starting point. For Freud's original investigations which led to the discovery of the unconscious were essentially symptom-analyses of conditions later described as 'transference-neuroses'.

We may be pretty certain therefore that, despite the exceptional case of Freud, sector-analyses conducted for a therapeutic purpose are not likely to give us more research information than we bring to them; from the research point of view they would tend to permit too much play to purely subjective theories. We may nevertheless ask whether in the case of what we might call researchanalyses, it is possible to apply a selective technique, to analyse only those parts and functions that seem to *bear on a particular problem*. The answer to this question must I think vary in accordance with the experience and predilection of the observer. My own view is that we cannot expect to establish from short-analyses more than some interesting (no doubt in their way essential) correlations between clinical observations and established theories.

But even if we assume that tendency-analysis is hampered by the absence of the dynamic factors which contribute to the success of a classical therapeutic analysis and that it is liable to be vitiated by the existence of subjective bias in the observer, we are not thereby deprived of any possibility of selective research. The way out of this difficulty is only too obvious. It lies in psycho-analytic specialization, i.e. in the *selection of cases*. From the research point of view the bulk of ordinary psycho-analytic practice is quite useless. Therapeutically, perhaps, the time may be well spent. And no doubt investigations of therapeutic failures would be exceedingly informative not only from the point of view of therapy but because of the light it would throw on the developmental significance of various types of resistance. The serial approach to resistance is as essential as any other serial investigation. Nevertheless, the research energies of the psycho-analytical practitioner are constantly frittered away by the random selection of clinical material incident to consulting practice.

For a number of reasons which for lack of time cannot be closely specified here, few psycho-analysts can be persuaded to specialize. They may embark on child analysis or psychiatric analysis (i.e. analysis of the psychoses), but these specialities are mere microcosms of the macrocosm. Even so the fields are too large, and include too much, to be designated specialities except in the most general sense. In this connection I can recall efforts I made over twenty years ago to persuade some young analysts to specialize in the analysis of the epileptic group. Needless to say, this and similar suggestions regarding the analysis of specific disorders did not materialize. Yet I can see no way of accelerating the pace of psycho-analytical discovery without developing some system of specialization.

THE OPTION OF RESEARCH

As for what I have called the option of fields of research, i.e. the points at which researches might well be concentrated, it is not difficult to single out one of the clinical focal points. It is the examination and limitation of the *concept of psycho-somatic reactions and disorder*. As I have pointed out before, if we assume that the mental apparatus proceeds from the simple to the more complex, that we can differentiate between psycho-somatic disorders and symptom-formations in the Freudian sense, we should be able to learn from the former much greater detail regarding the primary functions of the mind. But this will involve a truly effective distinction between *functional disorders* and *symptom constructions*.[1] I need hardly add that by functional disorders I do not mean physiological reactions to fœtal impressions. Following this line I still maintain that the epilepsies and so-called narco-lepsies would repay a careful and concentrated re-examination.

Research is also indicated on the intermediate stages of mental development that lie between those main phases which are already roughly mapped out and have already been correlated with a developmental series of classical mental disorders. It seems logical to direct our attention to clinical conditions which although relatively infrequent in incidence, nevertheless present symptoms derived from two or more distinct phases, but having character-istics that are quite distinct and specific. In the drug addiction group, I have always maintained, lies the secret of that stage of development that lies between a largely narcissistic organization and an organized phase of super-ego regulation.

Similarly in the case of the development of reality sense; it is to the manifestations that lie between the psychoses and the psycho-neuroses, that we should turn our attention. And I have frequently suggested that the *essential psychopathies* provide a fruitful field for investigating this subject. On the other hand, dissociation and the relation of ego structures to consciousness is best observed in the classical groups of disorder and much more could be done by contrasting the mechanisms in hysteria and schizophrenia respectively.

A similar contrasting study is desirable in the investigation of guilt, and I recommend in particular a contrasting of the mechan-isms in delinquent psychopathy and depressive character respec-tively. These are even more illuminating than the classical contrast of melancholia and mania. Finally, and to conclude this brief list of suggestions, I would repeat that the examination of affective disorder is an open field.

STATISTICAL RESEARCH

In the introduction to this review I suggested that statistical investigation, particularly of clinical material, was not likely to add much to our existing knowledge and that to discover something

[1] See 'Functional Aspects of the Mental Apparatus' (Chap. XXIV).

new we must have some understanding, however dim, of what we are looking for. By this I did not imply that statistical investigation had no uses in analysis. Once promising discoveries have been made, statistical methods offer a means of rapid corroboration or correlation. They can also uncover possible sources of error. Unfortunately their application even in this comparatively restricted field is itself subject to gross sources of error. There is still a considerable lack of uniformity of approach in psycho-analytical science. Our standards of diagnosis and classification exhibit wide variation, and we have no certainty that our technical methods of approach are more than roughly uniform. Premature application of statistical methods even to alleged new findings is therefore still liable to perpetuate error rather than to advance our knowledge. Nevertheless, there are some fields in which they could be applied with some prospect of success provided their scope is restricted in the first instance to conscious, descriptive data. It is indeed high time that psycho-analysts paid more attention to (pre)conscious content. So far they have left this field to the normal or academic psychologist whose most elaborate classifications are devoid of that perspective or sense of value which can only be acquired through knowledge of unconscious forces and function. It is quite absurd, for example, that psycho-analysts should leave the study and differentiation of affects, emotions, sentiments to the mercies of the academic psychologist. However that may be it seems probable that, provided a standard terminology could be adopted, statistical surveys could simplify the task of examining the more elaborate compound affects.

CORRECTIONS FOR ERROR

This brings me to a final consideration of a general nature. During the controversies of the past ten years I have constantly maintained that students should be taught only those principles and practices of psycho-analysis that are established beyond all doubt. To this policy the criticism has been advanced that it is likely to obstruct the possibility of new advances, that psycho-analysis must advance and that undue concern with deviations from psycho-analytic principles is a reactionary attitude. Inaccurate findings, it is maintained, will automatically destroy themselves, or at any rate will do so sooner or later. All I can say is that there is no evidence of this. To judge from the healthy state of Jungian Societies, deviations are perfectly capable of surviving for lengthy periods. The transferences existing in training analysis are perfectly capable of perpetuating error. But it is not only the scientific training of students that is at stake. So long as no distinction is drawn between established theory and unconfirmed hypothesis, it is impossible to apply any standard technique of research either analytical or statistical. Time and energy is wasted prodigally. A great number of analysts 'try out' the new idea, as a rule in cases in which they have encountered difficulties – perhaps the most unsatisfactory of all tests. And since factors of transference suggestion can lead to symptomatic alleviations, any coincidental improvements they may observe are likely to bias them in favour of the new interpretation. Discussions in societies do not improve matters. One side says 'we find this', or quotes, 'so-and-so has found'; the other says, 'you have no proof'. And so the story goes on. This is not scientific research. And as analytic groups increase in size, research conditions will get worse. In the earlier days when only a few investigators were actively concerned with research, it was always possible to check the probable accuracy of their conclusions from the integrity of their disciplines of thought or investigation. In larger groups this control is weakened. I maintain therefore that we must fall back in every case of doubt on the accepted principles of psycho-analysis and in special cases on the committee system of investigation – a fallible instrument, I am well aware, but, under the circumstances, the method most likely to effect corrections for error.

XXIII

THE POSITION OF PSYCHO-ANALYSIS IN GREAT BRITAIN*

[1949]

To advance our knowledge of those obscure stages of early mental development which are not accessible to direct analysis and therefore can be outlined only by means of plausible 'reconstructions', it is necessary not only that the existing body of proven psycho-analytic theory should be maintained intact but that it should be preserved from encroachment by speculations which, uncontrolled, are little more than wild surmises. The sanguine assumption that these aims can be readily achieved through the training- and control-analysis of psycho-analytical students is not borne out by the facts; as witness, the frequent schisms developing in psycho-analytical groups. On closer examination most of these divisions will be found to arise from interpretations of clinical data which reflect the speculative pre-conceptions of their authors.

On the other hand the prompt ventilation and correction of these theoretical adventures has been greatly hampered by the fact that psycho-analysis, having in its early days suffered greatly from extra-mural criticism and sometimes obloquy, has felt under obligation to preserve a closed front to the general psychological public. This mistaken policy has fostered the still more unfortunate tendency to gloss over differences existing within the confines of the particular group concerned. If persisted in, these policies would make an end once and for all of the possibility of scientific progress in psycho-analysis, the more so that, under the transference conditions existing during training-analysis, it is difficult to prevent a teacher's error becoming a student's cult.

Under these circumstances it seemed desirable to break down the barriers of political reserve which fence off intestine psychoanalytical controversies. The object of the following survey is to promote a clear distinction between the standard findings of psychoanalysis and those more speculative accretions which, though

* First published in the *British Medical Bulletin*, 1949, Vol. VI, No. 1–2, pp. 27–31.

imaginative enough in their own peculiar way, do more credit to the hearts than to the heads of their sponsors.

The reader who turns expectantly to reviews of 'recent work' on psychology hoping to find therein evidence of outstanding 'progress' during the past ten years is doomed to some disappointment. In the case of the physical sciences, once the fundamental principles governing any particular branch have been laid down, one may expect to find that year by year extensive advances have been made in a number of directions. It is quite otherwise with psychological science. The more dynamic it is and the more it is concerned with the unconscious functions of mind, the more it works against a head of resistance and consequently the slower the pace of discovery. Even the impact of war, which, again in the case of physical sciences, usually accelerates the rate of discovery, produces little or no positive effect in the psychological field – rather the contrary. The tendency of psychology during the war and for some time afterwards is reactionary. The energies of psychotherapeutists are diverted to the application of short-cut forms of treatment, usually old methods dressed up as new. Hence no discoveries of consequence are made.

With this preamble, it can be stated that since the death of Freud in 1939 no advances of importance have been made in the field of psycho-analysis in Great Britain. Nevertheless, certain significant changes in the tendency and direction of the psychoanalytic movement have taken place. And these are worth recording.

I. DEVELOPMENT OF PSYCHO-ANALYSIS IN BRITAIN

Before doing so it is desirable to outline briefly the development of the psycho-analytic movement in this country. It commenced only a few years before the outbreak of the First World War. At that time Freud's theory of the unconscious, of dreams, and of the neuroses was well established; and a small group of pioneers centred in London, having founded the London Psycho-Analytical Society, devoted themselves to practising and teaching Freudian principles. After the close of the war this society was reconstituted as the British Psycho-Analytical Society. In the meantime Freud had developed and expanded his theories in a number of directions and was about to enter the second great phase of his theoretical formulations. Up to that time the concept of unconscious mental conflict, and with it the theory of neurosis, had presumed an antithesis of libidinal (in the general sense, sexual) instincts and the ego-instincts, in particular the impulses of self-preservation, together with certain reactive (aggressive) impulses. The neuroses were regarded as compromise formations representing both the repressed and the repressing forces, which latter were held to operate through the unconscious ego and to be activated by the ego-instincts.

The new orientation in Freud's theory was due to a number of factors. Most important of these were the extension of his researches into the structure of the unconscious ego, and fresh understanding of the part played by the impulses of aggression in ego development. The groundwork had already been prepared by his investigation of melancholia, from which Freud was able to postulate the existence of early differentiations of the unconscious ego. The modern psycho-analytical concept of the super-ego, or unconscious conscience, was developed from these studies. The function of the super-ego, which is derived essentially from an internalization of parental influences, is to exercise, or more accurately to instigate the unconscious ego to exercise control over primitive impulses threatening danger to its stability. At the same time Freud was able to demonstrate that the forces giving rise to disorder of super-ego function, of which melancholia is the exquisite example, were not only the narcissistic components of the libido with which the ego is invested, but the aggressive impulses which are loosened when any pathological disturbance takes place in the relation of the ego to its instinctual objects. These aggressive impulses, when let loose within the unconscious ego, give rise to a variety of pathological changes varying in accordance with its stability from mild neuroses to the most extensive psychoses.

Obviously a new orientation in the Freudian theory was necessary: and Freud did not hesitate to make the necessary changes. Abandoning his concept of special (non-libidinal) ego-instincts, he postulated the existence of an unorganized psychic institution, the Id, which is also a reservoir of all instinctual forces. He also distinguished at the periphery of this system ego-institutions, i.e. the super-ego, concerned with the supervision of libido and aggressive instincts, and the ego proper, concerned with the maintenance of adequate systems of discharge in reality. The self-preservative impulses were then regarded as libidinal in nature – an extension therefore of the earlier and more limited concept of narcissistic libido; and the instinctual antithesis between libido and ego-instincts was replaced by a deeper antithesis between the 'erotic' or 'life instincts' and the aggressive instincts which Freud held to be a derivative of a fundamental 'death-instinct' or 'innate tendency' of living matter to return to the inanimate state. These views he set forth in three monographs.[1]

The impact of these new ideas on the British Psycho-Analytical Society may be said to have taken effect roughly about 1926. Up to that time the Society was, on the whole, a conventional group undisturbed by schisms and controversies and, perhaps for that very reason, rather uninspired. The bulk of psycho-analytical research and discovery was the work of three groups, in Vienna, in Berlin and in Budapest, although it is undeniable that up to a few years before his death Freud himself was responsible for the lion's share of this work. In England, apart from the papers of Ernest Jones,[2] little of significance was published. Naturally, therefore, the new ideas were at first taken over without reservation, although a few members found difficulty in accepting Freud's concept of the 'death-instinct'. As, however, the fundamental discoveries regarding conflict, repression, symptom- and dream-formation and the nature of transference were not disturbed by this theoretical concept, there was at first no sign of scientific differences within the British group.

II. IMPACT OF THE EUROPEAN GROUPS

That changes soon took place was due to a number of factors. In the first place psycho-analysis, like all other sciences, is to some extent subject to the influence of fashion. It soon became the custom to see unconscious aggression in every analytic manifestation, and to speculate more and more on the organization of the ego prior to the classical Oedipus or incestuous phase of develop-

[1] Freud, S.: (1920) *Beyond the Pleasure Principle*, (1921) *Group Psychology and the Analysis of the Ego*, (1923) *The Ego and the Id*, Hogarth Press, London.

[2] JONES, E.: Papers on Psycho-analysis, Baillière, Tindall & Cox., London, 3rd ed., 1923 [5th ed., 1948].

ment, which is generally held to emerge about the age of three and a half years. These tendencies were greatly fostered by an increasing interest in the direct psycho-analysis of children. The first child-analyst in England, Mary Chadwick, started her specialist work about 1922. Between 1925 and 1927 two courses of lectures were given in Great Britain by a Berlin analyst, Melanie Klein, who had also specialized in child-analysis. By that time child-analysis had become a recognized speciality in Britain.

In any case, it was natural that interest should be focused on early stages of development. For although the Oedipus phase between three and a half and five years of age had been fairly accurately mapped out and although some working generalizations had been established regarding mental function in the first eighteen months of life, the gap existing between these hypothetical reconstructions and the established findings valid for later childhood called for attention. Ferenczi of Budapest and Abraham of Berlin had done extremely useful work in this direction, but their formulations were not completely satisfying. The main problem remained unaltered, namely, what are the forestages of the super-ego, i.e. before that period at which it is obvious that its main function is to enable the child to wean itself from its Oedipus longings, frustration and dependence. For until the age of roughly two and a half years, when it is first possible to establish a rudimentary 'psycho-analytical situation' and thereby to check theories of mental development by direct psycho-analytical investigation of children, all such theories are of necessity based on hypothetical reconstruction and therefore give play to subjective factors. Obviously this state of affairs was calculated to give rise to dissensions and controversies, in which these subjective factors were bound to play an increasing part. And this is in fact what happened. A controversial period in the development of the British Psycho-Analytical Society set in. This was greatly accentuated by the development of a new school of child-analysis founded by Melanie Klein, who by this time had settled in England.

The earlier formulations of this school were received on the whole with eager acceptance by most members of the British Society. This was no doubt in part a reaction to the previous absence of any very new or striking contributions to psycho-analysis from within the group; but it was due also to a genuine desire to see the gaps in knowledge of the early ego and of pregenital development filled up. Briefly, the new ideas included a number of legitimate extensions of the theories of Freud and Abraham, including the existence of early forms of super-ego and the rôle of introverted sadism in modelling these early forms. On the other hand, the new concepts already showed a distinct anti-Freudian tendency. A true Oedipus phase and a true super-ego were postulated for the sixth month of life and it was further maintained that libidinal positions or primacies are called out by struggles with the aggressive impulses, that is to say, the destructive impulses are more creative in effect than the libido.

These tendencies to deviate from accepted Freudian theory became quite obvious in the later formulations of Melanie Klein on the subject of depression.[1] It was laid down that a 'depressive position' is organized from the third month of life. This, it was maintained, is the result of a love-trauma due to the infant's imagined greedy destruction of a real loving mother whom it really loves. This depressive position is based on an earlier 'paranoid position' in which the child is believed to suffer from anxieties due to the projection of its own sadism. It was also stated[2] that all neuroses are different varieties of defence against fundamental depressive anxiety. The developmental importance of aggression rather than of libido was reasserted and it was maintained that unconscious phantasies occurring in the first few months of life exercise a far-reaching and uninterrupted influence on the development of the mind. The Freudian distinction between the unconscious system and the pre-conscious system was considerably blurred; the concept of narcissism was dropped in favour of an imagined system of 'internal objects'; and auto-erotism was regarded not as a narcissistic phenomenon but as a system of occult allo-erotic satisfactions in which the part of the body masturbated is actually an internal object representing a former external object.

Had these assumptions been valid, they would have involved a drastic revision of Freudian theory. But their sponsor had gone too

[1] Klein, M.: 'A Contribution to the Psychogenesis of Manic-Depressive States, *Int. J. Psycho-Anal.*, 1935, 17, 174; also 'Mourning and its relation to Manic Depressive States', ibid., 20, 1936.

[2] See, in particular, papers (*Int. J. Psycho-Anal.*, 1936, 17, 304, ibid., 395), by Joan Riviere, who, together with Susan Isaacs, provided most of the necessary metapsychology for the Kleinian system.

far. Although many members of the British Society espoused her cause in a most devoted manner, open opposition developed in other quarters. This was strengthened when, after the Nazi invasion of Austria, a large number of the Vienna group, led by Anna Freud, settled in London. Opposition to the penetration of the Society with Kleinian views became more organized and for a time the Klein group dropped their earlier and bolder suggestions that Freud was just a little antiquated and old-fashioned. Nevertheless, the important issue – whether students of psycho-analysis were to be trained in Freudian or Kleinian views – could not be burked. Discussions on the matter were just reaching a crisis when the Second World War put an end to them for the time being. The situation then was that the Society was divided, though not openly, into three groups: a classical Freudian group, a Kleinian group and a 'middle group' whose members, whilst accepting some of the earlier ideas of Melanie Klein, felt that her later formulations went too far.

Looking back it seems somewhat remarkable that the Kleinian deviations from Freud should not have led to more drastic action. It is now clear that the tendency of the later Kleinian theories is identical with the tendencies of those earlier schismatics, Jung and Rank. The Klein group follows Rank in attributing mental development, and all variations in mental disorder, to a traumatic situation occurring, not, it is true, at birth, but shortly after birth; it follows Jung in attributing dynamic and developmental power to archaic phantasies. The phantasies attributed to the suckling by the Kleinians do not differ from the archetypes of 'original sin' which Jung regards as a product of the (Jungian) 'collective unconscious'.

III. Post-War Development

Towards the close of the war, when members who had evacuated London or had joined the Forces began to return, the Klein controversy broke out again. For 18 months a series of discussions on the subject took place, but the result was inconclusive. Many ex-Viennese members, dissatisfied with the state of affairs existing in the Society, had transferred to the United States of America shortly after the outbreak of the war, and this weakened greatly the influence of the Freudian group. Hence, despite shattering criticism of their views,[1] Kleinian members retained their membership of the British Society. The Society, whilst nominally unchanged, split openly into two main groups: Kleinian and Freudian. A middle group sat rather timidly and uneasily in the centre.

After prolonged negotiations an attempt was made, not indeed to bridge the gap scientifically – because the differences between Freudian theories on the one hand and Rankian and Jungian ideologies on the other are scientifically irreconcilable – but to found some system of training which would obviate an official split in the Society. This, roughly, is the state of affairs at the present time. Students are at first taught only Freudian theory but after the first year their training is taken over by two groups teaching respectively Kleinian and Freudian theory and practice.

This camouflage arrangement, however, does not alter the situation and whether in the future the Society turns Kleinian or Freudian depends for the most part on the numbers trained by the respective groups. Mainly, but not exclusively: for after the war a new influence began to make itself felt in the British Psycho-Analytical Society. This was, in the first instance at any rate, a matter of policy rather than of science, and involved an almost formal rapprochement between psycho-analysis and psychiatry. Before the war, psycho-analysis and psychiatry reacted to each other with an aloof disregard bordering on contempt. Psycho-analysis would in fact have nothing to do with any body that did not profess exclusively Freudian principles. Suggestions that a closer contact might be made even with more eclectic medico-psychological clinics, such as the Tavistock Clinic, were frowned on. The Society itself contained only a sprinkling of young psychiatrists who had so far contributed nothing to psycho-analytical knowledge.

During the war psychiatry made spectacular advances in administrative authority. For no particular reason except that of favourable opportunity, psychiatry became a positive craze in the combatant services; and naturally once the war was over a number of young psychiatrists, who had whetted their appetite on psy-

---

[1] I have outlined the Klein system and summarized the relevant criticisms of it in a monograph entitled 'An Examination of the Klein System of Child-psychology', first published in *The Psychoanalytic Study of the Child*, Vol. I, 1945, Imago Publishing Co., Ltd., London: since reprinted separately.

chiatry in the Forces, evinced a desire for psycho-analytic training. The Society for its part began to overcome its earlier distrust of psychiatry. To cut a long story short: under the influence of its psychiatric members, plans were put into effect to train a number of psychiatrists; more remarkable still, psychiatric-minded analysts took up administrative positions in the previously non-analytical Tavistock Clinic, now the Institute of Human Relations.

This new development may in course of time influence the trend of psycho-analytical thought in Great Britain. Psycho-analysis in Britain was not, as in the United States of America, an offshoot of psychiatric activity. It derived its support partly from lay cultural sources and partly from doctors who before and after the First World War were interested in the Freudian approach to medical psychology. In short, it developed in the European tradition of psycho-analysis in which psychiatry, it is true, played a part but never exercised controlling authority. The older lay traditions of psycho-analysis, which Freud, although himself a physician, did much to foster, are thus threatened with extinction. On the whole it is not a very happy development and does not augur well for future progress in psycho-analysis. No doubt it will contribute to the general efficiency of psycho-analytic training, for most of the early medical analysts and all of the lay analysts in Britain were deficient in psychiatric training. Nevertheless, the specialized and restricted outlook of the psychiatrist does not qualify him to assume a directing rôle in psycho-analysis; in other words, the average psychiatrist has neither the education nor the cultural background necessary for psycho-analytical research.

Simultanously, with the development of this psychiatric bent, psycho-analysis has begun to play a larger part in the practice of child guidance. Unfortunately a new branch of 'child-psychiatry' threatens to offset any advantages that might accrue from this logical and essential development of psycho-analytic work. For if psychiatry exercises a too highly specialized and too rigid influence on adult psycho-analysis, it is still less suitable to act as a regulator of child-analysis. It is indeed imperative that the speciality of child-analysis should recruit its members from the most broadly orientated, soundly trained and scientifically disciplined groups.

IV. Present Situation

With this brief survey of recent developments in the British

Psycho-Analytical Society it is possible to indicate the present scientific status of psycho-analysis in Britain. The Society is now divisible into four groups: (*a*) an orthodox Freudian group, (*b*) a Kleinian group, (*c*) a psychiatric group and (*d*) the remnants of the old 'middle group' to which reference was made earlier. The orthodox group is concerned chiefly with the maintenance of Freudian standards of training and education, particularly in the field of child investigation. The Kleinian group has not produced any new orientations, although already its influence is responsible for a growing tendency to take the psychology of 'internal objects' for granted and to regard it as the most important factor in mental develpment. We shall, I think, soon see a 'schizoid position' added to the 'paranoid' and 'depressive positions' and 'manic defences' of early infancy already hypothesized by the Kleinians. No doubt in course of time most of these absurdities will be either watered down or eliminated, but in the meantime they constitute a threat to the scientific development of psycho-analysis in Britain. In other countries they have received no support and a good deal of overt criticism. The position of the third or psychiatric group has already been indicated. As for the fourth and rather nondescript 'middle group', there does not seem much hope that it will survive very long. People with a fanatical enthusiasm for a special point of view exert, in any case, more influence than those who, out of a wish for compromise, keep to the middle of the road. And although there is no scientific virtue in compromise, yet a strong middle group does serve to restrain the exuberance of enthusiasts.

On the whole, therefore, one can only hope that the first or orthodox group will extend its authority. Freudian principles are still vital to the development of psycho-analysis.

A similar comment can be made regarding the therapeutic aspects of psycho-analysis. Psycho-analytic therapy is not, as is often thought, just a matter of free association and *ex cathedra* interpretation. It depends on the development during analysis of what is called the 'transference neurosis'. Starting with a spontaneous transfer of friendly (or hostile) infantile attitudes to the personality of the analyst, the patient gradually 'transfers his neurosis' to the analytic situation, thereby rendering it more amenable to analysis and liquidation. When this is achieved the analyst sets about liquidating also ('analysing out') the transferences. This is what distinguishes psycho-analysis not only from hypnosis and suggestion but from all other forms of 'analytical' therapy or again from mixtures of suggestion and 'analysis'. Unless the transference is adequately analysed, the whole process of therapy, and whatever therapeutic results may accrue, depend on a state of infantile rapport, in other words they partake of the essential nature of suggestion. Naturally the 'transference neurosis' occurs in classical form only during the psycho-analysis of the psychoneuroses, hysteria and the obsessions, which for that reason are often called 'transference neuroses'.

During the war, when military necessity dictated the use of short cuts in diagnosis, treatment or selection of personnel, a number of old methods were resuscitated and given more pretentious names; hence the use of 'hypno-analysis', 'narco-analysis' and at a later date 'group-analysis'. It is often assumed and sometimes explicitly stated that these constitute 'advances' in psycho-analysis. The fact is, however, that they constitute merely advances in the technique, respectively, of hypnosis, narcosis and 'transference therapy'. They add nothing to our knowledge of psycho-analysis proper and in fact act as obstacles to the carrying out of classical analysis. Whether they produce results more quickly remains to be seen, and is in any case beside the point. No one ever suggested that an analysis should be evaluated by temporal measures. And as Freud, anticipating that some time or other necessity would lead to a mixing of methods, once remarked: the quickest way to carry out an analysis is to do it properly, i.e. in accordance with psycho-analytical principles. No doubt psycho-analysts have tended to neglect Freud's conservative views on the therapeutic applicability of psycho-analysis to cases indiscriminately selected, and have only themselves to blame when, goaded by the intractability of many non-neurotic cases (e.g. character disorders, psychoses and perversions), they hanker after quicker methods. But it is inherently unlikely that any method which canalizes rather than analyses the transference will in the long run prove more efficient or permanent in effect than psycho-analysis proper.

But when all is said, the present is an interesting phase in the history of psycho-analysis. However absurd some of the hypotheses recently advanced may have been, there is no doubt that the focusing of interest on problems of early ego-development and on the organization of mind during the phase of 'primary identification' (i.e. at the stage before the 'self' and the 'not-self' are accurately differentiated), will in the long run produce results of value both diagnostically and therapeutically. It will involve, as I have suggested in my 'theory of nuclear development of the ego', a molecular rather than a 'gestalt' approach to the subject; or rather, it will involve a distinction between rudimentary and organized gestalt-patterns of the unconscious.[1]

What psycho-analysis needs in the future is what it has always sorely needed, an accession of scientific workers, who must, it is true, be able to conduct therapeutic analyses – that is essential – but also whose interest in research or in the formulation of new theories is disciplined by scientific controls rather than regulated by 'intuitions', which are often little more than subjective reactions. If psycho-analysis could rally to its ranks the numbers of young, intelligent and imaginative men and women who flock to the service of physical science, progress in research would no doubt be spectacular. But alas for the prospect, the budding physical scientist may make a good academic or laboratory psychologist but he does not as a rule make a good psycho-analyst. Hence it is necessary for psycho-analytic institutes to go out into the highways and byways of cultural activity to seek promising recruits. These, when found, must be suitably subsidized to stand the financial strain of combined psycho-analytical and medical education, and, later on, prevented by appropriate rewards from choosing the path of professional success rather than the less lucrative road to scientific discovery. Psycho-analysis, which seeks to penetrate the mysteries of cultural development, must become and remain a cultural as well as a therapeutic or professional pursuit.

[1] Glover, E.: (1932) *Int. J. Psycho-Anal.*, **13**, 298, (1932) *J. ment. Science*, **78**, 819, (1933) *Int. J. Psycho-Anal.*, **14**, 486, (1943) ibid., **24**, 7. [See Chaps. XI, XII, XIII and XX.]

XXIV

FUNCTIONAL ASPECTS OF THE MENTAL APPARATUS*

[1950]

With every attempt to trace the development of the mental apparatus during the period before direct psycho-analytical technique can be applied to the growing child (and even the most sanguine child-analyst can scarcely claim that a true 'analytical situation' can be established before the age of two and a half years or that the 'accessibility' to analysis of the normal two-year-old is greater than that of an advanced psychotic), we are brought closer to the supreme test of psycho-analytical thinking, viz. its capacity to 'reconstruct' the rudimentary structure, economics and function of the mind during what has been described, a little too perfunctorily, as the 'oral phase', i.e. from birth to eighteen months of age.

It is true that by a comparative study of a series of mental disorders varying in depth (or regressional level) we can make some rough guesses as to the state of mental organization existing at the fixation levels of these disorders, and in this way reconstruct with some plausibility the total function of the mental apparatus at what is still called, again too casually, the 'anal phase'. But even at its earliest the 'anal-sadistic phase' pre-supposes an elaborate organization of the mental apparatus and gives us little notion of the state of affairs existing in the first eighteen months of life. In any case this method of approach is open to grave error in speculation. As we have seen in recent years the analytic study of adult disorders can lead to the postulation of organizations of the mind during the first year which bear a suspicious resemblance to the disintegration products of the psychoses. It is no solution to our metapsychological problems to job backwards using as counters clinical and theoretical findings applicable at best to the mind as it can be observed between the ages of four and forty-four years. And it will scarcely be disputed that the concept of orderly progression in mental development

* This paper was given in an abbreviated form at the 16th Psycho-Analytical Congress, Zürich, August, 1949; first published in *The International Journal of Psycho-Analysis*, Vol. XXXI, pts. 1 and 2, 1950.

lays us under obligation to describe the earliest stages as simply as possible.

As outlined in earlier papers my own attempts, first to classify mental disorders and then to educe from these classifications a potential order of mental development led to the rejection of the concept of an early synthesized 'ego' and the postulation of early 'nuclear' ego-formations more in keeping with our knowledge of the phenomena of regression (see Chaps. XI, XII, XIII, XVI and XX). But although this nuclear hypothesis seemed to promise increasing accuracy in etiological formulations, it did not fully satisfy either theoretical or clinical requirements. In the first place, it did not account for the wide scatter and age-incidence of 'psychosomatic' states; and in the second, it could not indicate the point at which unconscious 'conflict' becomes the decisive factor in psychogenesis. Obviously a purely structural approach could do little more than give a thumb nail sketch of the earliest stages of mental organization; and equally obviously the proper course was to concentrate on the dynamic aspects of early mental activity. The result was the postulation of a 'primary functional phase' which is outlined in the following paper. The idea has been more fully elaborated in a chapter on 'Psycho-somatic and Allied Disorders' in 'Psycho-analysis' and given further theoretical and practical extension in two monographs; Basic Mental Concepts *and* Psychoanalysis and Child Psychiatry.[1]

At the Amsterdam Congress of European Analysts I endeavoured to outline the most important of those sparingly stated basic concepts on which the theory and practice of psycho-analysis is founded and on which the validity of the most elaborate presentation of mental structure and function ultimately depends. On that occasion I pointed out that Freud's original description of the mental apparatus, as outlined in the theoretical part of his *Interpretation of Dreams*, provided us with a perfectly adequate reconstruction of the first stages of mental life. It is with this frequently misunderstood but nevertheless *master-concept of a mental apparatus* that I am concerned here.

The fact that in recent years psycho-analysts have neglected the concept of a mental apparatus is due to a number of causes some

---

[1] *Psycho-analysis*, 2nd. ed., London, Staples Press, 1949; *Basic Mental Concepts*, London, Imago Publishing Co., 1947; *Psycho-analysis and Child Psychiatry*, London, Imago Publishing Co., 1953.

of which cannot be distinguished from resistances. Chief of these is an inveterate tendency to anthropomorphize all mental concepts. Because, for example, we tend to identify ourselves with our ego, or, as the case may be, our super-ego, it is easy to neglect the purely *functional* aspects of these *psychic institutions* as instruments of adaptation. The tendency to anthropomorphize the mental apparatus, to personalize its parts and functions, was accelerated by the circumstance that Freud's original and mainly dynamic concept of the apparatus was considerably overlaid by his later expansions of structural psychology. This emphasis on ego-psychology has given rise during the past ten to fifteen years to attempts to describe early functional (dynamic) phases of the mental apparatus in terms of organized ego-institutions; or, to put the matter more simply, to attribute to the suckling the conscious mentality and unconscious organization of a four-year-old child.

Similarly, concepts of unconscious *conflict* appropriate to comparatively late symptom-formations such as the infantile psycho-neuroses, tend to be applied to earlier forms of developmental disorder; for example, to rudimentary psycho-somatic reactions, to convulsive seizures and to the essential (infantile) psychoses. We are inclined, that is to say, to look upon the earliest disturbances of mental function as if their etiology did not differ in any essential respect from the etiology of the psycho-neuroses.

It would be interesting and not altogether irrelevant to the purposes of this paper to speculate on the unconscious factors giving rise to these 'conceptual' resistances. For the moment, however, we must content ourselves with the suggestion that the main obstacle to understanding is narcissistic in nature, namely, a need to deny that the ego was at one time purely Id. This need can be readily satisfied by the tacit assumption that an 'ego-self' exists shortly after birth, in other words, by regarding the Id as if it were merely a primitive ego-institution. Moreover, since conflict implies some degree of ego-organization, the assumption that true conflict exists shortly after birth flatters the narcissistic vanity of the adult observer by its implication that the infant is already possessed of moral institutions. However that may be, it is undoubtedly a fact that the psycho-analytical observer starting his investigations with a fairly comprehensive understanding of the four-year-old and seeking to reconstruct the earliest phases of mental development tends to 'carry back' his established findings, to read the early unknown in terms of the later known. Inevitably these tendencies obscure our understanding of early mental development, and I consider it essential to work out in greater detail the functional aspects of mind at a period when mental structure is of the most rudimentary order and before the mind has acquired conceptual content.

To begin with it should be remembered that Freud's original description of the mental apparatus was intended to provide a theoretical basis for the processes of dream-formation. And since the dream-material he examined was almost exclusively adult material, his sketch of the mental apparatus had perforce to indicate its fully developed form. Thus, for example, when describing the essential characteristic of punishment dreams, Freud pointed out that it is not the repressed unconscious wish that is responsible for the dream but 'the punitive wish reacting against it, a wish pertaining to the ego, even though it is unconscious'. In a footnote to this passage, added some years later, he remarked, 'Here is the place to insert the idea of the super-ego which was later recognized by psycho-analysis.' In other words, Freud was then describing the operation of the mental apparatus during sleep at a stage at which the classical Oedipus complex is in process of being overcome, that is to say at the very earliest a three- to four-year-old mental apparatus. Nevertheless, he gave numerous hints as to the nature of mental activity in the earliest stages; as when he suggested that dreaming is 'a fragment of the superseded psychic life of the child'; that our dreams are 'remnants of the supremacy of the pleasure-principle and proofs of its power'; that the primary processes are *'residues'* of the phase of development 'in which they were the only kind of mental processes'; that in laying aside our mental acquisitions in sleep we approach remarkably close to the situation in which we began life; and that the master-mechanism responsible for dream activity is that of regression.

No matter, therefore, how many distinct levels we may ultimately postulate in the development of the mental apparatus, we are compelled to distinguish in the first instance *a primary functional level*. Metapsychologically this primary level can be described as a central psychic path lying between the sensory and the motor boundaries of the apparatus, along which unbound instinctual charges advance or regress according to the pleasure principle, activating and reactivating in their passage primordial memory traces. Stimulated by variations of affect this primitive apparatus seeks during the brief periods of waking infantile life to effect adaptation by mostly unco-ordinated motor discharges, and, during the much longer periods of sleep, to reduce excitation by regression, in course of which hallucinatory images are from time to time activated at the sensory end of the apparatus. The mental apparatus is in fact at this stage less a structural unit than *a series of dynamic (energic) sequences representing and recording the flow and ebb of psychic excitation.* Dealing as it does with unbound psychic energies, *its urgent need is to reduce traumatic stress due to damming up of excitation.* We may assume further that the favourable or unfavourable (retarded) development of the mental apparatus depends at first on a quantitative factor, since some degree of traumatic intensity is essential to the laying down of those memory traces which subsequently are used for purposes of reality adaptation.[1]

Pursuing this dynamic approach, we may assume still further that the first mental disorders occurring at this primary functional stage are simple *disorders of excitation and discharge* without fixed psychic content and giving rise to the purest form of psycho-somatic reaction (disturbances of affect, of organ innervations, of motor discharge and of sleep). At the same time we must remember that not all disturbed discharges can be regarded as pathological in type. Infantile convulsions are not necessarily a sign of idio-pathic epilepsy. Moreover, already at this stage the repetition-compulsion can take precedence over the pleasure-principle. Indeed, we can regard the operation of this repetition tendency as the first spontaneous attempt at active, autoplastic psycho-therapy, in that, in contradistinction to regression, it seeks to master rather than escape from dammed-up energies due to instinctual frustra-tion and over-excitation of whatever sort.

Before considering the means whereby the validity of these assumptions (regarding a primary functional phase of the mental

---

[1] This is not very clearly expressed. The passage is intended to convey that although we are accustomed to think in *clinical* terms of traumatic stresses that give rise to disordered function of an already existing apparatus, the *normal* structure of the mental apparatus itself depends on stresses which are intense enough to register permanent traces.

apparatus) can be tested, it is convenient to indicate briefly what is known regarding *later* functional phases of development. Of these later phases the easiest to recognize is that arrived at just prior to the latency period, when for all practical purposes the mental apparatus has achieved its final form. Needless to say, it is unnecessary to recapitulate here the familiar features of this well attested phase which is described clinically as the Oedipus phase. Of the *intervening* phases much less is known. Indeed, by the time we reach back to the two-year-old level of mental development, we are already compelled to have recourse to hypothetical reconstructions: and our conclusions have little more force than those we arrive at concerning a primary phase. Nevertheless, the progress of psycho-analysis depends on the accuracy with which we can isolate these intervening stages. No doubt the process of isolation does violence to the concept of total function: yet for both clinical and descriptive purposes we must ignore both the overlapping and the simultaneous functioning of transitional phases.

Of the many possible methods of isolation the most important are: first, the analysis of psychic stresses; second, the isolation of predominating defence-mechanisms characteristic of any given phase; third, the demarcation of Id-ego boundaries, or, to use the older terminology, of the unconscious-preconscious barrier; fourth, the distinction of increasingly complicated ego-object relations; and, fifth, the ordering in developmental sequence of symptom-formations. Naturally all of these approaches overlap.

Among the *stress factors* the most important are: the damming-up of instinct-quantities, the stimulus of reactive anxiety and the pressure of unconscious guilt. An essential part of this investigation is to distinguish *developmental order of stresses*. For although at the final stages of development of the mental apparatus, all three varieties of stress can be observed to operate simultaneously, this does not permit the assumption that all of them exist and operate with equal force in the earlier stages.

Here is the point at which it is necessary to define with some precision the concept of *conflict*. Some years ago Hartmann[1] suggested that this term is applied too exclusively to the processes of adaptation and that there is a 'sphere without conflict' which

[1] 'Ich-Psychologie und Anpassungs-Problem', *Int. Z. Psychoanal.*, **24**, 1939.

nevertheless records clashes between the organism and its environment. In the writer's opinion, Hartmann might have developed this idea further. Clearly, if such spheres exist they indicate that, at some stage of development, stress without conflict must have been a characteristic feature of mental activity which later on manifests itself in more limited 'spheres'. Stresses due to the opposing aims of instincts existing before the ego is organized cannot be labelled 'conflict' without making nonsense of the concept of the Id, to say nothing of the primary processes which take no cognizance of contradictions.

Neither can we proceed to the opposite extreme and limit the term conflict to stresses arising specifically from the super-ego, for that would be to ignore the rôle of traumatic anxiety in ego-development. Moreover, we cannot associate conflict exclusively with symptom-formation. That would be to confuse cause with a special group of effects. It would in any case be absurd to suggest that persons who are free from clinical symptom-formation have no unconscious conflicts. It would therefore seem reasonable to distinguish at least three stages in psychic stress: (1) stresses existing at a time when the ego is not yet organized. These belong to the primary functional phase. (2) Stresses existing when the ego is more organized and employs specific defence-mechanisms but is still subject more to anxiety than to guilt. This secondary phase overlaps with a third: (3) namely, the period when the super-ego stresses give rise to the purest form of endopsychic conflict.

The next method of demarcating stages in the development of the mental apparatus depends on the *isolation of defences* operating before the establishment of an organized repression barrier. Here again a distinction can be drawn between primitive phases when regression and reflexion of instinct predominate, and phases when systems of anti-cathexis are organized. The rôle of anti-cathexis in the formation of the early ego has been under-estimated in the past, largely because it has been almost exclusively associated with the process of primal repression. There is every reason to assume that for a prolonged period anti-cathexis is one of the chief agents not only in controlling frustration and the damming up of excitations consequent thereon, but in developing the pre-conscious system. In other words, anti-cathexis is in the first instance a response to traumatic stress rather than to conflict. It affords breathing space for the development of secondary processes, not only through the mechanism of primal repression but through a general function of mobilizing counter-interest.

This brings us to the third approach, namely, study of the development of the *barrier between the unconscious and the pre-conscious systems*. This is an approach to which much less attention has been paid in recent years, partly because the overriding importance attached to the Id has encouraged a certain indifference amongst psycho-analysts as to its boundaries. It is not hard, however, to distinguish three distinct phases, viz., a primitive imaginal phase when fluctuations in the cathexis of memory traces constitute the nearest approach to ideational activity, a phase when thinking is mainly symbolic in nature, and a phase when concep-tual thinking exerts a primacy over the earlier modes.

It is desirable at this point to stress the importance of this concept of *primacy of function*. Study of the relations of the Id and of the repressed to the pre-conscious ego illustrates very clearly the phenomena of simultaneous function and, in the structural sense, the 'overlapping' of different phases. With every approach to the demarcation of phases of development it is essential to remember that a primitive phase does not cease to function because it has reached the limits of its expansion and is overlaid by subsequent more organized layers. In contradistinc-tion to the atrophy of certain primitive physiological systems or organs, the earliest mental systems continue to function through-out life alongside more developed organizations or institutions.

Thus in the present instance, it is probably true to say that the phase of imaginal representation characteristic of the primary functional phase is gradually superseded during the period when symbolic thinking contributes to the organization of the deepest layers of the pre-conscious system; and that from the onset of conceptual thinking it is incapable of further development. But we have every reason to know that it does not abandon function. We know too that as the pre-conscious system expands the ego develops rapidly. But although the ego is more organized and the mental apparatus has clearly passed from a primary to a *secondary* phase, it is still concerned for the most part with the control of or flight from excessive excitation, using for the purpose automatic unconscious mechanisms. Stress rather than conflict is still the decisive factor in the earlier stages of this secondary phase. Only at the end of the secondary phase when conceptual thinking has to a considerable extent superseded symbolic thinking does the influence of super-ego organization begin to predominate. We can then speak with some justification of a *tertiary phase* in the organization of the mental apparatus in which true endopsychic conflict is a constant factor.

Within the limits prescribed by a summary it is scarcely possible to do more than indicate the scope of the fourth method of approach; viz., *a study of object relations and boundaries*. By far the greater part of psycho-analytical work has been and is concerned with ego-object relations. Indeed, when one considers the extensive observations that have been made on developmental phases of libido and of the aggressive impulses and on the influence of unconscious mechanisms such as projection, introjection and displacement on ego-object relations, it would appear that we are already in a position not merely to isolate one or two main phases in mental development, but to describe a lengthy series of phases. From the point of view of ego-psychology this is no doubt true; but when seeking to isolate phases in the development of the mental apparatus a great deal of this complexity disappears or, at any rate, can be reduced to a few simple generalizations.

Thus we can identify the primary functional phase of the mental apparatus with the period of 'primary identification' which includes the most primitive forms of (organ) object relationships and which is maintained largely by the mechanisms of regression and by commencing projections. We can also recognize without much difficulty the final and stable phase of object relations which occurs when introjection processes have reached their peak activity and are giving place to more elastic mechanisms of identification. There is in my view a good functional justification for including identification in this latest phase, namely, that it promotes and preserves a necessary fluidity in object relationships. Introjection by contrast expands the ego at the cost of object relationships.

Regarding the period that lies between these first and final phases it is difficult to speak with any precision. We may be certain that during this intervening phase object relations are influenced by three main mechanisms, introjection, repression and displacement. But although in this respect the mental apparatus functions in a much more complicated way than it does in the primary functional phase, we cannot presume that there is any direct ratio between the variety of instinctual experiences and the *complexity of the apparatus*.[1] However much it may add to the organization of the ego, the experience of a succession of instinctual primacies calls for no outstanding change in the function of the apparatus; although no doubt the development of the repression group of mechanisms gradually lessens the rigidity of introjections.

Turning now to the last or *clinical approach* to the mental apparatus, viz., by means of establishing *a developmental series of mental disorders*, we encounter the difficulty that, to be clear about a hierarchy of mental disorders, we must know something about the hierarchy of levels of mental development from which they spring. We can be certain that the constitutional factor exerts its maximum influence during the primary functional phase and contributes characteristic features to the simple disorders of excitation and discharge that appear during that phase. We can be equally certain that those classical symptom-formations, the infantile neuroses, first appear in what I have called the tertiary phase. But (to keep for the moment to the main groups of psychic disorder) the position of the infantile psychoses is still far from clear. Sharing with neurotic symptom-formations the characteristic of possessing occult meaning, they nevertheless present many functional features, in the sense that they are also responses to traumatic over-excitation and therefore have their roots in both primary and secondary phases. Uncertainties of this kind are naturally increased when we attempt to distinguish etiological formulæ for the various sub-groups of the psychoses and for transitional groups such as the drug addictions, and on the strength of these distinctions to outline transitions in the function of the mental apparatus.

The varieties of approach described above do not of course exhaust our means of investigating the problem. Nor is it intended

---

[1] [Note (1955): Neglect of this consideration is no doubt responsible in part for those 'reconstructions' of early mental development in which a degree of ego-structure is assumed that would be more appropriate for later phases and in which unconscious mental content is postulated which shows the hallmark of secondary processes, sometimes even of conscious rational thinking. The complexity of mental content is manifestly a derivative of pre-conscious activity as can readily be observed during the processes of falling asleep and awakening.]

that the brief descriptions of them given here should be more than a stimulus to orderly thinking and research on the subject. Nevertheless it is essential to submit the generalizations that have been put forward to a clinical test in order to determine their plausibility. Before doing so the following considerations should be borne in mind. In the first place it should be remembered that our metapsychological measures are highly artificial: the mind is best conceived of as being constantly in a state of energic flux. Secondly, what we call in the structural sense organization of mind is not to be thought of merely as a series of *superimposed* developmental levels. There is, to use a spatial image, a vertical as well as a horizontal development of the apparatus.

This fact is best expressed in terms of the *continuity* of functional systems within the apparatus. For instance, although, using the different methods of approach described above, it is comparatively easy to distinguish in each case primary, secondary and tertiary levels in the development of the mental apparatus (and no doubt with increasing accuracy in investigation other transitional phases will be established), it would be absurd to expect that the various functions of any one level would necessarily coincide in time, that is to say, that at a given developmental age-period *all* the manifestations of, e.g. the primary phase, would be found at the same time functioning in a closed system. What for the sake of convenience we describe as the superposition or overlapping of different horizontal layers can also be regarded as the continued function of a mental system, throughout more advanced stages of development.

Perhaps the best clinical illustration of the uses of a vertical rather than a horizontal approach is to be found in the case of paranoia. Here a primary fault in the function of the mental apparatus giving rise to excessive use of projection mechanisms continues to disturb development at various later stages and gives rise to characteristic disorders at each stage, e.g. some of the early infantile phobias and obsessions. Only when we reach the comparatively late period of infantile homosexual development, either primary or reactive, can we speak accurately of a true paranoid basis for the future psychosis. Yet it is clear that this *canalization of functional disorders* in a consistent system serves to some extent to preserve the integrity of the ego. For despite a gross disturbance of reality sense, the ego of many paranoiacs continues to manifest a remarkable degree of effective function.

Needless to say this factor of continuity of systems is constantly reinforced by the operation of the mechanism of regression. It is of considerable help to understanding the total function of mind to remember that none of these levels or systems ever goes out of operation. As has already been suggested, they continue to function simultaneously throughout life. This is clearly shown, by the existence at all ages of dream formations, of disorders of sleep, of convulsive seizures and of the deeper inhibitions of activity produced under hypnosis, all of which manifestations may be presumed to exist in simpler form during the primary functional phase.

If only for clinical purposes, therefore, it is justifiable to break down this state of functional flux, to isolate both horizontal levels and vertical (or serial) canalizations of mental activity, and to indicate the disorders that are associated with each level or canalization. Naturally the most important of these levels or canalizations is what I have described as the primary functional phase. And I think there is some advantage to be gained by describing this primary phase as, in the dynamic sense, a *traumatic phase*.[1] I have suggested, moreover, that at this primary period we find the simplest forms of psycho-somatic reaction, in other words, simple disorders of excitation and discharge. It is at this stage that individual factors combine with constitutional factors to form a *predisposition*, respectively, to the psycho-somatic disorders, to

---

[1] I realize fully that there are some drawbacks to the use of the term 'traumatic' in this connection. Traumatic hypotheses have in the past given rise to all sorts of confusion regarding mental development in general and pathogenesis in particular. It would perhaps have been better to keep to the term 'stress' and indicate the traumatic factor in quantitative and qualitative terms, i.e. the intensity and variety of excitation. Unfortunately, apart from clinical data, we have no accurate psychoanalytical measures of intensity, and must consequently fall back in the meantime on descriptive terms. The word 'traumatic' has therefore some descriptive value. Developmentally regarded it implies that under normal circumstances the infant's limit of effective tolerance of excitation is repeatedly exceeded during the primary functional phase. From the pathogenetic point of view, 'trauma' implies that, owing to constitutional factors or to individual factors (e.g. the degree of frustration) or to both, the threshold of effective tolerance has been seriously lowered either temporarily or permanently.

the psychoses and to the psycho-neuroses of later life.

These disorders of excitation and discharge do not, however, *give place to* more meaningful disorders such as the psychoses and neuroses. They continue to have, as it were, a history of their own. As the rudimentary ego develops during the secondary phase, we begin to distinguish more precisely different *varieties* of functional disorder which predispose, e.g. to hypochondria, to neurasthenia, and to the anxiety-neuroses.

On the other hand, although it is desirable to isolate a series of functional disorders preserving the primitive characteristics of excessive excitation and discharge, this does not prevent us making the usual correlations between the functional states and the development of psychoses and neuroses. The established correlations on the one hand between the damming-up of narcissistic libido and the development of hypochondriacal anxiety and on the other between the damming-up of object libido and the development of neurotic anxiety would remain unaltered; but they would acquire a more systematic value. Similarly with the relation of hypochondria to paraphrenia; and of the actual neuroses to hysteria and obsessional neurosis. We could then say that given the appropriate ego- and libido-fixations these different varieties of functional disorder provide the foundations on which are built up, first, the primitive[1] symptom-formations of the psychoses and later the true symptomatic compromise-formations of the psycho-neuroses.

This rough distinction of horizontal levels would enable us to follow with clearer understanding what I have called the serial development or canalization of mental disorders. In the case of two of the psychotic groups, the depressive group and the paranoiac group, we could distinguish more clearly *the early functional traumatic stages on which the later symptom-constructions are founded*. In both instances it is not difficult to establish by analysis and sometimes to confirm by anamnesis a traumatic factor, involving in the case of depression a damming-up of oral-sadistic excitations: in the case of paranoia a damming-up of mainly anal-sadistic excitations.

---

[1] [Note (1955): 'primitive' not only in structure and mechanism but in the sense that the diseased ego is governed by restitutive processes intended to re-establish object relations *via* symbolic thinking. In the psycho-neuroses the ego is largely intact and symbolic object contact is confined to the neurotic symptom formation.]

Moreover, by reversing the order of approach and studying the effect of sudden regression on a developmental series, we can throw some light on the phenomenon of suicide. In a paper on this subject I suggested many years ago that the act of suicide, although associated closely with depressive mechanisms, could be explained only by assuming an instinctual regression which simultaneously breaks down the defence-barriers existing at *every* stage of infantile development. To this formulation I would now add that in effective suicide the regression of dammed-up energies activates the primary functional level of the apparatus, producing an intolerable state of stasis which overcomes primary inhibitions and seeks autoplastic discharge through motor paths.

Following the same approach it would be possible to effect an orderly classification of that omnibus group of disorders frequently but often inaptly described as 'traumatic neuroses'. We could isolate those traumatic states in which the symptom-picture is determined mainly by the functional discharge or inhibition of excessive excitation from those traumatic states in which true psychotic or neurotic formations, respectively, complicate the clinical picture. We could also distinguish more clearly the psycho-somatic states in which the effects of summated excitation lead to purely functional discharges or inhibitions from those which provide a fixation basis for a subsequent conversion hysteria.

To take one last example: the concept of a primary functional phase can be usefully applied to the group of disorders known as the convulsive states. Both neurological and analytical observers have been prepared to recognize in these conditions a hierarchy of etiological elements derived from different levels of organization, and, although they express the basic reaction in different terms, agree that the convulsion is in the last event a violent archaic discharge consequent on damming-up of excitations or, as the neurologist would say, the blocking of stimuli. Examination of the different clinical conditions during which convulsive seizures occur bear out the assumption of a factor of traumatic stress. Psycho-analytic investigation shows, however, that the convulsive states constitute a group which can be sub-divided in accordance with levels of development, e.g. neurotic and psychotic epilepsies. And it seems likely that, as in the case of suicidal manifestations, a sudden and almost total regression breaks through the various barriers in series and lights up an archaic (motor and sensory) discharge which is seen in its simplest form in earliest infancy and is characteristic of the primary functional phase. Reversing the clinical order of events, we can surmise with some confidence not only that normal development consists in the superposition of increasingly effective barriers against the activity of primary discharges, but that the so-called mental disorders, when arranged in series, give a more accurate idea of the way in which these barriers originally functioned. But that is merely to say that in a serial classification of mental disorders the later elements represent more advanced systems of spontaneous attempts at 'cure' of excessive excitation.[1]

In this attempt to outline the serial development of the mental apparatus, I have confined myself for the most part to a consideration of a primary functional phase: and have referred to later phases mostly for purposes of contrast. I believe this procedure to be justified on a number of grounds, not the least of which is that by adopting the concept of early functional disorders of the mind we could eliminate some of the confusion in our existing etiological formulæ. But even if they should prove to have more theoretical than practical (clinical) value, the concepts of a primary phase and of primary functional disorders would at least prevent us falling into the grievous error of anthropomorphizing Freud's master-concept of a mental apparatus.

[1] This view is supplementary to the thesis I have advanced on many occasions that the various layers of mental disorder constitute serial defences against regression to earlier and less controlled forms of function, which come into operation when the 'normal' apparatus cannot counter existing stresses.

XXV

ON THE DESIRABILITY OF ISOLATING A 'FUNCTIONAL' (PSYCHO-SOMATIC) GROUP OF DELINQUENT DISORDERS*

[1950]

When I first introduced the concept of a 'primary functional phase' in the development of the mental apparatus, a phase at which endopsychic conflict – with its implication of opposition between ego and super-ego organizations – could not be presumed, I was inclined to think that its value might lie more in the theoretical than in the clinical field (Chap. XXIV). To be sure the concept of 'psychic functional' disorder promised to clarify the position of so-called 'psycho-somatic' states and to facilitate the distinction between these disorders and true 'symptom-formations' (Freud); but its more extended use in the clinical field was not at first apparent. A little reflection showed however that the concept could be applied usefully in three distinct fields, viz. in normal characterology, in character disorder and in child psychiatry. Since normal character is rarely subject or accessible to analytical procedure, the first step seemed to be to examine behaviour disorders which are uncomplicated by neurotic or psychotic manifestations (symptom formations). These are most conveniently studied in the field of forensic psychiatry. In the following article an attempt is made to isolate some functional behaviouristic syndromes. An extension of the concept to child psychiatry, in which behavioristic disorders and explosive tension states figure even more prominently than do classical 'symptom-formations', is described in Psycho-analysis and Child Psychiatry.[1]

It will scarcely be contested that progress in delinquency research depends to a considerable extent on the accuracy with which different clinical types can be isolated and classified. Unfortunately,

* First published in *The British Journal of Delinquency*, Vol. I, pt. 2, p. 104.
[1] EDWARD GLOVER: *Psycho-analysis and Child Psychiatry*, London, Imago Publishing Co., 1954.

criminal psychiatry, unlike other branches of mental investigation, suffers from the handicap that it must always take cognizance of the social labels already attached to the offender under criminal law. The pure psychiatrist is interested in the reality (social) sense of the schizophrenic; but most of the deluded cases he sees are neither under arrest nor threatened with a penal sentence because of their delusional formations. In forensic psychiatry the situation is quite otherwise. The group of pathological 'pilferers', for example, can be broken down under examination into a number of clinical types – neurotic, psychopathic, psychotic, mentally deficient and the like; but in recommending treatment or disposal the legal codes governing sentences for theft must of necessity influence the recommendation.

Moreover, in certain cases the criminal psychiatrist finds himself unable to attach a precise clinical label to the delinquent condition and is compelled to borrow for the time being mere descriptive socio-legal categories; as when he includes under juvenile groupings the headings 'behaviour problem' or cases 'out of control'. It is obvious, therefore, that before he can apply accurate standards to the classifications of pathological delinquency he must set his own house in order.

Earlier difficulties in formal psychiatric classification were concerned with the accurate definition of terms such as neurasthenia, hypochondria, psychasthenia, anxiety neurosis, and of their relation respectively to the psycho-neuroses and to the psychoses. Some of these difficulties have been overcome by the application of etiological formulæ based on psycho-analytical theories. But a number of confusions remain, in particular the precise connotation of the term psychopathy and the relation of the psycho-somatic states to conversion hysteria and to the traumatic neuroses.

In the case of psychopathy, attempts to clarify the situation have followed two directions; in the first place, the inclusion in the psychopathic group of certain clinical syndromes, e.g. schizoid, cycloid, and inferiority reactions; and, in the second, classifying psychopathic reactions in terms of ego-psychology. The former procedure is based mainly on descriptive criteria. It contributes to the understanding of psychopathy only in so far as it implies that psychopathy, though not strictly psychotic, has many and close relations with psychotic systems or mechanisms. The second system of classification is mainly psycho-analytical and involves recognition of specific groups of character disorder associated with specific stages of ego and super-ego formation. This is less a descriptive than a psycho-genetic approach. Thus some psycho-pathies can be described as due to morbid function of the super-ego paralysing the sense of guilt and further subdivided in accordance with whether mother or father elements in the super-ego are affected. Or again, some psychopathies can be grouped in terms of morbid function of the ego, e.g. its capacity for 'reality testing', and subdivided in terms of the particular instinct or pattern which produces the blind-spot in reality proving. Although some progress has been made in both of these main directions, the psychopathic group still contains too many unclassifiables. And many observers, including the present writer, prefer to limit the term in the meantime to the type originally described by Prichard,[1] distributing the so-called psychotic, alcoholic and epileptic types of psychopathy amongst other psychiatric groups.

In the case of the psycho-somatic states the situation is almost as complex. In the first place it was necessary to distinguish the somatic manifestations of a particular psycho-neurosis, viz. conversion hysteria, from those 'functional' disturbances of the body-organs or systems in which neither organic disease nor psychoneurotic formations could be detected. This was a perfectly legitimate procedure. But the correlation was too restricted. It left many psycho-somatic states in the air with a rather vague etiology and no very satisfactory method of subdividing the omnibus group, except, of course, by the rather obvious device of using descriptive criteria, e.g. the particular body-system involved, gastric neurosis, asthmas, skin neuroses, etc. This latter method gives no indication of the relative depth of the disorder, in particular of the correlation between some forms of psycho-somatic discharge and a psychotic predisposition.

[1] Prichard, writing of *moral insanity or moral imbecility* (1835) described it as follows: 'a form of mental derangement in which the intellectual functions seem to have sustained little or no injury, while the disorder is manifested, principally or alone, in the state of the feelings, temper or habits. In cases of this nature the moral and active principles of the mind are strongly perverted or depraved; the power of self-government is lost or greatly impaired, and the individual is found incapable, not of talking or reasoning upon any subject proposed to him, but of conducting himself with decency and propriety in the business of life'.

Recently, the writer,[1] using psycho-analytical categories and following a developmental (serial) approach, has endeavoured to clarify the position by relating both psycho-somatic formations and true 'symptom-formations', such as the psycho-neuroses and psychoses, to different stages in the development of the *mental apparatus* up to the age of roughly five years, preserving at the same time the essential distinction between psycho-somatic states and both neurotic and psychotic formations. As, however, this psycho-analytical approach involves the use of the term 'functional' in a new and specifically psychic sense, it is desirable to indicate briefly in what respects the term as here used differs from the term 'functional' as used in organic medicine.

The mind or mental apparatus is conceived in psycho-analysis as a central system whose function it is to receive, regulate, distribute and where possible discharge excitations arriving from without, whether from bodily or from environmental sources. The localization of this apparatus in space is not the concern of the psychologist, the more so since the concept of a mental apparatus is based on a system of analogies existing in his own mind. For the slipshod purposes of description we may say that it lies between the afferent systems of stimulation and the efferent systems of discharge. The periphery of this mental apparatus can be indicated by the use of certain psycho-physical *boundary concepts* such as that of instinct, which is a psychic stimulus traceable in the last resort to somatic sources, and achieving entry into the mental apparatus through the medium of what psycho-analysts call the *Id*.[2] Other stimuli may achieve more direct entry through the

[1] *Psycho-Analysis*, 2nd Edition. Staples Press, 1949. 'Functional Aspects of the Mental Apparatus.' 16th International Psycho-Analytical Congress, Zürich, 1949. Published in *Int. J. Psycho-Anal.*, 30, pts. 1 and 2, 1950 (see Chap. XXIV).

[2] The *Id* in psycho-analysis represents the primitive unorganized part of the psychic apparatus. Dynamically it can be described as a reservoir of instinctual energy, but its relations to the *ego* (and *super-ego*) can best be understood in structural terms. It is non-structural and therefore impersonal (non-ego). At the same time it is held to include the repressed, which, of course, has already been subject to ego (and super-ego) interference. Constitutional factors operate through the Id as do those psychic tendencies which develop into unconscious mental mechanisms. The ego and super-ego are therefore organized portions of the Id, a cortex developed as the result of experience of instinctual relations with the world of objects.

system called perceptual-consciousness and directly affect different parts of the ego either conscious or unconscious. But even so they also affect the working of the mind through their effect on Id-instincts. Thus the temporal series of events following psychic stimulation, whether from the body or the external world, is as follows: instinctual excitation, the appearance of instinctual deriva-tives, affects and ideations, the functioning of various mental mechanisms intended to control, distribute, inhibit or obliterate instinctual excitation, and finally the end-phenomena of discharge, by means of various somatic innervations, through either the sensory or the motor frontiers of the mental apparatus. *What we call behaviour consists for the largest part of these discharge pheno-mena.* Whether the discharge is partial or total it follows the channels of feeling, ideation, speech, action or changes in the body organs and systems. Needless to say, the largest part of the controlling process takes place unconsciously.

This psychic apparatus can be studied by three approaches: (1) structural (the differentiation of mental institutions), (2) dynamic (the varieties and modifications of mental energies), and (3) economic (mental mechanisms distributing or controlling excita-tion). We can then distinguish two groups of mental disturbance: (*a*) *disorders of the apparatus in which the apparatus itself is not diseased, but in which excessive stress or damming up of instinct produces certain pathological forms of excitation and discharge,* and (*b*) *conditions in which unconscious conflict produces characteristic compromise (symptom) formations (Freud) and thereby causes disease of the mental apparatus itself,* either structural, dynamic or economic. The essence of the distinction lies, however, in the structural concept. In the first group, to which I here apply the term 'functional', no structural alterations take place. Dynamic stresses occur giving rise to economic changes, but once the stress is relieved or discharged the mental apparatus resumes normal function. In the second group characteristic structural changes occur in the mental apparatus, varying in gravity, permanence and amenability to treatment.

Adopting this approach it is possible to claim for functional or psycho-somatic reactions a historical (developmental) priority over psycho-neurotic symptom-formations. For, in the first place, the rudimentary nature of mental structure in the first two years of life and the relative weakness of inhibitory processes during that phase, is likely to promote a fairly rapid discharge of mental tension through body-systems (and *vice versa*); and, in the second place, the unconscious conflicts which give rise to compromises between repressed and repressing forces (in other words, symptom-formations) begin to develop at a time when mental structure is already fairly elaborate, e.g. in the case of the neuroses from two to three years onward. Naturally it is not implied that the functional or psycho-somatic variety of discharge is abandoned when true symptom-formation appears. Abnormal functional discharge occurs at all stages of life; it can be exacerbated by unconscious conflict; and it can from later infancy onward exist in reciprocal relation to psycho-neurotic or psychotic disorder.

In both of these two main groups (the functional disorders and the symptom-formations) constitutional factors and current stresses (precipitating factors) play their part; and both groups can therefore be subdivided in terms of the variety of stress and the stage of development at which it first becomes operative. In the functional group, as has been indicated, therapeutic results can be obtained by the relief of stress; in the symptom-formation group it is necessary to analyse or by some compensatory device (general psychotherapy) reduce or compensate or counter-balance the conflict. By adopting the concept of a functional group, the position of the traumatic neuroses, anxiety neuroses, neurasthenia, organic reaction types, etc., can be clarified, and their tendency to promote subsequent 'symptom-formation' (Freud) plausibly explained, in that a functional disturbance of any organ or body-system renders it liable to over-libidinization and therefore to neurotic selection.

Turning to the criminological aspects of the problem, it is not surprising to discover that difficulties in psychiatric classification of delinquent disorder reflect with some fidelity the difficulties existing in formal psychiatry. The fact that, because of socio-legal standards, attention is directed primarily and mainly to the *behaviour* of the offender does not alter this problem. The popular view to the contrary is based on the misconception that behaviour is something concrete existing in its own right and therefore to be judged exclusively by common social standards. For those who believe that the mental apparatus is activated by instinctual energies, *behaviour is a psychic end-product and usually a discharge product*. We must, however, extend the term to include both positive and negative varieties of behaviour. Positive behaviour is thus either an active and mainly motor response to increased mental *excitation* or an end-product bringing about and signalizing the *discharge* of excitation. Negative behaviour refers to such phenomena as inhibition where, despite instinctual stress, behaviour which might have been expected is either absent or restricted.

To illustrate this distinction we may take the case of a simple rage affect. Should, for example, a person of 'normal' character be subject to provocation sufficient to drive him into a rage, he may get red in the face, clench his fists, utter threats of violence and under certain circumstances strike whomever has provoked him. All this can be regarded as positive behaviour. If, on the contrary, he reacts to strong provocation by becoming tongue-tied, and developing a limpness of the arms and hands, we may describe this as negative behaviour. In neither case need we assume that the individual suffers from unconscious conflict of a pathogenic type. This behaviour represents a form of discharge of tension, in one case externally, in the other internally directed. Nor need we presuppose the existence of unconscious pathogenic conflict if a person who is by nature prone to lose his temper but has from early years practised the arts of inhibition, develops muscular contractures of the arms or hands from a constant habit of clenching the fists. We can simply say that he suffers from the 'organic-functional' effects of a 'psychic-functional' disorder of discharge. *This is what is generally described as a psycho-somatic state.* Should, however, a person who has shown no particular sign of constitutional aggressiveness and, in fact, can behave reasonably or appropriately under provocation suddenly develop a paralysis of the right forearm and hand, and further, should we be able to establish not only that he had recently experienced frustration of his libido but that in childhood he had suffered from acute masturbatory guilt, we would be entitled to assume that this particular form of negative behaviour was a hysterical formation based partly on the symbolism of the hand and arm, and representing on balance a punitive compromise between his repressed impulses both sexual and aggressive and his unconscious conscience.

If now we were to report to the police persons manifesting

these four different types of behaviour the outcome would not be in doubt. No charge would be made against the tongue-tied inhibitionist, the psycho-somatic case or the hysteric. The positive behaviourist, on the other hand, might well find himself in the dock charged with a common assault or at least with uttering threats. The law, in short, is not primarily interested in psycho-pathology; it rarely goes further than to characterize certain end-products of psychic tension (behaviour) as socially undesirable or reprehensible, and to charge and sentence the offender accordingly. Even when, as in the case of the M'Naghten Rules, the law establishes the relative immunity from punishment of offenders suffering from some forms of mental disorder, its concern is less with the actual state of mind of the individual than with the lack of social responsibility ensuing therefrom. Psychiatry must carry this social classification further; indeed, except in the case of psychopathy and certain 'behaviour crises', has already done so with advantage.

Moreover, the behaviouristic (social) criterion cannot be limited to normal and delinquent groups. Many character disorders, such as miserliness, manifest themselves in social behaviour that is neither normal nor delinquent. And the same may be said of neurotic, psychotic and other mental disorders; these frequently give rise to eccentric behaviour, obsessional ritual, for example, which is nevertheless non-delinquent.

On the other hand, any attempt to classify pathological delin-quent behaviour solely in terms of classical mental disorders (neurotic, psychotic, psychopathic, mentally deficient, sexually perverted, alcoholic, epileptic), or of recognized character abnor-malities (schizoid, paranoid, cycloid, obsessive, hysterical and the like) is bound to be unsatisfactory; first because it does not permit correlation of pathological delinquency with the delinquencies of 'normal' persons, and, second, because a number of pathological delinquencies do not fall into either of these two comprehensive groupings.

Take, for example, the case of boys or girls of ten to fifteen years of age recommended for examination, because of outbreaks of hostile and aggressive behaviour (wilful destruction, lying, stealing, truancy or wandering) at home, school or in general social contact; or because of sexual misdemeanour or assault. In many cases of sexual or social violence occurring in early adolescence it is possible to establish that the individual is neither hysterical nor psychopathic nor again pre-psychotic, with the consequence that he or she is finally classified as a 'pubertal behaviour problem', meaning usually that his delinquent conduct is due to sexual stress, lack of sexual instruction or traumatic seduction. Can we improve on this rather vague or at best merely suggestive terminology?

At this point it would seem desirable to consider whether the broad distinction which can be applied in non-delinquent psychiatry is also applicable in criminal psychiatry; namely, the distinction between functional disorders of the mental apparatus and true psychic symptom-formations (Freud). Is there, for example, a 'functional delinquency' as distinct from a 'conflict delinquency'? Can we distinguish between delinquent reactions that represent a temporary phase of exaggerated discharge of dammed up instinctual tension and delinquent reactions that follow a hysterical pattern, in which, for example, instead of a *phobiac* (morbid fear) reaction to certain (symbolic) objects or situations, we find a phase of violent conduct *directed against* certain (symbolic) objects or situations? If so, we could, following the example of formal psychiatry, speak of *psycho-somatic* delinquency. Or, since the term psycho-somatic is sometimes misleading and often inadequate, we could speak of (in the psychic sense) *functional delinquency.*

There is certainly a good deal of evidence that such a distinction is desirable. For not only do criminal statistics[1] suggest that spontaneous[2] abandonment or mitigation of delinquent conduct has *some* relation to increasing age, and presumably therefore to diminishing instinctual stimulation, in particular the activity of the sexual impulses, either conscious or unconscious, but that there are a number of transitory delinquent states which can be subdivided according to age-groups. And these latter can be readily correlated with the current state of libido imbalance, e.g. frustration and damming up of quantities of instinctual energy.

[1] See Roper. *Brit. J. Delinq.*, 1950, I, p. 15.

[2] The use here of the term 'spontaneous' requires qualification. Strictly speaking it means only that improvement has occurred in the absence of concerted psycho-therapeutic or other form of treatment. But, of course, many 'spontaneous cures' are due to altered conditions either in the (internal) state of mind of the individual or in his environmental (psychologically significant) setting.

The type of case which, after pubertal delinquent crises, comes most readily to mind is that of the middle-aged shoplifter, often a solitary spinster who steals, usually inefficiently and alone, and who tends to develop later into an involutional[1] type. The kleptomania of males between 40–50 years of age who suffer from an increasing but usually unconscious fear of impotence is also frequently of the functional type. Following this approach it is not hard to distinguish 'transitory' delinquencies occurring between 6–8, 10–12, 13–15, 17–20, about 25, 40–50 and over 55 years of age. These are, in fact, the periods when instinctual crises are prone to develop or when a transition from one stage of libidinal organization to another takes place. Having established the existence of a particular variety of crisis, it is not hard to effect further sub-division in terms of predisposing (infantile) factors; whether, for example, the individual has developed during childhood strong instinctual fixations, or has made an over-rapid (preconscious) progression from one stage of instinctual development to another, or has suffered infantile regressions at critical phases of childhood. Incidentally, some of the 'atypical' psychopathies in which, contrary to the rule, no consistent history of psychopathic reaction can be traced from childhood, yet the individual passes through a temporary phase of psychopathic behaviour, belong to one or other of these functional groups.[2]

Naturally, the work of sub-dividing these psycho-somatic or functional delinquencies would involve the isolation of factors other than age. Different constitutional types prone to damming up and excessive discharge would have to be isolated. And here some correlation between 'traumatic delinquencies' and the so-called 'traumatic neuroses' of formal psychiatry could be effected,

---

[1] Signifying disorders of a regressive type commonly associated with the climacteric.

[2] *A propos* the correlation of criminal behaviour with psychopathic states and with psychosomatic disorder, some interesting observations have been made by M. Schmideberg (unpublished communication). In quite a number of instances persons deprived by imprisonment of the opportunity of delinquent activity developed psycho-somatic symptoms; and in private practice too some cases who prior to treatment had already abandoned their delinquent practices because of fear developed psychosomatic disturbances. These observations may shed new light on the relation of certain cases diagnosed as 'malingering' to the psychosomatic states and in particular to hypochondria.

and would permit a more accurate valuation of various 'environmental' factors than exists at present. In the 'war-neuroses', for example, it was never hard to detect both constitutional sensitiveness and a sharpened (predisposed) emotional reaction to the traumatic environmental setting. The delinquencies associated with 'organic reaction types' could also find a place in the new functional groupings, together with delinquencies due to endocrine and metabolic imbalance. In fact, the time seems not far off when criminal psychiatrists need no longer depend on socio-legal descriptive terms to distinguish a number of forms of delinquency which up to the present have been only imperfectly understood, and have therefore gone without a specific clinical label.

Should it prove possible to establish these clinical distinctions, we may also look forward with some confidence to effecting much closer correlation than at present exists between 'social' and 'individual' disorders, that is to say, between the disorders in which the individual seeks to discharge his mental tensions on the environment (the world of instinctual objects) and those in which he discharges them through pathological changes in his body or mind. To take one example, we could correlate such apparently distinct conditions as a gastric conversion hysteria (psycho-neurosis), pathological excess of appetite (psycho-somatic state), gastric hypochondria (actual neurosis), persecutory delusions of food-poisoning (psychosis), sporadic pilfering of food (functional delinquency), kleptomanic sweet-stealing (psycho-neurotic delinquency), or, for the matter of that, black market food offences, shop-breaking or railway offences involving stores of provisions ('normal' crime).

Needless to say, the clinical distinction of a functional or psychosomatic group of delinquencies should not be too rigid. Even with the best of classifications it is desirable to retain the category 'unclassifiable' to cover those cases whose etiology is unknown. And in any event 'transitional forms' lying between any two main groups, or 'mixed forms' presenting features drawn from a number of main groups are essential to an orderly classification. Moreover, the factor of 'superposition' of symptom constructions should always be borne in mind. Psycho-neuroses are often superimposed on anxiety neuroses, psychoses on hypochondrias, and it seems likely that many of the conflict or symptomatic delinquencies are superimposed on functional delinquencies.

XXVI

RESEARCH METHODS IN PSYCHO-ANALYSIS*

[1952]

It will scarcely be disputed that progress in the understanding of mental development, and in particular of those early stages which are incapable of direct analytic observation, calls not only for an elaborate research organization but also for a lengthy period of preparation during which the working concepts of psycho-analysis can be re-examined and re-defined, and standardized units of comparison established. This in turn will involve a careful scrutiny of existing psycho-analytical literature in order to distinguish contributions which conform to scientific standards from those which are either elaborations of unchecked hypotheses or are based on unchecked interpretations of data. Actually the greatest hindrance to psycho-analytical progress lies in the unrestricted licence to interpret, which although unavoidable in therapeutic work, gives rise to a degree of fabrication in clinical researches which tends to vitiate any conclusions arrived at. The aim of the following review was frankly political, namely, to promote the development of an international psycho-analytical research organization; and it is gratifying to be able to record that a few tentative steps have since been taken in this direction. The success of any such venture will depend however on the thoroughness with which the existing ground is explored and scientific criteria applied.

The aim of this paper is to discuss methods of psycho-analytical research, ultimately to promote the development of an international psycho-analytical research organization. The views expressed are based, first, on personal clinical experience, second, on experience gained as Director of Research of the London Institute of Psycho-Analysis over a period of sixteen years, and third, on reflections stimulated by recent experience of the

* Read at the 17th International Psycho-Analytical Congress, Amsterdam, August, 1951; first published in *The International Journal of Psycho-Analysis*, Vol. XXXIII, pt. 4, 1952.

activities of the Research Committee of the International Psycho-Analytical Association.

As a preliminary to discussion of method, it is necessary to review the somewhat unusual conditions that prevail in the field of psycho-analytical research. Two factors in particular call for prior attention. The first has from time to time been referred to in psycho-analytical literature; namely, the fact that, owing partly to the conditions under which clinical analysis is conducted, and partly to the use of interpretative techniques of investigation, it is not possible either to employ fully or fully to depend on the forms of scientific control customary in most other sciences. This difficulty is unavoidable but not insuperable: it can be met by sustained application of such scientific checks as *are* appropriate to the special conditions of psycho-analysis.

The second and much more important factor, though clearly avoidable, has significantly enough received little attention. It cannot be denied that there is an increasing tendency *not* to apply to the data of observation or to the methods of interpretation such scientific controls as *are* available. The consequence is that a great deal of what passes as attested theory is little more than speculation, varying widely in plausibility.

Let me give the commonest instance of this state of affairs. An analyst, let us say, of established prestige and seniority, produces a paper advancing some new point of view or alleged discovery in the theoretical or clinical field. Given sufficient enthusiasm and persuasiveness, or even just plain dogmatism on the part of the author, the chances are that without any check, this view or alleged discovery will gain currency, will be quoted and requoted until it attains the status of an accepted conclusion. Some few observers who have been stimulated by the new idea may test it in their clinical practice. If they can corroborate it they will no doubt report the fact: but if they do not, or if they feel disposed to reject it, this scientific 'negative' is much less likely to be expressed, at any rate in public; and so, failing effective examination, the view is ultimately canonized with the sanctioning phrase, 'as so-and-so has shown'. In other words an *ipse dixit* acquires the validity of an attested conclusion on hearsay evidence only.

If now we assume that the author is also a training analyst – and it must be admitted that most analysts of moderate prestige and seniority are likely to be training analysts – the process of acquiring untested value is accelerated. Whatever may be the ideal of training analysis, it is indisputable that the margin of scientific error introduced by factors of transference and counter-transference is extremely wide. It is scarcely to be expected that a student who has spent some years under the artificial and sometimes hothouse conditions of a training analysis and whose professional career depends on overcoming 'resistance' to the satisfaction of his training analyst, can be in a favourable position to defend his scientific integrity against his analyst's theories and practice. And the longer he remains in training analysis, the less likely he is to do so. For according to his analyst the candidate's objections to interpretations rate as 'resistances'. In short there is a tendency inherent in the training situation to perpetuate error. Such a state of affairs clearly calls for the application of special safeguards.

To these two considerations may be added a third, namely, that however ideal their training analysis may have been, individual analysts tend to express opinions which reflect in however distant a form their *own* instinctual preferences, their own forms of thinking, their characteristic emotional reactions, their *conflicts and their favourite pathological devices or mechanisms.*

The summated effects of these three factors is easy to observe in the scientific proceedings of such branches of the Psycho-Analytical Association as I have been able to observe at first hand. Three observations are sufficient to bear this out; first, that discussion has an almost entirely stereotyped form, each contributor reacting to each subject of discussion with opinions that can easily be surmised beforehand; second, that in a majority of instances, the opinions expressed bear an unmistakable resemblance to those of the contributor's training analyst; and third, that both individual and team research on any given subject is not only peculiarly difficult to organize but when organized ends as a rule merely in the discovery of individual differences which were already apparent before the research began and which persist after it is finished.

Less easy to demonstrate conclusively but in its way more significant than the sources of error already indicated is the fact that with the development of analytical 'schools' and a consequent increase in the number of points of divergence, no fool-proof system exists to prevent the attrition of established theory. Psycho-analytical groups are peculiarly susceptible to fashion, canalized no doubt through a hierarchy of transferences and counter-transferences. No one who has followed analytical discussions over a period of, say, twenty-five years, can have failed to observe how psycho-analytical theory and treatment are influenced by the slogans of the moment and how these slogans ('narcissistic inaccessibility', 'sadism', 'unconscious homosexuality', 'analysing the negative', 'projection and introjection', 'internal objects', 'good and bad organs', 'schizoid reactions', 'the transference first and last', 'here and now', etc.) acquire a prestige which intimidates the average analyst into loosening his grip of more fundamental concepts. I need hardly instance the present precarious position of Oedipus-theory in modern psycho-analysis or the significant down-grading of the mechanism of repression from its position as a leading defence mechanism.[1]

To all this it may be replied that it is scarcely fair to expect analysts selected originally on conditions of *suitability to practise* analysis, conditions incidentally which not only vary from branch to branch but in any case are somewhat arbitrary and haphazard, to produce more than a small proportion of *research workers*. So much is of course undeniable. Nevertheless the general conviction persists in psycho-analytical circles, a legacy from those early days when most students of psycho-analysis were natural investigators, that anyone who is qualified to practise therapeutic analysis is also qualified to conduct research. These times have changed. In fact candidates are seldom chosen because of their suitability for research work, and even those who have a flair for research are hampered by conducting a busy psycho-analytical practice. Actually the proportion of qualified research workers in psycho-

---

[1] [Note (1955): Perhaps the best example of this down-grading is to be observed in the recent emphasis laid by both analysts and non-analysts on the importance of the 'broken-home' or of 'separation-anxiety' in the etiology of psycho-neuroses, psychoses and character-disorders. In delinquency work, for example, the term 'broken-home' has become a cliché, and has been elaborately sub-divided in purely environmental terms. With every step he takes in this direction the analyst is, no doubt unwittingly, detracting from the central significance of the Oedipus situation in mental development. The proper assessment of early separations from the mother (or father) is in terms of predisposition to disordered reactions the ultimate form of which is determined by the vicissitudes of the Oedipus phase. To link up delinquency with predisposing factors alone is to ignore the unconscious reactions which determine the formation of the super-ego, or unconscious conscience (see footnote on team-research, p. 401).]

analysis is much lower, not higher, than that to be found in the natural sciences, a figure which is in any case low. But none of these facts constitutes an extenuation of the lack of organized research: it is rather an indication that research disciplines should be instituted and organized on a stricter and more comprehensive basis than in other sciences and that a qualifying distinction should be drawn between the analytical practitioner and the research worker. At present it is left to the predilection of the individual analyst whether he interests himself in research activities, with the result that there is no discrimination between controlled research and individual opinion.

To the reasons for these special difficulties in developing psychoanalytical research, reference will be made in a later part of this paper. In the meantime we may start with four working assumptions; first, that psycho-analytical research is almost totally unorganized; second, that the conditions of clinical analysis and of analytic training militate against objectivity in research; third, that in consequence a large proportion of current theorizing and clinical finding is little more than unchecked speculation; and fourth, that so far no system exists whereby the scientific authority of research workers can be distinguished from the prestige of senior analytical practitioners and teachers.

Turning from the obstacles to research to actual methods of research, the first and most pressing problem is that of applying scientific controls. And here, two closely interlocking factors have to be considered. There is no reason in the world why the ordinary statistical controls should not be applied to psycho-analytical work. That after all depends mainly on having a sufficiency of trained research-workers and a sufficiency of clinical observations. The real difficulties are, first, that the data of observation are rarely or never defined, so that the observations of one worker can be compared with the observations of another; and, second, that definition is itself hampered by a serious lack of control of interpretation.

To take a simple instance: no one to my knowledge has yet defined the term 'castration-complex' in a form which would permit statistical correlation, i.e. there are no accurate qualitative distinctions. Moreover, psycho-analysis has not yet provided quantitative measures, for example, measures of the intensity of psychic stimulation determining the persistence or absence of any given mental state. The most approximate quantitative measure, that of symptom-formation, is constantly vitiated by our incapacity to measure the forces promoting mental stability. The severity of symptom-formation measures only the *margin* of instability. The most acute and dramatic symptom may require only a slight re-adjustment of the mental apparatus to bring about its resolution: whilst, on the other hand, a comparatively mild symptom may prove intractable to persistent analysis. Yet more difficult is the attempt to measure degrees of transference or counter-transference.

Even this lack of definition of particulars would not prevent the application of statistical controls, if only there were agreed definitions of basic concepts. It must be confessed that no such agreement exists. For example, all research regarding superego activity is in my opinion, completely sterile so long as we persist in regarding the superego purely from a functional point of view or as an organized and unified institution, neglecting its clinical development from a number of contributing sources, both instinctual and egoistic.

And not only are the ordinary statistical measures of magnitude for the time being impossible to apply because of the lack of suitable psychic 'entities' and of a more precise definition of the relationship between them, but, as Carroll pointed out some years ago, the application of a mathematical 'operator' system, by which properties as distinct from magnitudes can be examined, tested, and new combinations or relationships predicted, is held up by the absence of *defined* sequences of mental processes, to successive members of which any appropriate mathematical symbols could be attached and a calculus developed. Here again the isolation of elements as distinct from the products (psychic end-results) of combinations of elements is no easy task, a circumstance, however, which does not justify neglect to explore the avenues of definition.[1]

The second point, namely, that in any given case interpretation is an essential part of the process of psycho-analytical investigation and that nevertheless there is as yet no effective control of con-

---

[1] I am indebted here to Denis Carroll who, working in conjunction with John Carroll, the mathematical physicist, has re-examined his original formulations on the mathematical representation of mental processes. For reasons of space I am unable to give here more than a bare hint of his approach; the details will, I understand, form the subject of a paper by these authors.

clusions based on interpretation, is the Achilles heel of psycho-analytical research. Clearly until we establish such controls, it is impossible to arrive at the dependable definitions on which accurate statistical research depends. The earlier hope that therapeutic criteria would provide an effective check is now recognized as illusory, first, because, despite all dogmatic and puristic assertions to the contrary, we cannot exclude or have not yet excluded the transference effect of 'suggestion through inter-pretation',[1] and, second, because we have in any case no reliable statistics of therapeutic results.

To this it may be added that even under the most favourable conditions, the process of psycho-analysis is only a fractional process and, still further, that the scientific statement of clinical situations is still more fractional, representing at most a personally selected 'sample'. One of the remarkably rare disservices which Freud rendered his own science was when, with a tolerance born of his own scientific integrity and of his incomparable flair for reconstruction, Freud gave sanction to the individual manipulation of 'samples'. Writing in 1912 on the propriety of taking notes during analytical sessions, he remarked that this procedure could be justified provided it was the analyst's intention to make any given case the subject of a scientific publication. He was careful, however, to warn the investigator against cultivating 'Scheinexakt-heit' by producing voluminous notes of case-histories, which, as he said, were often boring to read and no substitute for actual experience of the analytic situation. 'Altogether, experience shows that a reader who is willing to believe an analyst at all will give him credit for the touch of revision to which he has subjected his material.'[2] No doubt when someone of Freud's calibre appears in

[1] See Glover: 'The Therapeutic Effect of Inexact Interpretation', *Int. J. Psycho-Anal*, (1931), **12**.

[2] 'Recommendations for Physicians on the Psycho-Analytic Method of Treatment'. *C.P.* Vol. II.

[Note (1955): The translation of Freud's phrase 'bisschen Bearbeitung' by the euphemistic 'touch of revision' is both inaccurate and misleading. The 'elaboration' or 'working up from raw material' implied in 'Bear-beiting' describes exactly the procedures followed by most analytical writers, not only in their case-descriptions but in their reports of inter-pretations. And there can be little doubt that the process derives from the unconscious mechanism of 'secondary elaboration' observed when analysing the manifest content of dreams. Scientifically regarded, it is a

our midst he will be freely accorded and will in any case freely exercise this privilege. Until that time comes the uncontrolled licence should be revoked. Granted that intuition is the most precious of all instruments of research, we must nevertheless take steps to prevent its debasement to the level of the casual 'hunch' and still further to the authoritarian level of the *ipse dixit*.

The conclusion to be drawn from this brief preliminary survey is that before we can even begin to conduct systematic research on psycho-analysis, *a preparatory phase is essential during which a process of standardization and definition of terms and concepts can be effected.* Without this no research worthy of the name can be conducted. The provision of reliable units of comparison is no doubt an immense task which, with sufficient staff, might be effected in not less than ten years of careful correlation. Perhaps it would be safer to allow twenty years. But it is an essential task. Nevertheless, definition and classification alone will not fully prepare the ground. An essential ancillary to research is the organization of a clinical system of psycho-analysis. We are still hampered by the fact that our clinical systems and classifications have been largely borrowed from formal psychiatry. New psycho-analytical appraisements tend to slip through the gaps of formal psychiatry: and we cannot pursue comparative study of psycho-pathological states until our psychiatry is ordered, in particular until the existing groups of unclassified conditions are reduced to some system. The most obvious case is that of the psycho-somatic states, understanding of which is unnecessarily hampered by the absence of adequate differential diagnosis from the psycho-neuroses, by preconceptions regarding stages of mental function and symptom-formation, and by prejudices regarding the applicability of psycho-analytic therapy. For the matter of that the position of the anxiety neuroses, neurasthenias, hypochondrias and other states still cries aloud for more accurate definition. In any case the scope of psycho-analytical psychiatry is immensely

slipshod and tendentious habit of an essentially defensive type. Admittedly, case description is essential to scientific communication between analysts. But however condensed, it should be accurate, and in doubtful cases should aim at understatement rather than overstatement. The 'well-rounded case history' is no doubt seductive: but it owes a good deal of its appeal to witting or unwitting fabrication.]

wider than that of school psychiatry. The various character disorders, including disorders of sexual and social adaptation (e.g. delinquency), have yet to be accurately rated and correlated with psycho-pathological classifications of the standard of mental disorders.

This is not just a clinical counsel of perfection. Accurate investigation involves not simply the definition of clinical entities but the provision of defined units of statistical comparison. It is not only in the literature of classical psychiatry that one is impressed by the absence of well-defined diagnostic standards. Psycho-analytical literature is almost as deficient in this respect. Even in the comparatively simple matter of rating neurotic disorders there is no satisfactory consensus of opinion. No two observers follow the same diagnostic or differential systems. Consequently such psycho-analytical records as exist are useless for any exact therapeutic assessment; and, what is even more important, do not afford any statistical information that can be exploited by research workers.[1]

Even the apparently simple task of collecting data, both clinical and methodological, is not without its peculiar difficulties. Nothing in my experience is harder than to get psycho-analysts to disclose their clinical views on any subject outside their immediate personal interest, or for that matter to say how they actually apply and control their technique. On several occasions I have adopted the questionnaire method for these purposes with results that were as a rule scanty and, unless subjected to secondary interpretation, uninformative. On the most recent occasion I was able to test the approximate percentage value of this method. A questionnaire was circulated to members of the International Psycho-Analytical Association asking them to record such of their contributions during the past twelve years as appeared to break *new* ground in psycho-analysis. The object of this was threefold: first, to collect data, if any; second, to advertise fully the necessity for research; and, third, to test and measure the general impetus to research.

[1] I can think of no more discouraging or aggravating experience than the examination of clinic records that are useless for any but the most elementary research purposes. In the paper quoted above Freud suggested that spurious accuracy was a characteristic of many 'modern' psychiatric records. It must be admitted, however, that for one reason or another psycho-analytical records run these more scholastic productions a close second.

For this last purpose emphasis was deliberately laid on the necessity of recording 'new' observations. My anticipation was that although in principle the actual response under favourable circumstances could be as much as 75 per cent, the *effective* response was not likely to exceed 5 per cent.

In point of fact both anticipations proved correct. Excluding special sources of error, it was demonstrated that, particularly in smaller groups, a satisfactory and representative return could be obtained, yet when it came to assessing the research value of the material, the proportion of effective contributions could not be rated as much higher than 5 per cent.[1] This is possibly an excessive measure of the spontaneous drive to research, but in any case is as much as can be expected of any professional group. Of particular interest, however, was the doubt or searching of heart that in many cases resulted from the insertion of the qualifying term 'new'. Some contributors indeed maintained that it was not possible for any worker to say whether his own contributions were new or not, one more instance of the fact that preliminary work on definition and classification is a prerequisite of effective research. Unsatisfactory as the questionnaire method is in many respects, it is one that should be applied from time to time if only for its stimulus value. At the very least it brings us nearer to the facts than does the accumulation of an increasingly extensive but unorganized literature.

None of this preparatory work would, however, be effective, unless some attempt were made to control the validity of interpretation. As has been noted this precaution has been unduly neglected, partly no doubt because of the lack of working standards or

[1] The reactions of psycho-analytical groups to scientific research are worthy of close investigation. The frequently adduced argument that the procedures of natural science are in many important respects incapable of application to the 'analytic situation', though sound enough in its way, is something of a rationalization. The truth seems to be that, perhaps because of his constant exercise of intuitive interpretation, the psycho-analyst is fundamentally hostile to those scientific methods which seek to control intuition. And it is certainly true that a good deal of the analyst's scientific curiosity is directed less to the discovery of new formulations than to finding corroborative material to strengthen his own convictions. The 'rediscovery' of psycho-analysis in his case-material is of course a sovereign remedy for the analyst's inner doubts and resistances; but it can scarcely be regarded as research. To this day the bulk of psycho-analytical literature is devoted to this self-imposed task of corroboration.

criteria of interpretation. It seems to be thought that the only safeguard in this direction is the satisfactory training analysis of the worker. But training analysis, as has also been noted, is no guarantee of research capacity and in many instances indeed blunts this capacity. The facts are that the actual criteria of interpretation have never been satisfactorily worked out and that the method of case-presentation generally adopted, namely that of secondary elaboration, leaves the very widest gap for error. It is no uncommon experience to hear papers read in which the justification of interpretation is confined to the general statement that 'the material of the patient showed this' or 'that'. Failing corroborative evidence all we are entitled to conclude from such a statement is that the analyst convinced himself that his interpretation was suitable or plausible, not that it was necessarily correct.

Here again a tendency to neglect ordinary scientific precautions must be recorded. Whatever may be the difficulties in checking interpretation, it is surely not too much to ask that in the case of new theories the author should produce convincing evidence that he has applied all the available criteria of interpretation. And here the need for preliminary work in checking each criterion is again essential; that is to say in establishing the criteria of criteria. To take an obvious case, viz., the criteria of symbolic interpretation, no really satisfactory work on this subject has been carried out. Many years ago in a brief pilot research on dream symbolism I was able using the questionnaire to establish two points, first, that reasonable tests of validity could be applied and, second, that only a minority of workers took the trouble to apply them. Incidentally the application of tests of criteria provides a point at which the statistical methods of normal psychology might be fruitfully and rapidly applied. In the meantime it would promote progress if individual workers were to *apply* their own tests and, what is much more important, to *disclose them when applied*. There is no evidence that this is done except by a small minority. There is in fact no systematic approach to the application of valid criteria.

This brings me to what is perhaps one of the most striking deficiencies in psycho-analytical research, namely, the absence of any effective organization. Owing possibly to his hermit-like mode of professional life, possibly to his distrust of anyone's methods but his own, the psycho-analyst is not a very good team worker. Many years ago, seeking to promote an organized approach to the problems of the psychoses, I succeeded in compiling with the help of some interested colleagues a systematized list of the points requiring immediate attention. This was duly circulated within the British Society with so far as I could observe no obvious result whatever, a fact which soon convinced me that research cannot be left to the good will or predilections of a mixed group. It can scarcely be denied that a small selected committee of research-minded workers could sit round a table with pencils and paper and at the end of three-quarters of an hour produce a respectable list of key-problems in any given field of psycho-analysis. They might even be able to make a number of fruitful suggestions regarding their solution. But unless there were a sufficiency of trained and dependable workers sufficiently co-operative to dovetail their researches, such preparation would be largely an exercise in forlorn endeavour. To distribute researches in a mixed analytic group would be still more frustrating. For the strength of a research group is the strength of its weakest link.[1]

But even with the best laid plans and the best possible research teams, the co-operation of all members of psycho-analytical groups is essential to success. I have in mind not so much the fact that many members working outside a concerted plan can, nevertheless, produce individual observations and conclusions of value; or that they can test the conclusions of others in their own clinical work. Their co-operation is essential in yet another direction. In my opinion the main obstacle to the progress of psycho-analysis is the absence, first, of reliable statistics of results and, second, of any follow-up investigation. By this I do not mean to suggest that the therapeutic criterion is a dependable measure of the validity of any psycho-analytic theory. I mean that the absence of statistics of

[1] [Note (1955): This applies with even greater force to those team researches in which psycho-analysts collaborate with normal psychologists, psychiatrists and sociologists to investigate the relation of environmental to endopsychic factors in any given problem. For some years now I have observed closely the operation of these 'team methods' in the study of delinquency, and, although I fully agree that the psycho-analyst must play a leading part in such work, it has always seemed to me that in the process of co-operation, he has tended to water down psycho-analytical values to meet the limitations of the (pre)conscious, descriptive approach favoured by non-analytical members of the team (see also Chap. XXVIII 'The Frontiers of Psycho-analysis', pp. 421–441). A good example of this dilution of values is mentioned a propos the significance of the Oedipus complex (see footnote, p. 393).]

therapeutic results, in particular the absence of information regarding failure, introduces grave possibilities of error. Unless we know with some precision the exact therapeutic limitations of psycho-analysis in different groups of mental disorder, we run the risk of providing new theories to explain away failure. This raises again a number of old problems: of duration and termination, of technical procedure, of the theory and criteria of cure: it raises in particular the problem of dosage of regulated or unregulated analysis. If we assume that an analysis ought to succeed merely because the case has seemed to be suitable and if in fact the case proves refractory, the natural tendency exists to broaden the point of application of analysis, to say, for example, that the case needed broader or deeper or more active analysis, finally to postulate some hitherto unrecognized unconscious factors. This, however, may throw our proven etiological systems out of gear and encourage the advancement of theories which have little bearing on the clinical facts, but are necessitated to cover bad selection of cases.[1]

[1] Despite the frequent, if guarded, comments made by Freud on the therapeutic limitations of psycho-analysis, the tradition still runs unchecked in psycho-analytical circles that psycho-analysis can or should produce a high proportion of therapeutic successes in all but manifestly 'inaccessible' cases. And although it would be inconsistent to criticize the absence of reliable statistics of results (and of follow-up records) and in the same breath draw conclusions from scattered and uncontrolled observations, the latter may provide a useful corrective to the exaggerated expectations and sometimes even exaggerated claims of over-enthusiastic practitioners. Having had unusual opportunities of observing the results obtained by workers both in clinic and in private practice, I have formed the impression that, except in the classical psycho-neuroses and in conditions of a clinical rating equivalent to that of the neuroses, the therapeutic results of classical psycho-analysis are not particularly impressive. In particular there are too many cases in which the improvement leaves unresolved too many of the symptoms of which the patient originally complained.

Admittedly the percentage results obtained must vary in accordance with the system of selection followed by each practitioner. Those who by force of circumstances or by choice undertake the analysis of intractable cases must be content with meagre results; on the other hand, those who wish to enjoy the satisfactions of frequent therapeutic success must resign themselves to a rigid selection of 'favourable' cases. All this merely points the necessity of publishing detailed statistics of psycho-analytical results, checked by a follow-up of at least five years' duration. Only by so doing can any conclusions of theoretical value be drawn from therapeutic data.

These dangers can and should be avoided by complete frankness on the matter of results. But we can scarcely expect frankness so long as we foster the tradition that a recommended analysis followed *secundum artem* ought automatically to succeed – a tradition incidentally which intimidates the experienced analyst as much as it burdens the conscience of the training candidate. It is, moreover, a tradition which encourages the interminable analysis, and with the interminable analysis both clinical and theoretical perspective go by the board. No doubt the analyst's marked reserve regarding his therapeutic results has also been fostered by an earlier need to maintain prestige in the face of the hostile criticisms of non-analytical schools. That was never a desirable reaction and is in any case no longer necessary. Like the desire to turn at all costs a united psycho-analytical front to non-analytical psychology, it cripples objectivity at source.

In any case the historical fact should be remembered that psycho-analysis, starting as a method of investigation, developed into a therapy. There is still considerable confusion between the aims of research and those of therapy. To the present day an incongruous alliance is often effected between these two distinct aims; as witness the tendency of many workers to re-discover the facts of psycho-analysis in the course of their therapeutic work, and of others to model their therapy in accordance with their theoretical preconceptions, whether these are germane to the case or not. As we have seen, even the simple issue whether or not to take notes during a session brings out the confusion of aims between research and treatment. This is a confusion which should be finally resolved.

The influence of prestige or of hyper-sensitiveness on the traditions of psycho-analytical teaching is a subject that requires the closest consideration, but does not come within the scope of this paper. I have the impression, however, that psycho-analytical teaching preserves many of the disadvantages of mid-Victorian pedagogy and few of its advantages. Authoritarian spoon-feeding is never a good pedagogic system, and its deficiencies cannot be remedied, as is so often thought, by the candidate's training analysis. They are much more likely to be rendered permanent thereby. I cannot refrain, however, from mentioning a point that is often advanced when discussing methods of examining and clarifying tendencies and divergencies in psycho-analytic thinking, viz., that young analysts are not interested in differences but prefer constructive summaries or identities. This is tantamount to maintaining that the young are not interested in the proliferating margins of research. I must confess that although the age of a research worker does not seem to me to be of great moment, yet I find it hard to believe that this attitude of parental solicitude on the part of analytical teachers is an appropriate reaction to the enthusiasms of youth. It may serve well enough the needs of those who like to follow a quiet profession of psychotherapy, but it is entirely alien to the needs of research workers. Identities, it is true, can be built up on points of similarity; but they can only be organized through the sharp distinction of differences.

I am well aware that in this brief review I have not advanced any original arguments. Most of the views I have presented, with the exception possibly of the references to training and to the absence of reliable statistics of results or of follow-up records, have been discussed from time to time throughout the development of psycho-analysis. Nor have I attempted to indicate with what immediate practical measure the peculiar difficulties attendant on psycho-analytical research can be met. That surely is a matter to be dealt with by special Research Committees that should be set up in every Branch of the International Association and organized by research personnel having some security of tenure. I have not even indicated the necessity of establishing Research and Biblio-graphical Centres serving suitable regional areas. My main concern has been to bring together some of the points that must be con-sidered in detail by these Branch and Regional Research Com-mittees if and when they are brought into being.

The problem of organizing systematic research becomes more and more urgent every year. Branches increase rapidly in size; the number of new candidates increases equally rapidly; journals multiply; and an already extensive literature threatens to swell unchecked to gargantuan dimensions. But so far, there exists at no point of the psycho-analytical organization an adequate system of scientific controls. Nowhere is it fully recognized that research students are not born from therapeutic training but have to be made, that is to say, selected for the purpose and suitably trained in scientific disciplines; a comment, incidentally, which also applies to the provision of psycho-analytical teachers. And I do not believe it is fully recognized how far the whole future theory and practice of psycho-analysis depends on making, as soon and as thoroughly as possible, a complete survey of the subject – as it were, a Domesday Book of the science.[1] While there is no reason to suspend or hamper any of those existing systems of investigation which conform to scientific standards, and every reason to proceed forthwith to their more thorough organization, it would save a good deal of fruitless effort and much disappointment if we recognize that one of our first tasks, without which research is threatened with stagnation and sterility, is to settle down to the long and arduous task of defining terms, verifying criteria and developing reliable statistics.

[1] [Note (1955): Since this was written a few steps have been taken in this direction, including the publication of an 'Annual Survey' of psycho-analytical papers and monographs. Unfortunately this suffers from the fatal defect that the papers are not assessed in accordance with the degree to which 'research criteria' are applied. The assumption that all papers published under an official psycho-analytical imprint are of equal quality or relevance leads to endless confusion. It is very much to be hoped that a recently projected 'official index' will be unflinchingly edited and given appropriate annotation.

In the meantime the outlook for the International Research Committee, appointed in 1951 following a Congress Resolution by the present writer and acting at first under his Chairmanship, is distinctly bleak. During its first two years a useful preliminary survey was made of recent research and of training method in the international field, somewhat limited in scope, though by no means marred, by the pointed abstention, on parochial grounds, of the British Psycho-analytical Society. To meet this punctilio the Committee was re-constructed in 1953, a move that coincided with an immediate drop in its activities; and there is some reason to believe that it will be allowed quietly to expire, unwept, unhonoured and unsung. Research, however, cannot be controlled too long by punctilio; nor should the conclusion be drawn that international organisation of research is futile. What is lacking at present to give it effect is an adequate organization in each of the Branch Societies.

Regarding the prospective organization of training methods on a continental basis, it can only be said that until the leading Branch Societies set their own houses in order in this respect, it cannot be anticipated that a *gleichschaltung* of training methods can do more than give official sanction to existing disorder and discrepancy. Without unbiassed training no research worthy of the name is possible.]

XXVII

THE INDICATIONS FOR PSYCHO-ANALYSIS*

[1953]

When I was invited to give this lecture, my attention was called to the existence amongst general psychiatrists of an impression that psycho-analysts can rarely be prevailed upon to give exact indications of the clinical scope of psycho-analysis. Some of this reluctance is no doubt due to the fact that the scope of psycho-analysis is not limited to the classical psychiatric groups of disordered mental function. I believe, however, that the analyst's reserve on this subject is due mainly to the fact that, although he is concerned, more perhaps than any other clinical psychologist, with the theory of mental development, he tends to neglect the developmental approach within the confines of his consulting room and consequently is much more prone to errors in prognosis than the non-analytical medical psychologist, who, having no particular system of developmental standards, falls back on purely clinical criteria for treatment. While therefore it might seem more appropriate to include this article in a collection of therapeutic papers I decided to include it in this volume in illustration of the advantage of applying developmental standards in the clinical field.

If the standards of psychotherapy approximated to those in vogue in the field of organic medicine a lecture on the indications for psycho-analysis would be a comparatively brief and possibly tedious affair. Since, however, there is no uniform diagnosis of mental disorders, no exact account of the rationale of psycho-analytic treatment and no assented list of the modifications of treatment required in different forms of disorder, it is obvious that before we can usefully discuss indications for psycho-analysis or, in other words, the scope of psycho-analytic treatment, we must arrive at a certain amount of agreement regarding the diagnosis and prognosis of mental disorders and the nature of psycho-analytic therapy.

* A Maudesley Bequest lecture delivered before the Royal Medico-Psychological Association, 3rd Nov., 1953: first published in *The Journal of Mental Science*, 1954, Vol. 100, No. 419.

SOURCES OF BIAS

Before attempting to do so we must recognize a subjective source of bias, which although not unknown in general psychotherapy is particularly obstructive in the case of psycho-analysis. Owing to the early and widespread opposition with which they were faced, psycho-analysts developed and still maintain a number of protective reactions. Being put on the defensive they naturally buttressed their own position, maintaining, for example, that psycho-analysis was the most radical form of treatment for disorders of varying gravity; and sometimes, if only by implication, casting doubt on the depth and permanence of the results obtained by non-analytical treatment in such cases. To which it may be added that, within their own walls, they gave short shrift to any followers who might be tempted to dally with short-term methods of treatment.

This was an unfortunate policy; for like most psycho-therapeutists, the psycho-analyst is a reluctant and inexpert statistician. No accurate records or after-histories of psycho-analytical treatment exist: such rough figures as can be obtained do not suggest that psycho-analysis is notably more successful than other forms of therapy: and in any case none of the figures is corrected for spontaneous remission or resolution of symptoms. In consequence of all this psycho-analysis has developed a so far unacknowledged *mystique* which borders on the esoteric, and, like most esoteric products, springs from inferiority feeling. The attitude is in any case as ill founded as it is aggravating to non-analysts. The validity of psycho-analytic theory never did depend on therapeutic results nor, for the matter of that, does the validity of any other theory of mental function. The fact that a very large proportion of schizophrenics are inaccessible to the ordinary expectant techniques of psycho-analysis does not invalidate analytical etiologies of schizophrenia. Research and therapy though frequently combined in psycho-analysis are clearly different things.

DEFINITIONS OF PSYCHO-ANALYSIS

To begin therefore with definitions of psycho-analysis and of psycho-analytic treatment: it used to be said, up to twenty-five years ago, that whoever believed in the existence of the unconscious, in infantile sexuality, in repression, in unconscious

conflict and in transference believed in psycho-analysis.
Such was the definition of the late T. W. Mitchell, an acute and
sympathetic student; and, despite the passage of time, despite
emphasis on the factor of unconscious aggression and a corresponding burgeoning of psycho-analytical terminology, it is still
a satisfactory definition, on which criteria of psycho-analytical
therapy can also be based. In short we may say that whoever holds
these fundamental concepts, understands the processes of mental
development by which they are arrived at, has taken steps by
personal analysis to eliminate, as far as that is possible, the errors
of subjective bias, has learned to apply the technique of association and interpretation and is capable of analysing as far as
possible the transferences and counter-transferences that arise in
an analytic situation, can call his treatment psycho-analytic
therapy.

Of those conditions, the capacity and determination to analyse
the transference is decisive when drawing a distinction between
psycho-analysis and other forms of psycho-therapy. It was
Ernest Jones I think, who was in the habit of saying that there are
only two forms of psycho-therapy, namely, psycho-analysis and
suggestion. And although this must appear an unduly sharp saying
to psycho-therapeutists who spend a good deal of devoted energy
and ingenuity on analysing the material or symptom-formations
presented by their patients, it is certainly true in the sense that an
analysis which does not analyse the transference is no different
from any other form of psycho-therapy: it depends ultimately on
the state of therapeutic rapport existing between the psychotherapeutist and the patient.

General psycho-therapeutists may, however, take comfort from
the reflection that however sharp the saying, it is also two-edged.
For should the analyst not succeed in analysing the transference, or
should his modifications of technique, e.g. in the direction of
active measures or of moral support, prevent his successfully
analysing the transference, then his treatment depends for its
success or failure as much on factors of rapport as on his analytical
activities.

A further case exists. Should the analysts' interpretations be
consistently inaccurate then quite clearly he is practising a form of
suggestion, whatever else he himself may call it. It follows then
that when analysts differ radically as to the etiology or structure of a

case – as they nowadays do with increasing frequency – one side or the other must be practising suggestion. And since analyses, in private practice at any rate, tend to be lengthy, seldom less than two years' and frequently of four years' duration, it can easily be imagined how powerful the force of such analytical suggestion must be.[1]

Regarding the question of modifications of analytical technique it is obvious that the necessity for such modification depends on how widely the analyst casts his therapeutic net. For it is clear that if one attempts the analysis of, e.g. drug addicts, psychopaths and psychotic cases, the situations existing during crises do not usually permit continuance of the expectant technique used in the psycho-neuroses and equivalent states. It can, however, be fairly claimed that provided the usual techniques of association, interpretation and transference-analysis are followed whenever possible, such modifications as are entailed by the clinical necessities of the case or by the need to safeguard such of the patient's interests as he is for the time himself incapable of safeguarding, can justifiably be called psycho-analysis.

Classification of Mental Disorders

Having arrived at a working definition of psycho-analytic therapy, we may proceed to consider the difficulties arising from variation in classifications of mental disorders and in methods of diagnosis and prognosis. Here I think psycho-analysis may justly be said to have added considerably to our understanding both in diagnostic and in prognostic respects. Although ready to accept most of the clinical distinctions advanced by psychiatry, psycho-analysis has chosen to adopt a developmental approach to these clinical data. In the first place it regards all adult disorders, most adolescent disorders and a few pre-pubertal disorders (notably the obsessional neuroses) as end-products, the pre-disposition to

[1] This argument has acquired additional force since the beginning of the post-war period. Psycho-analysts are beginning to play an active part in the work of various projects of social amelioration, e.g. child-guidance clinics, marriage and social advisory councils. A feature of this work is that a large number of the conditions treated have no established etiology and that the patients are frequently treated by short-term methods of rapid interpretation given sometimes through the medium of social workers. Obviously unless these interpretations are accurate, the results obtained are due solely to transference-suggestion.

which is established during the first five to six years of life. The
nodal points in maldevelopment, mostly unconscious to be sure,
are termed fixation-points, which vary in number, depth and scatter. Following the theory of fixation-points, psycho-analysis has
arranged adult mental disorders in accordance with the developmental level to which the mind regresses when faced with
precipitating factors of frustration or traumatic excitation or both.
Thus to take a few instances, anxiety hysteria is regarded as having
an etiology based on disturbances at the fourth and fifth years of
mental development when genital anxieties constitute the main
pathogenic factors and repression is the main defence, the obsessional states as having fixation-points about the three to four year
level, when pre-genital factors are decisive and defence is mainly
reactive in type, and most psychoses as products of maldevelopment occurring during the first three years of life when both
libido and ego-development are extremely primitive. Classifications on this basis have not yet been worked out for various intermediate or transitional conditions, but there is every prospect
that a fairly accurate hierarchy of pathological elements based on
developmental criteria will some day be established. Alcoholism
and some cases of psychopathy, for example, illustrate transitional
forms lying between the neuroses and the psychoses.

The validity of this developmental approach is borne out by
two circumstances of considerable therapeutic significance. The
first of these concerns the degree of ego disorder, and the second,
the degree of 'transference potential' or, 'accessibility' as it is often
called. It is in accordance with theoretical considerations that the
more profound mental disorders, having early and scattered
fixation-points, should show greater instability and lack of synthesis of the ego than, for example, the neuroses. For therapeutic
purposes, this factor can best be described in two ways, first, by
the degree of capacity of the ego to withstand stress and trauma,
and second, the degree of capacity to make accurate reality
estimations. It is obvious, for example, that if the faculty of
reality-proving is gravely disordered, there is little prospect that
the ordinary techniques of expectant analysis will be effective, if
indeed they are even applicable.

Similarly with the transference factor. The earlier the fixation-
points the more tenuous the positive transference bond and the
less accessible the patient is to that opening up process of analysis

which depends on a working transference. In this connection it is useful to recall that Freud originally designated the hysterias and obsessional states as 'transference neuroses' and that psycho-analysis achieved and still achieves its greatest number of successes in this particular field. In illustration of the value of the developmental approach, and of the practical (therapeutic) significance of ego-synthesis, and of 'transference potential', we may consider the fact that whereas the hysterias are readily accessible to analysis, cases of 'pure' obsessional neurosis (i.e. unmixed with hysteria) are extremely difficult to resolve, and require an extremely lengthy analysis. This can be understood partly in terms of the earlier fixation points of the obsessional states and partly in the ambivalence of the transference. But it is much better understood if we reflect that the obsessional states behind which we can occasionally detect unconscious depressive or even paranoid layers, seem on the whole to protect against psychotic regressions. Although they may persist and expand up to the forties, they rarely regress to a psychotic state. Their refractoriness to analysis is thus seen to be a function of their *defence of the ego against further regression.*

But although psycho-analysts like most other psycho-therapeutists concentrate a good deal of their energy on the classical psychiatric disorders, they have also turned their attention to two other large psychopathological groups, viz. the so-called character disorders and the psycho-sexual disorders. Both types of disturbance are commonly found in association or conjunction as in marital difficulties; and it is tempting to suppose that both groups are also capable of subdivision according to developmental (predisposing) level. Although plausible in theory, this correlation between developmental layer and pathological end-products is much more difficult in character cases and sexual disorders than it is in the case of psychiatric symptom-formations, where the clinical symptoms afford relatively easy means of identification. This is easy to understand. Most symptom-formations carry the hallmark of their origin: a character disorder does not have the same developmental hallmarks, a psycho-sexual disorder still less.

Fortunately for diagnosticians there are many exceptions to this rule. An obsessional character, for example, is so close in pattern to an obsessional neurosis that it is not hard to find common developmental origins. And where homosexual or anal-

sadistic sexual perversions are accompanied by obsessional
characteristics it is not difficult to suppose that they too spring
from roughly the same level. On the other hand, the condition of
impotence may occur as frequently in the psychoses as it does in
persons of an anxiety type and diagnosis of its clinical importance
can be effected only on the strength of accompanying characteristics or symptom-formations.

EQUIVALENCE OF DIFFERENT DISORDERS

Despite these difficulties there are considerable diagnostic,
prognostic and therapeutic advantages to be gained by ordering
symptom-formations, character disorders and psycho-sexual
difficulties in roughly parallel series and by establishing rough
states of equivalence between the three groups. Perhaps the best
illustration is afforded by those transitional states that lie between
the psychoses and the psycho-neuroses. Analytical examination
of alcoholism, for example, shows that these states can be divided
roughly into four groups, those that show a predominantly projective character, veering towards persecutory feeling and reaction, those in which there is a depressive basis to the addiction,
those in which obsessive (compulsive) tendencies predominate,
and those in which the periodic bouts of alcoholism coincide with
excessive anxiety and/or inferiority manifestations. Running
parallel to the persecutory type of alcoholism are certain forms of
active homosexuality associated with strong contamination fears;
the psycho-sexual manifestations etiologically equivalent to the
depressive types of alcoholism fall mainly in the inhibited group,
and express themselves commonly in impotent forms of homosexuality: obsessional types of alcoholism find their psycho-
sexual parallel in fetichism; and anxiety types of alcoholism
correspond with the familiar forms of psycho-sexual impotence
which have, however, a strong latent homosexual disposition.

Correlating the same four groups with character difficulties,
we find the persecutory type of alcoholism corresponding with
severe difficulties in social adaptation, querulance, suspicion,
aggressiveness and incapacity in social relationships; the depressive
type corresponding with chronic incapacity and lack of success in
work, the obsessive type with obsessive indecision in life and work,
and the anxiety type with marked social inferiority.

As has been admitted these correlations have not been very

fully worked out, but already they enable us to arrive at useful prognostic assessments. The obvious difference in therapeutic response between the persecutory and the anxiety type of alcoholism can also be detected in the equivalent character and psychosexual disorders. It is important to be clear about this, otherwise the whole problem of indications for analysis is liable to be confused. Unless we make such etiological distinctions, it is in fact impossible to give a straight answer to the simplest questions, such as, 'Is psycho-analysis indicated in alcoholism?' Similarly with the equally simple question 'Is psycho-analysis indicated in impotence?'; the answer is, of course, 'It depends on the underlying states of disordered defence'. Again, although psychoanalysis obtains some of its best results in the treatment of anxiety hysteria, he would be a reckless prognostician who would recommend it in the case of monosymptomatic phobias without first of all examining the character structure to see whether this belongs also to the uncomplicated hysterical group or whether there is evidence of larval psychotic reaction, as there often is.

PROGNOSIS

So much for the symptomatic aspects of the problem. But symptomatic criteria alone do not resolve the many difficulties attendant on making a prognosis. Nor for the matter of that is it possible to give an exact prognosis by estimating however shrewdly the transference potential. A patient may appear and in fact be quite accessible to a psycho-analytic approach, yet the analysis may miscarry or end in stalemate simply because in the process of diagnosis, too little attention has been paid to the total function of his mind and in particular to the factors of primary and secondary gain.

Now the *primary gain*, that is to say, the part played by the symptom-formation in maintaining however inefficiently and at whatever cost to the individual the dynamic balance of the mental apparatus, or in simpler terms, in avoiding a break through of unconscious conflict, is not easy to estimate during preliminary examination. One may in all cases suspect that it is powerful enough, particularly where the form of the symptom-formation suggests either a reinforced masochistic predisposition or a defence against acute sadistic conflict or again violent psycho-sexual anxiety. The primary gain in some depressions, in most obsessional neuroses and in many forms of hysteria or marital disorder is extremely hard to deal with. But it is rarely possible to estimate it with accuracy until after a probationary period of analysis.

Secondary gain is quite a different matter. There should be no great difficulty in estimating whether by virtue of his neurosis or other disorder the patient succeeds in securing a favoured situation in his family environment, or is able to conceal his deficiencies from himself, or whether his conditions of life are such as to maintain a high level of frustration which keeps a symptomatic regression alive. When, for example, an anxiety hysteric within, say, ten years of the climacteric is caught in a loveless marriage from which, owing to her obligations as a parent, she is unable to free herself, it is foolish to suppose that psycho-analysis or for the matter of that any form of psychotherapy will liquidate even the simplest forms of phobia. When a latent male homosexual finds himself in the middle forties still unmarried and without adequate male friendships it is equally foolish to suppose that his working inhibitions will respond to however dexterous an analysis. Nor should we expect the multitudinous fifty-year-old anxiety depressions automatically to respond to a therapy which depends ultimately on an analysis of the transference and on the capacity of the patient to face squarely the emotional deficiencies of his life. Fortunately it is not hard to estimate the strength of secondary gain, for, as a rule it is equal and opposite to the precipitating factor.

Summing up the prognostic situation, we may say that roughly there are three factors to be taken into account; first, the depth of symptom-formations in which constitutional, predisposing (developmental) and precipitating (immediate) elements have to be assessed; second, the degree of transference potential, which must have a sufficiently strong positive side to withstand the stress incident to the uncovering of unconscious conflict (here the primary gain factor operates); and, third, the strength and persistence of the precipitating factors which determine in turn the strength of secondary gain. Where no major symptom formations are present and the disorder lies in malfunction of the ego and super-ego, prognosis is not so easily arrived at but can be estimated roughly in accordance with the total characteristics of the ego and the degree of primary and secondary gain; where the disorder takes the form of inhibition or perversion of function, particularly in work and love the prognosis is again variable but can be roughly estimated by an examination of ego-characteristics and by such minor symptom-formations as may accompany the inhibitions and give some clue as to their depth.

Although in principle the groups of factors we have considered cover the prognostic field, there are some items of sufficient importance to call for special mention. The *factor of age* for example is of more importance in psycho-analysis than in any other form of psycho-therapy. As has been pointed out earlier the hall mark of analysis is in the last resort the analysis of the transference, but analysis of the transference is not only a test for the analyst, it is a pretty searching test of the patient's capacity to free himself from fixations as well as from symptoms. With increasing age this feat is more difficult to compass. Non-analytical therapies in which transference support or exploitation is the rule have no such difficulties to face and consequently can be applied more readily to cases of advanced age. Despite these difficulties psycho-analysis which was originally confined mostly to the under-forties is now freely applied up to the sixties. Owing, however, to the factors of regression and of secondary gain it is doubtful whether many analyses of persons over the age belt of 45–50 are ever completed in the strict sense of the term. After this age the strength of the precipitating factors is in most cases the decisive prognostic test.

It is equally doubtful, although for different reasons, whether analysis of young children is even completed, and incidentally the therapeutic standards are also different from those applicable in the case of adults. In the first place the persistence of symptoms in a modified form need not be regarded as a failure provided there is evidence of strengthened character formation. Secondly, the success of a child analysis cannot be satisfactorily checked until an after-history of fifteen years has been secured. Indeed, in estimating the therapeutic efficacy of psycho-analysis it would be well to exclude children under the age of puberty and adults over the age of 45–50. In the case of adults whose age lies between these lower and upper limits, an after-history of at least five years is essential. Unfortunately it has to be admitted that satisfactory after-histories are seldom forthcoming; consequently our knowledge of the therapeutic range of psycho-analysis is vitiated by unchecked surmise.

Therapeutic Groupings

We are now I hope in a better position to deal with the main topic of this paper, viz., the indications for psycho-analysis. It will, I hope, also be clear that there can be no question of subdividing these indications in accordance with the clinical group. Nor strictly speaking is there any need to do so. From the therapeutic point of view it is sufficient to subdivide cases into those in which cure can reasonably be expected, cases in which considerable improvement may be anticipated, cases in which only slight improvement is likely to occur and cases which are not likely to improve except possibly in minor respects. Any notion that psycho-analysis is a panacea or that it should be recommended to every case coming for consultation is obviously absurd and the analyst who proceeds in this preposterous assumption is destined for early disillusionment. *From the point of view of analytic therapy, therefore, we can divide cases into three main groups, viz. accessible, moderately accessible and only slightly accessible.*

(1) *Accessible Cases*

The first of these groups is comparatively easy to delimit. It is constituted of the anxiety hysterias, the conversion hysterias, cases of mixed neurosis in which obsessional and hysterical elements are associated, and some cases of anxiety depression of a mainly reactive type. Care should of course be taken not to include in this category, mixed neurosis where there is an underlying system of endogenous depression. To these may be added disorders of sexual, social, marital and occupational life which I have described as 'equivalents' of a neurotic symptom formation. They include, simple impotence, ejaculatio praecox and vaginal frigidity, early marital frictions, facultative bisexuality, anxiety of an inferiority type and phobiac types of working inhibition (e.g. examination anxiety), neurotic confusional states and lack of powers of concentration leading to incapacity to work. The feature of such equivalent cases is that the predominant anxiety arises from the later infantile genital phases of development.

(2) *Moderately Accessible Cases*

At the head of the moderately accessible group I would put the average organized obsessional neurosis and obsessional character cases. These are by no means readily accessible to analysis, but on the other hand I cannot think of any other method of treatment which has better prospect of penetrating the structure of these conditions. In this group come also a number of sexual perversions having their roots mainly in pregenital layers of development. Typical examples are fetichism, tranvestism, and cases of active homosexuality in persons under the age of 40: the younger the better in fact. Alcoholism and drug addiction having a psycho-neurotic or mildly depressive basis also come in this category. As a rule treatment requires to be combined with a course of abstinence conducted by another physician. However difficult it may be to obtain cure by analysis, it occurs to me that to deal with alcoholism and drug addiction solely by abstinence methods and without any analysis is to leave the patient at the mercy of a psychopathological process which he was originally unable to withstand.

The second group also includes cases of phobia formation, conversion hysteria and the equivalents in sexual and social disorder which owing to the operation of an earlier type of pregenital fixation are more resistant to analysis. And to these I would add a number of milder cases of psychopathy under the age of 25.

I am in some doubt whether to include in the second group some cases of endogenous depression. There are certain types of both larval and manifest endogenous depression in which the traumatic fixations at late pregenital and genital levels of childhood have apparently been of greater significance than the more usual oral fixations, and in which in consequence the sado-masochistic predisposition does not offer so much resistance to analysis. Certainly a number of these cases although long drawn out respond satisfactorily. But to err on the side of caution I usually include the endogenous depressions in the third or intractable group.

(3) Intractable Cases

As in the case of the second group, the third or intractable group includes cases which would ordinarily come in the earlier groups but for evidence of deeper or wider ego disorder. The best example is afforded by types of alcoholism which cover either an endogenous depression or a paranoid predisposition. The third group also includes cases of anxiety hysteria which appear to have a psychotic sub-structure. Many severe monosymptomatic phobias are of this type. But the main constituents of the group fall under four subheadings, the pure psychoses, the psychotic characters, severe cases of psychopathy and sexual perversions and inhibitions of an equivalent order, including incidentally some apparently simple cases of impotence and frigidity and a large number of marital disorders. Needless to say amongst the psychoses the endogenous depressions are the most favourable and the pure paranoias the most unfavourable.

FUNCTIONAL DISORDERS

It will be observed that no mention has been made in any of these divisions of the expanding group of 'psycho-somatic' cases. My reason for omitting these is really to raise a special problem, viz. of cases suitable for psycho-analytically directed therapy as distinct from pure psycho-analysis, which as you know is a lengthy and more or less standardized procedure, involving under the present usages of private practice, a period which, unless curtailed by extrinsic circumstances, runs in the average from eighteen months to two years, with an average of five weekly sessions and involving fees that are likely to tax the resources of all except the well-to-do. The decision to recommend straight analysis in psycho-somatic cases depends on whether the patient also presents neurotic or psychotic symptom-formations or again sexual or social inhibitions or perversions of the kind already tabulated. In such cases psycho-analysis is indicated, but with the same sub-divisions of prognostic groups, mild, moderately accessible and intractable. It should be remembered that psycho-somatic conditions contribute to what are sometimes called patho-neuroses or organ-fixation-neuroses, also that a pure psycho-neurosis can be readily built round a psycho-somatic core. When, however, no such complications exist the case can well be dealt with by short-term exploratory and abreactive methods, which however I have no hesitation in maintaining should be based on psycho-analytical principles and orientation. For I do not conceal my view that alone amidst the welter of present day psycho-therapeutic systems, psycho-analysis offers a reasonable theory and etiology not only of mental disorders but of those disturbances of mental *function* which follow from states of mental over-excitation of whatever cause.

Recommendation of Treatment

Having roughly divided the cases that appear most commonly in the psychiatric consulting room into three prognostic groups, it is possible to give an equally rough indication of recommendations. The first group comprises those cases in which psycho-analysis, in my view, ought to be recommended forthwith and with a reasonable expectation of cure. The second group comprises cases in which substantial improvement may be expected but where there is no certainty of cure. In the third group certainty of cure or even of major improvement cannot be expected and should never be promised. It is true that well-selected cases taken from this third group may from time to time give surprisingly good results, but it would be absurd to pretend that on the average more than a mild degree of betterment can be expected.

Nevertheless, as I have suggested in the case of alcoholism, the indications for psycho-analysis should not be determined exclusively by prognosis. No organic physician would refuse to treat a case of rheumatism because it was chronic, intractable and promised at best only a mild degree of improvement. So long as there is reasonable chance of an improvement which could not be obtained more rapidly by some other form of psycho-therapy, it is perfectly justifiable to recommend psycho-analysis in difficult cases. Particularly in the psychoses, psychotic characters and severe sexual disorders therapeutic failure is an honourable failure which may in course of time lead to an improvement of the therapeutic instrument. Other things being equal, what should determine the recommendation is an objective assessment of the will to recovery as opposed to the primary and secondary gains secured through illness. A favourable balance justifies the recommendation.

Lay Analysis

A short postscript on lay-analysis. A properly qualified lay-analyst can safely be entrusted with any of the cases listed above with the exception of certain well-defined groups (*a*) cases of somatic disturbance of whatever kind that call for clinical (medical) discrimination (*b*) cases in which crises may arise involving danger to life. This latter condition automatically excludes the psychoses and psychotic characters. In any case these should be excluded since lay-analysts undergo no adequate training in psychiatry. To be on the safe side it might be desirable also to exclude such cases as call for concurrent sedation and for a decision as to periods of institutional supervision. But of course this difficulty can be overcome provided there exists an adequate liaison between the lay-analyst and the psychiatrist recommending the case. In many instances it is essential for the medically trained psycho-analyst to maintain similar communications. In cases of alcoholism involving complete abstinence the necessity for this is obvious, for the analyst cannot well conduct the abstinence; but also in cases involving supervision it is essential for the analyst to have ready means of support in the event of crises developing which require hospital supervision. The psycho-analyst who throws his therapeutic net widely is faced with frequent uncertainties, anxieties and harassments and it is of considerable moral and professional support to him on occasions of difficulty to know that he has behind him the expert knowledge and co-operation of an understanding psychiatrist.

XXVIII

THE FRONTIERS OF PSYCHO-ANALYSIS*
[1954]

In the early days of psycho-analysis, such diplomatic relations as existed with other sciences were, to say the least of it, rather cool. Psycho-analysis was on the defence and inclined to meet attack with counter-attack. In other instances no diplomatic relations existed. Gradually a change has come over the situation, due in part to the extension of psycho-analytical psychology to the dimensions of a theory of mind and partly to the fact that, even from early times, psycho-analysts, seeking for corroboration of their findings outside the clinical field, took to trespassing on psychiatry, social psychology, sociology, anthropology, aesthetics and even politics. In recent years a limited amount of team-work has brought psycho-analysis in closer contact with cognate sciences, although, it has to be admitted, often with the result that psycho-analytical concepts have been scaled down to meet the necessities of inter-communication with 'conscious' psychology.

Even so there still remains a good deal of distrust, scepticism and depreciation of psycho-analysis in the minds of psychiatrists, sociologists and normal psychologists, a state of affairs which is not improved by the psycho-analyst's reactive tendency to pontificate on subjects of which he has much less direct experience than he has of 'abnormal psychology'. So long as these reactions persist there is little hope of effective liaison in research work. The aim of the following article is to expound the developmental theories and discoveries of psycho-analysis and to clarify the relations between the different disciplines bearing on psychology, without, it is hoped, adding to the state of alienation that exists between them.

For the purposes of this survey the term 'frontier' can be used in two senses – domestic and political. The domestic approach includes the range of psycho-analysis as set by its own concepts and the nature of the material it studies: the political approach refers

* An address delivered at the Department of Psychology, University of Manchester, 2nd Feb., 1954.

to the spheres of influence of other branches of psychology and biology, and to the degree of liaison, actual or potential, existing between these branches of science and psycho-analysis.

RANGE OF THE MENTAL APPARATUS

From the domestic point of view the range of psycho-analysis is set by Freud's theory of a mental apparatus the functions of which are to receive, control, distribute and discharge excitation. This apparatus Freud originally described in terms of 'psychic systems' which could be distinguished by their dynamic relations to perceptual-consciousness, i.e. the dynamic unconscious (ucs), the preconscious (pcs) and the conscious (cs) systems. The 'boundary' or 'frontier' concepts employed in this earlier description were of two kinds. In the first place they designated the 'afferent' and 'efferent' aspects of this central apparatus. Roughly speaking these corresponded respectively to the sources of psychic excitation, and the products of psychic discharge. Amplifying this peripheral approach to the mental apparatus, it was found convenient also to speak of the sensory approaches to and motor ends of the mental apparatus. The relations of the psychic apparatus to somatic activity were further indicated by the use of the term 'instinct' in the sense of energic drive (*trieb*). Instinct in psycho-analysis is a boundary concept par excellence: a stimulus to psychic activity, derived ultimately from somatic sources, indicating at the same time the boundary between the somatic and the psychic and therefore the limits of psychology though not, of course, of psycho-somatic discharge.

This earliest attempt to describe the mental apparatus suffered from the disadvantages of a linear or serial approach. These disadvantages Freud sought to reduce in his second and more structural approach to the problem. This was governed by two polar concepts, namely of the *Id* and of the system 'perceptual-consciousness'. On the one hand the new concept of the Id – viz., of an unorganized and perpetually unconscious psychic system through which instinctual energy operates on the organized parts of the mental apparatus indicated more accurately the internal boundary between the somatic and the psychic. On the other hand, subjective experience both of internal excitation and of external stimulation passing through the system perceptual-consciousness to form 'memory traces', leads to the organization of psychic systems or nuclei which can be grouped respectively as ego and super-ego institutions. Both of these latter can be divided into unconscious and (pre)conscious fields or layers or belts, the ego system having, however, a closer relation to external reality through perceptual consciousness than the super-ego system, the nuclei of which lie closer to the Id.

It will be seen that the new boundary concept of the Id, being more circumferential than linear, was much more convenient than the original boundary concept of 'instinct', and more suited to expansion of the idea of an organized central mental apparatus. It enabled psycho-analysis to clarify its relation to both constitutional and environmental factors in mental activity. On the one hand constitutional factors, however described, defined or classified, can be conceived of as operating through the Id; and on the other hand the effect of environmental stimuli can be seen to depend primarily on the amount of Id-excitation aroused by them. In other words the effect of a congenital club-foot, of the state of the endocrine system, of hypersensitiveness to frustration, of the physiological or anatomical state of the central or other nervous systems, of infantile traumatic experiences, of organic disease, infectious or otherwise, of a motor accident, of a rural district council by-law, of the inheritance of a fortune or the experience of financial disaster, of celibacy or promiscuous sexuality must be reckoned primarily in terms of Id-excitation, including instinctual stress, and secondarily in terms of ego or super-ego response to the excitation or stress.

In this connection it is interesting to note that amongst psycho-analysts themselves a constant tendency exists to undermine this Id concept. Working back from the organization of mind as they find it about the age of three or four years and seeking by observation, interpretation and inference to reconstruct those earliest phases of mental function which cannot be directly examined by psycho-analytic methods, some analysts are tempted to postulate such hybrid concepts as 'psyche-somas' or 'body-egos', in some cases held to exist during the later months of foetal life. This tendency is due to loose thinking about the nature of the Id. It attributes ego organization to the Id, implies the existence of an ego at a time where there can be no possible ego-object differentiation, and obliterates the heuristic distinction between body and mind. Regarding mind as a central psychic apparatus operating between the processes of stimulation and discharge and having the function of regulating the intervening states of excitation, there is no point in stepping outside the conceptual range of this apparatus to dally with hybrid concepts. It is like putting one's head out of the bath-room window and maintaining that one is thereby sitting on the front-lawn.

All this you may say is of little interest to you. You are not concerned with the slipshod thinking of psycho-analysts. Nevertheless I was bound to start with the boundary concept of the Id, the energy of which activates the organized parts of the mental apparatus. In the first place, and as we shall later see, it clarifies the relation between psycho-analysis on the one hand and *neuropsychiatry* on the other. The second reason concerns the relation of psycho-analysis to *normal psychology*. Whoever accepts the concept of the Id is in a position to indicate the external frontiers of psycho-analysis. For the environment of the mind, which includes body as well as the world of external objects, is not only a source of stimulation to the Id but is the playground or battle-ground of the ego seeking to control or effect discharge of Id excitation. It follows, therefore, that *all* behaviour under whatever circumstances is the legitimate concern of the psycho-analyst.

LIAISON WITH COGNATE SCIENCES

You will observe that with this sweeping statement I have passed from the domestic to the political relations of psycho-analysis. There is no concealing the fact that psycho-analysis, whether it officially advances the claim or not, is sooner or later bound by its own principles to claim matriarchal rights over all other branches of psychology, individual and social. This I am sure is what psycho-analysts really have in prospect; although most of them would be ready to admit that, so far, they have neither sufficient workers nor the technical experience necessary to make the claim good. Indeed, it is interesting to inquire how far psycho-analysis *has* already succeeded in infiltrating other branches of psychological science.

In the sense of *direct co-operation* on the basis of common principles, the answer is of course 'very little indeed'. A marginal infiltration of psychiatry by psycho-analysis has occurred in this country but only marginal. In the United States, it is true, psychiatry has been extensively permeated by psycho-analysis and many psycho-analysts hold key positions in psychiatric training – a manœuvre incidentally which is essential to success in all psychological politics. But in any case this rapprochement between psycho-analysis and psychiatry has been offset by a wave of psychiatric interest in physiological methods of treatment both medical and surgical (e.g. shock therapy, pharmaco-therapy, leucotomy, etc.) which has widened the existing gulf between psychiatry and psycho-analysis. Not only so, psychiatry as a whole and particularly at its research stations has shown a readiness to move towards and co-operate with normal psychology, sometimes in a directive and sometimes in a subordinate capacity. This is not unnatural since neither psychiatry or normal psychology takes kindly to psycho-analytic views on unconscious psychic determination; and although psychiatry and normal psychology differ very much in methods of examination and of control, they have a good deal in common, in particular an absorbing interest in the (pre)conscious aspects of any given problem.

PSYCHOLOGY OF THE PRE-CONSCIOUS

This, incidentally, is where the psycho-analyst shows a major neglect of his plain duty. He has neglected 'to study the normal limits of (pre)conscious function at different ages, and under varying circumstances. It is only recently that, stimulated, in this country at any rate, by the nursery work of Anna Freud and her followers, psycho-analysts have begun to observe children as distinct from analysing them. The earlier neglect of observation was due partly to the fact that in the case of neuroses and other mental disorders analysts had found that the unconscious factors giving rise to predisposition were more important in bringing about the disorder than the immediate environmental or precipitating causes; added to which the recent urge to observation of children has been stimulated by the fact that under the age of, say, three years it is not possible to produce the conditions essential to true psycho-analytical investigation.

The situation is even more deplorable in the case of the conscious psychology of the so-called 'normal' adolescent and adult. Again due to the fact that psycho-analysts are compelled by the conditions of their therapeutic work to pay more attention to unconscious pathological factors than to the normal aspects of the conscious personality, there has been a gross neglect of (pre)conscious factors. In particular the examination of varying 'norms' of thought, action, speech, emotional expression and somatic variations in function, in other words of conduct, has been neglected. But it is not only a matter of establishing norms of conduct. The whole field of mental mechanisms operating under normal circumstances from the period of latency (say six to eleven years) onwards has been left to the almost exclusive attention of the normal psychologist.

PSYCHOLOGY OF THE EMOTIONS

The same can be said of the field of the emotions. The adult affects with which the psycho-analyst is concerned are those which either constitute pathological data in themselves, e.g. morbid anxiety states, morbid guilt states or morbid depressive states, or such primary affects as themselves give rise to morbid reactions, e.g. to depersonalization. The whole field of normal affects, their history and development, including various combinations or fusions of affect, has been left fallow. It is here indeed that the difference between descriptive and psycho-analytical psychology is most marked. Left to his own resources the normal psychologist can do no more than 'catalogue the different affects he encounters, observe their emergence under different experimental conditions and possibly attempt to measure their intensity. But unless he adopts psychoanalytical techniques he cannot very well break down apparently pure affects into their constituents; whereas the psycho-analyst having studied the various unconscious factors which give rise to an apparently pure jealousy or depression is in a position to break down a 'fused' affect into its emotional constituents. Depression, for example, is compounded of disappointment, hate, jealousy and the special type of anxiety that is commonly called inferiority-feeling. Moreover the concept of negative affects, loosely but inaccurately termed 'unconscious' or 'repressed' affects is without the scope of descriptive psychology. Even the psycho-analyst is compelled to describe affects which give rise to end results but do not themselves appear in consciousness by behaviouristic labels; as when he traces the 'need for punishment' to 'unconscious guilt'.

EDUCATIONAL PSYCHOLOGY

Perhaps the best illustration of the position is provided by *educational psychology*. Although the psycho-analyst believes that the processes of education during the period of latency, in adolescence and in adult life are radically influenced by unconscious mechanisms that are laid down during the period of infantile education (up to five years), he has made practically no attempt to link up these unconscious processes with the more sophisticated mechanisms listed by the pedagogue.[1] True, he does pay attention to certain pathological manifestations observed amongst schoolchildren, e.g. to inhibitions of learning; but here again he is concerned mainly with unconscious dynamic factors in the situation. To his credit be it said that he does pay attention to the influence of sexual education and development as distinct from personality and social education, but again his interest is directed mainly to pathological manifestations, for example, to pathological character changes, to sexual disorders and to social abnormalities such as delinquency. This apart, the whole field of normal pedagogy has been left severely alone. So much so that educational psychologists and pedagogues have taken the matter in their own hands and are building up an educational psycho-pathology of their own.

PERCOLATION OF PSYCHO-ANALYTICAL CONCEPTS

To be sure a good deal of *indirect* psycho-analytical influence has been exerted on other branches of psychology, as in the case of general psychiatry and to a certain degree educational psychology: and it is not uncommon to find both psychiatrists and educational psychologists using terms and concepts which were originally minted by psycho-analysts, without too accurate an understanding of the unconscious conditions they connote. But the fact has to be faced that largely owing to absence of interest, to a shortage of specialized workers and to unfamiliarity with the necessary techniques, psycho-analysts have woefully neglected the extensive field of normal preconscious psychology and have in consequence handicapped themselves with a number of uncontrolled or unchecked preconceptions about the nature of so-called normal mental function. This is all the more surprising when we reflect that psycho-analysts have not hesitated to plunge into the fields of anthropology, folklore, language, literature and art, latterly into politics and ethnology; although to be sure their

[1] See Chapter XVII.

activities in these fields have been limited mostly to looking for (and of course discovering) the influence of primary mental processes in these end-products. Psycho-analysts have made no systematic effort to trace the process of psychic events that links primary to secondary mental processes in the more mature stages of mental development.

Summing up these preliminary considerations we may say that although, according to its basic concepts, there is no department of psychology but comes within its range, psycho-analysis has not yet seriously attempted to make more than a few scientific, sometimes merely speculative forays into the territories of normal psychology or social psychology. Whether it will even establish direct authority in these territories is itself a matter for speculation. For quite apart from the pitiful scarcity of workers trained in psycho-analytic method and capable of research, it is open to question where the application of psycho-analytic techniques to normal individuals (and after all the study of individuals is the first and last resource of psychology) can mobilize sufficient force to be effective. We know that even within the customary range of psycho-analytic therapy, *it is necessary to select cases according to their accessibility*, their will to recovery. And the will to recovery can be freely translated as the reaction to suffering. Suffering less than his mentally disordered fellows, the normal individual has no will to recover from normality and in the therapeutic sense of the term is as inaccessible as the psychotic or the psychopath, a fact which explains in part why we learn so much about the normal person from a study of abnormality, why indeed we can learn little in any other way, unless of course we condense great masses of descriptive data, categorize them and subject them to psycho-analytic interpretation. Interpretation, I ought to add, is not simply a matter of drawing conclusions but of decoding, and in the case of disordered mental states is also one of the main methods of securing *access* to unconscious data – a scientifically perilous enterprise no doubt and open to grave sources of errors, yet in point of fact the most valuable instrument of psycho-analytical investigation and research.

It is tempting at this point to enter in greater detail into this concept of normality; to contrast, for example, the concept of the 'continuum' ranging from the normal to the abnormal (a concept which is a product of descriptive psychology) from the more qualitative classification of end-products in terms: (*a*) of their instinctual origin, (*b*) the economic functions that determine them, and (*c*) the structural peculiarities that give them their characteristic form, all of which is a product of psycho-analytical psychology. But perhaps it would be better to touch on these aspects of the subject when making a brief political survey of the psychological field.

PSYCHOLOGICAL MEASURES

Before attempting this survey it is desirable to take with us some *psychological measures.* I have just indicated one set, viz. the application of dynamic, economic and structural criteria. Another set of measures is derived from the study of mental symptom-formations, which according to psycho-analysis, are determined by three sets of etiological factors, the *constitutional*, the *predisposing* and the *precipitating.* Of these, the second or predisposing factors require special definition. In psycho-analysis a predisposing period is postulated stretching from birth through infancy to the end of the first period of childhood – in other words the first five pre-school years. During this period it is not simply a question of environmental factors operating on constitutional factors, though that may be roughly true of the first few months of extra-uterine life, but of environmental factors operating on an increasingly complicated series of *endopsychic factors*, comprising mainly what are called the *primary psychic processes*, as a result of which the mental apparatus acquires characteristic forms and functions which are already capable of division into normal and abnormal – the latter comprising the psychiatric disorders of early childhood. After this predisposing period, which in the case of normal mental products ought be described as a 'predetermining period', the environmental factor can be rated as a true precipitating factor and can be conveniently measured in terms of stress, in particular frustration stress.

NEURO-PSYCHIATRY, EMBRYOLOGY, BIO-CHEMISTRY, ENDOCRINOLOGY

To begin then with our survey: we must first consider the relations of psycho-analysis to *neuro-psychiatry*, in particular to neuro-anatomy and physiology, both normal and pathological, to *embryology*, to *bio-chemistry* and *endocrinology*, especially in their pharmacological aspects, and to *genetics*. Apart from their empirical uses as auxiliaries in diagnosis and treatment, information derived from most of these sources is concerned with what the psycho-analyst would call constitutional factors and environmental factors respectively – for as has been suggested already, both constitutional and immediate somatic factors have to be reckoned in terms of their influence on the Id, in other words, the body-factor regarded psycho-analytically is an environmental factor operating ultimately on the ego and super-ego, as it were, by courtesy of the Id. To be sure the psycho-analyst cannot help being interested in somatic changes, variations and modifications detected during maturation – a concept which, however, must be clearly distinguished from that of mental development. And he is particularly interested in such somatic changes as may be detected as the result of psycho-therapy either individual or social. These are issues that have been brought to the fore by recent work on the anatomy and physiology of the central nervous system and in particular on electro-encephalography in some groups of delinquents. Even so the psycho-analyst's interest is motivated less by his interest in somato-psychic correlations than by his concern to increase knowledge of the function and limits of function of the mental apparatus. Hence, he must translate the language of somatic biology into its psycho-biological equivalents. When the psycho-analyst thinks of constitutional factors his main concern is with variations in dynamic instincts, in stress, sensitivity, frustration-tolerance, anxiety-tolerance and hate-tolerance, (transmitted possibly, as Ernest Jones once suggested, through the genes). It is, by the way, an open question whether guilt-readiness and guilt-tolerance which are after all the pivots of human mental development and reach their height in the early years of life can also be regarded as factors derived from the anxiety group or whether they are acquired individually during the period of pre-disposition formation.

How much use will in future be made of these extramural studies is a question that cannot be answered until our present appalling ignorance of the early stages of mental development and of the primary mental processes has been dissipated. In the meantime the most we can derive from these studies is some tempting but quite often misleading analogies. It is of course interesting but not at all surprising to find correspondences between cybernetic ways of thought and psycho-analytic views as to the control and distribution or flow of mental energies; but at present this correspondence means no more than that conceptual analogies of a similar kind are used in both fields. In ʿhe meantime 'Information Theory' and the 'Theory of Symbolic Thinking' can usefully go their several ways.

SOCIAL PSYCHOLOGY

Let us now turn our attention to the relations of psycho-analysis to *social psychology*, keeping in mind all the while the psycho-analytic conception of predisposing developmental factors. Now the concern of social psychology (which nowadays can be held to include familial psychology in the sense of cultural pressures on the individual operating through the family) lies in two main directions, charting the social manifestations, structure and function of groups, and tracing the influence of social factors on the psychology of the individual. For example, using controlled statistical methods the social psychologist has discovered that in the U.S.A. sexual offences are much commoner amongst negroes than amongst whites in the same areas. And having tried to eliminate sources of error, he is now seeking to discover what group (environmental) factors may contribute to this manifestation. Or again in this country he has discovered and seeks by classification of his data to explain the fact that the so-called 'broken home' is a significant social (familial) factor in outbreaks of delinquent conduct. Now this discovery of the extent of the problem of the broken home is a valuable one. But in his attempts to break down this factor, the social psychologist's classifications are still descriptive and he ultimately comes up against the stone-wall of a flat, descriptive rating.

Enlisting at this point the services of the individual psychologist who has personal access to cases and, through the social worker, to their homes, he can establish that there are, say, fifteen different types of broken home. Here he is up against an obstacle which, unless he has psycho-analytical orientation, he is liable not to recognize, much less to surmount. For when he comes, as he must come, to consider the question of susceptibility on the part of the children, he must remember that pre-disposition is due not merely to the interaction of constitutional and environmental factors, but also to the specific interaction of environmental and endopsychic developmental factors. Taking the alleged fifteen factors in turn the psycho-analyst can sub-divide most of them into as many as ten different types in accordance with predisposition or suscepti-bility. Some of these psycho-analytical types present problems that are difficult to assess except through individual analysis, and they must sometimes appear to the social psychologist as, to say the least of it, aggravating complications. To be sure it is sometimes recognized by the social psychologist that the hostility of child to parent must be measured when estimating the effect of a 'broken home'; but it is not commonly recognized that a child who for reasons of unconscious jealousy unconsciously wishes to separate the parents, in other words, to break up the home, is liable because of his unconscious guilt to be unusually susceptible to actual disruption of the home initiated by parents. And it is interesting to reflect that most of the broken home investigations do not include an essential control group drawn from those who deal with their unconscious home-breaking tendencies by various degrees of 'running away from home'.

Time does not permit me to elaborate this point and many others of a similar nature: so I will content myself with making the following modest claim: viz. that, although there are obviously not enough analytically trained psychologists to carry out the investigations undertaken by social psychologists, the services of a psycho-analyst should be enlisted at three points in any social research; first, when drawing up the terms of reference; second, when preparing the case-frames, questionnaires and interview techniques; and third, when interpreting the results of examina-tion. To the statistical factor 'P', indicating significance and estimations of chance must be added the psycho-analytical factor 'Pa-bp' indicating psycho-biological probability as checked by existing knowledge of unconscious factors. Should you respond with the counter claim that a Jungian, an Adlerian, a Stekelian, a Suttieite, a Horneyite and a Kleinian have as much right as a Freudian to be included in the research team, I shall remain entirely unmoved, stating merely that, despite the optimism of modern eclectics, the period of isolated schools of clinical thought is *not* at an end. The unconscious psychology of the Freudian remains incompatible with that of any deviations from it, or of any eclectic composts of it with other systems.

SOCIOLOGY AND ANTHROPOLOGY

Needless to add that what applies to the social psychologist applies also to the *sociologist* and the *anthropologist*. In so far as their sciences are concerned with the functioning of groups, there seems no reason to suppose that the metapsychological principles found so useful in the case of the individual mind should not be applied to group phenomena. This implies that three distinct approaches should be made to each problem – dynamic, economic and structural, leading up to an examination of the technique whereby the group succeeds in maintaining its organization in spite of the turbulent forces with which it has to deal. In this connection it is essential to find a set of energy-measures comparable with those that are available in the case of the individual. Of these latter the most reliable are found in psycho-pathological manifestations, during the analysis of which some estimate can be made of the strength of controlling forces in the face of instinctual stress and of the affects engendered by stress. We may also assume that the same forces and the same types of controlling mechanism operate in the group; and, following this assumption, it would appear essential to decode the end-products of group activity in terms of their unconscious components, a task which again would require the co-operation of the psycho-analyst.

This recommendation applies with particular force to those anthropological and sociological researches which endeavour to trace *the relation of group-psychology to individual psychology*. I am only repeating myself when I say that to assess the relation of cultural influences to so-called culturally determined traits we must know at least as much of the pre-disposing (endopsychic) factors as we do of environmental factors. In this connection it should be remembered that what the sociologist regards as plasticity of the individual to cultural pressure operates at its maximum during childhood and is influenced at all points by the organization of the mind during its formative phases. And in any case we must consider how far the culture-pattern is itself a projection-product – a consequence of modelling society and its rules on the pattern of endopsychic conflict. In short to be a good sociologist one must be a good child psychologist.

Needless to say this last statement is reversible. A good child-psychologist requires more than clinical insight: he must also be a good anthropologist. When in doubt about the theoretical conclusions he derives from his clinical observations, he should subject them to the test of psycho-biological probability. He should consider whether they are consonant with the main tendencies of racial development. For it is not only the mental history of the individual adult that lies buried in the mind of the child but also the mental history of the race. It was one of the virtues of Freud's formulations regarding mental disorders that they could be plausibly correlated with reconstructions of racial development; the best examples being of course his correlation of the obsessional neuroses with the animistic and magical phases of mental development of primitive man, and his suggestion that hysterical states are essentially atavistic. That cyclothymic, paranoid and schizoid characters had also their group equivalents in prehistoric times is also possible but by no means so probable.

This correlation between the mental disorders of adult life, the predisposition to them developed during early childhood, the early unconscious phases of mental development, and the (hypothetically conceived) prehistoric phases of mental evolution of the race leads to the further assumption that *major unconscious mental conflicts of the individual adult correspond to difficult phases of adaptation in racial history.* At one time or another the psycho-analytical therapeutist cannot help wondering what primary conflict is common to all mental disorder. As you no doubt know Freud's earliest view on the matter was that Oedipus conflict is the kernel conflict and the greatest part of psycho-analytical anthropology has been devoted to tracing, with a considerable amount of success, the influence of the incest-barrier on racial organization. Later modifications of this view have taken the form either that unconscious homosexual conflict (the specific 'negative Oedipus conflict') is the main trouble or that guilt over unconscious sadism and anxiety over unconscious masochism are the root sources of conflict. Some speculators whose enthusiasm has outrun their discretion have even postulated a root conflict over sadism directed towards the mother in the first few months of life. However all this may be, and the last of these assumptions flies in the face of psycho-biological probability, there is little doubt that the science of anthropology can be quickened by psycho-analytical conceptions and that descriptive field-work in anthropology together with any statistical evaluation of it must be finally subjected to *interpretation* in terms of unconscious function, in which task psycho-analysis is entitled to play a leading rôle.

'ANIMAL PSYCHOLOGY'

Here would be a suitable point at which to indicate the relation of psycho-analysis to what is sometimes called *animal psychology* but is better described as a form of behaviourism derived from observation of set experimental situations. Here the psycho-analyst's main difficulty is that when examining the infant he is deprived of his own main instrument of investigation, the interpretation of introspections. True it is tempting to use the technique of play therapy to reconstruct early stages of development, but this is subject to the danger of displacing backward knowledge that is reliable enough in the case of three- or four-year-olds but may not be applicable to earlier ages. The same danger applies to any attempt to equate the terms 'neurosis' or 'conflict' as used in animal behaviourism with the 'psycho-neuroses' and 'endopsychic conflicts' of the young human. The issue turns as I have suggested before on the date of onset of unconscious guilt. The period when analogies drawn from animal behaviour may be of interest to the psycho-analyst is most surely the first few months of life. We do not know when unconscious guilt is sufficiently organized or permanent an influence to be clearly distinguished from social anxiety, but it is already certain that we must distinguish an early series of what I have called *functional disorders of the mental apparatus*, due to difficulties in mastering simple stress and oppositions of stress, from the later symptom-formations such as child-neuroses and child-psychoses. And this in turn means that we must know much more of the early combination and fusions of affect than we do at present.

NORMAL PSYCHOLOGY

Having made this somewhat erratic survey of the range and frontiers of psycho-analysis it is high time to return to what is after all the most important political relation of psycho-analysis, namely, to *normal psychology*, including under this caption that branch of normal psychology which studies the influences of formal education on the individual. And to judge from the extensive literature on test-psychology it seems legitimate to concentrate on this last activity, particularly that form known as *personality testing*. It is, I think, true to say that in the past the psychoanalyst has tended to ignore the enormous amount of valuable work done in these fields. But this has been due to a large extent to the influence of his own system of dynamic values and his belief that such unconscious values have not been taken much into account in those 'set and controlled situations' commonly described as tests. This attitude seems to be undergoing modification in two directions. In the first place, when pressed by the sheer weight of clinical material the analyst is now more ready (particularly, I think in America) to extract from test reports such information as will shorten his consultation; and, in the second, there are now signs that in the near future he will seek to manufacture tests of his own. Only the other day I glanced at a 'Dynamic Personality Inventory'[1] which consists of 369 items based mostly on psychoanalytic orientations, each item established on a five point scale. No doubt experiments of this kind will in course of time add greatly to the value of personality estimations, yet I could not help thinking that however inadequate, slipshod, variable and uncontrolled the psychiatric interview or consultation may be (and when one considers how difficult it is to acquire reliable information even from a continued and lengthy psycho-analysis, it is obvious that the single, double or triple interview is a hit or miss procedure unless conducted by observers of ripe experience) the time is approaching when personality tests may become so elaborate as to make examining the patient more worth while than testing him.

Otherwise the issues between the psycho-analyst and the psychological observer in the matter of personality tests are simple enough: first of all, what particular manifestations of mental activity are under examination, secondly, how far are these aspects or functions of mental activity subject to influence by dynamic factors, e.g. instincts, affects, conflicts, defence-mechanisms and what the psycho-analyst calls transferences, and thirdly, how far do these instincts, affects, conflicts, defence-mechanisms and transferences operate unconsciously; or, to use structural terminology how far are the end products observed and measured in the

[1] Formulated by Grygier, Krout and Krout-Tabin (unpublished communication).

accessible (pre)conscious system influenced by Id factors, unconscious ego-factors and no doubt some of the deeper and less accessible pre-conscious factors? If, of course, you hold that these so-called deeper factors are merely residual products without dynamic force you can go ahead happily enough selecting your factors in accordance with their probable relevance and without reference to any unconscious factor. And it must be admitted that this system works well enough not only in the case of intelligence tests but in a number of personality tests which are used for *prediction of conduct*. The Gluecks, for example, based their predictive delinquency scales on as many as 402 factors which they subsequently condensed to three tables each made up of five factors that at first sight seemed to be non-specific. For example, their 'character structure scale' comprises: assertiveness, defiance, suspiciousness, destructiveness and emotional lability. The factors were of course chosen on clinical experience of delinquents. Their 'psychiatric scale' is based on Rorschach tests and their 'social background scale' on the degree of affection, discipline and cohesiveness existing in the family. Yet using these sets of general factors it is apparently possible to distinguish potentially anti-social from potentially social children, both normal and neurotic. That they should distinguish normal and delinquent children from neurotics is of course obvious from *a priori* considerations – a neurotic child is rarely assertive, defiant, suspicious or destructive though frequently emotionally labile. And the psychiatric scale would pick up differences between the delinquent and the normal child. What strikes me, however, about all these tests is that, however useful they may be as short-cut diagnostic or prognostic tests – and sometimes they are not so very short – they depend finally on *a priori* information: they tell us no more about the structure, function and dynamics of any condition, whether normal or abnormal, than we already know. In the Szondi test, for example, certain characteristics are rated as having an anal-erotic significance. But who told the Szondi operator about anal-erotism and its potential character reactions? Certainly not a tester looking for anal-erotism but an investigator, Freud, who originally had no conception that there was any such thing.

CHARACTEROLOGY

And here, I think, we can qualify to some extent a criticism of psycho-analysis advanced earlier in this paper, namely, that it has been guilty of gross neglect of the normal psychology of later childhood, adolescence and adult life. All this is true enough. But there is one direction in which, by tracing the influence of un-conscious factors on waking life, psycho-analysis has not only made important contributions to normal psychology but has actually revolutionized it; although to be sure the normal psycho-logist is as a rule blandly unaware of the subversive events going on around him. I refer of course to *psycho-analytical characterology*. This has taken three main forms, dynamic, economic and struc-tural. Dynamic characterology traces the influence of early instinctual endowment not only on abnormal character formation but on the character of the ordinary, so-called 'normal' individual. This is indicated by the use of such terms as oral, urethral or anal character, in which the imprints of early component sexual instincts on the reality ego are studied and recorded. Economic characterology investigates the effect on ego-formation of the various unconscious controlling or 'defence' mechanisms which deal with instinctual stresses, e.g. positive or negative character traits, active and reactive characters, projective characters and the like. Structural characterology is, in the main, a study of the effect of early unconscious introjection of and identifications with important family imagos, e.g. father, mother or sibling identifica-tions.

But psycho-analysis has gone much further in the delineation of normal character. It has investigated the effect of early and transient psycho-pathological states on adult character and is ready, for example, to distinguish hysterical, obsessive, depressive, manic, paranoid and schizoid characters amongst the normal population. The most convincing examples are of course; first, the obsessive character, in which the individual's reactions to the details of life and conduct are similar to those observed in the obsessional neuroses, e.g. hyperconscientiousness, over-scrupu-lousness, doubt, indecision, double thinking, flattening of emo-tional tone and ritualistic behaviour; and second, the so-called cyclothymic character in which phases of hyperactivity and relative euphoria alternating with bouts of moody inertia are found corre-sponding in kind with the sequences of manic-depressive insanity. There are in fact almost endless possibilities of extending this clinical characterology. The character-formations that accompany the four main types of alcoholism can also be isolated amongst the more bibulous of the 'normal' population; the epileptic character is not unknown amongst 'normal' persons who have never had a convulsive seizure; and of course the at present rather vaguely defined psychopathic character has its counterparts amongst people who are usually regarded as no more than eccentric and/or ego-centric.

All this, although of tremendous significance for normal psychology, is still in the embryonic stages. Like many original psycho-analytical discoveries, what appeared at first to be a set of irreducible formulations proved in the long run to be rough approximations, capable not only of expansion and sub-division, but of correlation with other factors. With increasing interest in ego-development, libido characterology gave place for a time to structural characterology, and structural characterology gave place in its turn to a study of the effect of 'combined mechanisms'. In other words the atomistic approach has had to be supplemented by recognition of certain specific products of various syntheses of unconscious factors, or gestalts as you would no doubt prefer to call them.

It is here, too, that close co-operation is possible between the normal and the psycho-analytical characterologist. In the first place, when selecting the various factors on which test-techniques are based, the normal psychologist would do well to enlist the services of a psycho-analytical characterologist, and, in the second, once the psycho-analyst has formulated his various traits and described them in a form capable of statistical investigation, he in his turn would do well to enlist the services of a normal psycho-logist who, using his own special techniques, could examine the normal population in order to ascertain their incidence and significance.

So it comes to this: whoever seeks to correlate the work of normal psychology with that of psycho-analysis must surmount two difficulties, both of which are due to deep-seated suspicion. The normal psychologist has a profound distrust of psycho-analytical methods of clinical observation and interpretation and prefers the more controllable examination of behaviouristic end-products. The psycho-analyst, on the other hand, has a deep distrust of taking things as they seem, unless their form and function correspond with what he knows of unconscious forces and mechanisms. This is a situation that seems to call for the creation of a group of psychological frontiersmen familiar with the disciplines and languages of both sides.

MATHEMATICS

And talking of disciplines and languages it will be one of the tasks of the frontiersmen to produce a sort of psychological pidgin-English, a *lingua franca* in which such terms of one science as are capable of paraphrase into the dialect of another are so paraphrased. Psycho-analysts are frequently reproached for their neglect of *mathematical coding techniques* and systems of control: and, in so far as this applies to clearly definable data and terms, the reproach is not without justification. On the other hand, it would be a waste of time, energy and good temper to seek to apply the method to data and terms which are either undefined or undefinable, that is to say relate to properties which cannot be given mathematical symbols and measured as magnitudes are. Psycho-analysis has contributed more than any other branch of psychology to our knowledge of mental properties. But it has not so far been able to establish clearly defined units for purposes of statistical comparison. Nor, with the exception of rough psycho-pathological standards, has it been able to suggest a working series of energy measures, a task which is rendered immeasurably difficult by the operation of the mechanism of repression, and by the mere suggestion, made by Freud, that there are specific qualities of different quantities of psychic energy. In spite of these difficulties there remain certain qualities and quantities which can be estimated using clinical standards, provided of course these standards take into practical account the existence of unconscious factors. It is at this point that co-operation between psycho-analysts and mathematicians is possible and should be encouraged.

And with this brief reference to a science with which psycho-analysis has so far only the most distant contact, I must conclude this survey of the frontiers of psycho-analysis. I need hardly say I am well aware of its shortcomings, but hope that a frank admission of these may help to surmount some of the difficulties of discussion. Having claimed matriarchal rights for psycho-analysis I must be ready to meet with equanimity the counter-assertion that, from the point of view of the physical scientist and the descriptive psychologist, psycho-analysis was born under the bar-sinister.

Appendix

EDWARD GLOVER

BIBLIOGRAPHY

I

RESEARCHES IN ORGANIC MEDICINE

(1) 1914 The 'Albumin Reaction' of the Sputum in Pulmonary Tuberculosis, *Brit. J. Tuberc.* 8, 4, Oct. 1914.

(2) 1915 The Diagnosis of Early Tuberculosis, *Tuberc. Yearb.*, London, 1915.

(3) 1915 Subcutaneous Tuberculin Injections in the Diagnosis of Pulmonary Tuberculosis, *Brit. J. Tuberc.* 9, 4, Oct. 1915.

(4) 1915 The Early Diagnosis of Pulmonary Tuberculosis, *Quart. J. Med.*, 8, 32, July 1915.

(5) 1916 The Significance of 'Abortive' Cases in the Classification of Pulmonary Tuberculosis, *Practitioner*, Nov. 1916.

(6) 1918 Tuberculosis and Toxaemia, *Brit. J. Tuberc.*, 12, 3, July 1918.

(7) 1918 The Diagnostic Significance of Haemoptysis, *Practitioner*, Aug. 1918.

(8) 1919 A Note on the Treatment of Laryngeal Tuberculosis with Intravenous Gold, *Tubercle*, Lond., Dec. 1919.

II

PAPERS ON PSYCHO-ANALYSIS

(9) 1922 The Psychology of Crime, *National Union of Societies for Equal Citizenship, Summer School for Women Magistrates*, Oxford, 1922.

(10) 1923 Psycho-Analysis and General Practice, *Brit. Medical Association*, Catford Branch, 1923.

(11) 1924 Active Therapy and Psycho-Analysis, *Int. J. Psycho-Anal.*, 5, 269–311, 1924.

11853   (12) 1924   **Critical Notice of 'Entwicklungsziele der Psychoanalyse,' von S. Ferenczi und Otto Rank,** *Brit. J. med. Psychol.*, **4**, 319–25, 1924.

11903   (13) 1924   **The Significance of the Mouth in Psycho-Analysis,** *Brit. J. med. Psychol.*, **4**, 134–55, 1924.

        (14) 1924   **Abstract and Criticism of 'Das Trauma der Geburt" von Otto Rank,** *communication to Brit. Psycho-anal. Soc.* (with James Glover) April 2nd, 1924.

11880   (15) 1925   **Notes on Oral Character Formation,** *Int. J. Psycho-Anal.*, **6**, 131–54, 1925.

11877   (16) 1926   **The Neurotic Character,** *Int. J. Psycho-Anal.*, **7**, 11—30, 1926. (Published also in *Brit. J. med. Psychol.*)

11908   (17) 1926   **A 'Technical' Form of Resistance,** *Int. J. Psycho-Anal.*, **7**, 377–80, 1926.

11860   (18) 1926   **Einige Probleme der psychoanalytischen Charakterologie,** *Int. Z. Psychoanal.*, **12**, 326–33, 1926.

11855   (19) 1926   **Abstract and Critical Notice of Freud's 'Hemmung, Symptom und Angst,'** *Brit. J. med. Psychol.*, **6**, 121–36, 1926.

11850   (20) 1926   **Contribution to Discussion of Dr. Bernard Hart's paper 'The Conception of Dissociation,'** *Brit. J. med. Psychol.*, **6**, 261–3, 1926.

11873 (21) 1927   **On Lay Analysis.** (Symposium contribution), *Int. J. Psycho-Anal.*, **8**, 212–20, 1927. Published also under the title of **Laienanalyse,** *Int. Z. Psychoanal.*, **13**, 229–36, 1927.

11846 (22) 1927   **On Child Analysis,** (Symposium contribution), *Int. J. Psycho-Anal.*, **8**, 385–7, 1927.

        (23) 1927   **Some Observations on Suicidal Mechanisms,** *Int. Psycho-Analytical Congress,* Innsbruck, Sept. 1st, 1927.

11874 (24) 1927-28 **Lectures on the Technique of Psycho-Analysis,** *Int. J. Psycho-Anal.*, **8**, 311–38; 486–520; **9**, 7–46; 181–218, 1928. Published as *Supplement No. 3 to Int. J. Psycho-Anal.* under the title **The Technique of Psycho-Analysis,** Baillière, Tindall & Cox, London, 1928.

11909

11861 (25) 1928   **The Etiology of Alcoholism,** *Proc. R. Soc., Med.* **21**, 45–50, 1928.

        (26) 1928   **'Forerunners' of Conscience,** Address to the Heretics Society, Cambridge, March 4th, 1928.

        (27) 1928   **Memorandum on Psycho-Analysis,** Presented to the Psycho-Analysis Committee of the British Med. Assoc., Nov. 22nd, 1928. *Proceedings of same.*

11902 (28) 1929   **The 'Screening' Function of Traumatic Memories,** *Int. J. Psycho-Anal.*, **10**, 90–3, 1929.

11893 (29) 1929 **Psycho-analytical Groundwork in Group Psycho-logy,** *Int. J. Psycho-Anal.*, **10,** 162–9, 1929. Also published under the title **Zur analytischen Grund-legung der Massenpsychologie,** *Int. Z. Psychoanal.*, **15,** 297, 1929.

11896 (30) 1929 **The Psychology of the Psychotherapeutist,** *Brit. J. med. Psychol.*, **9,** 1–16, 1929.

11866 (31) 1930 **Grades of Ego-Differentiation,** *Int. J. Psycho-Anal.*, **11,** 1–11, 1930.

11915 (32) 1930 **The 'Vehicle' of Interpretation,** *Int. J. Psycho-Anal.*, **11,** 340–4, 1930.

(33) 1930 **Lectures on the Theory of Psycho-Analysis,** Inst. of Psycho-Analysis, April–June 1930.

11870 (34) 1930 **Introduction to the Study of Psycho-analytical Theory,** *Int. J. Psycho-Anal.*, **11,** 470–84, 1930.

(35) 1930 **The Psychotherapy of the Psychoses,** *Brit. J. med. Psychol.*, **10,** 226–34; 1930. A reply to the discussion of this subject : same Journal.

11906(36) 1931 **Sublimation, Substitution and Social Anxiety,** *Int. J. Psycho-Anal.*, **12,** 263, 1931.

11855(37) 1931 **The Prevention and Treatment of Drug Addiction,** *Brit. J. of Inebriety*, **29,** 13–18, 1931–32. Also published in *Lancet*, 587, March 14th, 1931.

(38) 1931 **The Collection of Self-Interpreting Data, with illustrative examples,** *Brit. Psycho-Anal. Soc.*, March 4th, 1931.

(39) 1931 **The Psycho-Pathology of Flogging,** published by the Howard League for Penal Reform under the title *Corporal Punishment*, 1931

11833 (40) 1931 **Pathological Character Formation; the Neurotic Character,** published in *Psychoanalysis Today*, edited by Sandor Lorand, London, Allen & Unwin, 1933.

11910 (41) 1931 **The Therapeutic Effect of Inexact Interpretation; a Contribution to the Theory of Suggestion,** *Int. J. Psycho-Anal.*, **12,** 397, 1931.

11938 (42) 1931 **Critical Notice of Flugel's 'Psychology of Clothes,'** *Brit. J. med. Psychol.*, **11,** 2, 158–63, 1931.

(43) 1931 **Pacifism in the Light of Psycho-Analysis,** *Proc. Int. Federation League of Nations Union Societies.* Summer School, Geneva, 1931. Later published in *War, Sadism and Pacifism*, London, 1933.

11862 (44) 1932 **The Etiology of Drug-Addiction,** *Int. J. Psycho-Anal.*, **13,** 298, 1932.

11847   (45) 1932 **Common Problems in Psycho-Analysis and Anthropology : Drug Ritual and Addiction,** *Brit. J. med. Psychol.*, **12,** 1932.

11928   (46) 1932 **Critical Notice of Alexander's 'Psycho-Analysis of the Total Personality,'** *Brit. J. med. Psychol.*, **12,** 1932.

11876   (47) 1932 **Medico-psychological Aspects of Normality,** *Brit. J. Psychol.* (General Section), **23,** 2, 152–66, 1932.

11892   (48) 1932 **Psycho-Analytical Approach to the Classification of Mental Disorders,** *J. ment. Science,* Oct. 1932.

11899   (49) 1932 **The Relation of Perversion-Formation to the Development of Reality Sense,** *Int. J. Psycho-Anal.*, **14,** 486, 1933.

** *   (50) 1932 **Contribution to Symposium 'On the Psychology of Crime,'** *Brit. J. med. Psychol.*, May 28th, 1932.

(51) 1932 **Contribution to Symposium ' Psychology and Psychical Research,'** Brit. Psychol. Society (Medical Section.)

11876   (52) 1932 **Die Normalität vom medizinisch-psychologischen Standpunkt,** *Psychoanal. Beweg.*, **6,** 1932.

(53) 1933 **Report on a Questionnaire on Technique,** Brit. Psycho-Anal. Society, Apl. 5th, May 3rd, Oct. 18th, 1933. Final Report May, 1934.

11917   (54) 1933 **War, Sadism and Pacifism,** (1st Ed.) London, Allen & Unwin.

(55) 1933 **On War and Sadism,** *Socialist Rev.*, **5,** 5, Aug. 1933.

(56) 1933 **The Psychology of Peace and War,** *Brit. J. med. Psychol.*, **11,** Dec. 13th, 1933.

11862   (57) 1933 **Zur Aetiologie der Sucht,** *Int. Z. Psychoanal.*, **19,** 170, 1933.

11868   (58) 1933 **Das Institut zur wissenschaftlichen Behandlung der Kriminalität, London,** *Psychoanal. Beweg.* **5,** 1933.

11911   (59) 1933 **Unbewusste Wünsche im Alltagsleben,** *Psychoanal. Beweg.*, **5,** 1933.

(60) 1934 **The Psychology of Pacifism,** *XXth Century*, **6,** 34, March 1934.

(61) 1934 **Some Aspects of Psycho-analytical Research,** Communication to Brit. Psycho-Anal. Soc., Oct. 3, 1934.

(62) 1934 **Lectures on ' The Theory of the Neuroses,'** Inst. of Psycho-Anal., Apl.-June, 1934.

(63) 1934 **The Need for ' Reality Thinking,'** (with Prof. Levy), *Listener*, 13 June 1934; also published in *The Web of Thought and Action*, edited by H. Levy, London, 1935.

(64) 1934 **War and the Aggressive Impulses,** Inst. of Psycho-Anal., London, 1934.

11875 (65) 1934 **Medical Psychology or Academic (Normal) Psychology. A Problem of Orientation,** *Brit. J. med. Psychol.*, **14,** 1934.

11894(66) 1934 **Psychologisches über Krieg und Pazifismus,** *Alm. der Psychoanal.*, Vienna, 1934.

11843 (67) 1935 **The Application of Psycho-analytic Principles in Psychiatry,** *Proc. R. Soc. Med.*, **28,** 1935.

11913(68) 1935 **Introduction to Symposium ' Psycho-Analysis and Education,'** Brit. Psycho-Anal. Soc., May 8 and 21, 1935. *Int. J. Psycho-Anal.*, **18,** 2–3, 1935.

——(69) 1935 **Theft as a Symptom of Disease,** *J. ment. Hyg.*, **14,** 1935.

11857(70) 1935 **A Development Study of the Obsessional Neuroses,** *Int. J. Psycho-Anal.*, **16,** 2, 131, 1935.

11886 (71) 1935 **Das Problem der Zwangsneurose,** *Int. Z. Psychoanal.*, **21,** 235, 1935.

11907 (72) 1935 **Symposium über die Psychologie von Krieg und Frieden,** *Alm. der Psychoanal.*, 1935.

——(73) 1936 **On the Treatment of Neurotic Patients by the Family Doctor,** *Lancet*, Apl. 1936.

——(74) 1936 **Psychological Obstacles to Learning,** *Adult Education*, **9,** 2, Dec. 1936.

(75) 1936 **Contribution to Symposium ' Criteria of Success in Psycho-Analysis,'** Brit. Psycho-Anal. Soc., March 4, 1936; abstracted in *An Investigation of the Technique of Psycho-Analysis*, London, Baillière, Tindall & Cox, 1940.

11854 (76) 1936 **The Dangers of Being Human,** London, Allen & Unwin, 1936.

(77) 1936 **Four Lectures on Physical Aspects of Mental Disorder,** Inst. of Psycho-Anal., Jan.-March 1936.

under *(78) 1936 **Medizinische Psychologie oder akademische (normale) Psychologie; ein Problem der Orientierung,** *Imago*, **22,** 1, 5, 1936.
11875
add

11916 (79) 1936 **War and Pacifism : Some individual (unconscious) Factors,** *Character and Personality*, **4,** 4, 305–18, 1936.

——(80) 1937 **Psychology and the Social Sciences,** from *Further Papers on the Social Sciences*, edited by J. E. Dugdale, Le Play House Press, 1937.

11852(81) 1937 **Symposium on The Theory of the Therapeutic Results of Psycho-Analysis,** *Int. J. Psycho-Anal.*, **18,** 2/3, 125, Apl. Jly, 1937.

11914 (82) 1937 **Utopien,** *Almanach der Psychoanal.,* I. P. V. Vienna, 1937.

—— (83) 1937 **The Psychopathology of Flogging** (2nd and revised ed.), Howard League for Penal Reform, London, 1937.

11913 (84) 1937 **Unconscious Functions of Education,** *Int. J. Psycho-Anal.,* **18,** 2/3, 190, 1937.

11878 (85) 1938 **A Note on Idealisation,** *Int. J. Psycho-Anal.,* **19,** 91, 1938.

11913 (86) 1938 **Die unbewusste Funktion der Erziehung,** *Almanach der Psychoanal.,* I. P. V., Vienna, 1938.

11877 (87) 1938 **Psycho-Analysis,** *Brit. Encyclopaedia of Med. Practice,* **10,** London, Butterworth, 1st ed. 1938.

—— (88) 1939 **Sigmund Freud (May 6, 1856–Sept. 23, 1939): a Broadcast Tribute,** *Listener,* 28 Sep., 1939.

11891 (89) 1939 **The Psycho-Analysis of Affects,,** *Int. J. Psycho-Anal.* **20,** 3/4, 297, 1939.

11888 (90) 1939 **Psycho-Analysis,** 1st ed., Pocket Monograph Series. John Bale, Son and Daniellson, London, 1939.

11845 (91) 1940 **The Birth of Social Psychiatry,** *Lancet,* 239, Aug., 1940

—— (92) 1940 **Social Institutions,** *Med. Pr.,* **204,** No. 5297, 1940.

11895 (93) 1940 **The Psychology of Fear and Courage,** A Penguin Special, Penguin Books, Harmondsworth, 1940.

—— (94) 1940 **Über die durch den Krieg verursachten Anderungen in unserer psychischen Oekonomie,** *Int. Z. Psychoanal.,* **25,** 3/4, 1940.

11871 (95) 1940 **An Investigation of the Technique of Psycho-Analysis,** Baillière, Tindall & Cox, London, 1940.

—— (96) 1940 **On the So-called 'War-Neuroses,'** Conference of the Brit. Psychol. Society, Birmingham. Published as Chap. VI of *War, Sadism and Pacifism,* 3rd ed., 1947.

—— (97) 1940 **Mental First Aid,** *Nurs. Mirror,* Dec. 14, 1940.

—— (98) 1941 **Man—the Anachronism,** *World Rev.,* Dec. 1941. Subsequently published in *This Changing World,* Edited by J. R. M. Brumwell, Routledge & Kegan Paul, London, 1944.

—— (99) 1941 Foreword to **The Nursing Couple,** by Merell P. Middlemore, Cassell & Co., London, 1941. Reprint 1953.

11881 (100) 1941 **Notes on the Psychological Effects of War Conditions on the Civilian Population.** Part I: **Introduction**; Part II: **The Pre-Blitz Period,** *Int. J. Psycho-Anal.,* **22,** 2, 132, 1941.

11858 (101) 1942 **The Diagnosis and Treatment of Delinquency,** I.S.T.D. Publications, London. Extended from a paper of the same name published in *Mental Abnormality and Crime*, Macmillan, 1944.

— (102) 1942 **The Secret Places of the Mind,** *Listener*, 4, Jne, 1942.

11781 (103) 1942 **Notes on the Psychological Effects of War Conditions on the Civilian Population,** Part III : **The Blitz,** *Int. J. Psycho-Anal.*, 23, 1, 17, 1942.

(104) 1943 **The Abolition of Tolerated Prostitution,** Proceedings of an International Meeting of the International Bureau for the Suppression of Traffic in Women and Children, Oct. 1943.

— (105) 1943 **Towards an Adult Society,** *Listener*, 30, No. 775, 571, 1943.

11849 (106) 1943 **The Concept of Dissociation,** *Int. J. Psycho-Anal.*, 24, 1, 2, 1943.

—(107) 1944 **Persuasion or Compulsion ? Views on National Service for Boys and Girls in Their Teens,** *Listener*, Feb. 17, 1944.

—(108) 1944 **The Case of Bill Williams** [*with* **Maxwell Jones and Anna Kavan**], *Horizon*, 9, 50, 96, 1944.

— (109) 1944 **State Parentalism,** *New English Weekly*, Mch. 23, 1944.

—(110) 1945 **Psychology at the Peace Conference,** *World Rev.*, Nov. 1945.

—(111) 1945 **Psychology and the Public,** *Horizon*, 11, 63, Mch. 1945

11904 (112) 1945 **The Social and Legal Aspects of Sexual Abnormality,** *Med.-leg. Rev.*, 8, 3, 1945. Also published as a monograph by I.S.T.D. Publications, London, 1945.

1186³ (113) 1945 **An Examination of the Klein System of Child Psychology,** in *The Psychoanalytic Study of the Child*, 1, Imago Publishing Co., London, 1945. Published separately as a monograph, London, 1946.

1189⁷ (114) 1945 **The Psycho-Pathology of Prostitution,** I.S.T.D. Publications, London, 1945.

1185⁹ (115) 1945 **David Eder as Psycho-Analyst,** in *David Eder : Memoirs of a Modern Pioneer*, (Ed. J. B. Hobman), Goilancz, London, 1945.

(116) 1945 **The Psychology of Frustration and Fulfilment : the Psycho-analytic Approach,** The Provisional National Council for Mental Hygiene, Oct., 1945.

—(117) 1946 **Right, Left or Centre : A Psychological Approach to Party Politics,** *Horizon*, 14, No. 83, 275, 1946.

(118) 1946 **Reactionary Aspects of Modern Psychology,** *Polemic*, **1**, 1, 1946. Originally delivered as an address to the Progressive League, London.

(119) 1946 **Zest or Apathy : A Psychological Enquiry Into the Nature of Incentive,** *World Rev.*, 33, Jan. 1946.

(120) 1947 **War, Sadism, and Pacifism,** 3rd and enlarged edition of the essays first published in 1933 (q.v.) Allen & Unwin, London, 1947.

(121) 1947 **A Psycho-Analyst Looks at Town-Planning,** *Town and Country Planning*, **15**, 57, 14, 1947.

(122) 1947 **Basic Mental Concepts,** Imago Publishing Co., London, 1947.

(123) 1947 **The Investigation and Treatment of Delinquency,** *Brit. med. J.*, Mch. 29, 1947.

(124) 1947 **Youth in Trouble,** Rotary Club of London, Oct. 1947.

(125) 1947 **The Role of Illusion in Society,** Second Conference of Rationalist Press Association, Aug. 1947. Abstracted in *Literary Guide*, London, 1947 and published *in extenso* in same, **62**, 9, Sep. 1947.

(126) 1948 **Freud or Jung,** Part I, *Horizon*, **18**, 106, Oct. 1948.

(127) 1948 **Freud or Jung,** Part II, *Horizon*, 107, Nov. 1948.

(128) 1948 **Ideas and Beliefs of the Victorians,** No. 16. **Ideas of Sex : A Psychological Interpretation,** *Listener*, **39**, No. 1008, May 20. Subsequently published in *Ideas and Beliefs of the Victorians*, Sylvan Press, 1949.

(129) 1948 **Conceptos mentales basicos ; sus valores clinicos y teoricos,** *Rev. Psicoanal.*, **6**, 1, 1948.

(130) 1948 **The Juvenile Delinquent : A summing-up,** *Rotary Service*, **14**, 59, 3, 1948.

(131) 1948 **The Future of Psycho-Analysis.** An Address to the Dutch Psycho-Analytical Society, Amsterdam, Nov. 1948.

(132) 1949 **Freud or Jung,** Part III, *Horizon*, Apl. 1949.

(133) 1949 **The Social Psychiatrist at Large,** *New English Weekly*, **35**, 11, 23 Jne, 1949.

(134) 1949 **The Position of Psycho-Analysis in Great Britain,** *Brit. med. Bull.*, **6**, 1/2, 27, 1949.

(135) 1949 **Psycho-Analysis: a Handbook for Medical Practitioners and Students of Comparative Psychology,** 2nd ed., (being the second and enlarged edition of a pocket-monograph of the same title published by John Bale, Sons & Daniellson, London, 1939), Staples Press, London, 1949.

11865 (136) 1950 **Functional Aspects of the Mental Apparatus,** *Int. J. Psycho-Anal.*, **31**, 1/2, 1950.

(137) 1950 **Fuchs : the Mind Behind the Man,** *Leader,* **7,** 20, Mch. 18, 1950.

(138) 1950 **The Psychopathic Personality,** Lectures to the Psychiatric Week-end Course, Roffey Park, 1950.

(139) 1950 **The Psychological Effects of Child-Bearing,** Brit. med. Assoc., Annual Meeting, Section of Psychiatry, Jly. 18, 1950. Abstracted in *Brit. med. J.*

(140) 1950 **Memorandum on 'Capital Punishment'** submitted to *The Royal Commission on Capital Punishment* on behalf of the Institute for the Study and Treatment of Delinquency, H.M.S.O., Apl. 1950.

11856 (141) 1950 **On the Desirability of Isolating a ' Functional ' (psycho-somatic) Group of Delinquent Disorders,** *Brit. J. Delinq.*, **1**, 2, Oct. 1950.

(142) 1950 **Critical Notice of D. H. Stott's " Delinquency and Human Nature,'** *Brit. J. Delinq.*, **1**, 2, 135, Oct. 1950.

(143) 1950 **Psychology in the Law Courts,** *World Rev.*, New series, Nov. 21, 1950.

11864 (144) 1950 **Freud or Jung,** Allen & Unwin, London, 1950.

(145) 1950 **A Note on Psychology and Education,** *New Era*, 31, 2, Feb., 1950.

(146) 1951 **Freud O Jung** (Spanish trans. of *Freud or Jung*, 1950), Editorial Nueva, Buenos Aires, 1951. *add to 11864*

(147) 1951 **On the Alleged Preventive Effect of Capital Punishment and Methods of Prevention of Crimes of Violence: Research and Methodology,** *Brit. J. Delinq.*, **2**, Oct. 1951.

(148) 1951 **Vue analytique des Troubles Nerveux, du Caractère et des Psychoses de l'Enfant,** Psychiatrie Sociale de l'Enfant, Ed. C. Koupernick, p. 101. Centre International de l'Enfance, Paris, 1951. Originally delivered as two lectures to the Cours de Psychiatrie Sociale de l'Enfant, London, 1950.

11851 (149) 1951 **Contributions of Psycho-Analysis to Psychiatry,** *Indian J. Psychol*, **26**, 1/4, 1951.

(150) 1951 **Preliminary Notes on the Application of Individual Methods of Research to the Problem of Psychopathy,** *Brit. J. Delinq.*, **2**, 2, 149, 1951.

(151) 1951 **Projected Researches on the Alleged Preventive Effect of Capital Punishment and on Methods of Prevention of Crimes of Violence** (with Dr. T. Grygier) *Brit. J. Delinq.*, **2,** 144, Oct. 1951.

(152) 1951 **Critical Notice of August Aichhorn's 'Wayward Youth,'** *Brit. J. Delinq.*, **2**, 2, 167, Oct. 1950.

(153) 1952 **Research Methods in Psycho-Analysis,** *Int. J. Psycho-Anal.*, **33**, 4, 1952.

(154) 1952 **Forschungsmethoden in der Psychoanalyse,** *Psyche*, **6**, 481–93, 1952.

(155) 1952 **Society and Crime.** An Address to the London Personalist Group, May 13, 1952.

(156) 1952 Introduction to **Society and the Homosexual,** by Gordon Westwood, Gollancz, London, 1952.

(157) 1952 **The Law, Psychology and the Criminal.** Address to the Romilly Association, Reading, Sep. 29, 1952.

(158) 1952 **Psycho-Analysis** in *Brit. Encyclopaedia of Medical Practice*, **10**, (2nd rev. ed.), Butterworth, London, 1952.

(159) 1953 **Psycho-Analysis and Child Psychiatry,** Imago Publishing Co., London, 1953. Extended from a paper of the same title published in *Samiksa* **6**, 3, 1953.

(160) 1953 **La Psicoanalisi,** Fratelli Bocca, Milano, 1953. Italian Translation of *Psycho-Analysis*, item 135.

(161) 1953 **Crime and Punishment,** London University Extension Lectures, Feb. 28, 1953.

(162) 1954 **Team-Research on Delinquency: A Psycho-analytical Commentary,** *Brit. J. Delinq.*, **4**, 3, Jan. 1954.

(163) 1954 **A Symposium on the Report of the Royal Commission on Capital Punishment: II Psychiatric Aspects,** *Brit. J. Delinq.*, **4**, 3, Jan. 1954. Reprinted with annotations, *Modern Law Rev.*, July, 1954. Subsequently reproduced as a pamphlet with contributions by Gerald Gardner and Dr. Jur. H. Mannheim, under the same title. I.S.T.D. Publications and Howard League, London, 1954.

(164) 1954 **The Indications for Psycho-Analysis,** *J. ment. Science*, **100**, 419, Apl. 1954.

(165) 1954 **On Psychopathy,** abridged in *Proc. R. Soc. Med.*, 1954.

(166) 1954 **The Frontiers of Psycho-Analysis,** Address to the Psychological Dept., University of Manchester.

(167) 1954 **Freud ou Jung,** French trans. of item 144. Presses Universitaires de France, Paris, 1954.

(168) 1954 **Recent Developments in the Psycho-analytic Study and Treatment of Delinquency,** 4th International Course on Criminology, London, Apl. 12, 1954.

(169) 1954 **Therapeutic Criteria of Psycho-Analysis,** *Int. J. Psycho-Anal.*, **35**, 1954.

(170) 1954 **Critical Notice of G. Zilboorg's ' The Psychology of the Criminal Act and Punishment,'** *Brit. J. Delinq.*, **5**, 2, 152, Oct. 1954.

(171) 1955 **The Technique of Psycho-Analysis,** combining a second and enlarged edition of "Lectures on the Technique of Psycho-Analysis, 1928" (Item 24), together with an abbreviated edition of " An Investigation of the Technique of Psycho-Analysis, 1940 " (Item 95) and reprints of three clinical and theoretical papers on psycho-analytic therapy (Items 41, 81 and 169), Baillière, Tindall & Cox, London, 1955.

(172) 1955 **Obituary Notice of Walter Schmideberg,** *Int. J. Psycho-Anal.*, **36**, 3, 1955.

(173) 1955 **Psychopathy and Character Disorder.** Lecture to I.S.T.D. Whitsun School, May 1955.

(174) 1955 **Psycho-Analysis and Criminology: a political survey,** paper given at the International Congress of Psycho-Analysis, Geneva, July 1955.

(175) 1955 **Prognosis or Prediction: a psychiatric survey,** *Brit. J. Delinq.* **6**, 2, Sept. 1955.

(176) 1955 **Memorandum on Homosexuality,** edited on behalf of the Institute for the Study and Treatment of Delinquency and presented to the Departmental Committee on Homosexuality and Prostitution, September 1955.

(177) 1955 **Delinquency Work in Britain:** a Survey of Current Trends, *J. Criminal Law, Criminology and Police Science (U.S.A.)*

INDEX OF AUTHORS

SUBJECT INDEX

Abnormality, concept of, 235–7
Aboulia, 272
Absolute normality, myth of, 219, 225
Abstinence, drug, 28, 198, 206, 211
Academic psychology, 45, 78, 253–4, 311–12
Accessibility, 364, 410, 416, 428
Accumulation and discharge systems, 3
Active and passive
  aims, 7–8, 22, 28
  therapy, 42, 65
  types, oral, 8–9
Actual neuroses, 73, 281
Adaptation, 82, 103
  and character, 61
  and normality, 24–8
Adolescence, 241
Adolescent taboos, 20
Affect, 75, 137, 255
  and ambivalence, 300
  analysis of, 79, 364–5
  of bursting, 302
  classification of, 299
  and conceptual mesh-systems, 271
  and depression, 302
  and destruction, 305
  and erotism, 300
  expressive, 312
  fixed or labile, 299, 301
  and frustration, 300
  fusions of, 80, 300, 344, 426
  and hysteria, 303
  infantile, 276
  and instinct, 298–9

mixed, 300
negative, 426
and obsessional neurosis, 302–3
potential, 344
primary, 80, 298, 306
psycho-analysis of, 79, 297–306, 364–5
reactive, 312
and sadism, 303–4
simple or compound, 299
and sublimation, 147–9
and super-ego, 304
Affective
  anxiety, 302–3
  balance, 312
  defences, 344–5
  discharge, 301–2
  disposition of candidates, 105–6
  layering, 299
  matrix, 301
  obsessions, 272
  resistance, 295
  states, infantile, 299
Age-factor in prognosis, 415
Aggression, 14, 188, 191–2, 354
  and alcoholism, 84–5
  and drug addiction, 189, 191, 195
  and education, 286
  libido, 357
  and melancholia, 164
  oral, 8–9, 11, 23, 29, 31, 38
  and sublimation, 148, 150, 155–7
  in therapy, 104

Racial
 history, 434
 impressions, 122
Rage
 in alcoholism, 85
 oral, 23–4, 31
 (*see also* Aggression and
 Sadism)
Rapport
 in drug addiction, 304
 and projection, 313
 therapeutic, 102
Rationalization, 52, 59, 60, 62, 98
 and alcoholism, 84–5
 and normality, 250
 and sublimation, 147
 in therapy, 101
Reaction formation, 21, 35, 40,
  43, 53, 71, 77, 98, 137–9,
  310
 and sublimation, 139–40
Reactive ego function, 119
Reading addiction, 205–06
Real
 anxiety, 68, 76, 78, 246–7
 ego, 9, 87, 115–19, 121, 340
 ego in therapy, 100–01, 103
 object, 128
 (*see also* Anxiety)
Reality, 62, 178
 definition of, 179–80
 disorders of, 180
 estimations, 410
 flight from, 82
 function, 6
 and magic, 217–18
 principle and normality,
  246–7
 psychic, 340
 qualitative, 173
 testing, 178, 184, 341
 testing and psychopathy, 381
 reality sense, 57

in adult and child, 221
and anxiety, 220
and component impulses, 233
development of, 27
and drug addiction, 209, 222
and fetichism, 231–3
and homosexuality, 223–5
and instinct, 220
and introjection, 222, 229
in neurosis, 57–8
oral-anal, 222
order of development, 226
in paranoia, 278
and perception, 219–20
and perversion, 216–34
preservation of, 222, 224
projection, 222, 229
in psychoses, 57–8
research on, 349
stages of, 231
and symbolism, 220
Reassurance, 189
 in drug addiction, 210
 and obsessional neurosis, 210
 by sublimation, 210
Reconstruction, 352, 364, 369,
  378
 fallacies of, 25
Rediscovery of psycho-analysis,
  399, 403
Re-education, 95–101
Reflex arc, 254
Reflexion, of instinct, 370
Reform movements, 250
Reformatory cases, 66
Refusal of food, 19
Regression, 129, 183, 200, 370,
  377
 in alcoholism, 83, 85–6
 and defence, 275
 and drug addiction, 189–90
 of ego, 121
 genital, 18